C000218716

The Lefties' Guide to Britain

POLITICO'S

The Lefties' Guide to Britain

From the Peasants' Revolt to the Granita Restaurant

Edited by

Peter Clark

POLITICO'S

First published in Great Britain 2005 by
Politico's Publishing, an imprint of
Methuen Publishing Limited
11-12 Buckingham Gate
London SW1E 6LB

1 3 5 7 9 10 8 6 4 2

Copyright © Peter Clark 2005

Peter Clark has asserted his rights under the Copyright, Designs & Patents Act, 1988, to be identified as the editor of this work.

A CIP catalogue record for this book is available from the British Library.

ISBN 1 84275 144 1

Printed and bound in Great Britain by St Edmundsbury Press Ltd, Bury St Edmunds, Suffolk.

This book is sold subject to the condition that it shall not by way of trade or otherwise be lent, resold, hired out, or otherwise circulated without the publishers' prior consent in writing in any form of binding or cover other than that in which it is published and without a similar condition being imposed on the subsequent purchaser.

Oh trust me, every thought that yet
In greatness rose and sorrow set,
That Time to ripening glory nurst
Was called an 'idle dream' at first.

Ernest Jones (1819–69)

The great use of history is to teach us how laws, usages and institutions arose, what were their effects on the people, how they promoted public happiness, or otherwise.

William Cobbett (1763–1835)

Some had name, and fame, and honour, learn'd they were, and
wise and strong;
Some were nameless, poor, unlettered, weak in all but grief
and wrong.

William Morris (1834–96)

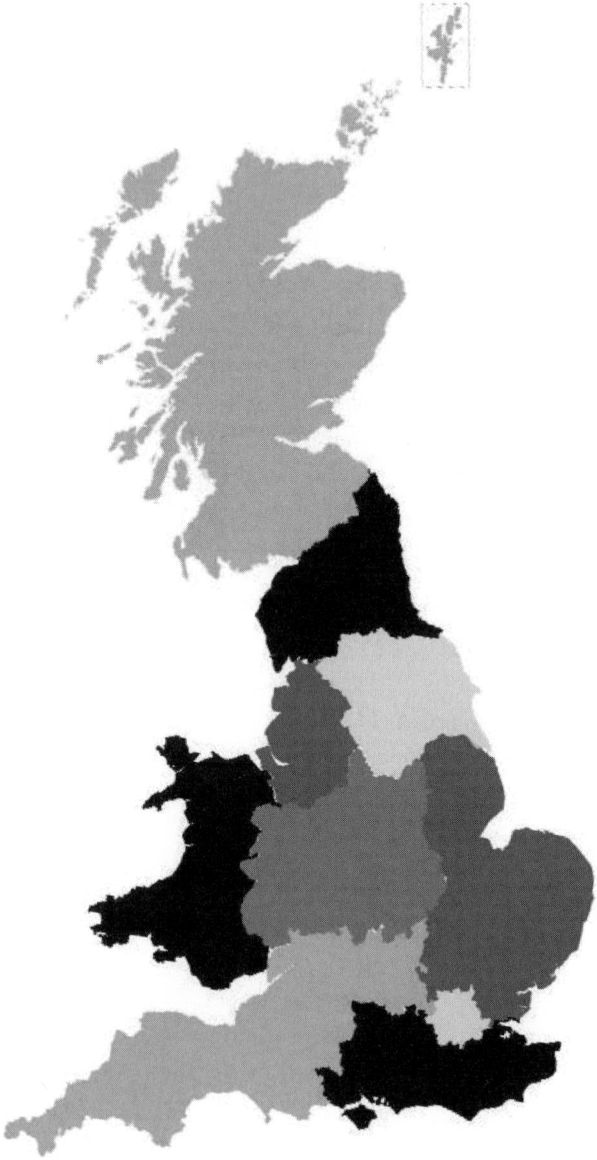

Contents

Acknowledgements ix

Foreword, Michael Foot xi

Contributors xiii

Introduction, Peter Clark 1

1. South West England,
   Kristine Mason O'Connor and Terence O'Connor 19
2. South East England, Penny Young 47
3. London, John Shepherd 77
4. Eastern England, Peter Clark 119
5. The Midlands, Mark Allen 143
6. Wales, Joe Hillaby and Caroline Hillaby 169
7. Lancashire and Cheshire, John Belchem 225
8. Yorkshire, Keith Laybourn 253
9. The North, Paul Routledge 281
10. Scotland, Alan Campbell 207

Index 357

Acknowledgements

The idea of this *Guide* emerged during a chat I had with Sean Magee in 2003. We both insist on being the originator of the idea. Disputed paternity apart, Sean has, throughout the gestation period, been supportive, providing access and introductions, and full of ideas and encouragement. But for Sean, the *Guide* would be a different and a lesser book.

This *Guide* owes an enormous amount to many people: the authors' partners above all, but friends, relations and colleagues; writers and historians, alive and dead; and many people whom the authors have met on site – guides, museum curators, librarians, journalists, fellow fans of Britain's alternative history. Hundreds of people have shown enthusiasm for the project and helped us on our way.

To all, fraternal thanks.

Acknowledgements

Foreword

Michael Foot

Most of the men who built our trade union movement (and all the women too, we should hastily add before any old misogynist sneers are revived) first learned their trade unionism from the flaming injustices they saw inflicted on their fellow human beings.

How the original heroes and heroines in these struggles made their discoveries, and prepared the way for an exposure of the wrings and the provisions of remedies, is a story often suppressed altogether for generations and may still not be published to this day. The owners of the newspapers or the producers of books often had the most interest in the suppresssion of the stories of the men and women who first felt they must risk their own lives to win their battles. The mere name Tolpuddle can still illustrate this truth most sharply. These trade unionists across the whole country, indeed across the world, meet every year to commemorate the first meeting in their cause. Or perhaps they assemble in the harbour of my native Plymouth where they have a special place to record the Tolpuddle exiles returned from their prison camps in Australia – a homecomihg for us Plymouthians to set beside the *Mayflower* to commemorate some other famous freedom lovers.

There is one other source for his idea I am sure Peter Clark would be eager to acknowledge. Once upon a time our Museum of Lbaour History had its home in George Lansbury's Limehouse Town Hall, a most fitting arrangement since the whole Labour movement owed so much to Lansbury. But then suddenly, we had to find a new home. Jack Jones and John Monks of the TUC came to the rescue but, considering the massive delicacy of our treasures, it was still touch and go.

But then came three strokes of luck or genius. One was Graham Stringer of the Manchester Labour Council. He gave us the kind of welcome to Manchester which, I am sure, Karl Marx's Engels owuld have approved. Next came the moment when Nick Mansfield applied for the job of General Director. He has from the start been the inspired leader of the whole enterprise. From the very beginning he had at his side Stephen Bird who had been in charge of the Labour Party's libraries in London. He too, like Nick Mansfield, will not be there forever. But Peter Clark's journeys should start and finish there. The two women who succeed them, Cath Birchall and Catharine Rew, will have a special welcome.

Michael Foot

Contributors

MARK ALLEN is a native of Derby and worked in Nottingham for a time before doing his degree at the University of Hull. He moved to King Alfred's College, Winchester to do his PhD on historical demography, which he obtained in 2000. He now lectures on nineteenth- and twentieth-century British history at the University of Winchester.

JOHN BELCHEM is Professor of History at the University of Liverpool. Having published extensively on nineteenth-century radicalism, including a biography of Henry 'Orator' Hunt, his research now focuses on Liverpool. During his current Leverhulme Major Research Fellowship he is writing a cultural history of the Liverpool Irish, and is leading the team working on the urban biography *Liverpool 800: Culture, Character and History*, to mark the eight-hundredth anniversary, in 2007, of the granting of letters patent to the borough.

ALAN CAMPBELL taught anthropology at Edinburgh University for 20 years. In the late 1970s, he made contact with a group of Amazonian Indians called the Wayapi in an isolated area in Brazil. He maintained contact with them over the years and wrote about them in his book *Getting to Know Waiwai* (1995).

PETER CLARK worked for over 30 years with the British Council, mostly in the Middle East. He has written books on Henry Hallam, Marmaduke Pickthall and Wilfred Thesiger, and has translated contemporary Arabic literature extensively – history, fiction and drama. His last translation was *The Woman of the Flask* by the Iraqi novelist Selim Matar (2005). He is also a travel consultant for tours to

Syria and Turkey. He has been interested in Leftie history since he studied history and politics at the University of Keele.

CAROLINE HILLABY was born and bred in Berkshire. After Exeter University, Caroline entered the Lord Treasurer's Department under Lord Hailsham, later transferring to Social Security. Always a traveller, she awarded herself a gap year in 1957 to travel overland via Iran and Afghanistan through Herat, Bamyan, Kabul and the Khyber Pass to Pakistan and India, and, thence, after trekking in Nepal, to Australia. On her return she entered local government service. Since retirement, she has organised group travel with friends, including visits to Armenia, Iranian Azerbaijan and Kurdistan, and Georgia, with the exacting journey to Mestia in Svaneti in the High Caucasus.

JOE HILLABY is an Honorary Research Fellow at the University of Bristol. Early schooling under Cader Idris in Merioneth, and beneath Wharfedale's Buckden Pike and Simon's Seat, engendered his love of the countryside. Political education included Yugoslavia after Tito's break with Stalin, Algeria during the Revolution, and leading student groups in Dubcek's post-invasion Czechoslovakia. He is a former chairman of the Worcestershire Archaeological Society, of the Herefordshire Council for the Preservation of Rural England and the Woolhope Club. He is a member of the Hereford Diocesan Advisory Committee and of the Jewish Historical Society. His studies have included medieval Jewries of London, Bristol, Gloucester, Worcester and Hereford. His *Ledbury: A Medieval Borough* is in its third edition and his *Leominster: Minster and Priory c660–1548* is forthcoming.

KEITH LAYBOURN is Professor of Modern British History at the University of Huddersfield. He has written and edited 37 books and about 60 articles, including *Britain on the Breadline* (1991, 1996), *The General Strike* (1993), *Under the Red Flag* (1999) and *A Century of Labour* (2000). He is about to publish a book on the 1924 Labour Government, with John Shepherd, entitled *In Office but not in Power* (2006) and a book on *Marxism in Britain since 1945* (2005). He edits the *Annual Bulletin of Historical Literature* for the Historical Association.

KRISTINE MASON O'CONNOR is Dean of Teaching and Learning at the University of Gloucestershire. In her doctoral thesis she researched the education and employment of young women in rural areas. Early in her career she taught sociology of education and was active in her local Labour Party. In recent years her political energies focused on researching the biography of Joan Maynard (*Joan Maynard, Passionate Socialist,* 2003). She shares Joan Maynard's commitment to improving and widening access to education.

TERENCE O'CONNOR studied Fine Art as a mature student, and later, the Social History of Art at Leeds University. He joined the Labour Party in 1979 and was an active member for a number of years. He lectures in art and art history, and is also a painter. His interests are generally around European history, culture and ideology, and particularly in issues of representation and nature.

PAUL ROUTLEDGE is a political columnist with the *Daily Mirror*, and also the author of biographies about Labour figures as diverse as Arthur Scargill, Betty Boothroyd and Gordon Brown. His last publication was *The Bumper Book of British Lefties.* A former labour editor of *The Times*, a political correspondent of the *Observer* and the *Independent on Sunday*, he lives in a former mill village in North Yorkshire, opposite the birthplace of Labour's first Chancellor, Philip Snowden.

MARTIN ROWSON is an award-winning cartoonist whose work appears regularly in *The Times*, the *Guardian*, the *Independent on Sunday*, the *Daily Mirror* and many other publcations. In addition to being Ken Livingstone's official 'Cartoonist Laureate' (in return for one pint of beer per annum) he was also, until the summer of 2005, a vice-president of the Zoological Society of London. He lives with his wife and their two children in South East London.

JOHN SHEPHERD is Visiting Professor at Anglia Polytechnic University, Department of History, in Cambridge, and is a Fellow of the Royal Historical Society. He was educated at Borough Road College and gained his doctorate at Birkbeck College, University of London. He is president of the Cambridge branch of the Historical Association. His recent publications include *George Lansbury: At the Heart of Old Labour* (2002). Currently, he is completing a book with Keith Laybourn on the first Labour government. John is an Arsenal season ticket holder.

PENNY YOUNG graduated from the University of York and worked on regional newspapers before joining the BBC, where she worked in local radio, on Radio Four's *Today Programme* and regional television. In 1991, she bought a bicycle and cycled to Turkey via Eastern Europe. She lived abroad for two years, studying Turkish and Arabic, and working on the *Turkish Daily News* in Ankara and the English-language version of *Al-Ahram*. She also freelanced for BBC Radio Four, BBC World Service and CNN. She has published an account of a cycling trip along the Euphrates in Syria for *Intrepid Arabia* (1999), and is currently working on a book about the working relationship between William Cobbett and Henry Hunt.

Introduction

Peter Clark

The people's history has been rooted in place. Struggles for rights have often been localised and have involved local issues, such as resistance to enclosures, the rights of trades unions, or peace campaigns around specific military bases. But rights, once secured, are often taken for granted, and we forget the struggle and the people involved in making the lives of the vast majority of British people better, safer and more meaningful.

The Lefties' Guide to Britain aims to offset this neglect or indifference. Tolpuddle, Jarrow, Greenham Common and Orgreave are places that have resonance in the history of the British Left. But other sites – where Chartists met on Pennine moors, where women demonstrated to secure more equal rights, sites where a phrase became part of the Lefties' political currency, birthplaces, residences and graves of famous Lefties – are less well known.

Organised by region, with each contributor providing an overview of that area's particular significance for the history of the Left, the ***Guide*** lists seven hundred or so sites that are as much part of the British heritage as those cathedrals, stately homes and battlefields that have usually been part only of the history of an elite, and often a privileged and conservative elite.

As we have worked on the ***Guide***, we have become aware how provisional the list is. While we hope all major sites are included, we know that many may have been overlooked. It is hoped that the ***Guide*** will stimulate an interest in Leftie history and its connection with place. The People's History Museum at Manchester is a model, but every region should commemorate its popular past. Just as every regiment has a museum, so every trade union should have one. The Jarrow March against unemployment in October 1936 made that town a byword for human suffering and social devastation, caused by indifference and a stern economic theory. Jarrow rightly celebrates the Venerable Bede, but why is there not a museum dedicated to the Jarrow March? The last marcher died in October 2003. There is ample material – banners, diaries, recorded personal memoirs, press cuttings – for a museum to remind the present and future generations that human beings matter more than economic theory.

Popular protest has a long history. The ***Guide*** goes back to the Peasants' Revolt of 1381, when John Ball proclaimed that 'things will never go well in England so long as goods be not in common'. A chapel is dedicated to the Blessed John Ball at the parish church at Thaxted, Essex. The ***Guide*** includes the location of the debates during the English civil war – at St Mary's Church, Putney – when a challenge was made, in the name of the people, to the class nature of society. And protest intensifies with nineteenth-century campaigns for political rights, improved economic conditions, trade union rights and women's rights. Socialism in all its varieties provided an ideological framework for the improvement of the conditions of the people. The words of 'The Red Flag' were written on a train between Charing Cross and New Cross. Liberty for the common people was upheld by writers – Hazlitt, Byron, Shelley, Cobbett, Ruskin, William Morris, H. G. Wells, George Orwell, J. B. Priestley. Socialist theorists, trade union leaders, Labour politicians, suffragettes and peace activists have all contributed to making the world a better place. Where were they born? Educated? Where did they live? Where are they buried? George Lansbury's ashes were scattered off Land's End, H. G. Wells's from a boat off Poole, Dorset, Aneurin Bevan's – and Jennie Lee's – above Tredegar in South Wales.

The location of sites illustrates the fabric of British social history. Geography shaped the contours of industrial Britain, the cities and the economic life of the countryside. The Independent Labour Party was launched in the West Riding of Yorkshire. A Scottish Labour Party preceded a national Labour Party. London has witnessed the catalyst between ideas and agitation on the one hand and the implementation of reforms on the other. But each corner of Britain has seen a distinctive contribution to the British Leftie tradition. Villages throughout the country witnessed a spread of rural nonconformity, especially (but not exclusively) Methodism and Primitive Methodism, which challenged class assumptions of the alliance of Church of England, squire and wealthy farmer. The poor did not have to be the passive recipients of messages delivered by and in the interests of the more comfortable. Nonconformity helped the excluded to articulate concerns. In Methodism, working men preached to other working men and women. A huge number of nineteenth- and twentieth-century trade unionists had a background in Methodism. The Primitive Methodist pulpit was a political training ground as much as the Oxford or Cambridge Union.

The ***Lefties' Guide*** celebrates Leftie history through location. Some areas are richer than others, but no corner of Britain lacks a site that is a reminder of the development of British liberties, rights and a better life. These reminders may be in unexpected corners. The remains of Beatrice and Sidney Webb, who had a major influence on British socialist thought in the twentieth century, are buried in Westminster Abbey, as are those of Clement Attlee. But John Smith, leader of the

Labour Party, 1992-94, is buried in the kirkyard of Iona Cathedral. Eton College produced Shelley, George Orwell, the Labour Chancellor of the Exchequer from 1945–48 Hugh Dalton, and Tam Dalyell.

Serious methodological questions have perhaps inhibited the production of such a guide in the past. What is a Leftie? Where do you start? How do you cope with the ideological – almost theological – interpretations of Leftie history?

A Leftie is seen as one who has been ready to challenge the status quo in the name of the people and works to change society, and to make life for the mass of people richer ethically, culturally and materially. The Leftie is never on the side of the Establishment – though he/she may be sucked into it. The Leftie has a vision of a better world and is often idealistic and impractical. Lefties are not often good team players. The Leftie hates war and militarism. She/he aspires to ensure that the good things of life are in the grasp of all. This may be through work, education, literature or leisure. He/she is not complacent: there is always a Leftie agenda. The Leftie has, in the last two centuries, been found politically on the fringes of Liberal radicalism or in the Labour Party. But she/he may have nothing to do with politics directly. The Leftie may be obsessively concerned with one or two issues, such as the extension of rights to particular groups. Lefties may be in conflict with other Lefties. As G. D. H. Cole said of one Leftie hero, 'Cobbett had none of the liberal virtues. He was not broad-minded or tolerant, or considerate or forgiving, or humble or charitable, or slow to anger or plenteous in mercy.' Lefties may not practise the universal brotherhood that they preach. Indeed, sectarianism can be as bitter as any *odium theologicum*. But it takes a Leftie to recognise, sometimes reluctantly, another Leftie.

In the ***Guide*** we go back to the Middle Ages. From time to time there were isolated or individual demands for a justice that implied the necessity of wide social changes. Wat Tyler, Jack Cade and Robert Kett expressed these demands in the fourteenth, fifteenth and sixteenth centuries. In the seventeenth century, England underwent a revolution that seemed, at times, to spill over into a social revolution. The middle decades of that century produced debates and statements that mixed a late medieval messianism with a concern for rights that has a very modern ring. Then things went quiet for a century or so.

Resistance to foreign occupation, under the leadership of Boudicca or of Harold, is not seen as early anti-imperialism. Nor is the Reformation seen as part of the Leftie heritage.

The pace of references quickens with the late eighteenth and nineteenth centuries. Vast social and economic changes forced people to question the ethical basis of society. Poverty and repression led to political action that is recognisably modern. There is a 'whig interpretation' of Leftie history, to which this volume subscribes. The Chartists were the heirs of the revolutionaries and advocates of reform during and after the Napoleonic war. The early socialists at the end of the nineteenth century picked up the debate after the Chartists. And from the foundation of the Labour Party in 1900 there is an institutional continuity to the present day.

There is a great library of Leftie history. In the nineteenth century, many in the Leftie tradition wrote vigorously – William Cobbett, Samuel Bamford, William Lovett, Thomas Cooper. They illustrate the struggles of the early years of the century. Comparable volumes of memoirs do not appear again until after the First World War. But in the years before and after the First World War, a Leftie historiographical tradition was established. Three married couples created that tradition: Sidney and Beatrice Webb, J. L. and Barbara Hammond, and G. D. H. and Margaret Cole. Since then, there have been revisionists and tweakers of the tradition. Lefties have been prolific writers – autobiographers, journalists, theoreticians, pamphleteers. The Communist Party had its own group of historians that included people of the calibre of Christopher Hill, E. J. Hobsbawm, E. P. Thompson, George Rude, John Saville. Their influence extended far beyond either the Communist Party or the world of the Left. Sometimes their writings on Leftie history were excessively ideological: there were identifiable good guys and bad guys. In this ***Guide*** we have tried to be broadminded. Ramsay MacDonald and Philip Snowden may not be heroes to the metropolitan Left. But in Lossiemouth and Cowling they are local boys made good. And this ***Guide*** draws attention to the local roots of many who played glorious or ambiguous roles in Leftie history.

In Scotland and Wales there are particular problems. Both countries have had a national consciousness that has sometimes been allied to, sometimes in conflict with, a pan-British Leftie-ism. In Wales, religious Dissent, language and education have been the weapons of challenge to an English, Anglican establishment. Scotland has had distinctive institutions, a large Irish immigration, and a land situation that produced in the Highlands huge economic asymmetries (that is, a few people were very rich and very powerful, while most people were very poor and vulnerable). But Scotland has also had a comparatively egalitarian educational system that has enabled individuals to break out of a cycle of disadvantage. The sources of the distinctiveness of Welsh and Scottish Leftie-ism are explored in the sections devoted to those parts of Britain.

Each contributor in this ***Guide*** has defined the scope in his/her own way. Leftie history is local and often personal. My own paternal grandfather, William Clark (1877-1956), was a Scottish watch-repairer, from the same county – Morayshire – as Labour's first Prime Minister, James Ramsay MacDonald. He served on the western front in the First World War, loyally but without distinction. Poor health brought him, and his family, to the sea air of the Thames Estuary. His experiences of war and poverty made him a socialist, and he and my grandmother were pioneers in establishing the Labour Party in Southend-on-Sea. Politics was the preoccupation of the household throughout the 1920s. Many of the leaders of the national party – George Lansbury, Charles Trevelyan, Arthur Ponsonby, Robert Smillie, Emanuel Shinwell, Katherine Bruce Glasier – came to Southend-on-Sea to inspire and rally. Some stayed overnight with my grandparents. Many wrote messages in a family autograph book. The family felt part of a world that was working for a better tomorrow.

Often during the summers of that decade my grandparents arranged, through the Labour Party, for Welsh miners to come and stay, to enjoy some east-coast sea air: a contrast to the coal dust of the valleys. My grandmother would lead a singsong round the piano. The miners would harmonise Welsh anthems and the family would join in. To the end of his life, my father, who died in 1971, was able to sing songs such as 'Sosban Fach' in Welsh.

The political world of the Welsh miners in the 1920s and the world of my grandparents were polls apart. Southend-on-Sea was never promising socialist territory: unlike Brighton it has never had a Labour MP. The Welsh mining valleys may be conservative, but have never had a Conservative MP. My grandparents were part of a socialist culture that went beyond Southend-on-Sea, and beyond politics. The mingling of the miners and my grandparents was a family memory that brings home how localised political experience was in the last century. But it was the Labour movement that brought them physically together.

The Labour movement was a coalition of the Labour Party, trades unions and various Leftie societies. For a century or more it had a religious ethos. Socialism was morality. The movement was often inward-looking, socially self-contained and self-righteous. It was moulded in the nineteenth century and, as a political force, lasted until the later decades of the twentieth. It still lingers in some families and communities, but it has become an endangered species, a survivor from the past. The movement had its own heroes and heroines, its own interpretations of history and like religious movements, had its dogmas, its heretics and its apostates. The greatest of the apostates was Ramsay MacDonald. His apostacy was all the greater because he had been a most charismatic leader of the Labour Party, a miracle worker, an organiser, a spellbinding orator and a prolific theoretician. My grandfather, like Ramsay MacDonald, periodically returned to Morayshire for filial visits. More than once he met MacDonald on the train. In the family autograph book is a cutting from a diary in which Ramsay MacDonald wrote a message: '. . . It becomes more and more clear that Socialism is the only hope of the world.' When MacDonald formed a coalition with the Conservatives to deal with the financial crisis of 1931, and turned his back on the party he had done so much to create, the sense of loss and betrayal was massive. It disillusioned many, and the Labour movement was never quite the same again. The next man to be Labour Prime Minister fourteen years later – Clement Attlee – lacked the charisma of MacDonald. But as a conscientious and methodical bureaucrat, he led the faithful into a Promised Land – the Labour government of 1945 – with its extensive nationalisations, the creation of the Welfare State and the beginning of the dismantling of Empire. The poverty, desperation and indignities of the past became a historical memory.

But for many on the Left, the Promised Land, for much of the twentieth century, was two thousand miles to the East – the Union of Soviet Socialist Republics. The 1917 Russian Revolution and the collapse of Tsarist rule were welcomed by many across the political spectrum. But the Bolsheviks who took over used the language of the Left. Their inspirational apostles were Karl Marx and Friedrich Engels. Both had spent decades in Britain; had developed their theories of revolution from observations of the working out of the Industrial Revolution in Britain. Both had good relations with leaders of Labour and with socialists in Britain. Lenin had also been a political refugee in Britain – his office is preserved at the Marx Memorial Library in Clerkenwell. After he had assumed power, Lenin maintained a close and flattering interest in the British Labour movement. The British Communist Party was set up in 1920 and worked on political and industrial issues. For many, the Communist Party represented an uncompromising purity. Its enemies were the enemies of the working class. In their ruthless pursuit of positions of power and influence in Britain, communists created bitter hostility to the extent that their most ferocious enemies were others on the Left. The party continued to attract poets and intellectuals until the 1950s: their cultural influence extended far beyond the Communist Party and the Labour movement. But the Communist Party of Great Britain became, in effect, an instrument of Soviet foreign policy. The party and the party newspaper received subsidies from Moscow. Its leaders used to travel to Moscow several times a year – wondering sometimes whether they would be allowed to return – and the leadership lost any intellectual credibility by parroting the never-constant Soviet line. Individual communists, open and creative in other spheres of activity, had closed minds about the evils that were perpetrated in the name of socialism. A massive self-delusion enabled many for decades to believe that the Soviet Union was not as other states. And yet, many of the causes they embraced at home were shared by Lefties of a more sceptical turn of mind.

Disillusion with the Soviet Union checked the heady idealism of many on the Left. A further cause for the disintegration of the Labour Movement arose from the success of the Labour government of

1945. Life became freer for the great majority of people. Later Conservative governments were unwilling to dismantle Labour's achievements. Indeed Harold Macmillan, Conservative Prime Minister from 1957–63, went so far as to describe Toryism as 'paternalistic socialism'. Full (or high levels of) employment brought social mobility. Extended educational opportunities undermined class loyalties. Leftie thought became more pragmatic. Socialism was no longer an ideological system that would replace capitalism. It no longer suggested an ethical code. Indeed the word is never used nowadays – even negatively by the opponents of the Labour Party.

Leftie-ism, like the face and smile of the Cheshire cat, is fading away. The 2005 General Election may well have been the most un-ideological election since the nineteenth century. But this makes it all the more vital to record what is vanishing, and to note the sites that belong to a tradition that has shaped the face of modern Britain, almost always for the better.

I have traced the heyday of Leftie-ism and its decline in the last three generations. But the Leftie tradition goes back much further. History is never static, and deference was accompanied by movements of social protest in the Middle Ages. The Christian tradition includes messianic ideas of justice on earth that have been used by people who have wished to improve the human condition. But much Christian social teaching was geared to conditioning the poor to accept their lot and their place in the divine order of things. This was convenient for the wealthy and powerful. Privilege from medieval to early modern times was often tempered by notions of fairness within the context of a paternalistic society. But authority and decision-making was always with the rich and powerful. Popular interests, such as access to common land, could be overruled legally and legitimately. For the poor, the common lands provided fuel and folk medicaments, and a place to shoot a rabbit for the family pot, to tether a goat or to allow a cow to graze. The enclosure movement 'privatised' common land, forcing people to accept a cash economy, and served overwhelmingly the interests of the possessing classes. It made agro-industry more efficient and, in the long run, may have prevented Britain from starving, but in the short term, forced thousands to face starvation, emigration or the humiliations of the workhouse.

The French Revolution, which transformed the continent socially and culturally, had its echoes in Britain. It quickened a demand for parliamentary reform to enable the passing of laws to reflect the interests of a wider number of people. But the governments of the time, for these very reasons, stamped on reformers and popular demonstrations. The inequitable distribution of authority was aggravated by an Industrial Revolution that made some people very rich but pauperised the majority. The country's economic centres of gravity shifted from south to north, from London, Bristol and Norwich to Birmingham, Lancashire, Yorkshire and Scotland. New methods of producing textiles and industrial goods brought thousands of people together, into conditions of squalor and hopeless poverty. There was no state protection for men, women and children, who toiled twelve or fifteen hours a day and more for the most meagre of wages. The concerns of these people were articulated by some remarkable individuals, such as William Cobbett and Henry Hunt. Both were outstandingly fluent communicators, Cobbett as a writer and pamphleteer, Hunt as an orator. Both were farmers from southern England, but both had a political base in Lancashire. Both were involved in the demands for parliamentary reform, which – in a limited way – was achieved in the Reform Act of 1832.

This reform extended the franchise, not to the labouring masses, but to the newly enriched middle classes. But at least the reform indicated that the parliamentary system was not sacrosanct. Social conditions for the unenfranchised did not improve, and the decade after 1832 saw a distinctly working-class movement in Chartism. There were many strands to Chartism but the basis was a charter that called for an extension of parliamentary reform – universal suffrage, secret ballots, annual Parliaments, equal electoral districts, no property qualification for MPs and payment for MPs. (All have subsequently been secured – or conceded – except for annual parliaments.) Chartism went through several phases, sometimes seeking an improvement in social conditions, sometimes revolution. One strand sought land reform, another the creation of ideal rural communities. There were charismatic orators among the leaders – Feargus O'Connor, Henry Vincent – who, thanks to the new railways, were able to move rapidly around the country.

Although politically Chartism achieved very little, those with authority took note. Reform alleviated the worst of social abuses, especially when it dealt with matters of public health: cholera was no respecter of social boundaries. The middle of the century saw an economic improvement in wages and conditions, and many in the new working class saw opportunities in self-improvement, emigration, education, religion, temperance and (among the skilled working class) a trade unionism that aimed to negotiate for improved conditions. Samuel Smiles' gospel of self-help had a great appeal for working people in the middle years of the century. The Liberal leader, W. E. Gladstone, appealed to this upwardly mobile class. His Liberal Party was able to recruit working men into Parliament and even to governmental office. The political world was cautiously extended with Reform Acts in 1867 and 1884, enfranchising working men in the towns and countryside. Women, however, continued to be excluded. And there was still an excluded underclass – best documented in the work of Henry Mayhew – that was disadvantaged and dependent for survival on handouts from their social betters. Charity was organised according to the perceived moral worth of those in need.

Trade depression in the 1880s put a check on widespread hopes for a steady amelioration of conditions. From the 1840s to the 1880s Engels and Marx had been observing political and social developments in Britain, but their direct impact was minimal. But from the 1880s, their ideas of class struggle and the transformation of capitalism to socialism seemed to make some sense. As with Chartism half a century earlier, there were several strands in early British socialism, from the would-be revolutionary – H. M. Hyndman and the Social Democratic Federation – to the pragmatic – represented by George Bernard Shaw, Sidney and Beatrice Webb and the Fabian Society – to the desperately practical – represented by a new unionism in London and Yorkshire. The new unionism led to the formation of the Independent Labour Party (ILP) in Bradford in 1893. Hyndman and the Fabian Society sparred over socialist ideas. The Fabian Society was London-based and saw itself as a pressure group that aimed to permeate the existing parties with its ideas. Hyndman did at least get to know Burnley and stand for election there.

The Lefties in the generation before the First World War did not concern themselves with politics alone. Shaw wrote plays with a sharp content of social comment, dealing with housing, war and prostitution. H. G. Wells produced novels that portrayed upwardly mobile individuals from the working class, inspired by ambition, science and education. Robert Blatchford, a gifted journalist, edited a socialist journal called *The Clarion* that had a vast appeal. In the north of England especially, there were Clarion Clubs where socialists met together and played together. The bicycle was a social liberator and leveller. There were socialist cycling clubs, socialist churches. One Clarion Club still survives at Newchurch-in-Pendle, Lancashire.

Many of these groups gathered together to increase the representation of the working class in Parliament. In February 1900, these groups founded a Labour Representation Committee, with a young Scot, James Ramsay MacDonald, as secretary. In 1906, the Committee was formally renamed the Labour Party.

The new party was an alliance of trades unions and socialist organisations. Under its banner, 29 MPs were elected in the 1906 General Election. They were joined by fourteen miners' MPs who had, at first, stood aloof from the new party. The Labour Party was a coalition of interests. The leading figure was the charismatic James Keir Hardie, a former Scottish miner. The parliamentary party was made up mostly of working men – trade unionists who were primarily concerned about negotiating better conditions. Some saw themselves as socialists, but many did not. In the years before and during the First World War, programmes were devised largely by middle-class members of the ILP or of the Fabian Society. Arthur Henderson and Sidney Webb drafted a new constitution for the Labour Party, which thereafter was based on trades unions and an aggregate of constituency Labour Parties. These new arrangements permitted a huge expansion in the years after the War. The constitution included the specifically socialist Clause Four, which declared the party's aim to be 'to secure for the producers by hand and brain the full fruits of their industry, and the most equitable distribution thereof that may be possible, upon the basis of the common ownership of the means of production and the best obtainable system of popular administration and control of each industry or service.'

The Labour Party in Parliament before the First World War acted as a radical ginger group of the reforming Liberal government, supporting the distributive 1909 Lloyd George budget and the introduction of old-age pensions and national insurance. Individual

Labour MPs supported the public agitation for equal political rights for women, and after the outbreak of the war, many Labour MPs – including Keir Hardie, Ramsay MacDonald and Philip Snowden – opposed British entry into the war. Most of the party, however, backed the war, and were rewarded by the appointment of Labour MPs Arthur Henderson, George Wardle and George Barnes as ministers in the Lloyd George coalition government during the latter period of the war. Some old socialists – H. M. Hyndman and Robert Blatchford – were strident in their support of the war. But unease about how the country conducted its affairs brought others into the party, especially from the radical wing of the Liberal Party. They personified a switch in allegiance on the part of the electorate.

The increasingly well-organised party increased its representation in the elections after the war, effectively replacing the Liberal Party in Parliament. In January 1924, Ramsay MacDonald formed the first Labour government.

Thereafter, the Labour Party either formed a government, or participated in government, or was in parliamentary opposition and expecting to form a government. But much political activity – both effective and ineffective – was outside Parliament: the mob in the eighteenth century; the huge rallies addressed by Hunt at Spa Fields in London and St Peter's Fields in Manchester; mass Chartist rallies outside the large cities of Northern England; demonstrations in Trafalgar Square; the 1926 General Strike; since the Second World War, marches organised by the Campaign for Nuclear Disarmament to protest against the British possession of nuclear weapons; and in February 2003, the largest demo ever, the million plus march against the Iraqi war. Sometimes the demos have achieved their ends, not necessarily directly – five of the six points of the Chartist programme, for example – but the demos have always been part of British political discourse. The extension of the franchise in 1867, and to women after the First World War, would not have happened without the street politics, and the threat of disorder. The Left has not had a monopoly on street politics, as the Countryside Alliance has shown, but the Left has shown the way.

The Labour movement saw itself as the party of the working class. If this was absolutely so, then it would have won all elections in its history. But political allegiance has never been absolute, and during the twentieth century there has been a steady erosion of working class consciousness. Even a century ago, loyalties were mixed. As in the United States many working class people did not accept the socialist message. They saw either education, or enterprise and the taking of opportunities as the way out of the cycle of poverty. Governments, including Labour governments, sometimes seemed remote and ineffectual. Many of the poor accepted a deferential society. The rich and well-educated, men from families steeped in tradition and privilege, were, just for those reasons, better trained and equipped to make decisions affecting everyone. A Winston Churchill from a ducal family had intrinsically greater authority than an Ernest Bevin, an illegitimate and ill-educated working man from Somerset. There were also interests that captured the allegiance of working class men and women and diverted them from voting Labour. In Lancashire Irish immigrants competed for jobs and brought down wage levels. Workers were often allied to a Protestant 'Orange' Conservatism. Paternalist employers could undermine the socialist case against wicked capitalists. Labour repudiated militarism. This won the Labour Party no friends in parts of Sheffield where a steel industry was involved in the building of battleships, or in garrison towns such as Portsmouth or Chatham.

But the Labour Movement and Leftie-ness have had an irreversible influence on the whole of British society. The Welfare State, the idea of equality of opportunity, the inclusiveness of education, the abandonment of deference have – as conservatives and traditionalists recognise – been the result of a huge spread of Leftie ideas. Indeed some twentieth-century Conservatives look to Disraeli (and Oastler and Shaftesbury) – good nineteenth-century Conservatives – as examples of how the ruling classes can be as passionate in their hatred of poverty, and sometimes as effective in remedying social abuses, as any Leftie. Conservative governments have not wished to upset all the social and political changes brought in by Labour governments. Some Conservatives, especially between 1945 and 1975, have been sensitive to the ideas and ethos of Leftie-ism. In the latter year, Margaret Thatcher became leader of the Conservative Party and launched an intellectual and political challenge to a century of Leftie-ism, but she did not dismantle the Welfare State, abolish old-age pensions, or deprive women of the vote. Nobody publicly comes out with the unfeeling comments about the poor or disadvantaged that were uttered in the nineteenth century.

The Lefties' Guide to Britain has been divided geographically into ten areas. The authors of each chapter have selected the sites. The aim has been to be authoritative and reasonably comprehensive. Each writer has his/her own approach. It has not been possible to be exhaustive. Readers will spot omissions. And I hope people will write to me, care of the publisher, to make corrections and offer suggestions for possible later editions.

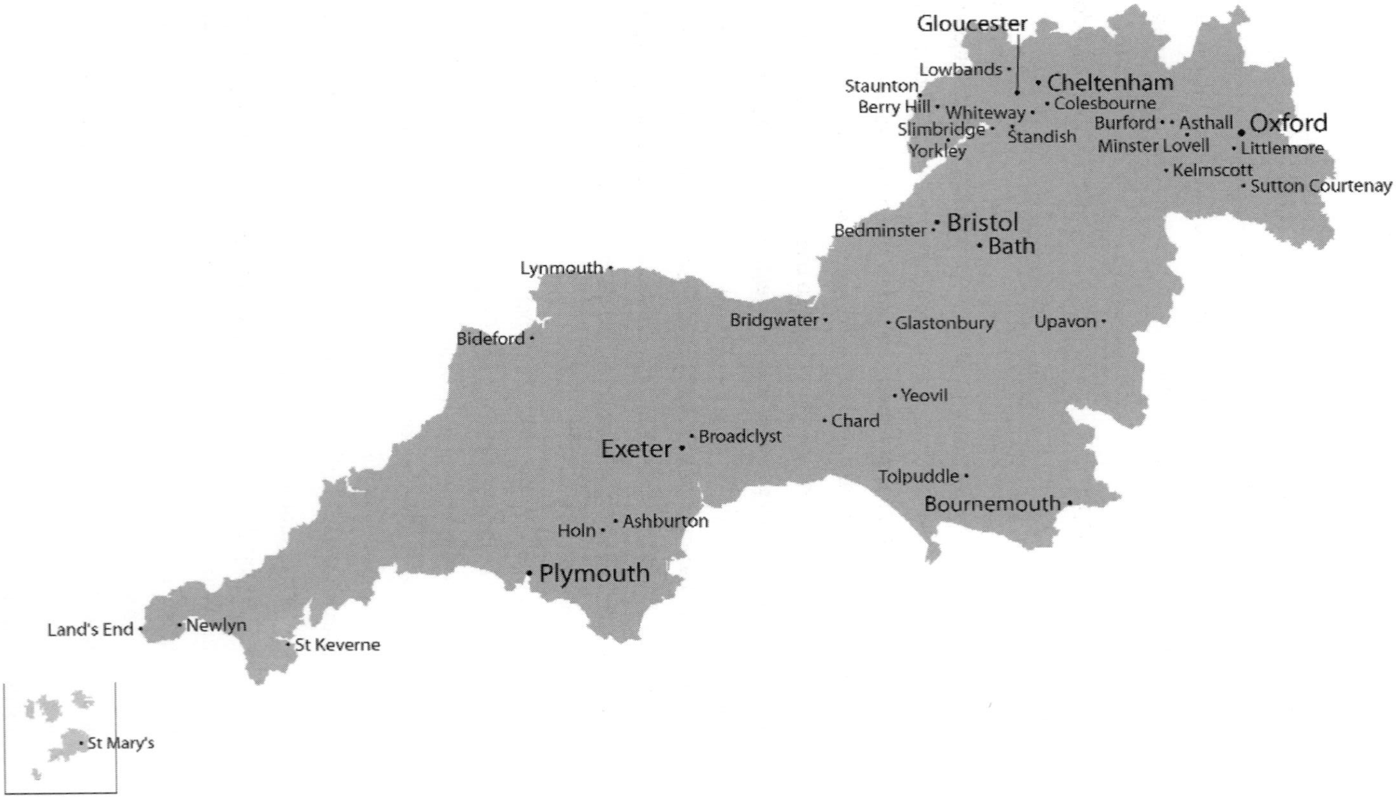
Gloucester
Lowbands
Cheltenham
Staunton
Berry Hill
Whiteway
Colesbourne
Slimbridge
Standish
Yorkley
Burford
Asthall
Oxford
Minster Lovell
Littlemore
Kelmscott
Sutton Courtenay
Bedminster
Bristol
Bath
Lynmouth
Bridgwater
Glastonbury
Upavon
Bideford
Yeovil
Chard
Exeter
Broadclyst
Tolpuddle
Bournemouth
Holn
Ashburton
Plymouth
Land's End
Newlyn
St Keverne
St Mary's

1.

South West England

Kristine Mason O'Connor and Terence O'Connor

In our selection of entries for the gazetteer we have not applied a narrow benchmark of Leftie-ism, but have chosen to include events and people that have, in some manner, pointed the way towards co-operative living in the interests of all. There are good reasons for this approach, not least in that the very meanings of terms in Leftie discourse were/are unstable. Socialism, communism, liberalism, democracy, anarchism – all have been subject to variation over the last two centuries, overlapping, contrasting and trailing nuances depending on who was speaking. For example, at a time when 'socialism' was often equated with atheism, William Morris, the towering figure in the development of English socialism, uses the word 'communism', which then carried the meaning of primitive, co-operative and spiritual forms of social organisation.

An earlier example in the evolution of 'socialist' is that until the 1840s it was associated with a range of other terms: co-operative, mutualist, associationist, phalansterian, agrarianist, radical. Bound up with some of these terms was an idea, common among socialists in Britain and in France, that industrialisation, and the urban ghastliness that went with it, were solely the result of capitalism, and that the truly progressive society would be rural.

The South West lends itself to the idea/fantasy of getting away. With its coastal cliffs and coves, its high moorlands and secret valleys and creeks, its pretty villages and pastoralism, gardens lost and found, Eden et cetera et cetera, the region can be imagined as the antithesis of modernity. Cider with rosy-coloured spectacles. But to see the land as landscape is to prise one aspect of it away from its material wholeness, and to deprive it of its history. The men and women, who worked the land without owning it, experienced the full force of history at any given time.

In the 1640s Gerard Winstanley, the Digger leader, estimated that two thirds of England was common land, that is, was owned in common by the people, with ancient rights. Whatever the accuracy of his estimate, the common land did give landless people the possibility of subsistence, independent of the landed employer. A band of his followers established a community on Slimbridge Waste, by the Severn in Gloucestershire. Their beliefs were simple and generous: equality, and common ownership of the land. In Winstanley's words, 'The Earth was made a Treasury for all.' Like other Digger settlements, this one was most likely oppressed out of existence.

The Levellers were less radical, but more dangerous to Parliament and the grandees, as they comprised whole regiments of Cromwell's New Model Army. They pressed for manhood suffrage, reform of government in favour of the less privileged, the reopening of the commons and the loosening of trade monopolies. When the demands were rejected, some sections of the army rebelled, but were faced down by Cromwell in 1649 at Oxford, or in the case of those at Burford, Oxfordshire, put down by exemplary execution. The Parliament for which they had fought and risked all turned out to have rather different ideas. As the Leveller Colonel Rainborrow exclaimed, 'I wonder we were so deceived.' No change there, then.

Throughout the nineteenth century, the increasing pace of enclosure of the commons for the benefit of existing landowners corralled the poor into dependency on paid employment. In the

Martyn Seat, Tolpuddle

aftermath of the war against Napoleon, employment, too, was put under pressure.

In the 1830s, in our region, Gloucestershire, Wiltshire, Somerset and Devon were all known to the landed gentry as 'Swing' counties – that is, that the agricultural workers in those counties, following the example of 'Captain Swing' in Kent, resisted the introduction of threshing machinery that put them out of work, and threatened violence in support of claims for better wages and reductions in rents and tithes. It was noted at the time that it was in the 'Swing' counties that enclosures had been carried out at the greatest rate. The situation for the labourer had been deteriorating since the end of the war with France, and though the grievances were not political, revolution was always in the background. E. P. Thompson in *The Making of the English Working Class* quotes a letter from around Yeovil, signed with a bleeding heart, 'The Burthen that is now laid on us we are Determin'd to bear no longer, Blood and Blood and Blood, A General Revolution there mus [sic] be . . .'

Technological change was coupled with recession; and a great increase in the pool of labour, brought about by the demobilisation of the army, led to depressed wages in agricultural and dependent trades and, above all, in the wool and woollens industries. These were key to the economy and culture of the region, especially the Cotswolds. The valley of the Windrush is an example, as are the valleys around Stroud, which saw the most vehement protests against lowered wages and conditions. At Randwick, near Stroud, between 1831 and 1833, a self-help scheme was set up for the benefit of redundant woollen workers. In exchange for labour – road improvement, say – vouchers were given which could be exchanged for food, clothing, and books, weavers traditionally being autodidacts, at least in the cottage-industry phase. Famously at Tolpuddle, in 1834, the farm workers who combined to demand increased wages were subjected to a punitive sentence of transportation to Australia, on a charge of conspiracy. The liberal conscience of the nation was stirred through the energetic campaign mounted on their behalf, and they were repatriated in 1836.

In the whole South West, only Cornwall had virtually no 'Swing' incidents. And yet it was from Newlyn that William Lovett came. It was he who drew up the People's Charter, the founding document of the Chartist movement. Lovett was a ropemaker before he left Cornwall in 1821 to try his luck in London. Ropemaking was a trade whose members were known as articulate, self-educated and radical. Chartism gave protest an organisation, a focus and leadership. There were riots in Bristol, and many meetings of crowds numbering tens of thousands, addressed by leaders of the South West such as Henry 'Orator' Hunt. There was now a perceived threat of a 'General Revolution'.

It is said that Chartism was not really socialist – more a working-class reform movement. However, the Chartist Land Co-operative in the 1840s has, in some respects, the appearance of Fourierist strategy (that is to say, that the settlements at Staunton and Minster Lovell, and others in the country, were conceived as a sort of phalanstery, after the influential idea of Fourier). The neat alignment of the Charterville cottages and their symmetrical design evokes working-class respectability, but also the shoulder-to-shoulder power of the military phalanx – in marked contrast to what, at the time, would have been the immiseration in the cottages of Minster Lovell, down by the Windrush. Small wonder that Parliament would not find a legal basis for the Chartist Land Bank. There were other reasons for the rapid failure of the scheme, some practical, some ideological. Some, such as the improvement in wages and conditions in industry after 1850, made rural subsistence less attractive. In any case, the fortunate lottery winners had little or no agricultural experience, and the land purchased was relatively unproductive. For the time being, no doubt they would experience the joy of freedom from alienating factory work, of equality among comrades. Fourier wrote joyfulness into his prescription, as did the young Marx, in his vision of the classless society.

Low wages and technological change in agriculture increasingly drove workers off the land to find work in the woollen mills, which were themselves doomed by the competition from the North of England in the form of larger mills, and broader looms powered by steam. (The remaining mill building in Minster Lovell village is now part of a conference centre, and a leading member of the 2005 Labour Cabinet has a weekend retreat nearby. Present Imaginary, based on Imagined Past.)

Another kind of centre emerged in the early nineteenth century – Cheltenham. The Spa was thrown up quite swiftly, in a series of entrepreneurial developments, starting at the end of the eighteenth century, but mostly after the 1830s. The city of Bath had earlier demonstrated that a spa could be a money-spinner. What was required was an army of women domestic workers and men skilled in trades such as ornamental ironwork, decorative plasterwork and interior decoration in the latest fashions, as well as in the basic trades of construction. Many of these workers came down from London, where most of the trades involved were in recession, and they were already familiar with radical ideas. It was the presence of a ready audience that brought Thomas Willey to Cheltenham to sell, among other songs, his Chartist ballads.

The relative peace that generally characterised the South West after the 1850s can, in large measure, be explained by the fact that the centres of industrial tension had either disappeared or were disappearing, and farm workers had settled into a resigned silence. Some writers have explained the widespread morality of acceptance of one's lot as the influence of Wesleyanism in the South West. Presumably, the lot of the farm worker who stayed was, on balance, preferable to the available alternatives – indigence, vagrancy or emigration.

Some time around 1870, William Morris purchased the Tudor/Jacobean Manor farmhouse at Kelmscott in Oxfordshire, close to the border with Gloucestershire. The house was shared for a time with his friend, Dante Gabriel Rossetti. In spite of the unhappiness caused by Rossetti's relationship with his wife, Jane, at the house, Morris retained the deepest love for the place. 'So much has the old house grown up out of the soil,' he wrote, 'and the lives of those that lived on it: some thin thread of tradition, a half anxious sense of the delight of the meadow and acre and wood and river: a certain amount . . . of common sense, a liking for making materials serve one's turn, and perhaps at bottom some little grain of sentiment . . .'

His vision of a communistic Utopia is described in *News from Nowhere*, which ends with the narrator, Morris himself, arriving at Kelmscott, where he finds the people of the future society living a life of simple joy. (He, too, was interested in Fourier, not to mention Marx and the anarchist Pyotr Kropotkin.) 'The house itself was a fitting guardian for all the beauty of this heart of summer.' Morris is buried in the village churchyard under a simple tombstone designed by the architect, Philip Webb.

In the quotations above, Morris draws together some of his key ideas about socialist society – the worker is a whole, creative person at one with the natural world in which he or she lives; the product of that work embodies and expresses that integrity, and is Art. The proper aim of socialism, therefore, is the unfettering of the creative human spirit. Morris's ideas had a widespread impact, especially on people in the craft trades and in the arts, and the South West of the country was the place to try them out. We might now discern, after Morris, two kinds of movement: one, of Lefties native to the region, who leave it to go to London, seeking a wider stage; the second, of people who came to the region to live out, if they can, their ideals. We note that Morris used Kelmscott Manor for relaxation and dreaming; he set up the Kelmscott Press in London – wisely, as the case of C. R. Ashbee demonstrated.

C. R. Ashbee, artist, designer and socialist, was influenced both by Morris and by Ruskin. He saw that the handcraftsman was trapped in the mandibles of bourgeois culture: on the one side the exaltation of the individual, on the other the requirement to fulfil a brief determined by the customer. His inspiration was to found a workers' movement that combined craft production with craft teaching – an extended atelier system run as a co-operative, called the Guild and School of Handicraft. The workshops moved from

London to Chipping Campden in Gloucestershire in 1902, with 150 men, women and children. By 1908, the enterprise was bankrupt, because of the expense of transportation back to London, on top of the inherent cost of craft production, as compared with cheap, machine-made copies. Furthermore, the patrons of Liberty's were finding the gratuitous flourishes of Art Nouveau too, too delicious.

Joyfulness was certainly a feature of the community that was set up at Whiteway in Gloucestershire at the turn of the century. It is moving to contemplate those young Londoners, liberated by Tolstoy's social vision, and by their bicycles. Gloucestershire was within cycling range and yet far enough from London for land to be affordable. From the commerce and squalor of London's East End, they bicycled into Nature. They had liberated attitudes to sex, and went in for nudism. In all of this – recovering human nature in Nature – they exemplified both the underlying anarchist belief in the essential goodness of freed humanity, and a pervasive socialist vision. An imagined future was to be created out of an imagined past.

So-called fine artists have a particularly difficult task, since highly individuated practice – part of the ideology in this specialised area of commodity production – must also be politically cautious, if their product is to sell. As Clement Greenberg observed, the artist is tied to the rich by 'an umbilical cord of gold'. The artists' colonies that were set up around 1900 at Newlyn, St Ives and Lamorna were certainly inspired by some version of progressive idealism. But the visual representation of those ideals is, to say the least, indirect and uncontentious; scenes of ordinary working people, scenes of sensuous enjoyment of the sea and shore, and, later, adoption of a naïve style, demonstrating the unfettered – that is, unschooled – creative spirit. None of that would distress the liberal art world. Several of the artists who worked in those communities (for example, Laura Knight, Ben Nicholson and Patrick Heron) also joined the

Artists International Association (AIA). This was formed in the 1930s to oppose fascism and to advance socialism. With the onset of the Cold War, advancing socialism was seen by the younger members as not such good branding, and the AIA folded. One artist member of the AIA who kept faith was Wogan Philipps of Colesbourne. He was wounded in the Spanish Civil War, was turned down for military service in 1939, and took up farming. He was an influential member of the farmworkers' union. His paintings are never polemical, but express, almost in a puzzled way, the complex and contradictory aspects of places and people. For example, the flight of a heavy bomber casting its shadow across the Cotswolds, or the beauty and threat of Didcot's cooling towers.

Rutland Boughton established himself at Glastonbury in 1914. His project – to put in musical form the essential myths in the formation of The People, hence the Arthurian legend, hence Glastonbury – has overtones of Yeats, of Wagner, of Blake, and of William Morris. He was very widely supported in that project by the greats of the musical establishment, which says something about a degree of ambiguity in the political thinking. After the abrupt termination of the Glastonbury Arts Festival he settled at Kilcot in Gloucestershire, putting on further festivals – at Stroud and at Bath. He joined the Communist Party in 1929 and was one of the early vice-presidents of the Workers' Music Association.

Like Boughton and many of his contemporaries, Gustav Holst drew inspiration from what was seen as the directness and simplicity of folk music. He was born in Cheltenham in 1874, went to the Grammar School and, after holding a couple of minor musical appointments in Wick Rissington and Bourton-on-the-Water, went on to the Royal College of Music. In London, he joined the Hammersmith Socialist Club, and conducted the Hammersmith Socialist Music Society at William Morris's house in Hammersmith Mall.

Of those who left the South West, we have identified some who have made a contribution with lasting impact. Emmeline Pethick-Lawrence was able to use her social position and socialist principles to advance the cause of women's suffrage. Beatrice Webb had already achieved national significance in the Labour movement, when her husband, Sidney, took the title Lord Passfield. She refused on principle to be called Lady Passfield. Albert Mansbridge, the son of a carpenter, left school in Gloucester at the age of fourteen. While employed as a clerk in London, he furthered his own education in extension classes at King's College, then taught evening classes in industrial history, economics and typing. In 1903, he and his wife, Frances, founded the Workers' Educational Association, followed by similar organisations in Australia, New Zealand and Canada. In 1918, he established the World Association for Adult Education, in 1919, the Seafarers' Educational Service and, in 1921, the British Institute of Adult Education. Frances and Albert Mansbridge lived by the words inscribed on their memorial in Gloucester Cathedral: 'The multitude of the wise is the welfare of the world.'

Gazetteer

ASHBURTON, Devon. Church of England Elementary School. Here studied until the age of twelve, Richard Carlile (1790-1843), champion of a free press, campaigner for parliamentary reform, women's rights, the abolition of child labour and the improvement of wages and conditions for agricultural workers. As a child he saw Tom Paine's effigy burnt. He left Ashburton to be apprenticed as a tinplateman in Plymouth. He went on to London to find work as a tinsmith, and encountered other radicals. From 1817 he published Paine's works in pamphlets, and founded and published *The Republican*. His eyewitness reports of the Peterloo massacre in Manchester on 16 August 1819, and the publication of Paine's *The Age of Reason*, resulted in his imprisonment at Dorchester for seditious libel and blasphemy.

ASTHALL, Oxfordshire. Asthall Manor. Birthplace of Jessica (Decca) Mitford (1917-1996). In 1926, the family – sisters included Diana who married Oswald Mosley, sometime Labour minister – moved to a newly built house in nearby Swinbrook. Jessica, in her memoirs, *Hons and Rebels*, said the house had the 'utilitarian look of frankly institutional architecture. It could be a small barracks, a girls' boarding school, a private lunatic asylum.' She married Esmond Romilly, cousin of Winston Churchill, who fought with the International Brigade in the Spanish Civil War. She moved to the United States in 1939 and joined the Communist Party and, with her second husband, campaigned on human rights issues.

BATH, Somerset. Henry Vincent (1800-70), known in Chartist circles as the 'Demosthenes of the West', was the leading Chartist in the South West. He set up a paper, *The Western Vindicator*, in Bath, in which he gave weekly accounts of the meetings he had attended and speeches delivered. Bath is the birthplace of Edward Vansittart Neale (1810-92), Christian Socialist and founder of the first co-operative store in London. He became general secretary of the Co-operative Union.

BEDMINSTER, Somerset. Birthplace of Thomas Willey (1795-1861), Chartist and ballad printer. Willey moved to Cheltenham where he set up as a printer in the High Street, and where he chaired Chartist Land Plan meetings. Although most of the ballads he printed could be described as light entertainment, many addressed issues of parliamentary reform, a highly effective method of broadcasting radical ideas in an age of mass illiteracy.

BERRY HILL, Gloucestershire. Brick House, Joyford Hill. Birthplace of Dennis Potter (1935-94), the most innovative and important television playwright of his time. Viewers can be grateful to the electors of Hertfordshire East who, in 1964, did not elect him as their Labour MP. He found the whole process so dispiriting that he did not even vote for himself. The experience put him off party politics for ever, though he remained committed to the Left.

BIDEFORD, Devon. The Manse, Westcroft. Birthplace of Evan Durbin (1906-48), economist and Labour MP for Edmonton. After elementary schools in Plympton and Exmouth, he went on to Heles School, Exeter, and Taunton School, and then New College Oxford, to read Zoology. He switched to read Philosophy, Politics and Economics (PPE). A friend and associate of Hugh Gaitskell, he eschewed Marxist social and economic theory in favour of a British socialist tradition. His publications include *The Politics of Democratic Socialism* (1940), and he was the editor of *War and Democracy: Essays on the Causes and Prevention of War* (1938). Intellectual opponents acknowledged his integrity and fearlessness in the defence of his principles. He was drowned in heavy surf after rescuing his daughter and another child at Strangles Beach, North Cornwall.

BOURNEMOUTH, Dorset. St Peter's Church. In a vault are the remains of radical writer William Godwin (1756-1836) and his first wife, feminist Mary Wollstonecraft (1759-97), author of *Vindication of the Rights of Women* (1792). Both had first been buried in Old St Pancras churchyard, London. The family vault was built by the poet Shelley who married Mary, daughter of Godwin and Mary Wollstonecraft.

BOURNEMOUTH, Dorset. Stirling House. A fashionable girls' school in the 1870s. Beatrice Potter, later Webb (1858-1943), was a boarder here in 1875 and spent her time 'in lonely study and religious meditation'. The young and studious Beatrice was disconcerted to find that despite her religious studies she found herself talking 'frivolously' on the day of her confirmation. Shortly after leaving Stirling House she abandoned the Christian faith.

BOURNEMOUTH, Dorset. Conference Hall. Site of Labour Party Conference, 1985, when then Leader, Neil Kinnock, said, 'I'll tell you what happens with impossible promises. You start with implausible resolutions, which are then pickled into a rigid dogma or code. And you end up with the grotesque chaos of a Labour Council – a Labour Council – hiring taxis to scuttle around a city handing out redundancy notices to its own workers.'

BRIDGWATER, Somerset. St John's School. Attended by Leah Manning (1886-1970), who was born in the town as Leah Elizabeth Perrett. Socialist, teacher, president of the National Union of Teachers and MP for East Islington, and later Epping. She trained at Homerton College, Cambridge, and started her teaching career in Cambridge where she encountered at first hand the poverty and malnutrition of her pupils. During the Spanish Civil War she assisted with the evacuation of four thousand Basque children to Britain, and witnessed the bombing of Guernica. She resumed teaching in Harlow, where the Leah Manning Centre cares for the senior citizens of the new town. Her autobiography, *A Life for*

Education, was published in 1970.

BRISTOL. 39 Saxon Road, St Werburgh's. A plaque records the one-time home of Ernest Bevin (1881-1951), General Secretary of the Transport and General Workers' Union, Minister of Labour in Winston Churchill's war-time coalition and Secretary of State for Foreign Affairs in Clement Attlee's government, 1945-51. He was born at Winsford, Somerset.

BRISTOL. 8 John Street, Easton. Birthplace of Ben Tillett (1860-1943), President of the TUC, Labour MP for Salford North, a founder of the Independent Labour Party and the Labour Party, General Secretary of the Dock, Wharf, Riverside and General Labourers' Union, which was later merged into the Transport and General Workers Union. After an unhappy childhood, Tillett ran away to the circus and worked as an acrobat before joining the Royal Navy at the age of thirteen. He was invalided out, and worked in east London as a dock labourer, and espoused Christian socialism. An inspirational orator, in his retirement this pugilist for socialism tried to set up a trade union for boxers. John Street was overshadowed by the Easton Coal Pit. Now neither street nor pit exist. In 1991 the street was demolished and replaced by a small park as part of the Easton renewal scheme. The adjacent pub recalls the past, 'The Pit Pony'.

BRISTOL. 20 Charlotte Street, Clifton. Birthplace of Emmeline Pethick (1867-1954), later Lady Pethick-Lawrence, suffragist, pacifist and writer. In London she worked with the Methodist West London Mission and met the Pankhursts through James Keir Hardie. She was repeatedly imprisoned and force-fed following her uncompromising campaigns for women's suffrage. Her Old Etonian husband, Frederick Lawrence (who on marriage, adopted her family name), was editor of *Labour Record and Review*, and, together, they launched and edited the suffragette newspaper, *Votes for Women*. She was secretary of the Women's Social and Political Union and later president of the breakaway, militant, though non-violent, Women's Freedom League.

BRISTOL. University. From 1970 to 1988 the Chancellor of the University was Dorothy Crowfoot Hodgkin (1910-94). A Nobel Prize laureate, chemist and crystallographer, committed socialist, internationalist, and peace campaigner. She was a founder of the Pugwash group of scientists committed to peace and, in 1987, was a recipient of the Lenin Peace Prize. She was Margaret Thatcher's science tutor at Somerville College, Oxford.

BRISTOL. Public toilets on Stoke Road on the Downs. A blue plaque honours Victoria Hughes (1897-1978) who 'befriended and cared for prostitutes when she worked here as a lavatory attendant from 1929 to 1962'.

BRISTOL. Seven Stars Inn, 1 Thomas Lane, Redcliffe. A blue plaque commemorates Thomas Clarkson (1760-1846), anti-slavery campaigner, whose work was pivotal in engaging the commitment of William Wilberforce. He rode thousands of miles on horseback, conducting empirical research into the slave trade in Bristol, Liverpool, Bath and Gloucester. His first-hand accounts furnished abolitionists in parliament with irrefutable evidence of the horrors of the slave trade. When the slave trade was abolished in 1807, William Wordsworth wrote a sonnet acknowledging Clarkson's contribution: 'Clarkson! It was an obstinate hill to climb.'

BRISTOL. 68 Park Road, Stapleton. A blue plaque honours John Frost (1784-1877), Chartist leader and social revolutionary. In 1839, he led miners in the Newport Rising where he was arrested, tried for high treason, and sentenced to be hanged, drawn and quartered. Public outcry resulted in the sentence being first commuted to transportation to Van Diemen's Land, and later to permanent exclusion from Britain. In 1856, he was permitted to return. He retired to Stapleton and wrote newspaper articles on universal suffrage, and revisited earlier haunts where, as a young man in 1804, he had been employed as an assistant woollen draper and trader, before encountering the radical ideas of Thomas Paine and William Cobbett.

BROADCLYST, Devon. Killerton House. Family home of Richard Acland (1906–1990), hereditary baronet who, with J. B. Priestley, founded the socialist Commonwealth Party in 1942. The party was committed to the public ownership of land. Acland lived by his party principles by handing over the nineteen thousand acres of the Killerton estates to the National Trust in 1943. Support for the Commonwealth Party collapsed in the heady days of Labour's landslide victory of 1945. In 1947, Acland became Labour MP for Gravesend, but resigned his seat in 1955 in protest against the hydrogen bomb. He was a founder of the Campaign for Nuclear Disarmament. No advocate of any third way, he wrote in *The Forward March* (1941), 'Either the great resources of a country can be owned by private individuals, or they can be owned by all individuals in common. It is most important that anyone who vaguely hopes for any third alternative should sit down and write out in black and white what the alternative can be. Otherwise he should accept my contention that there are only these two alternatives.'

BURFORD, Oxfordshire. Parish Church. Levellers were incarcerated and executed here in 1649. 'Leveller' was originally a term of abuse. Levellers advocated manhood suffrage, exclusion of the aristocracy from government, radical reform of trade laws, abolishing tithes and reopening the enclosures. Many had fought for Cromwell in the Civil War, 1642-48. One of their leaders was John Lilburne. In May 1649, Leveller soldiers who refused to fight in Ireland were captured and imprisoned for four nights in the church. One soldier has carved his name on the font, 'ANTHONY SEDLEY. 1649. PRISNER'. On 17 May, prisoners were forced to the roof to witness the execution by firing squad, in the churchyard, of three of their members, Corporal Perkins, Cornet Thompson and Private Church.

In 1975, the Oxford Industrial Branch of the Workers' Educational Association organised the first Levellers Day at Burford. The following year, the Secretary of State for Energy, Tony Benn, accepted an invitation to speak at the church. This caused some outrage among local Conservatives, and the local MP, Douglas Hurd, questioned whether the WEA was misappropriating public funds. 'No one,' he wrote to the Secretary of State for Education, 'suspects that . . . [he] is coming to talk to my constituents about North Sea oil.' Benn fulfilled the engagement. As he approached the church, two elderly church wardens were wiping off a slogan with paraffin and wire brushes: 'Bollocks to Benn', graffiti that, in Benn's words, 'embarrassed the vicar but not me'.

CHARD, Somerset. Cemetery. Grave of Margaret Bondfield (1873-1953), born by Furnham Reservoir and educated at High Street School. Feminist, trade unionist, Labour MP for Northampton and, later, for Wallsend. Ramsay MacDonald appointed her as Minister of Labour in his 1929 government, and so she became Britain's first woman Cabinet Minister. She worked in Chard as a pupil teacher before moving to be apprenticed in a drapery in Brighton. There she was befriended by a customer, the women's-rights activist Louisa Martindale, to whom she described the miserable life for young women who, as shop workers, lived in dormitories owned by the employer. She went on to become assistant secretary of the Shop Workers' Union, and Secretary of the Women's Labour League.

CHELTENHAM, Gloucestershire. Montpellier Gardens. A tree commemorates Bill Bickham, Allan Chambers, John Cook, Mike Grindley, Brian Johnson, Clive Lloyd, Gareth Morris, Gerry O'Hagan, Alan Rowland, Robin Smith, Harry Underwood, Dee Goddard, Graham Hughes and Roy Taylor – the fourteen trade unionists at the Government Communications Headquarters (GCHQ) who refused to surrender their right to trade union membership, in response to the Conservative government's ban on trades unions at GCHQ in January 1984. The campaign to restore their rights, marked by annual rallies of support every January, lasted until May 1997, when the new Labour government partially restored the rights of trade unionists at GCHQ.

CHELTENHAM, Gloucestershire. Cheltenham Ladies' College. Attended by Dorothy Jewson (1884-1964). Labour MP for Norwich and author of *The Destitute of Norwich*.

COLESBOURNE, Gloucestershire. Butler's Farm. Former home of Wogan Philipps (1902-93), who inherited the title of Lord Milford. He was a farmer and painter, and the only communist in the House of Lords. In his maiden speech he proposed the abolition of the Upper House. He served in the International Brigade in the Spanish Civil War, as an ambulance driver, and was wounded.

GLASTONBURY, Somerset. Assembly Rooms. The composer, Rutland Boughton (1878-1960) moved to Glastonbury in 1914 to establish an artistic community, together with the poet Reginald Buckley, and the artist Christina Walshe. Boughton, who became a member of the Communist Party, sought to develop a specifically English form of 'music drama', grounded in folklore, such as *The Immortal Hour*, 1914, and *The Birth of Arthur*, 1920. These were presented at annual festivals, held in the Assembly Rooms. His work *Bethlehem*, with words by William Morris, was performed a number of times. In 1926, in sympathy with the miners and the General Strike, *Bethlehem* was given in modern dress, with Jesus born in a miner's cottage and Herod shown as a capitalist in a top hat. The ensuing furore spelled the end of the festivals in the Assembly Rooms. Walshe's portrait of Boughton hangs in the National Portrait Gallery.

GLOUCESTER. India House Inn, Barton Street. Nearby, in one of the now-demolished six Albert Cottages, India House Lane, was born Albert Mansbridge (1876-1952), founder, with his wife, born Frances Pringle, of the

Workers' Educational Association (WEA). He attended St James' Elementary School in Gloucester, and left school at the age of fourteen. Mansbridge's family moved to London. Later he and Frances established a precursor to the WEA, the Association to Promote the Higher Education of Working Men, in their home in Oxford. In 1903, the WEA was formally founded, and collaborated with universities to provide tutorial classes. Young, enthusiastic academics, keen to promote access to and widen participation in higher education, included R. H. Tawney, A. D. Lindsay, G. D. H. Cole, Hugh Gaitskell and E. P. Thompson. WEA graduates included Joan Maynard for whom the WEA 'opened up a completely new world'.

GLOUCESTER. Cathedral. The ashes of Albert Mansbridge and his wife, Frances, are laid in the north aisle.

HOLN, Devon. Vicarage. Birthplace of Charles Kingsley (1819-75), writer, churchman, and a founder of the Christian Socialist Movement. His children's book *The Water Babies: A Fairy Tale for a Land Baby* decries the harsh conditions endured by the poor, and the 'pollution of rivers and streams'. His political writings resonate to this day. In *Cheap Clothes and Nasty* and *Alton Locke, Tailor and Poet,* he rails against sweatshop conditions in which cheap clothes are produced, and in the novel *Yeast*, he denounces the working conditions in which food is processed.

KELMSCOTT, Oxfordshire. Kelmscott Manor. The country home of William Morris (1834-96), socialist, writer and designer craftsman. The manor can be visited on Wednesdays from the spring to the early autumn.

KELMSCOTT, Oxfordshire. St George's Church. Grave of William Morris, his wife Jane and their daughters.

LAND'S END, Cornwall. Off Land's End were scattered the ashes of George Lansbury (1859-1940), former Leader of the Labour Party. 'There are abler men in the Labour movement; minds more subtle and distinguished,' wrote Harold

Laski, 'but George Lansbury is its soul . . . Others may see further or more clearly; no man sees more justly.'

LITTLEMORE, Oxfordshire. Village school. Attended, until he was twelve, by Henry Broadhurst (1840-1911), trade unionist, campaigner for the extension of the franchise and MP, successively, for Stoke-on-Trent, Bordesley, Nottingham and Leicester. Broadhurst was then born in the village, the youngest of twelve children, worked as a blacksmith and was apprenticed to his father's trade of stonemason. He went to London and became an official of the stonemason's union. He became secretary of the Labour Representation League, founded, in 1869, to secure the return of trade unionists to Parliament. He served in Gladstone's third government as Under-Secretary of the Home Department and was out of sympathy with the Labour Party. He published his autobiography in 1901, with the title *Henry Broadhurst MP: The Story of his life from a Stonemason's Bench to the Treasury Bench Told by Himself.*

LOWBANDS, Gloucestershire. Here in the Forest of Dean, in 1846, the first of the Chartist land settlements was established, with 250 families.

LYNMOUTH, Devon. In 1812, while working on *Queen Mab*, Percy Bysshe Shelley walked along the shore, tossing bottles containing copies of his *Declaration of Rights* into the Bristol Channel. Reputedly, these were recovered in Avonmouth and in South Wales. His servant, Dan Healy, was imprisoned for six months for flyposting the *Declaration of Rights* in Barnstaple. In the notes on *Queen Mab*, Shelley wrote, 'there is no real wealth but the labour of man. Were the mountains of gold and the valleys of silver, the world would not be one grain of corn the richer: no comfort would be added to the human race.'

MINSTER LOVELL, Oxfordshire. Charterville. An estate bought by the Chartist Co-operative Land Company in June 1847. As at Snigs End, so in Minster Lovell, the aim of the Company was to purchase farms and estates to be divided into smallholdings. Workers saved to buy shares to be entered into a lottery for the smallholdings. Lottery 'winners' were provided with initial supplies of fuel and seed. Many of the original cottages can be seen in the area between the A40 and the B4047. Built with two bedrooms, an all-purpose main room, an outside privy and a well, they are now mostly much gentrified, extended, improved and priced beyond the reach of most workers.

NEWLYN, Cornwall. Birthplace of William Lovett (1800-77), the Chartist leader who drafted the People's Charter in May 1838. Lovett was an apprentice ropemaker in Penzance before moving to London in 1821. Finding no employment in his trade, he obtained work as a cabinetmaker. In his autobiography, *Life and Struggles in Pursuit of Bread, Knowledge and Freedom,* he describes what happened when fellow cabinetmakers found out that he had not served an apprenticeship as a cabinetmaker, and 'talked of "setting Mother Shorney at me"; this is a cant term in the trade, and meant the putting away of your tools, the injuring of your work, and annoying you in such a way as to drive you out of the shop.' Lovett displayed his leadership skills by calling a meeting, where, over 'a quantity of drink', he explained his circumstances and satisfied his critics. A plaque in the village commemorates Lovett's link with Newlyn.

OXFORD. The Dragon School. This smart prep school was attended in the early 1930s by Edward Palmer Thompson (1924-93), born at Boars Hill, the son of a Methodist missionary. After war service he worked as an extramural tutor at the University of Leeds. He joined the Communist Party at the age of eighteen and left in disgust in 1956. A peace activist – he was a founder of European Nuclear Disarmament – he is best remembered as a historian, the biographer of William Morris, and author of *The Making of the English Working Class* (1963), which he described as 'a biography of the English working class'. He was a charismatic teacher and campaigner who saw himself as a permanent member of the awkward squad. 'One must,' he wrote, 'to survive as an unassimilated socialist in this infinitely assimilative culture, put oneself into a school of awkwardness. One must make one's own sensibility all knobbly – all knees and elbows of susceptibility and refusal.'

OXFORD. Gloucester Green. A plaque commemorates the execution of Leveller soldiers Private Biggs and Private Piggen, 'executed', as the plaque records, 'like their Leveller colleagues at Burford by forces loyal to Cromwell. They were shot near this place for their part in the second mutiny of Oxford Garrison on 18th September 1649.'

OXFORD. 3 Merton Street. Birthplace of Henry Marten (1602-80), regicide. A plaque reads, 'In this house was born Col. Henry Marten, Gentleman Commoner of University College Oxford, MP for Berkshire, Republican and Wit.'

OXFORD. New College. This College has seen the university education of a disproportionate number of Lefties, including Richard Crossman, Douglas Jay and Tony Benn, who were all in Harold Wilson's Cabinet; Hugh Gaitskell, a Leader of the Labour Party; Evan Durbin and Harold Laski, intellectuals; Victor Gollancz, publisher; William Jowitt, Lord Chancellor, and Kenneth Younger, Minister of State for Foreign Affairs in Clement Attlee's government.

OXFORD. Magdalen College. Bill Rodgers was an undergraduate here. G. D. H. Cole and A. J. P. Taylor both taught.

OXFORD. Jesus College. Harold Wilson was a hardworking undergraduate here before he went to work for Lord Beveridge, another workaholic.

OXFORD. University College. John Ruskin, John Strachey and Clement Attlee were all alumni.

OXFORD. Balliol College. Four members of Harold Wilson's cabinets were educated here: Anthony Greenwood, Denis Healey, Roy Jenkins and Frank Soskice. As also were influential intellectuals such as G. D. H. Cole and R. H. Tawney.

OXFORD. Ruskin College.

Founded for trade unionists, this College has educated Moss Evans, Jack Jones, Dennis Skinner, John Prescott and Norman Willis.

OXFORD. St John's College. The alma mater of Tony Blair.

OXFORD. Somerville College. Shirley Williams and Margaret Jay were undergraduates.

OXFORD. St Hugh's College. Barbara Castle studied here.

PLYMOUTH, Devon. 1 Lipson Terrace. Birthplace of Michael Foot (1913-). Son of Isaac Foot, solicitor and bibliophile, he was editor of the *Evening Standard* in his twenties, co-authored the wartime book, *Guilty Men*, excoriating the pre-war Conservative-dominated governments, and was elected MP for Plymouth Devonport from 1945 to 1955. He wrote books on Swift, Byron, and H. G. Wells, and brilliant essays on politics and literature. In 1960 he was elected MP for Ebbw Vale after the death of his political hero, Aneurin Bevan, whose two-volume standard biography he wrote. An inspiring and amusing political orator, he became Secretary of State for Employment in Harold Wilson's government, 1974-76, and Lord President of the Council and Leader of the House of Commons in the 1976-79 government of James Callaghan, whom he followed as Leader of the Labour Party, until after Labour's defeat in the 1983 General Election on a manifesto described by Gerald Kaufman as 'the longest suicide-note in history', a manifesto on which – as Michael Foot has pointed out – Gerald Kaufman was re-elected.

ST KEVERNE, Cornwall. The Cornish Rebellion of 1497 is commemorated by bronze statues at the entrance to the village. The village blacksmith, Michael Joseph An Gof, led a march to London to protest against the taxes imposed by King Henry VII to fund his war in Scotland. His following was joined in Devon by that of Thomas Flamank of Bodmin, and by the time they reached the outskirts of London, their 'army' was estimated as forty thousand strong. They were decimated by Henry's troops at

Blackheath, and the two leaders were hanged, drawn and quartered.

ST MARY'S, Isles of Scilly. Old Town Church. Grave of Harold Wilson (1916-95), Labour Prime Minister, 1964-70 and 1974-76. Wilson and his poet wife, Mary, spent peaceful holidays enjoying the rocky coastline, flowers and birds of the Scilly Islands. After many years of illness, Wilson died in St Thomas's Hospital, London. 'The final tragic years,' wrote Geoffrey Goodman in his *Guardian* obituary, 'in which the jewel of his extraordinary memory became increasingly destroyed by terrible illness robbed him – and probably the nation – of an opportunity to demonstrate a matured wisdom that, undoubtedly, was there.'

SLIMBRIDGE, Gloucestershire. Slimbridge Waste. A Digger community was set up on the Waste around 1650; the precise location, somewhere in the neighbourhood of the Wildfowl and Wetlands Trust, is unknown.

STANDISH, Gloucestershire. Beatrice Potter, later Mrs Sidney Webb, (1858-1943) was born and raised at Standish House. Her father, Richard Potter, was a wealthy railway entrepreneur, and an associate of radical politicians and intellectuals. In long discussions with one of the visitors to the house, the sociologist and philosopher Herbert Spencer, the young inquiring Beatrice learned the value of 'seeking and sorting facts'. Much of her education was acquired through governesses, extensive travel and reading. Before her marriage in 1892, she had become well known in some circles with her writings on social and economic matters. Together with Sidney, she was influential in the Fabian Society and in the Labour Party. In 1913 they founded *The New Statesman*. Overlooking the Severn Vale, Standish House, with its extensive grounds inhabited by peacocks, became a sanatorium in 1922 for the treatment of tuberculosis patients. In 2004, health services and patients were transferred to Gloucester, and the peacocks to Prinknash Abbey.

STAUNTON, Gloucestershire.

Snigs End. As at Minster Lovell in 1847, the Chartist Co-operative Land Company purchased over 250 acres, which was divided into 81 holdings. In addition to the construction of cottages, an infrastructure of schools and roads was also provided. One of the smallholdings, now a Grade II listed building, provides Bed and Breakfast accommodation in 'cosy but deceptively spacious all ground floor accommodation'.

SUTTON COURTENAY, Oxfordshire. All Saints Church. In the churchyard is the grave of George Orwell (Eric Arthur Blair) (1903-50). He was buried in a country churchyard in accordance with his will. It could have been any country churchyard and he had no particular connection with Oxfordshire. However, the All Saints plot was secured through the influence of his friend, David Astor, whose family were landowners in the area. The churchyard is distinguished by several dozen fine yew trees. The tranquillity of the place is conflicted with the overwhelming presence of Didcot Power Station. Orwell's grave has a simple headstone, inscribed with his real name. David Astor, who died in 2001, is buried in the adjacent plot. Malcolm Muggeridge observed that Orwell's death on Lenin's birthday, and burial by the Astors, seemed to cover 'the full range of his life'.

TOLPUDDLE, Dorset. The Tolpuddle Martyrs' Museum. The Tolpuddle Martyrs – George Loveless, James Loveless, James Hammett, Thomas Standfield, John Standfield and James Brine – were brought to trial at Dorchester in March 1834, and sentenced to seven years' transportation. Their 'crime' was establishing a Friendly Society of Agricultural Labourers 'to preserve ourselves, our wives, and our children from utter degradation and starvation.' The men were charged with administering illegal oaths: combinations (trade unions) were not, in themselves, illegal. George Loveless is buried in Tolpuddle churchyard. Every July, a rally, and a march through the village to the grave, serve as a reminder that trade union rights were hard-won. The museum presents the history of the martyrs. The six TUC Memorial Cottages were built in 1934 to mark the centenary of the martyrs' conviction. Nearby, a bench – made in her native North Yorkshire – commemorates Joan Maynard (1921-98), twentieth century champion of agricultural workers.

UPAVON, Wiltshire. Chisenbury. Birthplace of Henry ('Orator') Hunt (1773-1835). During his trial in 1800 – for killing some pheasants – Hunt met a Radical lawyer, by whom he became politicised. Farmer, orator and businessman, his power base was the working class of northern England. He was a star speaker at Peterloo in 1819, and at Spa Fields in London for the last 20 years of his life.

WHITEWAY, Gloucestershire. Colony. Tolstoyan anarcho-communists founded a colony here in 1898. They had cycled out from London in search of land to be communally owned. Police, concerned about – or fascinated by – free love and naturism, infiltrated the colony. 'Manners had they none and their customs are beastly,' wrote an official in 1925, when the Home Office tried to close the place down. The commune, it was alleged, attracted an assortment of socialists, pacifists, freethinkers and refugees. Today the colony is still called 'Colony', and the inhabitants refer to themselves as colonists. Many of the original clapboard houses remain, surrounded by high trees and bushes, and a fair number of rusty vehicles. The feel of the place is more Appalachian than Cotswold.

YEOVIL, Somerset. Unitarian Chapel. Henry Solly (1813-1903) was Minister here for two years from 1840. His tenure was terminated because of his support for Chartism and his participation in the Chartist Conference in Birmingham. Although a champion of many initiatives to better the conditions of working people, Solly is best remembered as the founder of the Working Men's Club movement. In 1862 he established the Working Men's Club and Institute Union in London, and was employed as its secretary. By the time of his death, he had successfully established nearly a thousand clubs in towns and cities the length and breadth of the land. He completely failed, however, in requiring them to be teetotal.

YORKLEY, Gloucestershire. Birthplace of Lena May (1915-), later Lena Jeger, Labour MP for St Pancras and Holborn South. She campaigned for the release of Yashar Kemal, the imprisoned Turkish novelist and editor of the marxist weekly, *Ant*. On 3 July 1967, Barbara Castle recorded an all-night sitting on the Sexual Offences Bill, which decriminalised homosexuality. 'Trailing through the lobby at 4.00 a.m., I ran into Lena Jeger who put her arms round me and said in a piercing voice, "Aren't we good, doing our bit for the boys!" She really is a joy.'

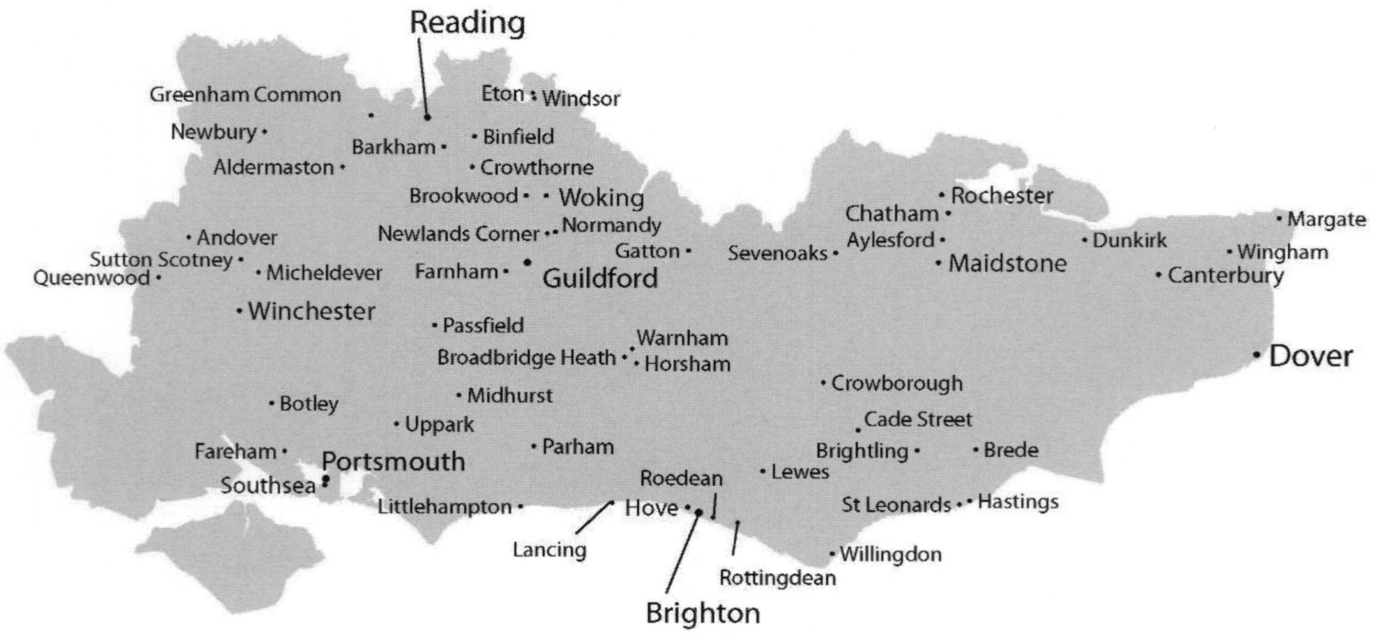

Reading
Greenham Common
Eton
Windsor
Newbury
Barkham
Binfield
Aldermaston
Crowthorne
Brookwood
Woking
Rochester
Chatham
Margate
Newlands Corner
Normandy
Andover
Gatton
Sevenoaks
Aylesford
Dunkirk
Wingham
Sutton Scotney
Queenwood
Micheldever
Farnham
Guildford
Maidstone
Canterbury
Winchester
Passfield
Warnham
Broadbridge Heath
Horsham
Dover
Crowborough
Botley
Midhurst
Uppark
Cade Street
Fareham
Portsmouth
Parham
Brightling
Brede
Southsea
Roedean
Lewes
Littlehampton
Hove
St Leonards
Hastings
Lancing
Willingdon
Rottingdean
Brighton

2.

South East England

Penny Young

I embarked on my own rural rides on behalf of the *Lefties' Guide,* through Berkshire, Surrey, Hampshire, Kent and Sussex, with great expectations. My car was crammed with holiday brochures, together with various guide books, *Highways and Byways* and Arthur Mees, unearthed in second-hand book shops. Every so often I would pull off the leafy lane or busy motorway to consult them. I was on the trail of desperate peasants in revolt, radical writers and reformers such as William Cobbett, Tom Paine and the handsome Henry 'Orator' Hunt. I was going to track down the country hideaways of the Fabians, Sidney and Beatrice Webb, and the commune of Queenwood, the most ambitious of Robert Owen's 'Villages of Co-operation' or, as Cobbett outrageously called them, 'Mr Owen's Parallelograms of Paupers'. I wanted to find the old haunts and inspiration of socialist writers including H. G. Wells and George Orwell, take a look at that bastion of privilege, Eton College, which turned out so many early socialists, and to remember what the Aldermaston marches and Greenham Common protests were all about.

The brochures jingled with information about where to stay and eat, and the leisure attractions. The books, rustling nostalgia, wound through slumbering villages and churches, respectfully pointing out the castles and stately homes of Britain's aristocracy. Sometimes, it is true, Wat Tyler, leader of the Peasants' Revolt of 1381, would jump out, or Jack Cade, a century later, would loom large, challenging the Establishment. William Cobbett would amble safely by, in carefully selected picturesque moments of *Rural Rides,* with just a taste of his more quixotic adventures. H. G. Wells even took a stiff bow. 'It is generally understood that in Mr H. G. Wells' *Tono-Bungay,* Bladesover corresponds to Uppark and Wimblehurst to Midhurst.'

But there was no flesh on the bones. Where were the villages cleared away by land enclosures? Where were the peasants, oppressed by corruption, unjust laws and heavy taxes to fund foreign wars, marching furiously with aching feet, along muddy tracks for miles a day, seeking revenge? Was there any whiff in the air of the hayricks being set on fire in 1830, or the crash and clang of the threshing machines being smashed up by starving labourers, who saw the new invention only in terms of taking away their jobs? How could these picturesque cottages, now costing hundreds and thousands of pounds, ever have been cold, windowless, derelict hovels, many of their inhabitants tortured (not too strong a word) and humiliated by the Poor Relief system, thought up in Newbury on 6 May 1795? I put the questions to the organiser of one of the many museums displaying rural machinery. The response was an astonished, 'That's politics.'

That other side of our history can be found, but it takes a lot of searching, much scrabbling around in corners for dusty information. Staff of the Visitors' Centre in Woking looked hard to find their last copy of the excellent booklet detailing the sites used by H. G. Wells in *The War of the Worlds*. It is written and published by a local enthusiast who was delighted to tell me that the Centre ordered more shortly after my visit. In Lewes, I was surprised to discover that the house where the author of *The Rights of Man*, Tom Paine, lived is owned by the Sussex Archaeological Trust, and closed to the public in spite of the streams of fans, mainly from the United States, who bang on the door. The Trust says it needs the space for its books and papers. It is a surprise, too, to discover that Field Place

Shaw Corner

outside Horsham, birthplace of the poet Shelley, remains a private house, behind a firmly locked gate. It can only just be glimpsed from the main road into Broadbridge Heath. Was I wrong to expect to find in Farnham far more about William Cobbett – father of parliamentary reform, the most prolific of journalists, whose works were read by everybody who could read, from farm labourers to heads of state all over the world, who began what we know as Hansard and for whom Hazlitt coined the phrase, 'the fourth estate'? Cobbett was born in an inn, The Jolly Farmer in Bridge Square, now named The William Cobbett. There are a few personal effects and a Cobbett library in the museum, but otherwise the lovely Georgian town is relatively silent about the man who is only briefly mentioned in the town's Heritage Trail brochure, despite being 'arguably Farnham's greatest son'.

Despite the surprises and frustrations, my journey of discovery was aided and abetted by a host of people – professionals, local experts and enthusiasts – whom I met along the way, and who entered into the spirit of things. They consulted libraries, maps and records, and sent me everything from a death certificate to specialist books. My e-mail inbox bristles with helpful information. I even got a couple of emails from Iraq, from the Squadron Commander of the Kitchener barracks in Chatham, where William Cobbett was based in 1784. For some people, the history is still very much the present. The story of young Henry Cook in Micheldever, who was hanged in January 1831 after aiming his sledgehammer at the hat of a member of the wealthy Baring family, was told to me by one man who still mourns the loss of the nineteen-year-old as if he was his own son. He continues to hold the Baring family responsible for the hanging. It was also exciting to discover the William Cobbett Society which is fundraising for, among other things, a life-size statue of Cobbett on horseback, in the town centre of Farnham. Then there are the Tom Paine enthusiasts who organise an annual Revolution to Revolution Festival in Lewes, from 4 to 14 July. They are planning big celebrations for the bicentenary of Paine's death in 2009, and intend to step up their campaign to have Paine's house opened up to the public. It was also good to find that, in Hastings, there is a Robert Tressell Festival – with music – celebrating the man who wrote *The Ragged Trousered Philanthropists* which is a gripping read, in spite of (or because of) its political label as a 'Socialist novel'.

Unlike most of my fellow contributors, I am not a historian or a political expert. I am not a member of any political party or group. I am an independent reporter who enjoys finding things out. I vaguely remember the Peasants' Revolt from my history lessons at school. I had heard of Cobbett and Paine. Thanks to my older sister, I had read *Animal Farm*. As I pursued my research, voraciously reading history books, novels, memoirs and biographies, I became hooked. I could not believe that I knew nothing of the Labourers' Revolt of 1830-31, which involved thousands of people across the country, rioting, in the name of Captain Swing, against low wages, unemployment and the general misery of their lives. In Kent in 1823, for example, nearly one third of the twenty-one thousand inhabitants in a group of parishes were paupers. And it was in Kent, in June 1830, that the Revolt began. The first hayrick was burned in Orpington, followed by the breaking of the first threshing machine in Lower Hardres. Rioting spread to Surrey, Sussex and Hampshire, where, momentously, the Poor Houses at Selborne and Headley were also burned down, and to Berkshire, followed by much of the rest of the country. By the end of riots in the South East, more than six hundred men and women had appeared in court, more than two hundred had been jailed, nearly two hundred transported, and ten men hanged.

It is significant that the 1830 Labourers' Revolt began in Kent, the county whose sign is the unconquerable free-spirited White Horse. When the history of Britain was first recorded, in the time of Julius Caesar, the Weald (Forests) of Kent, Sussex and Surrey was said to be the home of a proud and independent people. In the early thirteenth century, King John did not command but *appealed* to the men of the Weald of Sussex: 'We pray you for the love of us to assist us now in carrying our timber to Lewes, resting assured that we ask this not as a right but as a favour.'

In the fourteenth and fifteenth centuries, the Commons of Kent were among the first to rise in rebellion, first under Wat Tyler in the Peasants' Revolt, in the course of which the Archbishop of Canterbury, Simon of Sudbury, was beheaded, and then under Jack Cade, who soundly beat the troops of King Henry VI at Sevenoaks. in 1838, Kent also saw the last armed uprising on British soil, around the village of Dunkirk outside Canterbury. The leader was John Tom, or Sir William Courtenay, as he styled himself. He raised an 'army' of labourers and set out to overturn the establishment, starting in Bossenden Wood. It ended in the bloody deaths of twelve men. The affair had national consequences. The Church of England was blamed for the ignorance of Courtenay's followers, who believed he was the reincarnation of Jesus Christ. It caused a row in Parliament over the lack of proper schooling, and in July 1839 a Bill was introduced to enable Justices of the Peace to establish regular county police forces, instead of relying on local militias, and ordinary people forced into becoming 'special constables'. As for Dunkirk itself, the government decided that it should get its own church and school. The church is now redundant. The school thrives.

History, it is said, repeats itself, although a better appraisal might be that some things change for the better, some for the worse, while some other things stay the same. Visitors to Rochester Castle should pause for a moment to remember the burgher of Gravesend who was imprisoned here after refusing to work as a bondsman for Sir Simon de Burley, Lord Warden of the Cinque Ports. The burgher was freed by Wat Tyler's peasants. The title of Lord Warden dates back to 1226, and was the most powerful of royal appointments. In later centuries, it became a sinecure, bringing with it a nice annual sum of money and a palatial home at Walmer Castle, between Dover and Deal. William Pitt and the Duke of Wellington were among the Lords. Cobbett called people with sinecures 'dead weights' and 'tax eaters'. Queen Elizabeth the Queen Mother held the title until her death. Cobbett would have been proud of the people who wrote letters to the local papers questioning the whole concept, and suggesting that, if the position was to be filled, the people of the Cinque Port Towns should be allowed to choose.

As I scoured the south eastern counties looking for clues to the past and reasons for the present, I often felt I was following in former footsteps. It took quite a lot of driving to unearth the site of Robert Owen's social experiment, at Queenwood in Hampshire. The atheist and co-operator, George Holyoake, also had difficulty finding it in October 1843, as he tramped through the country lanes. He wondered at the settlement's remoteness from the seat of manufacture or commerce, and marvelled at the huge sums of money spent laying out the roads, clearing the land of flint and building the big house itself, Harmony Hall, with its panelled walls and mahogany decoration. There are still traces in the undergrowth. In Kent, there are bitter memories of a modern dispute between a government and a section of society – the miners' strike of 1984. The empty buildings of Snowdown Colliery (closed in 1986) are still there, mouldering away into the scrub and brambles. Nearby Aylsham village only got its memorial in 2003, a marvellous life-sized statue of a miner, a child perched on his shoulders, another holding his hand by his side. The bitterness continues, however, at Betteshanger (closed in 1989), where an industrial park and leisure facilities on the former mine site were still not completed in 2004. Although a pagoda has been sited over the mine head shaft, there were still no words about what lay beneath and around. It is strange, is it not, this fear of 'politics', of confronting or acknowledging what happened and why? As I browsed through a heap of booklets in a second-hand book shop, I came across one about Canterbury Cathedral. It mentioned the deaths of two archbishops during the

Black Death in 1348, but omitted to mention the one that was beheaded by Wat Tyler's men a generation later.

There was good news in Woking for enthusiasts of H. G. Wells and his *War of the Worlds* in which the town's mosque was blown up by the Martians. The Shah Jehan Mosque is the oldest in the United Kingdom and would have been just five years old when Wells moved to Woking. It is safe and sound, and thriving. Sadly, the splendid Oriental College of Learning that was built alongside did not survive the ravages of the town planners. A glance at the hulks of the superstores which now occupy the site – one was burned down in 2004 – gives the phrase 'war of the worlds' a whole new meaning.

There are some people who are not included in the gazetteer, but who ought to be remembered. These include Margaret Bondfield (1873-1953), the draper's assistant who went on to become the first woman chairman of the Trades Union Congress, the first woman Minister and the first woman in a Cabinet (that of Ramsay MacDonald, 1929-31). There is no mention of her that I could find, anywhere in Brighton or Hove, where her experiences led to her lifelong commitment to women's rights and the Trade Union movement. The satirist, Jonathan Swift (1667-1745), lived at Moor Park near Farnham, where he wrote *A Tale of a Tub*, that 75 years later, was to make such an impact on the fourteen-year-old William Cobbett, and described 250 years later by Michael Foot as 'a stupendous satire on almost every establishment, institution and custom of the age . . . Nothing was sacred.' Woodingdean, near Brighton, was the country home of the incredible Violet Van Der Elst (1882-1966), the coal porter's daughter who spent her life, and fortune, campaigning against capital punishment. George Attlee said she did more than anyone else to secure its abolition. Memory should also stretch back to the 'honest and industrious' shepherd with a wife and five children who, in 1830, was forced by the overseer of the parish to walk from Margate to Ash, thirteen miles away, six days a week, to collect his one shilling and sixpence (just over seven pence). He managed the journey for nine weeks before his strength gave out. A clerk told his story to the magistrates in Kent. Then there was Thomas Davis, the village hero of Swallowfield in Berkshire, the only man in the village to withstand pressure from squire and farmers to be sworn as a special constable during the Captain Swing riots. Last, and far from least, Charles Dickens (1812-70), who so vividly described the social conditions of his times, the Eatanswill of Politics, the fog of the Law. He wrote, as no other novelist did, about the way it was at the bottom of the pile. The Dickens Trail is well documented and includes Portsmouth, Rochester, Chatham and Broadstairs.

One of my favourite events happened at Wagstaff Farm in Biddenden, Kent. Although labourers were pitted against farmers in the nineteenth century, many farmers were sympathetic to their workers. In 1830 they worked together to win a reduction in rents and tithes, so the labourers could be paid higher wages. The fight against tithes was to continue, and, in February 1886, *The Kentish Express* described the extraordinary scenes at Wagstaff Farm, where the farmer, Will Weekes, was refusing to pay his tithes. The Rector had called in a London firm of auctioneers, who requisitioned a farm cart to help them sell off the farmer's property. The crowd rioted and pushed the wagon into a pond and roughed up the auctioneer. There was much throwing of rotten eggs. Mr Weekes and five others were brought before the magistrates and fined £5. One man got one month's imprisonment with hard labour. A petition to the Home Secretary won a week's reduction. Wagstaff Farm was bought by Vic Millen, whose father remembered the events. Mr Millen's grandson, Keith, runs the farm at present.

Another place which should be flagged up is another 'hotbed of sedition', Hurstpierpoint, Sussex, where lived a schoolteacher, Elizabeth Hitchener. In 1812, Shelley sent her a box of copies of his *Declaration of Rights* in favour of Catholic Emancipation in Ireland. Records show that Miss Hitchener, whose father was a former smuggler, was placed under surveillance by the Postmaster General, Lord Chichester. 'I shall have a watch upon the daughter and discover whether there is any Connection between her and Shelley.'

There is no reason why visitors and locals should not enjoy the glorious countryside, the fine castles, and magnificent stately homes in this truest of blue areas in the country. (Voters elected a solid swathe of Conservative MPs in 1992 with one exception, although by 2001 a few seats had turned red.) Nevertheless, they should also listen out for the distant echo of thousands of pairs of sore feet marching on London, the sobs of starving families, and the squeak of the pens of journalists and writers who dared to take on the establishment and confront 'politics'. My hat goes off to them all, but in particular to Tom Paine, whose *Rights of Man* is as relevant today as it was more than two hundred years ago. William Cobbett, were he alive today, would also have his work cut out. There is still the need for an independent journalist with robust and fearless integrity, whose work is read by *every* section of society, battling against what Cobbett called 'The Thing' of the establishment, and leading the fight for truth and justice.

Gazetteer

ALDERMASTON, Berkshire. The Atomic Weapons Research Establishment (AWRE). The Campaign for Nuclear Disarmament held its first public meeting in February 1958, and the first London to Aldermaston march took place that Easter. A sea of cardboard lollipops bearing the distinctive black logo, carried by thousands of demonstrators, marked the beginning of a movement that has endured over the decades. AWRE is in woodland, on the hill above the chocolate box village. The perimeter is sealed by a barbed-wire fence, with a no-man's-land watched by cameras. Cold War stuff: Orwellian buildings, tall chimneys, pipes, and conveyor belts or walkways. If you stop near the fence, security men will appear in seconds to ask you what you want.

ANDOVER, Hampshire. The Cloisters, Junction Road. The transformed buildings of a former workhouse, famed for a national scandal in 1845, when it became known that starving inmates, employed in pounding bones into bone-dust, had been gnawing at the stale marrow and gristle. The evidence of a House of Commons Select Committee filled two big volumes. The buildings today are an exclusive housing development, near the railway station. The flats fetch bone-crunching figures on the property market.

ANDOVER, Hampshire. Andover Museum. Life-size figures of a woman and child, miserably grinding bones, illustrate the 1845 Andover Workhouse scandal.

AYLESFORD, Kent. Preston Hall. The headquarters of the Kent and Medway Health Authority was, in March 1938, a sanatorium to which George Orwell (1903-50), writer and journalist, was admitted after coughing up blood. He spent nearly six months here, and sketched out the novel, *Coming Up for Air*, although doctors warned him against working too hard. Orwell enjoyed walking into the village, visiting St Peter's Church, and gazing at the medieval bridge.

BARKHAM, Berkshire. St James' Church. In the churchyard close to the south transept, is buried David Davies (1742-1819), who was Rector from 1782 to his death. He documented the effects of enclosures in *The Case of Labourers in Husbandry* (1795). In the 1790s, two thirds of the 40 families in the parish were dependent on parish relief. The cottager, he wrote, should be allowed some land about his dwelling to keep a cow, plant potatoes and grow flax or hemp. Today, the Barkham Mothers' Union has projects, including rehousing the homeless, and fair trade.

BINFIELD, Berkshire. All Saints' Church. Catherine Macaulay Graham (1731-91), radical historian, republican and pioneer feminist, was buried in the churchyard, although the grave has disappeared. In the church there is a portrait of her erected by her second husband, William Graham. Born Catherine Sawbridge at Wye, Kent, she wrote an eight-volume history of England. Her *Letters on Education* (1790) were admired by Mary Wollstonecraft (1759-97) who called Catherine Macaulay 'the woman of the greatest abilities that this country has ever produced.' Binfield's congregation was among the first to choose a woman priest.

BOTLEY, Hampshire. Opposite the Mill. William Cobbett (1763-1835) bought a house here on the River Hamble in 1805, going on to acquire other farms and woodland in the area. Here he saw the misery caused by land enclosures, and quarreled with the rector over tithes. He introduced new breeds and equipment, and paid his men well, although sometimes late. When he was in Newgate Prison they complained that he expected a month's work to be done in a week. Today, there is a Cobbett Trail, with markers depicting the silhouette of the Radical on horseback.

BOTLEY, Hampshire. Market Square. In the Market Hall are two engravings of William Cobbett. Opposite is a squat stone memorial, paid for by public subscription, and dedicated by the Hampshire members of the Institute of Journalists to 'a champion of free journalism'.

BOTLEY, Hampshire. All Saints' Church. The diamond-shaped clock with a gilded crown came from the stables at William Cobbett's Botley House.

BREDE, Sussex. Red Lion Hotel. On 5 November 1830, some labourers met here with farmers and a minister. They won a promise of higher wages, and agreed revenge against the assistant overseer of Poor Relief, Thomas Abell, who harnessed the needy to a cart, filled with stones for road mending, which they had to drag up the hill. Later that day, Abell was forced into the cart, pulled out of the parish, accompanied by a crowd of five hundred, and dumped at Vinehall. This Brede rising inspired other parishes – Burwash, Ticehurst, Fairlight, Brightling, Mayfield, Heathfield, Warbleton, Ninfield and Battle – to rise in the great labourers' revolt of 1830.

BRIGHTLING, Sussex. St Thomas a Becket. Women's-rights campaigner, artist, and a founder of Girton College, Cambridge, Barbara Leigh Smith Bodichon (1827-91), is buried here. Her tombstone is indecipherable. Her name is absent from the guidebook's list of notable people buried here – although it includes her brother Benjamin, the Arctic explorer.

BRIGHTON, Sussex. Cowley Club, 12 London Road. Named in tribute to Harry Cowley (1891-1971), the chimney sweep who stood up for the homeless and unemployed, and battled against Mosley's fascists. The Club provides refreshments, advice and enlightening literature.

BRIGHTON, Sussex. 2 Regency Square. Home of Dr William King (1786-1865), poor-man's physician, early Owenite, founder of benevolent and co-operative organisations, and publisher of *The Co-operator*. There is a plaque.

BRIGHTON, 36 Camelford Street. A plaque marks the home for 25 years of George Holyoake (1817-1906), Owenite, writer, founder of Secular Societies and, in 1842, the last man to be gaoled in Britain for atheism. By the middle of the 1850s, there were over 40 Secular Societies in Britain. Holyoake was the first President of the Brighton Equitable Co-operative Society.

BRIGHTON, Sussex. 6 Vernon Terrace. A plaque marks the lodgings, in 1873, of Eleanor Marx (1855-98), youngest daughter of Karl. She taught in Mrs Hall's school for girls in Sussex Square.

BRIGHTON, Sussex. 45 Brunswick Square. The socialist author, and advocate of gay freedom, Edward Carpenter (1844-1929), was born here. Carpenter hated the fashionable society, and felt 'an alien, an outcast and a failure'. A plaque was unveiled in 2004.

BRIGHTON, Sussex. Church Street. The Dome. Now a theatre, but in 1935, the site of the Labour Party Conference, when Ernest Bevin told the pacifist George Lansbury to stop 'hawking his conscience from conference to conference asking what he should do with it'.

BRIGHTON, Sussex. West Street. Site of Sports Stadium, demolished 1965. Site of the Labour Party Conference, 1957, when Aneurin Bevan denounced the Labour Left's unilateralism with the words, 'If you carry this resolution . . . you'll be sending a British Foreign Secretary, whoever he may be, naked into the conference chamber.'

BROADBRIDGE HEATH, Sussex. Field Place. Birthplace of Percy Bysshe Shelley (1792-1822), poet, atheist and democrat, and supporter of revolution, universal suffrage and women's rights.

BROOKWOOD, Surrey. Glades of Remembrance Cemetery, Plot 81. Grave of Rebecca West (1892-1983), feminist, journalist and writer, nee Cicely Fairfield. West chose the vast graveyard because it looked like a Victorian country estate. She bought the site, near a pink hawthorn, now embraced by a mistletoe, for £200.

CADE STREET, Sussex. Jack Cade, who led a rebellion against the oppressive policies and high taxation of King Henry VI, was allegedly cornered here in July 1450, and fatally wounded. A stone monument was erected in 1790 and reads, 'Near this spot was slain the notorious Jack Cade, by Alexander Iden, Esq, Sheriff of Kent AD 1450. His body was carried to London and his head fixed upon London Bridge. This is the success of all rebels and this fortune chanceth ever to traitors.' In fact, Cade Street had been in existence for a century before Cade was born. The site of Cade's fatal wounding has also been ascribed to nearby Heathfield; Iden, Sussex; Iden Green, Kent; and Hothfield, Kent.

CANTERBURY, Kent. Clarks Shoe Shop, High Street. A plaque marks the site of the Town Hall which, in June 1381, was attacked by Wat Tyler, leader of the Peasants' Revolt. Three rich citizens were beheaded as traitors.

CANTERBURY, Kent. The Castle. In 1381, Wat Tyler and his peasants in revolt took the castle and dragged the keeper to the basement jail, forcing him to release all the prisoners, burn all financial and judicial records of the county in his possession, and then take an oath of allegiance to the peasants. There are excellent information boards.

CANTERBURY, Kent. Cathedral. Helped by crowds of local volunteers, Wat Tyler and his peasants in revolt stormed the cathedral, terrifying the monks. They went on to sack the palace of the archbishop, Simon of Sudbury, next door. The palace lies behind stone walls and is marked OLD PALACE PRIVATE.

CHATHAM, Kent. Kitchener Barracks, next to Fort Amherst. Site of Chatham Lower Barracks, where William Cobbett (1763-1835) accidentally enlisted as a soldier in 1784 – he thought he was entering the navy. He became copyist to the garrison commander, Colonel Hugh Debeig, but made mistakes. A fanatical autodidact, Cobbett bought a grammar book and learnt it by heart, saving what he could, from his daily twopence, for books and writing materials, reading and writing 'amid the noise of half a score of the most thoughtless of men'. In 2004, the squadron commander decided to display, in the bar, a copy of Cobbett's description of his life there, for the soldiers of today to read, compare and reflect.

CHRIST'S HOSPITAL, near Horsham, Sussex. Christ's Hospital School. Leading Labour MP Michael Stewart (1906-90) won a scholarship to enter Christ's Hospital, wearing the blue robe and yellow stockings for seven years. He joined the Labour Party and became secretary of the school's Debating Society. His Headmaster asked if he had thought of becoming an MP. He went on to be Foreign Secretary in Harold Wilson's government, 1965-66 and 1968-70. John Edmonds (1944-), President of the TUC in 1998, also had a scholarship and was uncomfortable with what he saw as minor public school snobbery. Stuart Holland (1940-), Labour MP, is also an Old Boy.

CROWBOROUGH, Sussex. Uckfield Lodge, Church Street. Birthplace of Tom Driberg (1905-76). He attended The Grange Preparatory School, now a new housing development, down the road. Driberg hated Crowborough. It was, he said, dull, bourgeois and filled with stockbrokers drinking gin. He joined the Communist Party and was assigned 'the hopeless task' of selling its weekly paper. It is still hopeless to expect to find *The Morning Star* sold in Crowborough.

CROWTHORNE, Berkshire. Wellington College. A public school favoured by army officers. Not an obvious Leftie site, though it provided the schooling for Patrick Gordon Walker (1907-80), the lugubrious and luckless Foreign Secretary in Harold Wilson's first government. He lost his Smethwick seat in the 1964 General Election. Wilson appointed him Foreign Secretary, notwithstanding, but he lost the by-election, created for him at Leyton, in January 1965. In 1916, George Orwell (1903-50) was dispatched here with Cyril Connolly to sit an entrance exam, and was offered the first open scholarship in Classics. He spent the spring 1917 term here, enjoying skating on the lake, before going to Eton College.

DOVER, Kent. Buckland Hospital, Coombe Valley Road. Part of the hospital used to be the workhouse, where an exceptional teacher won the praise of a visiting inspector in 1889, with her decorations for the pauper schoolchildren of flowers, pictures and paintings. A photographic display near the chapel tells the history.

DUNKIRK, Kent. The woods close by saw the Battle of Bossenden Wood in 1838, when the unbalanced, but charismatic, Cornishman, John Tom, led a group of disaffected farm labourers, having persuaded them that he was Jesus Christ, and calling for a redistribution of property. 'The streets that have heretofore flowed with water shall flow with blood for the rights of the poor.' Tom had previously established himself as 'Sir William Courtenay'. His earlier antics had already taken him to Maidstone Prison and the lunatic asylum at Barming Heath. This time, troops were sent from Canterbury. In all, twelve people, including Tom, were killed in the ensuing battle. There is a Courtenay Road and a Courtenay Garage in the village. But the church refused to allow a memorial stone in nearby Hernhill churchyard, where Tom/Courtenay was buried. Today, one of the tea rooms at Mount Ephraim House, where the parson lived, is dedicated to 'Sir William'.

DUNKIRK, Kent. Red Lion Inn. After the Battle of Bossenden Wood in 1838, the body of John Tom, alias Sir William Courtenay, was displayed in the stables. Sightseers came from miles around. The stables are now a restaurant, and diners are regaled with newspaper cuttings, photographs, drawings and place mats telling the story of the last armed rising on British soil.

ETON, Berkshire. Eton College. The alma mater of a surprising number of Lefties. The poet Percy Bysshe Shelley (1792-1822), supporter of revolution, universal suffrage, trades unions, women's rights and radical reform of the Houses of Parliament, was severely bullied when he came here in 1804 – 'surrounded, hooted, baited like a maddened bull'. His first published work, *Zastrozzi*, was written here. In the 1880s, two teachers, Joynes and Salt, joined the Social Democratic Federation. Their suspicious activities included – in addition to the espousal of socialism – owning a tricycle. One of Attlee's Cabinet, the Earl of Listowel (1906-1997), became a socialist at Eton. This was well in advance of his contemporary, who also became an Attlee minister, the Earl of Longford (1905-2001), who worked for the Conservative Party before joining the Labour Party. George Orwell (1903-50) decided to 'slack off' after his Eastbourne cramming school. He recalled the school's 'one great virtue . . . and that is a tolerant and civilised atmosphere which gives each boy a fair chance of developing his individuality.' Lord Pethick-Lawrence (1871-1961), yet another Attlee Minister, loved Eton. John Strachey (1901-63), ditto, hated it. He claimed he became a socialist, or even a communist, 'from chagrin at not getting into the Eton Cricket XI'. His older contemporary, Oliver Baldwin (1899-1958), son of the Conservative Prime Minister, Stanley Baldwin, but nonetheless a Labour MP, described his years at Eton as 'a complete waste of time'. Tam Dalyell (1932-) is a more recent Old Etonian.

FAREHAM, Hampshire. Westbury Manor Museum. A reconstruction tells the story of the ill-treatment of three little boys in the Union Workhouse that became a national scandal in 1837. The children could not stand or walk without assistance. One nearly died. The staff were guilty of negligence, and the case was used to expose the harsh realities of workhouse life.

FAREHAM, Hampshire. St Christopher's Hospital. Site of the scandal-ridden Union Workhouse that became part of the hospital in 1948.

FARNHAM, Surrey. The William Cobbett Inn, Bridge Square. Birthplace, then called The Jolly Farmer, of William Cobbett (1763-1835), Radical writer. His father was innkeeper and small farmer. Here, as a boy, he chased away the birds from the turnip seed and the rooks from the peas, and fell in love with Merrie England.

FARNHAM, Surrey. Farnham

Museum, West Street. There is a bust of William Cobbett, various pictures and personal effects.

FARNHAM, Surrey. St Andrew's Church. In a family tomb, opposite the main porch, is buried William Cobbett.

GATTON, Surrey. A good example of a pocket borough that was sold before 1832 to the highest bidder who could stand for parliament unchallenged. The auctioneer selling Gatton advertised it thus: '. . . no tormenting claims of insolent voters to evade, no tinkers' wives to kiss, no impossible promises to make, none of the toilsome and not very clean paths of canvassing to drudge through: but, with his mind at ease and his conscience clear, with this elegant constituency in his pocket, the honours of the state will await his plucking and with its emoluments his purse will overflow.' It was bought for £90,000 in 1801. You can get a taste of the elegance of eighteenth-century life by a visit to the former Dower House near Ockley, now a splendid hotel and golf and country club, set in two hundred acres of ground.

GREENHAM COMMON, Berkshire. Site of the largest US airbase in Britain after the Second World War. The Thatcher government, in 1981, allowed the US government to site 96 Tomahawk Cruise missiles here. Greenham Common then became the focus for the longest and most determined women's protest against weapons of mass destruction in history. The protest lasted more than ten years. One demonstration saw thirty thousand women linking arms over fourteen miles. Missiles were removed in 1991, and the Americans left in 1992. The control tower and the huge nuclear bunkers remain. The Common, with cattle grazing, is again open to the public. Newbury Museum nearby has a room devoted to the Greenham Common story.

GUILDFORD, Surrey. The Mount Cemetery. Founding member of the Independent Labour Party and gay-rights campaigner, Edward Carpenter (1844-1929), is buried here with his companion of 40 years George Merrill. Carpenter died at 25 Mountside, off Wodeland Avenue.

HASTINGS, Sussex. 115 Milward Road. A plaque marks the home of Robert Noonan (1870-1911) who, as Robert Tressell, wrote the great socialist novel, first published in 1914, *The Ragged Trousered Philanthropists*. The novel's location is an inland town called 'Mugsborough', but Noonan, a master craftsman, worked on building sites in Hastings and drew on this experience for the novel. He was a member of the Hastings branch of the Social Democratic Federation.

HASTINGS, Sussex. Museum. In 1905, Robert Noonan, aka Robert Tressell, was commissioned to create a triptych for St Andrew's Church. The church was demolished, but one surviving panel is on display, inscribed 'Thy word is a Lamp unto my feet and a Light unto my path.'

HASTINGS, Sussex. Public Library. A commemorative panel for Robert Tressell, author of *The Ragged Trousered Philanthropists*, can be found in the entrance hall. It shows three workmen on a trestle with a quotation from the novel: 'The time will come when it will no longer be possible for a few selfish people to condemn thousands of men and women and little children to live in misery and die of want.'

HASTINGS, Sussex. The Cricketers Public House, South Terrace. The labourers of Robert Tressell's novel *The Ragged Trousered Philanthropists*, used to meet in a pub based on this. Now no longer an inn.

HASTINGS, Sussex. 9 Pelham Crescent. A plaque marks the family home of Barbara Leigh Smith Bodichon (1827-91), painter, a founder of Girton College, Cambridge, and women's rights campaigner. She wrote articles on women's emancipation from 1848 for the *Hastings and St Leonards News*, initially under the penname Esculapius. She was the inspiration for Dorothea, the heroine of *Middlemarch* by George Eliot.

HORSHAM, Sussex. St Mary's Church, Causeway. The plain memorial to the atheist poet Percy Bysshe Shelley (1792-1822) was erected in 1892, as part of the Shelley centenary celebrations. The parish magazine said, 'It is not intended as a monument in his honour and it is needless to say that there will be no ceremony or public function of any sort when it is put in its place.' In November 1830, 80-year-old Mr Hurst, owner of the great tithes (corn, hay and wood), was besieged in the church when a thousand labourers ganged up to demand a daily wage of two shillings and sixpence (12½ pence) and a reduction of rents and tithes. 'Mr Hurst held out so long that it was feared blood would be shed. The Doors were shut till the Demands were granted; no lights were allowed, the Iron railing that surrounds the Monuments were torn up, and the sacred boundary between the chancel and Altar overleapt before he would yield.' The people got their pay rise, and Horsham the reputation of being 'a hot-bed of sedition'.

HORSHAM, Sussex. Town centre, looming next to McDonald's. A memorial to Percy Bysshe Shelley, atheist and democrat, with the title Cosmic Cycle, by Angela Conner; variously described as a 'split pea', a 'mammoth ice lolly' and a 'lychee in a potato skin'. The Museum in Causeway has a room dedicated to the poet.

HOVE, Sussex. St Andrew's Church. The pioneer Co-operator and Owenite Dr William King is buried in the churchyard.

LANCING, Sussex. Lancing College. Tom Driberg (1905-76), socialist and socialite, attended this school, went to Brighton to join the Communist Party, became a house leader, and left the school in disgrace after making sexual advances to younger boys. He went on to teach at a prep school in Bournemouth. John Sankey (1866-1948), Lord Chancellor in Ramsay MacDonald's second Labour government of 1929, was also a pupil.

LEWES, Sussex. Bull House, opposite St Michael's Church. Various inscriptions commemorate the former workplace and home of Thomas Paine (1737-1809), radical journalist and revolutionary. He lived in Lewes from 1768 to 1774, working as an excise officer. During this time, he married Elizabeth Ollive at St Michael's Church, and took over his father-in-law's business as tobacconist and grocer. He agitated for higher wages for excise men, petitioning Parliament on the subject, and was sacked for neglecting his duties. Paine went bankrupt, parted from his wife and went off to a new life in America.

LEWES, Sussex. White Hart Inn. Venue of the Headstrong Club, in which Thomas Paine (1737-1809), revolutionary, human rights activist and writer, starred. A plaque commemorates the link. In 1963, a society was founded in Lewes to 'promote the recognition of Thomas Paine's contribution to the cause of freedom, and to spread a knowledge of his work and activities with a view to encouraging the growth of a similar spirit of constructive criticism in every aspect of public life.' The Headstrong Club still meets round the corner at the Royal Oak. Lewes celebrates an annual Revolution to Revolution Festival from 4 to 14 July.

LEWES, Sussex. Market Tower. A Painting of Tom Paine pointing west to America is on the wall.

LITTLEHAMPTON, Sussex. Green Lady Hostel, on the corner of Green Lady Alley and East Street. Emmeline Pethick-Lawrence, the suffragette, and Mary Neal, a Littlehampton magistrate and socialist, set up this hostel as a seaside holiday home for female factory workers. The building is now a nursing home. Green Lady Alley was so called after the green prison uniform worn by the imprisoned suffragettes.

MAIDSTONE, Kent. Penenden Heath. In June 1381, the commons of Kent chose Wat Tyler as their leader. The peasants overran the town and released John Ball, 'the mad priest of Kent', who preached social equality and had been imprisoned by the Archbishop of Canterbury. The Heath is now a public park, a venue for mums, dogs, kids and stroppy teenagers. The roar of the M20 replaces the roar of peasants.

MAIDSTONE, Kent. Registry Office, part of the former Palace of the Archbishop of Canterbury. John Ball was imprisoned here for heresy. In 1381, the peasants in revolt stormed the Palace and burned every scrap of manorial manuscripts that would have recorded the taxes, rents and services they owed.

MARGATE, Kent. Winter Gardens. Venue of Labour Party conferences in 1926, 1950, 1953 and 1955. In 1947, at the conference of the Electrical Trades Union, Emanuel Shinwell, Minister of Fuel in Attlee's Labour government, declared that 'we know that you, the organised workers of the country, are our friends . . . As for the rest, they do not matter a tinker's cuss.' The Winter Gardens, a white cake of a building sunk off the beach, now plays host to shows including the Elvis Revival and tributes to Chas and Dave.

MICHELDEVER, Hampshire. Church and Old Bakehouse. The village was the home of Henry Cook, a 20-year-old ploughboy, who, in 1830, during a time of rural distress, knocked off the hat of William Bingham Baring JP with a sledgehammer. Cook was tried for attempted murder at Winchester, sentenced and hanged. The whole parish turned out to pay tribute when Cook's body was brought back to Micheldever. He was buried in solemn silence, in an unmarked grave, probably to the north of the church reserved for 'villains'. Legend has it that snow never settled on his grave. This was probably true. The Old Bakehouse (still there), whose ovens worked all through the year, is directly north of the church.

MIDHURST, Sussex. Church Hill. A plaque outside the dental surgery commemorates the place of work of H. G. Wells (1866-1946), novelist and socialist, who, in 1881, was apprenticed to Mr Cowap, the chemist here. He lasted only a few months. His mother could not afford apprenticeship fees.

MIDHURST, Sussex. Grammar School. A plaque records its association with H. G. Wells (1866-1946). He spent two months at the school as a boarder in 1881, after the headmaster, Horace Byatt, recognised the brightness of the apothecary's apprentice. In 1893, Wells returned to the school as a teaching assistant on £20 a year. To his mortification, he had to be confirmed by the

Church of England. He lived in a garret over a sweetshop (now a cakeshop) next to the Angel Hotel. There is a plaque. Like a character in his novel *Love and Mr Lewisham*, Wells pinned up a timetable rationing sleep, food, leisure and reading.

NEWBURY, Berkshire. 2 London Road, Speenhamland, opposite the clock tower. Site of the Pelican Inn. The old gateway still opens into what was the stable yard. Here, in May 1795, Berkshire magistrates devised a system of poor relief. Wages would be subsidised in line with the price of bread. This gave the green light to employers to keep wages low, and intensified the poverty trap. The controversial so-called Speenhamland System was adopted throughout most of the country.

NEWLANDS CORNER, Surrey. Manor House Hotel. Birthplace of John Strachey (1901-63), Etonian communist, poet, and, later, Attlee Cabinet Minister. The building was constructed by his father, John St Loe Strachey, editor of *The Spectator*. It was a Cabinet rule that the Prime Minister had to approve any publication by a member of the Cabinet. Strachey submitted a volume of free verse to Clement Attlee. For some time there was no response. Strachey then asked the Prime Minister if there was any objection to the poems. Attlee replied, 'Can't publish. Don't rhyme. Don't scan.'

NORMANDY, Surrey. The Manor House, The Common. The site of Normandy Farm, leased by William Cobbett (1763-1835), reformer and journalist and author of *Rural Rides*. He died here after being carried around in a wheelbarrow to inspect his crops for one last time. The occasional visitor calls to ask to dig up the garden, in the hope of finding the bones of Tom Paine, brought back from the United States by Cobbett.

PARHAM, Sussex. Church. Grave of Henry Hunt (1773-1835), orator and reformer. The Bishop family of Hunt's beloved mistress, Mrs Vince, refused to allow his body to be admitted to their vault. Instead, he is buried in the vault of his forgiving friend, Mr (Colonel) Vince. The gravestones are barely decipherable.

PASSFIELD, Hampshire. Passfield Corner. Home of Sidney (1859-1947) and Beatrice Webb (1858-1943) from 1923 to their deaths. Both died here. Fabians, pioneer social scientists, founders of *The New Statesman* and of the London School of Economics. Sidney was in Ramsay MacDonald's first two Labour Cabinets and became Lord Passfield. Beatrice refused to use the title. She died here and was buried in the grounds. When Sidney died her body was exhumed, and the couple were buried in Westminster Abbey.

PORTSMOUTH, Hampshire. University, formerly the Polytechnic. Attended by Ron Davies, Cabinet minister in Tony Blair's first government, until a moment of madness on Clapham Common.

QUEENWOOD, near Broughton, Hampshire. The site of pioneer socialist Robert Owen's most ambitious self-contained community for 1,200 people, established in 1839. Robert Owen (1771-1858) governed for three years. Queenwood lasted another three years before running out of money. The farmyard is still in use. The walled garden is intact. Some of the buildings survive as private houses. The site of Queenwood's living quarters, Harmony Hall, can be traced in the undergrowth.

READING, Berkshire. Leighton Park School. Michael Foot (1913-) was a pupil here, excelling in history, English literature and mathematics, but also enjoying rugby, cricket and soccer.

ROCHESTER, Kent. Castle. In June 1381, peasants in revolt, supported by the citizens, seized the castle. Led by Jack Straw, and with Essex men among the several-thousand-strong rebels, they forced the Castle Governor, Sir John de Newton, to free the prisoners and march with them to London. King Richard II spent £500 repairing damage to the Castle.

ROEDEAN, Sussex. School. Margaret Postgate, later Mrs G. D. H. Cole, and even later, Dame Margaret (1893-1980), won a scholarship to this posh school at the age of ten. She hated it, resenting the censorship of reading – Macaulay was found too strong – and the lack of intellectual stimulation. But she discovered for herself the writings of Hazlitt. 'I was the wrong sort of cuckoo in a horribly alien nest.'

ROTTINGDEAN, Sussex. St Aubyn's School. Oliver Baldwin (1899-1958) attended this preparatory school. A son of the Conservative Prime Minister, he became a Labour MP. He recalled having to be patriotic, wave flags, march, beat drums, fire blanks from little guns and sing 'God Save the King'. 'We were trained just as seditiously and blasphemously as, in the eyes of certain Tory MPs, are the children of English Communists.' The School's blue flag still flutters on its flagpole.

ST LEONARDS, Sussex. 241 London Road. A plaque marks the home in 1907 of Robert Noonan (1870-1911). It is thought that much of the socialist novel *The Ragged Trousered Philanthropists* was written here. He wrote it under the name of Robert Tressell.

SEVENOAKS, Kent. Junction of Tonbridge Road and Solefields Road. A plaque marks the site of the battle where, in June 1450, men from Kent, led by Jack Cade, defeated forces of King Henry VI under Sir Humphrey Stafford, who was killed. In Shakespeare's *King Henry VI Part II*, Sir Humphrey addresses his enemy,

> Rebellious hinds, the filth and scum of Kent, Mark'd for the gallows, lay your weapons down.

One of the rebels was Dick, a butcher from Ashford, Kent. Shakespeare has Jack Cade congratulating him:

> They fell before thee like sheep and oxen and thou behavedst thyself as if thou hadst been in thine own slaughter-house.

SOUTHSEA, Hampshire. Kings Road. The socialist and novelist H. G. Wells (1866-1946), spent two miserable years from 1881 as a draper's apprentice in the Drapery Emporium – since bombed. Bored by the tedium, he later argued that workers should alternate work and education: 'Then the assistant would go behind the counter or into the stockroom with a sense of function instead of a sense of routine.' Wells contemplated suicide as he walked along the sea front, but he discovered the writings of Robert Owen and searched for God. His road to Damascus came in the Roman Catholic Cathedral with a sermon about Hellfire. He would have either to submit, or challenge. 'To deny was to assert that error had ruled the world so far and wisdom was only beginning – with scared little chaps like me. How could I dare?' The Roman Catholic Cathedral welcomes visitors, even those on the trail of H. G. Wells.

SUTTON SCOTNEY, Hampshire. Coach and Horses Public House. A plaque on the wall records the Captain Swing riots of 1830. In September that year, desperate people from local parishes met, as the Radical and Musical Society, in the White Swan Inn, (formerly opposite the Coach and Horses) to complain of taxes for 'unnecessary and unjust wars' and to protest against low wages. A petition for parliamentary reform was drawn up, and Joseph Mason walked to Brighton to deliver it to the King. William Cobbett threw a party here to celebrate the passing of the Reform Bill.

UPPARK, Sussex. National Trust house. The mother of socialist and novelist H. G. Wells (1866-1946) was housekeeper here from 1880 to 1893. The mansion was the model for Bladesover House in *Tono-Bungay*, and the underground passageways for servants provided the idea of the tunnels in *The Time Machine*. Wells was not impressed by the privileged, noting in *Tono-Bungay* that 'for the gentlefolk, the surplus of population, all who were not good tenants nor good labourers, Church of England, submissive and respectful, were necessarily thrust together, jostled out of sight, to fester as they might in this place that had the colours and even the smells of a well-packed dustbin.' But he discovered Thomas Paine's *Rights of Man* in the library, watched the heavens through a telescope he found in the attic and, at the age of fourteen, produced a satirical daily newspaper *The Uppark Alarmist*. The Uppark staff call their newspaper *The Alarmist*.

WARNHAM, Sussex. St Margaret's Church. Percy Bysshe Shelley (1792-1822), democrat, poet and atheist, was baptised here. A copy of the parish register recording this is on display.

WILLINGDON, Sussex. Chalk Farm Hotel. George Orwell (1903-50), walked from his Eastbourne prep school over the Downs here. It is thought the farm provided inspiration for Manor Farm in the village of Willingdon in *Animal Farm*:

> A little way down the pasture there was a knoll that commanded a view of the farm . . . the long pasture stretching down to the main road, the hayfield, the spinney, the drinking pool, the ploughed fields where the young wheat was thick and green and the red roofs of the farm buildings with the smoke curling up from the chimneys.

Animal Farm walks include the Red Lion pub (Farmer Jones got drunk in a pub of the same name); the present-day farm, still with its red roofs; Willingdon Mill; and the quarry (from which Boxer could have dragged up huge boulders to build *Animal Farm*'s windmill). Sheep and horses graze peacefully next to the quarry.

WINCHESTER, Hampshire. Winchester College. The alma mater of a number of influential Lefties such as Attlee's austere Chancellor of the Exchequer, Stafford Cripps (unkindly known as Sir Stifford Crapps) (1889-1952); the leader of the Labour Party from 1955 to 1963, Hugh Gaitskell (1906-63); Richard Crossman (1907-1974), a pillar of Harold Wilson's first government and later editor of *The New Statesman*, and Douglas Jay (1907-96), also in Harold Wilson's cabinets. One of Ramsay MacDonald's ministers, Oswald Mosley (1896-1980) was also at Winchester. He was briefly a Leftie in his trajectory from the Conservative Party to the British Union of Fascists. In 1936, an official College publication said that when 'we are called . . . a training ground of respectable conventionality, it is of interest to reflect that perhaps the two most vigorous and strongly contrasting aspirants to popular leadership are both Wykehamists, Sir Oswald Mosley and Sir Stafford Cripps.'

WINDSOR, Berkshire. HSBC Bank and Glorious Britain souvenir shop, High Street. Plaques mark the site of Rodgers and Denyers' Drapers, where, in 1880, the novelist and socialist H. G. Wells worked (or rather was employed) as an apprentice. For most of the time, he hid among the bales in the warehouse and read. After two months he was dismissed as 'a tiresome boring little misfit.'

WINGHAM, Kent. Village information board, High Street. The village is proud of its forebears who took part in the Peasants' Revolt of 1381, the Jack Cade Rebellion of 1450 and the Captain Swing labourers' riots of 1830. The village website wonders whether it might be time for another uprising.

WOKING, Surrey. Victoria Way subway. The novelist and socialist, H. G. Wells (1866-1946) lived in Maybury Road by the railway, in the 1890s. He used to tramp the Surrey countryside with his brother, Frank. 'Suppose,' Frank remarked, 'some beings from another planet were to drop out of the sky suddenly and begin laying about them here.' From this sprang The *War of the Worlds* (1898). The story of Martians wielding their lethal heat-rays on Woking's Horsell Common launched Wells's career. In the town centre towers one of the 'monstrous tripods'. The subway has a mural with scenes from the novel, and the house at 141 Maybury Road has a blue plaque.

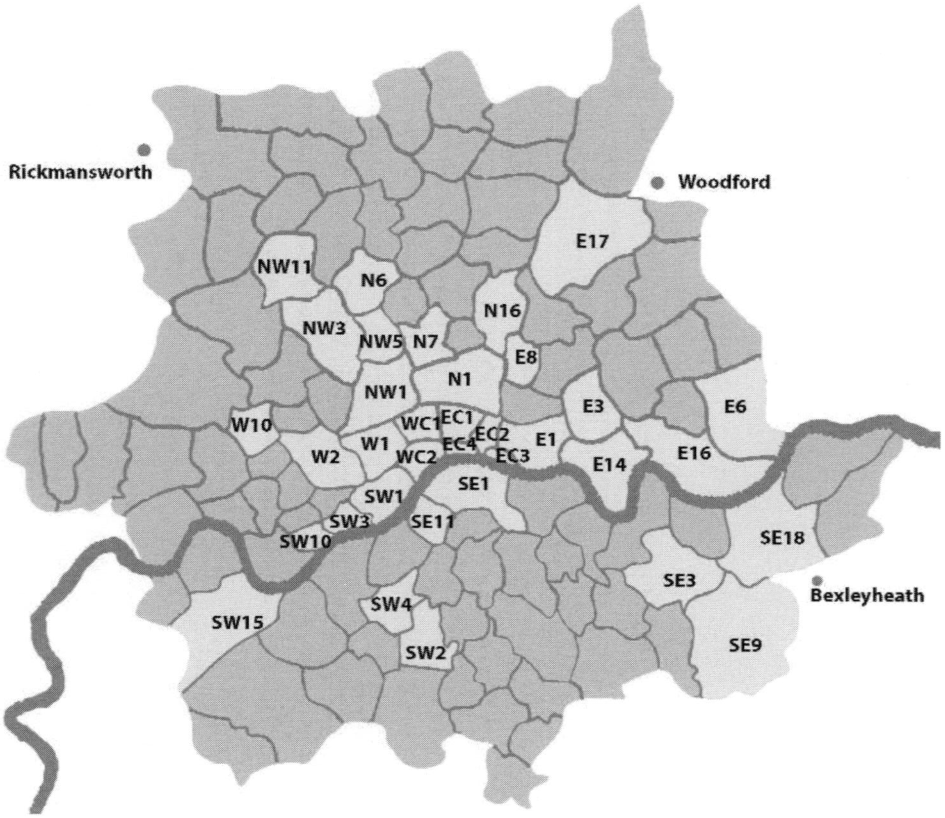
Rickmansworth
Woodford
Bexleyheath
NW11
N6
N16
E17
NW3
NW5
N7
E8
N1
NW1
E3
E6
W10
WC1
EC1
EC2
E1
W1
W2
WC2
EC4
EC3
E14
E16
SE1
SW1
SW3
SE11
SW10
SE18
SE3
SW4
SW15
SW2
SE9

3.

London

John Shepherd

Nearly a century ago, the novelist and Fabian socialist H. G. Wells observed in *Tono-Bungay* (1909) that 'London . . . takes a lot of understanding. It's a great place. Immense. The richest town in the world, the biggest port, the greatest manufacturing town, the Imperial city – the centre of civilisation, the heart of the world.' Wells wrote at a time when an Edwardian metropolis of around six million residents was the seat of the government of both the United Kingdom and a vast British Empire of around four hundred million subjects, on which officially the sun never set.

A century later, despite its greatly diminished industrial base and ailing infrastructure, cosmopolitan London remains a vibrant and intriguing world city. Much of the metropolis' rich history and tradition is expressed in its urban architecture and public monuments, which transmit and reinforce official values and mores across the generations. Culturally, the writings of Geoffrey Chaucer, William Shakespeare, Samuel Pepys, Charles Dickens and others evoke a colourful past of resplendent images, vistas and spectacle.

Tourist London is normally constructed from those places associated with the powerful and the wealthy, part of Britain's glorious imperial past. From an open-top tour bus visitors pass internationally famous attractions: Buckingham Palace, Trafalgar Square, the Houses of Parliament, Big Ben, St Paul's Cathedral, Westminster Abbey and the Tower of London, mostly close to the River Thames, historically London's main thoroughfare, now renowned for its bridges, *HMS Belfast* and the ever popular London Eye. Central

The Gay Hussar

London probably has more statues of its ruling and political elites than other world cities. The famous blue plaques (put up mainly by the London County Council and, subsequently, by English Heritage), often sited on less familiar residences, also identify the celebrated and eminent – but not the families or servants who lived and toiled there. Plaques exist for Labour leaders such as Clement Attlee and

Ernest Bevin; those commemorating writers include George Orwell; and in Mahatma Gandhi's case two plaques mark different sojourns in the capital, but overall, prominent figures on the Left are largely under-represented.

To all intents and purposes, London presents a fascinating panorama of Britain's social, cultural and political history, albeit one that is hardly all-encompassing in terms of official recognition. While the metropolis undoubtedly possesses a diverse and vibrant narrative of people, places and events connected with British socialism, the radical and political Left – particularly women – remain largely neglected in terms of public monuments, memorials and shrines.

Similarly, immigration over the centuries has played a significant part in shaping the evolution of cosmopolitan London. Migrants from Ireland, Europe, the West Indies, South Asia and other parts of the globe – often seeking a better life or escape from oppression – have broadened London's ethnic, religious and racial diversity, and enriched the economy and life of the city. In many cases, this aspect of London's history has only recently begun to be told and recorded for posterity.

The year 2005 marks the celebrations of the bicentenary of the birth in Jamaica of Mary Seacole, the remarkable nursing heroine who worked for sick British troops during the Crimean War. Voted recently the 'greatest black Briton', her fame lasted only briefly during her lifetime. Popularly known as 'Mother Seacole', she died in Paddington in 1881. Her restored grave is at St Mary's Roman Catholic Cemetery, Kensal Green, and her portrait, lost and found again, is now on display in the National Portrait Gallery. Interestingly, the individual life stories of many of London's ordinary citizens, previously unknown or neglected, are now being rescued by enthusiastic descendants taking advantage of the expertise and resources of the Family Records Centre in Finsbury, the National Archives in

Kew, and countless other London libraries and archives.

What then can also be rediscovered of a radical and socialist tradition in the metropolis – with its activists and citizens – from houses, public buildings, streets, theatres, railway stations, open spaces, cemeteries and similar places? If those on the Left (and others) glance around them, what monuments and other legacies remain to herald the past existence of a left-wing London and those who contributed to it?

In many instances, this radical past often stands side by side with the more familiar and authorised history of Britain. At the geographical centre of the capital – from which official distances are measured – no monument is more arresting than Trafalgar Square. Dominated by Nelson's Column, 176 feet high, supported by Landseer's four lions at its base, imposing fountains and a cluster of Victorian statues of monarchs, military leaders and other worthies, Trafalgar Square is indisputably one of London's most famous landmarks, designed to commemorate Admiral Nelson's heroic naval victories, culminating at Trafalgar in 1805. Two hundred years later, it still proclaims Britain's glorious imperial past – a perfect expression of public architecture transmitting official values and culture across the generations.

Historically, Trafalgar Square also has a different history as a central meeting place for political dissent and free speech, despite unfailing efforts by the authorities to ban rallies and protests. In the 1840s, the Home Office refused the Chartists access to Trafalgar Square but, by the 1880s, it had become a regular gathering point for 'Outcast London'. In 1886 and 1887, the Marxist Social Democratic Federation organised marches of the unemployed, which ended in the heavy-handed policing of a riot in the privileged clubland of Pall Mall and St James's and the arrest and subsequent trial of working-class leaders, including the future Cabinet minister

John Burns. Alfred Linnell also died in the hurly-burly on 'Bloody Sunday' of November 1887. The cortge of one hundred thousand mourners, stretching a mile and a half – the greatest since the funeral of the Duke of Wellington – snaked its way across London to Bow Cemetery, where William Morris declaimed the eulogy at Linnell's graveside.

In the pre-1914 years, the charismatic suffragette leader Emmeline Pankhurst was among those to address mass rallies in Trafalgar Square. In Edwardian London, the Women's Political and Social Union took militancy for 'votes for women' onto the capital's streets, chaining themselves to the railings of Downing Street and 'rushing' Parliament. Today, Mrs Pankhurst's statue stands defiantly in Victoria Tower Gardens, where it was unveiled in 1928 – the year all women were finally enfranchised in Britain.

In August 1914, as patriotic Britons prepared to answer Lord Kitchener's call to enlist, the British Labour movement held a large-scale anti-war rally in Trafalgar Square, a remarkable gathering addressed by a spectrum of the Left, including James Keir Hardie, Arthur Henderson and George Lansbury. Since then, along with Hyde Park and the Albert Hall, Trafalgar Square has been the venue of many left-wing demonstrations and pacifist rallies, from the 1936 Jarrow hunger march to the sit-in against the government's nuclear-weapons policy by the Committee of one hundred led by Bertrand Russell. Trafalgar Square has also witnessed violent confrontations over the Thatcher government's unpopular poll tax. In February 2005, Trafalgar Square was packed to capacity once more when the international statesman, Nelson Mandela addressed the anti-World-Poverty campaign.

Today, Greater London measures over six hundred square miles, and in terms of population – around ten million – is on a par with New York, Tokyo and Mexico City. As a major conurbation, London's sheer size and complexities defy definition, symbolised by the Edwardian cockney cab driver who told the visiting American writer Jack London that he did not know where the East End was. For those about to explore an imposing left-wing landscape, a gazetteer to its Leftie past should broadly feature the cosmopolitan capital's populace – the famous, the infamous and the unfamous – its buildings, historic scenes and notable visitors, as well as the social and political geography of the metropolis.

As a major international capital, historic London has long been synonymous with government and political power. It is also a city of contrasts – between rich and poor, the privileged and the dispossessed. Historically, as London rapidly expanded, divisions of wealth and power were reflected in the sharply differing economies and segregated metropolitan communities of west and east London. The West End, based on aristocratic estates, streets and squares, remains the fashionable district of residences, shops and entertainment. Nearby Westminster and Whitehall, comprising the Houses of Parliament, government and official buildings, lie at the heart of the British political system. Here much of London's radical past can be explored and recovered.

In 1898, Henry Broadhurst MP, after attending the state funeral of W. E. Gladstone, left Westminster Hall full of class pride. Thirty years before, an almost-penniless stonemason, he had laboured on the chilly clock tower high above Parliament. For some time, his stonemason's mallet and chisels have been displayed in the Pugin Room, among the parliamentary memorabilia of the political elite at Westminster. No socialist revolutionary, trade union secretary Broadhurst was an early representative of a radical tradition – centred later on the British Labour Party – that chose the parliamentary route to social and economic reform and improvement. Today, an official tour around the Houses of Parliament and its surprisingly compact chambers of Commons and Lords – the British symbol of democracy and freedom – also takes in Westminster Hall, the scene of the trial of King Charles I, as well as the statues, monuments and other mementoes to Parliament's largely aristocratic past.

Visitors to the Victorian Gothic precincts of the Houses of Parliament may also perch in the Strangers' Gallery. There a youthful George Lansbury was held spellbound by the great debates of Gladstone and Disraeli, and eyed the disruptive tactics of Charles Stewart Parnell and his Irish nationalist members. Fifty years later, no one was a more enthusiastic parliamentary guide than Lansbury. A firm believer in parliamentary democracy and accountability, the Labour leader would unhesitatingly point out to constituents where the Radical atheist Charles Bradlaugh, having refused to take his oath as Member of Parliament, stood steadfast at the bar of the House of Commons, and how Emily Wilding Davison hid in a cupboard during the 1911 Census.

At the time of the H. G. Wells' death in 1946, the social and political geography of the capital – which he portrayed as 'Dead London' in *The War of the Worlds* – had changed dramatically during his lifetime. In Edwardian Britain, the Liberals were in office, after the unprecedented landslide victory of 1906 when four hundred Liberal MPs were returned to Westminster. With only 29 MPs, the fledgling Labour Party seemed unlikely to replace its Liberal rivals.

With the heart of government at Westminster and Whitehall, London has attracted the embassies of foreign and Commonwealth governments, and the headquarters of the principal British political parties, even if for party conferences they prefer to go to locations by the seaside. In February 1900, the Congregational Memorial Hall in Clerkenwell was the setting for the two-day foundation conference, convened by the Trades Union Congress, that launched the Labour Party. This was the only one of four new groups founded in Britain that year with the objective of increasing working-class representation in Parliament that was successful. At the time, watched by only nine observers, this historic gathering of delegates from trades unions and socialist societies – the Independent Labour Party, the Fabian Society and the Social Democratic Federation – was barely noticed by the British press; the event took place in the middle of the Boer War. Since then, other comparable ventures have run into the sand. In January 1981, the Limehouse Declaration, issued at 78 Narrow Street by the 'Gang of Four' – former senior Labour politicians David Owen, Roy Jenkins, Bill Rodgers and Shirley Williams – announced the short-lived Social Democratic Party. The Memorial Hall, now rebuilt with a different function, also provided the backcloth to other notable Labour gatherings, during the 'Hands Off Russia' campaign in 1920, and the 1926 General Strike. However, Labour's historic sites abound in metropolis and suburbs.

To date, five Labour Prime Ministers – Ramsay MacDonald, Clement Attlee, Harold Wilson, James Callaghan and Tony Blair – have, with their families, been among the occupants of Britain's most famous political address, which serves as an official residence, government offices and family home. In 1924, Ramsay MacDonald, a widower after the tragic early death of his wife, Margaret, took up residence and promptly despatched his twenty-year-old daughter, Ishbel, to the Co-op sales to purchase furniture and household equipment, traditionally supplied by Prime Ministers on taking office. He also recognised the lack of an official library and appealed to friends and political acquaintances for spare scholarly volumes. It was Ishbel who undertook the formal duties of political hostess, traditionally performed by the Prime Minister's spouse at Downing Street. The MacDonalds' first home in Lincoln's Inn Fields had also served as the Labour Party's first office.

At Buckingham Palace, after wondering in his diary, 'What would Grandmama have thought?' – Grandmama was Queen Victoria – King George V soon expressed to MacDonald his concern about the singing of the 'Marseillaise' and 'The Red Flag' at the Labour victory rally at the Albert Hall in 1924. Inspired by the London Dock Strike of 1889 and revolutionary activity abroad, Jim Connell, an Irish journalist settled in London, had composed the words of 'The Red Flag' on a train from Charing Cross to New Cross. From its London origins in 1889, the song has been sung around the world, memorably in the House of Commons in 1945 by newly elected Welsh mining MPs.

In August 1931, MacDonald's second Labour government collapsed in the August financial and political crisis played out largely in Downing Street; this opened the way to the National governments of the 1930s. In 1945, after a memorable landslide victory, the first majority Labour government, under Clement Attlee, heralded a new socialist dawn with the Welfare State, the National Health Service, full employment, a start on colonial freedom, and support for the newly established United Nations Organisation. Since the 1980s, steel gates and armed police prevent, for security reasons, easy access to Downing Street, unlike in earlier years when the eight-year-old Harold Wilson was photographed – somewhat prophetically – outside Number Ten.

By the late nineteenth century, outcast London, nearly two miles downriver from Westminster and Whitehall, had become a city of about two million inhabitants. Andrew Mearns' classic pamphlet, *The Bitter Cry of Outcast London*, created a powerful contemporary image as a district peopled by the downtrodden and dispossessed in Victorian London, often perceived by the governing circles as the 'dangerous classes' or the 'residuum' of London society.

For many, East London was clearly associated with the working poor, radicalism and the threat of potential disorder. But, unlike other major European capitals – Paris, Berlin, Vienna – the capital, apart from a few occasions, such as the abortive Cato Street Conspiracy of 1820 and the monster Reform League demonstration that pulled down the Hyde Park railings in 1866, remained relatively free from revolutionary convulsions and political coups. In 1848 – the Year of Revolutions – as thrones toppled in Europe, Prince Metternich famously fled the Austrian capital. By comparison, in London, thousands of Chartists, led by the firebrand Feargus O'Connor, gathered on Kennington Common on 10 April to present to Parliament their third petition for democracy and reform. As a remarkable daguerreotype, unearthed in the Royal Archives, confirms, it was an orderly affair. Three years later, in 1851, in an age of comparative peace and prosperity, cheap train travel brought thousands of Britons to Hyde Park to see the wonders of Victorian technology on display at the Great Exhibition, in the Crystal Palace. This was later transferred to south London but destroyed by fire in 1926.

While in power, Labour governments have constructed some lasting, albeit controversial, public monuments in the capital. A. J. P. Taylor deemed 'Lansbury's Lido' with its mixed bathing on the Serpentine lake in Hyde Park, as the only memorable achievement of the second Labour government. It still survives, now marked by a plaque unveiled by Clement Attlee. On the centenary of the Great Exhibition, in the aftermath of the Second World War, the Labour government launched the Festival of Britain, constructing, on the derelict land of the South Bank of the Thames, the Dome of Discovery, the Skylon and the Royal Festival Hall. New homes with television sets promised a vision of a better tomorrow. Today, the Royal Festival Hall remains, as does the Lansbury Estate in the East End, named after George Lansbury, a revered son of Poplar. Ironically, 50 years later, this pioneering 'Living Architecture' project, of a working-class community, now survives cheek by jowl with Canary Wharf, the regenerated Docklands' conspicuous monument to contemporary capitalism.

Across the River Thames at Greenwich, the controversial Millennium Dome was largely the brainchild of Labour minister, Peter Mandelson. Hugely expensive and widely criticised, the Dome may well be a lasting but unwanted monument to New Labour. Fifty years earlier, the Festival of Britain had been one of the responsibilities of Mandelson's grandfather, Herbert Morrison, Deputy Prime Minister in Attlee's Labour governments. Strong allegiances with London, its local government and communities, including Hackney, Eltham and Woolwich, influenced Morrison's political make-up, and the identity he shaped as secretary of the London Labour Party, Mayor of Hackney, leader of the London County Council, MP for Lewisham and finally Lord Morrison of Lambeth.

Particular districts of London and its suburbs evoke strong memories of a radical and socialist past. Historically, Clerkenwell has a tradition of political dissent and revolutionary connections stretching over nine hundred years. In 1381, the rebel army from the north camped out on Clerkenwell Green during the Peasants' Revolt. Annie Besant and William Morris addressed the unemployed there before 'Bloody Sunday' in November 1887. Nearby is the socialist library and archive at the Marx Memorial Library, the oldest building on Clerkenwell Green, from where Lenin published his paper, *Iskra*. The two-mile Clerkenwell Historic Trail, officially opened in March 1998 by Chris Smith, Labour Secretary of State for Culture, Media and Sport, now guides the tourist around this historic quarter of London.

Both William Morris, poet, craftsman and revolutionary, and Annie Besant, Fabian and feminist, are associated with several parts of London. Morris's family home in Walthamstow now houses the

William Morris Gallery. After quarrelling with H. M. Hyndman in the Social Democratic Federation, Morris seceded, with his followers, from the Hammersmith branch to form the Socialist League. He died in Kelmscott House, Hammersmith, which also housed his Kelmscott Press. Morris's legacy was to influence a host of future socialists in London and beyond, including Margaret and G. D. H. Cole, Harold Laski, George Lansbury, Clement Attlee and Barbara Castle.

East London has witnessed much socialist and militant activity. Radical, feminist, and birth control advocate Annie Besant is famously remembered for organising a strike of Match Girls at the Bryant and May factory in Bow, East London in 1888. This inspiring struggle by an oppressed female workforce lit the fuse for the great Dockers' strike of 1889, under the leadership of John Burns, Tom Mann and Ben Tillett, which brought the Port of London to a standstill and captured the attention of the nation. The docks fell silent again in 1911 and 1912, and again during the General Strike of 1926. Karl's daughter, Eleanor Marx, addressed meetings of the Social Democratic Federation in Dod Street, Poplar, and was active in Will Thorne's Gasworkers' Union. Sylvia Pankhurst campaigned for the vote with the working-class women of Bow. And the 30 Labour councillors – 25 men and five women – went willingly to Brixton and Holloway prisons during the 1921 Poplar Rates Revolt, which put 'Poplarism' into the political vocabulary.

To the north, fashionable Hampstead, with fine views of London from Hampstead Heath, has attracted a host of leading politicians, intellectuals, politicians and writers. Among others on the Left, H. M. Hyndman, Hugh Gaitskell, Harold Wilson and Michael Foot have lived there. During the political crisis of 1931, the Labour Prime Minister Ramsay MacDonald confided in his diary that 'the lady of Frognal' – his home – beckoned him. More recently, Marxist historian Eric Hobsbawm has warmly recalled stimulating encounters with former Labour leader, Michael Foot, at their local bus stop, as the two stalwart Left-wingers made their respective ways from Hampstead to Birkbeck College and Westminster.

In central London, the streets and buildings of Fitzrovia supply diverse reminders of a rich radical past, from John Wilkes to Thomas Paine and onwards. Rabble rouser John Wilkes, MP for Middlesex and twice Mayor of London, regularly enjoyed mutton pies, claret and port at the Farthing Pye House (now the Green Man opposite Great Portland Street tube station). In 1792, Mary Wollstonecraft wrote her seminal *Vindication of the Rights of Women* in Store Street. In the same year, hiding from government prosecution in New Cavendish Street (now Upper Marylebone Street), Tom Paine penned his *Rights of Man* in which he declared 'all men are born equal and with equal rights'. The book sold two million copies in Britain, France and the United States. Another resident of Fitzrovia, and champion of the French Revolution, was the essayist, William Hazlitt, who lived in Percy Street and Rathbone Place, and died in Soho nearly 20 years after completing his four-volume *Life of Napoleon*. Prominent radical artisans of the London Corresponding Society, including the slave Olaudah Equiano, a leading campaigner for the abolition of the African slave trade, were also politically active in late eighteenth-century Fitzrovia.

Besides its memorable historic sites, London is handsomely endowed with libraries and archives, readily accessible to those who wish to study its Leftie past. In Bloomsbury, the British Museum is a powerhouse of knowledge, once used – among other researchers – by exiled revolutionaries Karl Marx and Vladimir Lenin. The famous domed Reading Room is still open to tourists, though the British Library, as it has become, has moved to a long-awaited new building next to St Pancras Railway Station. Lenin, who used to enjoy long rides on the top of London omnibuses, resided in Clerkenwell and elsewhere, an active exiled member of the Russian Social Democratic Party. However, the Brotherhood Church in Southgate Road, on the borders of Hackney and Islington, where radical American millionaire Joseph Fels, loaned Lenin and his fellow Bolshevik delegates their travelling expenses home, has been demolished. During his 34-year exile in the capital, Karl Marx and his family lived at several addresses in central London. His grave and headstone are probably the most famous in Highgate Cemetery, one of more than a hundred final resting places for London citizens within a nine-mile radius of Charing Cross.

Finally, London offers a unique opportunity to those who wish to follow in the footsteps of radicals and socialists. In University College, Gower Street, the preserved body of Jeremy Bentham, radical philosopher, economist and exponent of utilitarianism, who died in 1832, can be found gazing out of his display case, except when wheeled out for university functions. Fully clothed and sporting a straw hat and walking stick, this remarkable individual is not a wax replica like those at Madame Tussaud's. Engage Bentham in scholarly discourse – he was a candid critic of government and politics – though he remains silent now about London's radical and dissenting past.

Gazetteer

Places are distributed first according to postal address, starting EC, followed by WC, SW, SE, E, N, NW and W. Then outlying places, without the postal address, from Bexleyheath to Woodford Green.

EC1

CLERKENWELL. Named after the Clerk's Well, still to be seen at 14 Farringdon Lane, this was London's first suburb to the north of the city. It has had an association with popular radicalism and political unrest since the Middle Ages, situated as it was outside the City of London, which had an effective system of policing before Robert Peel established the Metropolitan Police in 1829. In the eighteenth century, Clerkenwell became the home of skilled French Huguenot craftsmen and their families, fleeing religious persecution. They set up workshops for making locks, clocks and jewellery. The River Fleet flowed openly through Clerkenwell until the construction of the Metropolitan Railway, when much slum dwelling was swept away. In 1900, the Labour Party was founded (as the Labour Representation Committee) in Farringdon Street, and three years later Lenin produced the newspaper of the Russian Social Democratic Party, *Iskra*, on Clerkenwell Green. The *Daily Worker* (later the *Morning Star*) was issued from Farringdon Street, close to the present day offices of the *Guardian* and the *Observer*.

CLERKENWELL. Clerkenwell Green. Important gathering point for radicals, dissenters and revolutionaries for at least six hundred years. Rebels from East Anglia and Essex camped here during the Peasants' Revolt in 1381. The Tolpuddle Martyrs, persecuted trade unionists of the 1830s, were first greeted here when they returned to Britain after transportation to Australia. Up to seven thousand people listened to Chartist speeches at regular meetings on the Green. At the time of the Paris Commune in 1871, a red flag, surmounted by a 'cap of liberty', was stuck on a lamppost on the Green, and on 13 November 1887 a 'Bloody Sunday' demonstration for the unemployed was addressed here by Annie Besant and William Morris. Two years later there was a London Dock Strike rally here.

CLERKENWELL. Spa Fields. Pleasure gardens in the eighteenth century, the open space of Spa Fields saw some of the biggest demonstrations for democratic rights in 1816 and 1817. Political gatherings were addressed by Henry 'Orator' Hunt (1773-1835), a prosperous Wiltshire farmer who had embraced the democratic cause. Establishment London quaked at the masses on the march, and over the next few years the government introduced repressive measures restricting freedom of expression and assembly. After the actual site for demos, Wilmington Square, was developed, mass meetings shifted to Clerkenwell Green. It is now a municipal park, but there is no plaque to commemorate its significance two centuries ago.

CLERKENWELL. Marx Memorial Library, 37a Clerkenwell Green. A socialist library and meeting place with around one hundred thousand books and other publications, including the original English translation of *The Communist Manifesto* by Marx and Engels. Built in the eighteenth century as a Welsh school, in 1872 the building became the headquarters of the London Patriotic Club, a meeting place for republicans and other Lefties, including Friedrich Engels and Eleanor Marx (but not Karl). In 1892 it housed the forward-looking Twentieth Century Press, socialist publishers who produced early editions of the work of Marx and Engels. The Press published the journal of the Social Democratic Federation, *Justice*. The Director of the Press, Harry Quelch, lent his office on the first floor to Lenin, 1902-03, to edit *Iskra*, the newspaper of the Russian Social Democrats. The office is now a shrine to Lenin, restored as it would have been when Lenin was there. The building became the Marx Memorial Library in 1933, on the 50th anniversary of the death of Karl Marx. In the first floor library is a 1930s fresco depicting 'The Worker of the Future Upsetting the Economic Chaos of the Present'. The artist was Jack Hastings, aka the Earl of Huntingdon, first father-in-law of Woodrow Wyatt. The fresco includes portraits of Marx and Lenin and other revolutionaries.

CLERKENWELL. 34 Clerkenwell Green. The address of Lunt's Coffee House, a venue for Chartists meeting in the 1830s, working for universal suffrage, secret ballots and annual parliaments.

CLERKENWELL. Coldbath Square. The site of Coldbath Fields, one of three sites in the area that were venues for radical gatherings in the early nineteenth century. Here in 1831, the National Union of the Working Classes met to hold a 'National Convention, The Only Means of Obtaining and Securing The Rights of the People.' Its objectives included the 'Extirpation of the Fiend Aristocracy; Establishment of a Republic' and many other demands, such as cheap and rapid administration of justice, 'emancipation of our fellow citizens the Jews', and the abolition of tithes.

CLERKENWELL. Mount Pleasant Post Office, Farringdon Road. The site of the Middlesex House of Correction, better known as Cold Baths Prison, closed down in 1877 and demolished in 1889. The ultra Radical Arthur Thistlewood, leader of the Cato Street Conspiracy, was held here in 1820 before being sent to the Tower of London, after which he was taken to Newgate Prison and hanged. The conspirators aimed to assassinate the Cabinet, and planned to place the heads of Sidmouth and Castlereagh, seen as the most oppressive members of the government, on pikes.

CLERKENWELL. Caroone House, Farringdon Street. This property was developed on the site of the Congregational Memorial Hall where the Labour Representation Committee (LRC) was founded, 27-28 February 1900. The conference brought together delegates of

41 trades unions, seven trades councils, and socialist societies. The objective was to increase support for working-class candidates for parliamentary seats. Pledges for Socialism and 'a recognition of the class war' were rejected. Instead, in words proposed by Keir Hardie, it was aimed to establish 'a distinct Labour group in Parliament, who shall have their own whips, and agree on policy'. The Secretary elected was James Ramsay MacDonald, then aged 33. The event was hardly noticed in the contemporary press. The LRC was renamed the Labour Party after the 1906 General Election. Under construction in 2004, Caroone House is dedicated to capitalism but is required to display a Greater London Council plaque to mark its historic significance.

CLERKENWELL. 75 Farringdon Road. The newspaper of the Communist Party, *The Daily Worker*, was founded in 1930. The first editor was William Rust, who lasted only two years but became editor again from 1942 to 1949, years of the heyday of the British Communist Party. The ownership of the paper was vested in a co-operative, with the name People's Press Printing Society. During Rust's editorship, a site was purchased there that became the editorial and printing base of *The Daily Worker*. The building became the William Rust House. *The Daily Worker* was renamed *Morning Star* during the editorship of George Matthews, 1967-81. Subsidies and guaranteed purchase (twelve thousand of each daily issue) from the Soviet Union continued until 1992. But by then the Farringdon Road building had been sold off – in 1987 for £2.1 million. The building has been replaced.

FINSBURY. 30 Holford Square. One of Lenin's London addresses, from where he walked to Clerkenwell Green to edit *Iskra*.

EC2

BISHOPSGATE. Bishopsgate Institute, opposite Liverpool Street Railway Station. Fascinating and helpful reference library, of particular interest to Leftie visitors and those investigating the history of their London-based firms. It contains the George Howell Library on trades union and Labour movements – including the papers of George Howell himself who was connected with most of the nineteenth-century Radical movements, from Chartism onwards. The George Holyoake collection on the Co-operative movement is also housed at the Library.

EC3

TOWER OF LONDON. Wat Tyler and his fellow rebels occupied the Tower during the Peasants' Revolt of 1381. Until the twentieth century, it was a prison. Arthur Thistlewood, Cato Street conspirator, was held here, as was Arthur Woodburn (1890-1978), a pacifist in the First World War and subsequently Secretary of State for Scotland, 1947-50, in Clement Attlee's Labour government.

EC4

BLACKFRIARS. Rotunda. Venue of Radical meetings in 1810s and 1820s, which was also the meeting place for the Owenite National Union of the Working Classes in the 1830s.

CITY OF LONDON. 6 Bouverie Street. Site of the home of William Hazlitt (1778-1830), essayist, supporter of the French Revolution and champion of liberty.

FLEET STREET. Bolt Street. The headquarters of the Social Democratic Federation (SDF), an important Marxist group founded in 1884 by Henry Mayers Hyndman (1842-1921), a wealthy Tory educated at Cambridge. He read Karl Marx in French and quarrelled with early members of the SDF, including John Burns and William Morris. The SDF leader had earlier played cricket for the Gentlemen of Sussex and bowled to W. G. Grace. The author of *England For All* (1881) and *Socialism Made Plain* (1883), Hyndman was an articulate socialist propagandist, though Marx and Engels disowned him for plagiarising their ideas. The SDF provided a formative influence on the early careers of many nineteenth-century socialists including George Lansbury, who became briefly 'the best organiser the

Federation ever had'. Hyndman later lived in Hampstead at 13 Well Walk. He recounted his colourful life in two readable volumes of autobiography, in one of which he described calling on Karl Marx in Hampstead: 'Our method of talking was peculiar. Marx had a habit when at all interested in the discussion of walking actively up and down the room, as if he were pacing the deck of a schooner for exercise. I had acquired, on my long voyages, the same tendency to pacing to and fro when my mind was much occupied. Consequently, master and student could have been seen walking up and down on opposite sides of the table for two or three hours in succession, engaged in discussing the affairs of the past and the present.'

FLEET STREET. Fetter Lane. A statue of John Wilkes (1727-97), populist would-be democrat – portrayed with a squint – is at the corner of Fetter Lane and New Fetter Lane.

FLEET STREET. Neville's Court, off Fetter Lane. The London home of James Keir Hardie (1856-1915), Labour leader, pacifist and socialist. His flat was later occupied by Fenner Brockway (1888-1988), who called on Keir Hardie at Neville's Court a Liberal, and left a socialist. It was bombed during the Second World War.

WC1

BLOOMSBURY. Birkbeck College, Malet Street. Famous college, which is part of the University of London, noted for its evening degree courses and postgraduate programmes for mature students. Originally founded as a Mechanics' Institute in the 1820s by George Birkbeck, the original plaque can be seen inside the main entrance. Above the doorway, the inscription *In Nocte Consilium* announces the Birkbeck philosophy towards higher education. Ramsay MacDonald was a former student. Among its distinguished Leftie academics have been J. D. Bernal, Tessa Blackstone, Bernard Crick, Eric Hobsbawm, Ben Pimlott and Michael Young. During the 175th anniversary celebrations, a packed Senate House audience heard Professor Hobsbawm lecture on

'Birkbeck and the Left'.

BLOOMSBURY. 2 Gower Street. Home of Millicent Garrett Fawcett (1847-1929), leader of the National Union of Women's Suffrage Society, the moderate and constitutional wing of the struggle for 'Votes for Women' before the First World War.

BLOOMSBURY. British Museum, Great Russell Street. The British Museum opened in 1759 in Montague House, daily for three hours. Readers were able to apply for tickets to do research. The mid-Victorian planning of the Library was the inspiration of the Italian revolutionary Antonio Panizzi. The dome became the second-largest dome in the world. Reader's tickets have been issued to Mahatma Gandhi, Prince Kropotkin, Karl Marx, Vladimir Lenin, John Ruskin, George Bernard Shaw, and Labour Minister and novelist John Stonehouse. Here Shelley was inspired to compose 'Ozymandias' and 'Ode to a Grecian Urn'. According to legend, Karl Marx occupied Seat 07 to research his major analysis of capitalism *Das Kapital*, and other works. He also studied treatises on medicine in an effort to cure his boils. In 1902 Lenin used seat L.13a under the name, Jacob Richter. The Reading Room today is a tourist site within the British Museum.

BLOOMSBURY. 21 Mecklenburg Square. Home of R. H. Tawney (1880-1962), historian (*Religion and the Rise of Capitalism*), President of the Workers' Educational Association, socialist theorist, author of *The Acquisitive Society* and brother-in-law of William Beveridge. Educated at Rugby School and Balliol College Oxford, he spent three formative years on social work at Toynbee Hall in the East End. A Christian socialist, Tawney had a distinguished career at the London School of Economics, where he became Professor of Economic History. He was an important influence on Labour Party policy, including the Hadow Report – which eventually shaped the 1944 Education Act – and the Labour manifesto *Labour and the Nation*. He is buried in Highgate Cemetery.

HOLBORN. 58 Doughty Street. Home of socialist, feminist and pacifist Vera Brittain (1893-1970). After her young fiance, Roland Leighton, was killed on the Western Front in 1915, she became a dedicated peace campaigner and joined the Labour party in the 1920s. An accomplished writer, Vera Brittain published her autobiography about the Great War, *Testament of Youth*, which became a bestseller. From 1919 to 1935, she had a long friendship with her fellow-writer Winifred Holtby, until the latter's death in 1935. Two years later, she joined the Peace Pledge Union and became its chairperson. She was also one of the founders of the Campaign for Nuclear Disarmament. Vera Brittain married the American political scientist George Catlin, in 1925. Their daughter is Shirley Williams.

HOLBORN. Red Lion Square. Named after the inn where disinterred bodies of the regicides Oliver Cromwell, Henry Ireton and John Bradshaw were kept, before being taken to Tyburn for hanging, after the restoration of King Charles II. No. 17 was the home of William Morris (1834-96), whose workshop was at No. 8. In the gardens there is a bronze bust of Bertrand Russell (1872-1970), philosopher, conscientious objector in the First World War and a founder of the Campaign for Nuclear Disarmament. There is also a statue of Fenner Brockway (1888-1988), pacifist, ILP and Labour MP, and campaigner against imperialism.

HOLBORN. Red Lion Square. Conway Hall. A centre for independent, political and cultural life, Conway Hall has been, since it was built in 1929, a venue for Leftie meetings – and still is. It is the headquarters of the Ethical Society and has the largest and most comprehensive humanist reference library. It is named after Moncure Daniel Conway (1832-1907), an American campaigner against slavery who lived occasionally in Britain, and was the biographer of Thomas Paine.

WC2

CHARING CROSS. 16 Charing Cross Road. Site of the tailor's shop of Francis Place (1771-1854), one of the great Radicals of the first half of the nineteenth century. This venue was an important meeting place for discussion of parliamentary reform.

COVENT GARDEN. 16 King Street. Headquarters of the Communist Party of Great Britain, founded in 1920 and feared for its Russian Bolshevik connections, and which the police raided several times. One early raid, in 1925, led to the arrest of twelve prominent Communists, including Harry Pollitt, Wal Hannington and Robin Page Arnot. At their trial at the Old Bailey they were found guilty of publishing seditious libels and breaches of the Incitement to Mutiny Act of 1797, and sentenced to periods of six and twelve months imprisonment. On another occasion, police mistakenly arrested Special Branch officers keeping surveillance on the premises.

HOLBORN. British Library of Political and Economic Science (BLPES), 10 Portugal Street. The BLPES, which has moved back into its handsomely refurbished premises, is a major powerhouse of knowledge for historians and social scientists researching the political Left. Among the major collections in the Archives Centre are the papers of William Beveridge, Hugh Dalton, George Lansbury, and Sidney and Beatrice Webb. The Archives also store the papers of Charles Booth and his mammoth survey *The Life and Labour of the People of London*. The BLPES is part of the London School of Economics, founded by the Webbs. Many famous Lefties, such as Clement Attlee and R. H. Tawney, have been members of the staff of the School.

HOLBORN. 3 Lincoln's Inn Fields. The family home of Margaret and James Ramsay MacDonald at the time of the foundation of the Labour Party in 1900. MacDonald was the first Secretary of the Party, and the backroom provided the office of the Labour Party. The MacDonalds, who had made a number of world tours, were committed internationalists, and their flat became a political salon for visitors from Britain and abroad. In 1924, Ramsay MacDonald took on the dual role of Labour Prime Minister and Foreign Secretary. Margaret died here in 1911. On the north side of Lincoln's Inn Fields is a memorial seat dedicated to Margaret MacDonald, acknowledging her contribution to the Labour movement. Margaret is sculpted as an angel, with a flowing cloak resembling wings, and is surrounded by happy children. The sculpture was by Richard R. Goulden and erected in 1914.

HOLBORN. 4 Clement's Inn. This building, near the Law Courts off Aldwych, was the London base for the Women's Social and Political Union, led by Emmeline Pankhurst and Christabel Pankhurst.

LONG ACRE. St Martin's Hall. The venue for the inaugural meeting, in 1864, of the International Working Men's Association, dubbed the First International. Among the trade union and socialist delegates attending from Britain and abroad were the Victorian trade union leader, Robert Applegarth, the first workman to be appointed to a Royal Commission; and Karl Marx.

STRAND. Shell Mex House, 80 Strand. An imposing office block on the site of the Cecil Hotel (used by H. G. Wells as Hardingham in his novel *Tono Bungay*). The hotel was largely demolished in 1920, but the façade was retained in the Shell Mex Complex which has the largest clock face in London. The building was taken over by the government in the Second World War, and here Clement Attlee told the post-war Labour Cabinet that Britain planned to develop the atom bomb.

SW1

HYDE PARK. One of London's largest Royal Parks and, the area just south west of Marble Arch, Speakers' Corner, a traditional gathering place for political meetings and demonstrations. May Day rallies have been held here since 1890. A lamppost now indicates the site of the 'Reformers' Tree', where the oak stood. For over 20 years, Donald Soper (1903-98), Methodist socialist and pacifist, and later Life Peer, addressed crowds here as well as on Tower Hill, earning his *Private Eye* nickname, Lord Soapbox. Speakers' Corner remains a popular part of the Park for visitors to hear and discuss a variety of dissenting political and religious views. On 15 February 2003, the one million plus march against the Iraq war ended up in Hyde Park.

HYDE PARK. 28 Queen Anne's Gate. London home of Richard Burdon Haldane, Viscount Haldane of Cloan (1856-1928), first Labour Lord Chancellor in Ramsay MacDonald's government of 1924. Philosopher and Liberal imperialist, Haldane was MP for Haddingtonshire (or Lothian) and was Secretary for War and Lord Chancellor in the Liberal governments of H. H. Asquith, 1905-15. Unlike some of his Liberal contemporaries, who switched their sympathies to Labour in the years after the First World War, Haldane never formally joined the Labour Party. MacDonald had met him at this house and at Cloan, Haldane's Perthshire home. Haldane played a part in recruiting Liberals and Conservatives (like Lord Parmoor and Viscount Chelmsford) into participating in the 1924 Labour government.

WESTMINSTER. Transport House, Smith Square. Headquarters of the Labour Party, 1928-80. Opened by Ramsay MacDonald on 15 May 1928, it also housed the headquarters of the TUC, 1928-57, and the Transport and General Workers Union, 1928-2000.

WESTMINSTER. Westminster Abbey. The ashes of Sidney Webb (1859-1947) and Beatrice Webb (1858-1943), and Clement Attlee (1883-1967) lie here.

WESTMINSTER. 5 Lord North Street. Former home of Harold Wilson (1916-95), Labour Prime Minister 1964-70 and 1974-76.

WESTMINSTER. 10 Downing Street. The official residence and office of the Prime Minister. Home of James Ramsay MacDonald 1924 and 1929-35 (the first two years as Labour Prime Minister), Clement Attlee 1945-51, Harold Wilson 1964-70 and 1974-76, James Callaghan 1976-79 and Tony Blair since 1997. In 1924, Ramsay MacDonald sent his daughter, Ishbel, to the Co-op to buy furniture and household equipment: Prime Ministers were expected to provide these items. His 1924 government removed ten-foot high wooden barriers, which had been erected during the Irish troubles. That year, the eight-year-old Harold Wilson posed for a photograph outside the door. Today access is heavily restricted.

WESTMINSTER. 11 Downing Street. The official residence of the Chancellor of the Exchequer. Home of Philip Snowden 1924 and 1929-31, Hugh Dalton 1945-48, Stafford Cripps 1948-51, Hugh Gaitskell 1951, James Callaghan 1964-67, Roy Jenkins 1967-70, Denis Healey 1974-79, and Gordon Brown since 1997. Only one of these, so far, has moved next door: James Callaghan (1912-2005).

SW2

BRIXTON. Brixton Prison. In 1921, during the 'Poplar Rates Revolt' 30 Labour councillors – mainly local working people – willingly went to gaol (25 men to Brixton and five women to Holloway) in defiance of the government and the national leadership of their party, to defend their local East End community of Poplar. As councillors, they refused to pay the precept rates imposed for central services, arguing that the people of Poplar were subsidising the most prosperous parts of London. The councillors, led by the former Mayor, George Lansbury, refused to reduce relief payments and were jailed for contempt of court. The prisoners disrupted prison routine, refused to work and demanded newspapers and footballs. Each day, George Lansbury addressed crowds outside from his prison-cell window. During their six-week imprisonment, the councillors held official meetings with council officials, and eventually they were released by the High Court. This memorable incident became part of 'Poplarism', the symbol in Labour history of local defiance against central authority. But it angered the national leadership of the Labour Party and, in 1924, Ramsay MacDonald did not appoint George Lansbury to his first Labour Cabinet.

SW3

CHELSEA. Glebe Place. Childhood home of Shirley Williams (1930-), Labour

Cabinet Minister and one of the 'Gang of Four' who left the party to form the Social Democratic Party in 1981.

CHELSEA. 4 Anderson Street. First of a number of London homes of Karl Marx and his family during his 34-year exile in London.

CHELSEA. 12 Bramerton Street. Home of the Coles. G. D. H. Cole (1889-1959), prolific Labour economist and historian, was Chichele Professor of Social and Economic Policy at the University of Oxford. In addition to his many works on the British Labour movement, often written in collaboration with his wife, Margaret, he also published *The Common People* with his brother-in-law, Raymond Postgate. Dame Margaret Cole (1893-1980), Fabian socialist, feminist, educationalist, historian of the Fabian Society and editor of Beatrice Webb's *Diaries*, was active in the First-World-War peace movement, and supported the miners during the General Strike. A member of the Labour Research Department and of the London County Council, she was chair of the Sidney Webb College of Education (for mature students) in her later years. In the 1930s, G. D. H. and Margaret Cole founded the Society for Socialist Inquiry and Propaganda, which held week-end socialist gatherings at the exotic and palatial Easton Lodge, the home of the Labour sympathiser, the 'red' Countess of Warwick, near Great Dunmow, Essex. The Coles also collaborated as writers of detective fiction.

SW4

CLAPHAM COMMON. 110 North Side. Home of John Burns (1859-1943), MP for Battersea 1892-1918 and hailed as 'the best known man in London'. Also known as 'The Battersea Bruiser', Burns was a socialist pioneer who joined the Social Democratic Federation in 1884, and played a leading part in the London Dock Strike of 1889, along with Ben Tillett, Tom Mann and Will Thorne. In 1892, Burns was one of three so-called independent Labour candidates elected to Parliament – the other two were Keir Hardie (West Ham) and

James Havelock Wilson (Middlesbrough) – but his political trajectory took him steadily rightwards. Elected to the London County Council, he associated with the Progressives (Liberals) and was active on transport and water-services issues. He became the first workman to become a Cabinet minister, as President of the Local Government Board in Campbell-Bannerman's Liberal government of 1905, though his former socialist allies were critical of his attitude on Poor Law policy. A lifelong pacifist, who had opposed the Boer War, Burns, in 1914, resigned from the Cabinet in protest against Britain's entry into the First World War. He withdrew from public life after 1918. Burns amassed a considerable private library with a specialist collection on the history of Labour and London. On his death, his estate was valued at £15,137 and his books were sold for over £25,000.

SW10

CHELSEA. 120 Cheyne Walk and 45 Park Walk. Two of the London residences of the suffragette leader Sylvia Pankhurst (1882-1960).

CHELSEA. 32 Elm Park Gardens. London home of Stafford Cripps (1889-1952), lawyer and Labour Chancellor of the Exchequer.

SW15

PUTNEY. St Mary's Church, Putney High Street. The New Model Army held the 'Putney Debates' in and around the church from 28 October to 11 November 1647 to discuss a new constitution after the English Civil War. Lieutenant-General Oliver Cromwell, chaired the intense discussions but with Commissary-General, Henry Ireton, opposed the demands of the Levellers' representatives, drawn from the more radical regiments, for manhood suffrage, parliamentary and constitutional reforms set out in the *Agreement of the People*.

SE1

BLACKFRIARS. 209-215 Blackfriars Road. Home of the

feminist Mary Wollstonecraft (1759-97).

SOUTHWARK. John Smith House, Walworth Road. Labour Party headquarters during the 1990s.

SE3

BLACKHEATH. Blackheath Gate. Site where Wat Tyler met rebel groups during the Peasants' Revolt of 1381.

SE9

ELTHAM. 55 Archery Road. Home, from 1929 to 1960, of Herbert Morrison (1888-1965). An expert administrator who built up the London Labour Party, he was Minister of Transport in Ramsay MacDonald's second government of 1929-31, became Home Secretary in Winston Churchill's wartime coalition government and Lord President of the Council and Leader of the House of Commons in Clement Attlee's 1945 Labour government. His role was to co-ordinate Labour's domestic and economic policy, and to drive the substantial legislation through Parliament. When Ernest Bevin had to quit because of ill-health he became Foreign Secretary for a few months in 1951.

SE11

KENNINGTON. Kennington Common. The site of Chartist rallies, including the assembly in south London on 10 April 1848, before the presentation to Parliament of the third petition, demanding rights. An early nineteenth-century photograph – a daguerreotype – found in the Royal Archives, shows an orderly gathering.

SE18

WOOLWICH. Beresford Square. Will Crooks (1852-1921), former cooper and member of the London County Council in 1903, crossed the Thames from his native Poplar to win a famous by-election and become the third Labour MP to enter the House of Commons. Photographs in his memoirs show enthusiastic crowds at his hustings in Beresford Square.

The victory was a landmark in the rise of the Labour Party as an independent political force. Many of Will Crooks' constituents were skilled artisans and co-operators who worked at the Woolwich Arsenal, the main government armaments works in Britain. As the local MP, he fought hard to maintain employment against the government's programme of discharges and short-time working.

WOOLWICH. Woolwich Arsenal. In 1886, the engineers, fitters and turners in the Dial Square workshops at the Woolwich Arsenal formed an amateur football club that maintained an exclusively proletarian identity for around twenty years, famously borrowing their first kit of red shirts from Nottingham Forest Football Club. The club struggled financially, as it was totally dependent on the military town of Woolwich and the Arsenal workers for its spectators. Eventually, Woolwich Arsenal embraced professionalism and became the second team to enter the Football League (second division), but was taken over by the predatory entrepreneur and local politician Henry Norris, chairman of Fulham FC. Controversially, in 1913 he moved his ailing club, lock, stock and barrel to upper-class Highbury in North London, where Arsenal became a world-class club in the 1930s, under the legendary Herbert Chapman. Today, the club motif of cannons, and the nickname 'The Gunners', as well as the red shirts, are all that survive of the club's working-class origins. Woolwich Arsenal is now open to the public as a heritage site and military museum.

E1

WHITECHAPEL. St George's Town Hall, 236 Cable Street. A large mural depicts and commemorates the 1936 'Battle of Cable Street', when Jews, socialists and communists fought Oswald Mosley's British Union of Fascists, preventing them from marching through the heavily Jewish East End.

WHITECHAPEL. Toynbee Hall, 28 Commercial Street. University settlement in East

London founded in 1884 by Canon Samuel Barnett and his wife, Henrietta, and named after Arnold Toynbee, Balliol historian and advocate of extending adult education. Social work among the poor and deprived of the East End was a formative experience for many middle-class figures at Toynbee Hall, in their early careers as settlers, such as Clement Attlee, R. H. Tawney and William Beveridge, who were later responsible for shaping the welfare state in Britain. Toynbee Hall remains an important centre today for its social-welfare and educational programmes.

E3

BOW. Fairfield Mills, Fairfield Road. The factory was the location, in 1888, of a strike of match girls at the Bryant and May works. The workforce of over one thousand women was organised by the Fabian socialist, Annie Besant, and was to demand better pay and conditions from its Gladstonian Liberal employers.

BOW. 105 St Stephen's Road. Home, now demolished, of Bessie and George Lansbury (1859-1940) and their family, when they occupied a cottage on the Isaac Brine Saw Mill and Timber Yard, after their return from an unsuccessful emigration to Queensland, 1884-85. In 1896, Lansbury took over the management of the timber yard, on the death of his father-in-law. The firm was often in financial difficulties, and Lansbury continued to work full-time while pursuing his political career, until around 1914 when his sons, William and Edgar, took over. Their sister, Daisy, started her career as secretary in the firm. Daisy married Raymond Postgate, brother of Margaret Cole.

BOW. 39 Bow Road. Bessie and George Lansbury moved with their family to this address in about 1917. As MP for Bromley and Bow, George Lansbury always lived in the heart of his East End constituency. No. 39 became famous as a haven for all, to which constituents brought their concerns and requests for help. In 1940, George Lansbury's body lay in state here. The house was destroyed during an early bombing raid in the Second World War. A plaque now marks the site.

BOW. Electric Clock, Bow Road. Memorial to Minnie Lansbury (nee Glassman), one of the 30 Labour Councillors imprisoned during the Poplar Rates Revolt of 1921. She died at the age of 32 after a six-week imprisonment in Holloway. A former school teacher, Minnie was an ardent supporter of Sylvia Pankhurst during the suffragette campaign, with her husband Edgar, son of Bessie and George Lansbury. Edgar's second wife was the actress and former suffragette, Moyna MacGill. The award-winning actress, Angela Lansbury, is their daughter.

BOW. Bow Cemetery, Southern Road. Grave of Alfred Linnell, crushed under police horses during 'Bloody Sunday', a demonstration of the unemployed in Trafalgar Square on 13 November 1887. William Morris wrote a poem which he declaimed at the graveside:

> They will not learn; they have no ears to hearken.
> They turn their faces from the eyes of fate;
> Their gay-lit halls shut out the skies that darken.
> But, lo! This dead man knocking at the gate.

Will Crooks, Labour victor in a landmark by-election at Woolwich in 1903, is also buried here, in a restored grave. Admired son of Poplar and famous for 'Crooks's College' providing open air discussion and political education outside the Dock Gates, Crooks made the employment of the Woolwich Arsenal workforce a prime concern.

BOW. Old Ford Road. Home, with plaque, of Israel Zangwill (1864-1926), writer, poet and philanthropist. He was the chronicler of Jewish migrants, the East End ghetto and an active supporter of Sylvia Pankhurst and the women's movement in East London.

POPLAR. Kingsley Hall, Powis Road. A blue plaque marks Mahatma Gandhi's fifth visit to London in 1932, when he chose to stay with the socialist and peace campaigners Muriel and Doris Lester, in deprived East London, rather than at a fashionable West-End hotel like the rest of the delegates to the London Round Table Conference on the future constitutional development of India. He crossed London each day. During his stay he also made a famous visit to the cotton-mill workers of Lancashire.

E6

WEST HAM. A Labour and socialist heartland. Railway workers founded the London Co-operative Society in West Ham in 1862. Thirty years later, former miner and journalist James Keir Hardie was returned as the first independent Labour MP for the constituency. West Ham also elected the first socialist municipal council in Britain, in 1889-90, with members of the Social Democratic Federation.

WEST HAM. 1 Lawrence Road. Home of Will Thorne (1857-1946), leading figure of the London Dock Strike of 1889, pioneering General Secretary of the Gas Workers' Union, and Labour MP.

E8

HACKNEY. 59 Mapledene Road. The first home of Cherie and Tony Blair, where they joined the local Labour Party. An end of terrace house, the Blairs bought it in 1980 for £40,000 and sold it in 1986 for £80,000.

HACKNEY. 373 Mare Street. Home of Mary Wollstonecraft (1759-97), early promoter of women's rights.

E14

LIMEHOUSE. 78 Narrow Street. Former home of David Owen, where, on 25 January 1981, four disillusioned Labour dissidents, Roy Jenkins, Shirley Williams, Bill Rodgers and David Owen himself ('The Gang of Four') made their Limehouse Declaration outlining the aims of the Council for Social Democracy. Two months later, the Social Democratic Party (SDP) was launched as a separate political party, with the objective of breaking the mould of British politics. In November 1981, Shirley Williams became the first to be elected as an

SDP MP, and the second woman to have been elected for two different parties. (The other being Megan Lloyd George.) Roy Jenkins won the Glasgow Hillhead by-election in 1982 and became the leader of the SDP. After fighting the 1983 and 1987 General Elections in alliance with the Liberal Party, the SDP's fortunes declined, with only five MPs elected in 1987, and the party split over the proposal to join with the Liberals. In 1988, the SDP voted for the merger and the new party eventually adopted the name Liberal Democrats.

POPLAR. Wade Arms Public House. Headquarters of the 1889 London Dock Strike.

E16

STEPNEY. Haileybury House, Durham Road. The home, at the beginning of the twentieth century, of Clement Attlee (1883-1967), Prime Minister of the Labour governments 1945-51 that introduced the National Health Service and established the Welfare State. Born into an upper-middle-class family in Putney, Attlee attended Haileybury School, Hertfordshire, and University College, Oxford. He was called to the bar and started a legal career in his family's law firm. But the experience of the very different world of the the deprived East End of London powerfully shaped his socialism. In 1905, he visited Haileybury House, a youth club founded by his old school. Two years later he became manager of the boys' club. He joined the Stepney branch of the Independent Labour Party and was elected Mayor in 1920.

E17

WALTHAMSTOW. William Morris Gallery, Lloyd Park, Forest Road. Formerly the home of socialist, poet and craftsman William Morris (1834-96), the Water House – as it was known – was given to the local council by the owners, the Lloyd family, to be part of a municipal park. In July 1900, Sam Woods, the Lib-Lab MP for Walthamstow, officiated at the opening ceremony, which was accompanied by local trade union banners and processions. Woods was general secretary of the TUC Parliamentary Committee and a former Lancashire miner, and had won a spectacular by-election in 1897. His connections with the Liberal Party brought political attacks from socialists, and he made no mention of William Morris in his speech. Today the Gallery is a museum displaying William Morris wallpaper and other artistic designs.

N1

ISLINGTON. 27b Canonbury Square. The home of Eric Blair, better known as George Orwell (1903-50), and his wife, Eileen, from 1944. It was then a war-damaged square: now a fashionable quarter for well-to-do academics and professionals. Wounded on the Republican side in the Spanish Civil war, he recounted his experiences in *Homage to Catalonia*. Orwell enjoyed his first major success with *Animal Farm*, parts of which were written here. Four British publishing houses – Jonathan Cape, Faber, Collins and Gollancz on the recommendation of T. S. Eliot – famously turned down the manuscript of what is probably Orwell's greatest work. *Animal Farm* became an international best-seller and has remained in print. Suffering from tuberculosis, and after his wife's death in 1948, Orwell would spend the summer with their son, Richard, on the Inner Hebridean island of Jura at Barnhill, and the winter in Canonbury. In writing *Nineteen Eighty-Four* he used the decaying no. 27 as the model for the rundown Victory Mansions, the home of the novel's hero, Winston Smith. In the novel – his depiction of a future servile state in which political freedom had been exterminated – the Senate House, University of London, served as his design for the Ministry of Truth. A blue plaque marks Orwell's time here.

ISLINGTON. Granita Restaurant, 127 Upper Street. In 1994, the new leader of the Labour Party, Tony Blair, and Gordon Brown allegedly sealed a partnership about the leadership of the party. Blair would yield to Brown at some future unspecified date. When this encounter was dramatised for television, the restaurant owner wrote to *The Guardian* to correct some of the details, in particular, the menu. By early 2004 the restaurant had been closed.

ISLINGTON. 1 Richmond Crescent. The home of Cherie and Tony Blair in the years up to May 1997, when they transferred their residence to 10 Downing Street. They have recently purchased a five-storey, stucco- and brick-fronted residence with five bedrooms, close to Marble Arch, for £3.5 million.

ISLINGTON. Copenhagen Fields. On the edge of the site of a meeting place for radicals and reformers in the eighteenth and nineteenth century, including the London Corresponding Society, a group that linked up sympathisers with the French Revolution. The large open space – later an important Victorian cattle market – witnessed the mass gathering in support of the six transported trade unionists, the Tolpuddle Martyrs. Chartists also gathered here.

N6

HIGHGATE. Cemetery, Swain's Lane. Grave of Karl Marx (1818-83). One of London's most famous, elegant, and landscaped resting places, Highgate Cemetery opened in 1839. Friedrich Engels found his lifelong friend Karl Marx dead in his favourite armchair in his study at 1 Maitland Road, Kentish Town (a street destroyed by Second-World-War enemy action and replaced by a six-storey block of London County Council flats). Marx was buried in the same grave as his wife, Jenny, who died in December 1881. At the graveside, attended by about 20 people, Engels read the main address: 'Just as Darwin discovered the law of development of organic matter, so Marx discovered the law of the development of human history.' In 1954, Marx's grave was repositioned and given a famous sculpted head by Lawrence Bradshaw, commissioned by the Communist Party of Great Britain. Nearby is the grave of Raphael Samuel, influential social historian of the East End of London, and initiator of 'people's workshops' in historical writing.

N7

HOLLOWAY. Prison. Suffragettes were imprisoned in Holloway before the First World War, and many went on hunger and thirst strikes, until released by the infamous 'Cat and Mouse Act'. Five women Labour councillors from Poplar were also incarcerated here during the six-week Poplar Rates Revolt of 1921. Constance Markievicz, a prominent figure of Sinn Fein, was held during the Irish troubles and, while in custody, was the first woman to be elected to the British Parliament, though she always refused to take her seat.

N16

STOKE NEWINGTON. Abney Park Cemetery. In the Victorian cemetery is the grave of the revolutionary Chartist James 'Bronterre' O'Brien (1805-64), the first advocate of 'physical force' and of the nationalisation of land.

NW1

CAMDEN. London Working Men's College, Crowndale Road. Fabian and Labour Cabinet minister Sidney Webb (1859-1947) taught here.

CAMDEN TOWN. 6 Oakley Square. One of the houses that Vladimir Ilyich Lenin stayed in, while in exile at the beginning of the twentieth century.

ST PANCRAS. Old St Pancras Churchyard. The original burial site of pioneer-feminist Mary Wollstonecraft (1759-97). She died giving birth to Mary Shelley, author of *Frankenstein*. Her body was moved to Bournemouth but the headstone remains.

ST PANCRAS. St Pancras Hospital, St Pancras Way. Place of death of Hugh Dalton (1887-1962), Etonian and Labour Chancellor of the Exchequer 1945-47.

SOMERS TOWN. Oakshott Court, Werrington Street. Home of Mary Wollstonecraft. A plaque marks the site.

NW3

HAMPSTEAD. St John-at-Hampstead Church. In the churchyard extension are the graves of Frank Soskice (1902-79), Labour Home Secretary 1964-65; and Hugh Gaitskell (1906-63), Leader of the Labour Party 1955 to his death.

HAMPSTEAD. 37 Belsize Park Gardens. Home of journalist and socialist H. N. Brailsford (1873-1958).

HAMPSTEAD. 9 Howitt Road. Home of James Ramsay MacDonald (1866-1937), first Labour Prime Minister, from 1916 to 1925.

HAMPSTEAD. 103 Frognal. Home of James Ramsay MacDonald (1866-1937) from 1925 to his death.

HAMPSTEAD. 8 Frognal Gardens. Home of Hugh Gaitskell (1906-63), Labour Chancellor of the Exchequer 1950-51 and Leader of the Party 1955-63.

HAMPSTEAD. 10 Fitzjohn's Avenue. 10 Netherhall Gardens. Homes of Sidney Webb (1859-1947) and Beatrice Webb (1858-1943), leading Fabians and social scientists associated with LSE and the *New Statesman*. Their famous partnership produced histories of local government, trade unionism and the British labour movement. Beatrice Webb served on the 1905–09 Poor Law Commission. Her *Diary* remains an important source for Labour historians. Sidney Webb was a Cabinet minister in Ramsay MacDonald's Labour governments, 1924 and 1929–31.

HAMPSTEAD. Hollycot, Vale of Heath. Home of the historians Barbara Hammond (1873-1961) and J. L. Hammond (1872-1949) from 1906 to 1913.

HAMPSTEAD. 13 Well Walk. Home of H. M. Hyndman (1842-1921), founder of the Social Democratic Federation.

HAMPSTEAD. Prompt Corner Café, South End Green. Site of Westrope's Bookshop where George Orwell (1903-50) worked as a part-time assistant from 1934-35

NW5

GOSPEL OAK. 9 (later 46) Grafton Terrace. Home of Karl Marx and his family during his political exile in London.

NW11

GOLDERS GREEN. Cemetery. The remains of Ernest Bevin (1881-1951), Foreign Secretary in the Labour government 1945-51; Arthur Henderson (1863-1935), Foreign Secretary in the Labour government 1929-31; Emanuel Shinwell (1884-1986), Minister in all Labour governments between 1924 and 1951; and A. J. P. Taylor (1906-90), socialist historian, are all buried here.

HAMPSTEAD GARDEN SUBURB. 10 (and 12) Southway. Home of Harold Wilson (1916-95), Labour Prime Minister 1964-70 and 1974-76.

W1

MARYLEBONE. Portland Rooms, Foley Street. Meeting place of the third Trades Union Congress (TUC) in March 1871.

MARYLEBONE. 1a Cato Street. The site, near the Edgware Road, of a plot, in 1820, by a group of conspirators armed with guns and swords, and led by ultra-Radical Arthur Thistlewood, to assassinate the entire Tory Cabinet of the Earl of Liverpool while they were dining at 44 Grosvenor Square. The 20 would-be assassins were exposed by an *agent provocateur*. There was a fight when police raided their cottage in Cato Street. Thistlewood escaped immediate capture, but was found the following day near Moorgate. He was executed at Newgate Prison where William Cobbett (also a prisoner there) was one of the last to see him.

SOHO. Gay Hussar Restaurant, 2 Greek Street, Soho Square. Hungarian restaurant, launched by Victor Sassie in 1953, it became associated with the Bevanites in the Labour Party, such as Barbara Castle, Michael Foot and Tony Benn. This Leftie haunt in bustling Soho remains popular with socialists and journalists and is now under the management of John Wrobel. Renowned for its cuisine and wines, the legendary restaurant is adorned by the portraits of its famous clients drawn between 1999 and 2005, by the outstanding cartoonist Martin Rowson, and now published in *Mug Shots*. In July 2003, the restaurant was packed for one of the celebrations for the 90th birthday of Michael Foot. Among many present were Cabinet Minister, Peter Hain, Jack Jones, General Secretary of the Transport and General Workers' Union, and former Conservative Cabinet Ministers, Ian Gilmour and Peter Walker.

SOHO. Coach and Horses, 29 Greek Street. Soho pub that was the venue of the fortnightly lunches held by the satirical magazine *Private Eye*.

SOHO. 26-29 Dean Street. A restaurant founded by Italian Peppino Leoni, unjustly interned during the Second World War as an enemy alien. Previously, no. 28 was the address of Jenny and Karl Marx, their family and their maid, Lenchen. Eleanor Marx was born in Dean Street in 1855 and three of the Marx children died here.

W2

PADDINGTON. 3 Cambridge Street. Place of death – according to the 1881 Census, she was lodging here – of Mary Seacole, Jamaican nurse and heroine of the Crimean War, and author of an autobiography, *Wonderful Adventures of Mrs Seacole in Many Lands* (1858). People are at last beginning to acknowledge her remarkable career.

W10

KENSAL GREEN. All Souls Cemetery, Harrow Road. Among the graves are those of Feargus O'Connor (1794-1855), Chartist leader; and George Birkbeck (1776-1841), founder of Mechanics' Institutes and after whom Birkbeck College is named.

And Beyond

BEXLEYHEATH. Red House, Red House Lane. Home from 1860 to 1865 of William Morris (1834-96), socialist, poet and craftsman.

BROMLEY. Allders Department Store, High Street. Site of the birthplace of H. G. Wells (1866-1946), novelist and Fabian socialist.

RICKMANSWORTH. Land of Liberty Inn, Heronsgate. Site of a Chartist land settlement under Feargus O'Connor, 1847.

WOODFORD GREEN. 17 Monkham's Avenue. Home of Clement Attlee in the 1920s. Woodford was the last constituency of Winston Churchill.

WOODFORD. West Dean, Charteris Road. Home of former suffragette, communist and pacifist Sylvia Pankhurst, and her common-law husband, Silvio Corio. They published a newspaper from here supporting the Emperor Haile Selassie, when his country, Ethiopia, was invaded by Fascist Italy in 1935. After 1945, Sylvia Pankhurst lived in Ethiopia until her death. West Dean was demolished but an anti-war memorial that she built – a falling bomb on a plinth – survives on Woodford High Road.

Grimsby
Gainsborough
Hogsthorpe
Skegness
St Faith's
Norwich
Oxburgh
Wymondham
Thetford
Burston
Kenninghall
Bressingham
Halesworth
Southwold
Cambridge
Bury St Edmunds
Cardington
Stowmarket
Framlingham
Leiston
Friston
Ashdon
Clare
Ipswich
Wallington
Hollesley Bay
Thaxted
Tilty
Ayot St Lawrence
Little Easton
Coggeshall
Hertford
Great Dunmow
Harlow
Greenstead-Juxta-Ongar
Upshire
Bradwell on Sea
Steeple
Laindon

4.

Eastern England

Peter Clark

First impressions of Eastern England are that it is not a very Leftie part of Britain. East Anglia – and Lincolnshire – is largely rural, supplying the capital and the rest of the country with the fruits of agriculture. The parts near to London – Hertfordshire, Buckinghamshire, Essex – are made up of dormitory towns, supplying the capital with labour and services. Bedfordshire, Cambridgeshire and Lincolnshire have large areas that have been saved from fen and flood. Fensmen and fenswomen have a quality of their own. They are close to the physical environment and so dependent on coping for survival that there is a sturdy bloody mindedness about them, which does not tolerate condescension from outside.

Eastern England has no great industrial base. Until the twentieth century, migration tended to be outward-bound. There has been no in-migration that has produced a working-class solidarity. But Lefties have come out of Eastern England; others have found a home there. Historically, East Anglia has resisted the assumptions of the possessing classes: the Fens provided a base of resistance to the Norman Conquest. Fenlanders filled the armies of the Parliamentarians and

Oliver Cromwell, himself from Huntingdon. In East Anglia there were many recruits to the medieval rebellion of Wat Tyler. And in the following century, the popular rebellion of Robert Kett in Norfolk, against enclosures, raised tens of thousands of men and required two government armies, ultimately, to crush them. Norwich was, until the nineteenth century, a city of small employers and independent weavers.

The Thomas Paine Hotel

In the rural areas of Eastern England, the Tory model of church and squire was under constant challenge from varieties of Dissent. Today nearly every village in East Anglia has its Dissenting chapels, offering physical testimony of a challenge to the legitimacy of the parson. Against the prescribed Anglican monopoly of Church and State, Norfolk has its alternative world-view – Baptist and Congregational, Unitarian and Quaker, but also the different branches of Methodism. Lincolnshire, where John Wesley was born, was strong in Methodism, and Norfolk was particularly receptive to Primitive Methodism.

If East Anglia and Lincolnshire have been isolated from the capital and industrial England, the long coastline has been the frontier to other worlds overseas. From the seventeenth century, Puritans from East Anglia had settled in New England: Boston and Springfield are only two names that allude to places in the homeland. But the ports were also open to continental influences. From medieval times a local textile trade exported to the Netherlands and the lower Rhine. Norwich received exiles and craftsmen from Europe. Boston and Great Yarmouth have been replaced by Immingham and Grimsby, Ipswich and Felixstowe as outlets to Europe and beyond.

With the exception of the railway towns and ironworking Scunthorpe, the Industrial Revolution passed Eastern England by. Enclosures in the eighteenth century and improved agricultural techniques produced prosperity for landowners and those serving them – architects, lawyers – but the increased wealth did not trickle down. After the Napoleonic wars the rich held their own, but the agricultural poor went to the wall. Despair led to the burning of ricks and the breaking of farm machinery. Industrial activity in towns was often closely related to agriculture – machinery, brewing and malting, fertilisers. The economies of larger towns offered specialised activities – Cambridge, the university; Norwich, mustard, and boot and shoe manufacturing; and, with the coming of the railway, Southend-on-Sea, Clacton, Sheringham and Cromer, Skegness and Cleethorpes became leisure centres. Indeed the coming of the railways transformed the region. Agricultural areas were more tied to the capital. Migration within the country was facilitated. Lincolnshire, Norfolk and Suffolk lost some of their cultural isolation. The counties of Hertfordshire and Buckinghamshire became commuter districts. Peterborough, Wolverton and Bletchley became major railway junctions and 'railway towns'.

Such is the background. Let us tour the region and draw attention to features that have produced the monuments of Leftie-ism.

Moving north from London is Hertfordshire, which has been politically dominated by the cathedral city of St Alban's and the Cecil family, the Marquess of Salisbury, and Hatfield Palace. In 1874 the MP for Hertford was a nephew of the then Marquess of Salisbury, Arthur Balfour. In 1974 the situation had not changed: another nephew (Lord Balniel) of the latest Marquess was MP. Hertfordshire has always been a Conservative county, with pockets of radicalism in Watford and Hertford. It nurtured a Leftie in Eric Heffer; provided schooling for one Labour Prime Minister, Clement Attlee (at Haileybury); and a final home for George Bernard Shaw at Ayot St Lawrence. Leftie influence in social engineering can be seen in the early new towns of Letchworth and Welwyn Garden City.

Moving west, we come to the irregularly shaped county of Buckinghamshire. To this day, the county has preserved a rural area. Such industry as there has been is relatively small scale. It has been a residential area, and since the railways, one with good transport links to London. But one small part has been popular with prominent mid and late twentieth-century Labour politicians. Barbara Castle, Aneurin Bevan and Jennie Lee, Clement Attlee, and Stafford Cripps all had homes within a few miles of each other.

To the north is Bedfordshire, which has always been difficult to categorise. It is not East Anglia, not Home Counties, not Midlands. Bedford, which boasts its connections with John Bunyan, was always a town with a huge presence of different nonconformist sects. It has also been, since the Second World War, a town that has favoured immigrants – first, Italians, who worked in the brickyards, and then Asians. Education in Bedford was dominated by the Harper Trust schools, which provided a relatively cheap independent secondary education with good sports facilities – not the obvious recruiting ground for Lefties. On the other hand, the Open University, one of the achievements of which Harold Wilson was proudest, is based at Milton Keynes.

In Cambridgeshire, the city of Cambridge has seen Lefties as transient residents of the University. King's College always had something of a Leftie reputation, in spite of its links with Eton College, although that link did produce Clement Attlee's first Chancellor of the Exchequer, Hugh Dalton. It was also the alma mater of Peter Shore, and the Marxist historian Eric Hobsbawm taught at the College. Cambridge has produced its radical intellectuals. Noel Annan's 'intellectual aristocracy' – with its Wedgwoods, Keyneses, Huxleys, Darwins and Trevelyans – had a secure base in Cambridge, as had the Bloomsbury Group in the twentieth century. Much of Cambridgeshire is former Fenland and, in the seventeenth century, was the base for Cromwell – a Cambridge undergraduate who matriculated from Sidney Sussex College. Among the Lefties who were born in Cambridgeshire, there are two whose writings had much influence in their time: William Godwin, author of *Enquiry Concerning Political Justice* (1793), and father-in-law of Percy Bysshe Shelley, was born in Wisbech; and Margaret Cole was born, the daughter of a Classics don, in Cambridge itself.

To the north is Lincolnshire. Lincoln Gaol has been a temporary home for some Lefties – Fenner Brockway did time here. The county has produced some Lefties who have, otherwise, not been associated with Lincolnshire. The childhood and early apprenticeship of the Chartist poet Thomas Cooper was passed in Gainsborough, which was also the birthplace of the trade unionist Vic Feather (whose forenames, redolent of early twentieth-century Leftie history, are Victor Grayson Hardie). Christopher Addison, who served in the Cabinets of both Lloyd George and Clement Attlee, was born in Hogsthorpe, and the pacifist theorist Norman Angell was born in Holbeach. Anthony Crosland became MP for Grimsby and identified himself with that town. His ashes were scattered, not very effectively, into the sea off the town.

Norfolk has been an agricultural county, and the county town of Norwich was, before modern times, the second (or, vying with Bristol, third) city of the country, with a cathedral and 50 parish churches. It was also an inland port and had a strong Dissenting community – old Dissent, Quakers and Unitarians – which provided its own liberal intellectual aristocracy with Frys, Buxtons and Martineaus. But there was also a more popular radicalism, manifesting itself in the societies during the 1790s. William Morris and Keir Hardie both found Norwich a fertile city for the promotion of late-Victorian socialism. Both radical trends converged with the life of Noel Buxton, who switched from Liberal to Labour, and became a minister in the governments of Ramsay MacDonald.

Norfolk boasts of being the birthplace of Nelson, but his contemporary who had a far greater impact was Thomas Paine, born and educated in Thetford. Paine is better commemorated in the United States than in Britain, but nearly all radical literature and thought during the last two centuries refers back to his writings. Another of the county's enduring radical legacies, which, nurtured by primitive Methodism, manifested itself in rural trade unionism. Joseph Arch established branches of agricultural workers' unions here, and two early-twentieth-century leaders of the National Union of Agricultural Workers – (Sir) George Edwards and Edwin Gooch – were born in the county. This union was behind the Burston School Strike of 1914 – 'the longest strike in history' – producing one of the most fascinating of Leftie sites in the whole country.

Suffolk has also been isolated, but there have been pockets of rural radicalism. The cathedral city of Bury St Edmunds was home to a medieval popular revolt against authority. Suffolk was also a county in which Captain Swing was in action in the 1830s, with outbreaks of rickburning in desperate protest against the repression of the poor. This distress manifested itself later in rural Chartism. Leftie individuals have been connected with the county: George Lansbury was born at Halesworth – his father worked on the railway; George Orwell lived in Southwold; A. S. Neill established his extremely progressive school of Summerhill at Leiston; and the communist historian A. L. Morton was from Ipswich, and lived and died at Clare.

Essex, like Hertfordshire, has been economically and politically linked with London. It has no *ancient* cathedral city and no great industry. It helped to feed London, and, with the railway, provided the capital with workers. The railway lines reached the termini of Liverpool Street and Fenchurch Street, in the City; so a large proportion of the workforce tended to service the financial houses – no automatic Leftie breeding ground. Southend-on-Sea, the largest town in the county, was a playground for the East End. Those East Enders who could afford to do so moved out, leaving their radicalism behind. They became a part of the socially upwardly mobile England that gave voting strength to Margaret Thatcher.

The sites in Essex are generally rural. Thaxted Church was a base for high-church-socialism. The Red Flag flew from the church tower, and the church associated itself with pageantry, beautiful things and – in collaboration with a Thaxted resident, Gustav Holst – music. The church living, which allowed all this to happen, had been in the possession of the amazing Countess of Warwick, of Easton Lodge. The Countess was immensely rich, but saw herself as a socialist. She was a Labour parliamentary candidate (for Warwick), and offered her stately home to be used for TUC Conferences and Leftie summer schools during the 1920s and 1930s. H. G. Wells was a tenant and lived in the village. The Countess inherited her Essex estate, but other Lefties have chosen to live there – Tom Driberg had his stately home in Bradwell and not too far away is Stansgate, Tony Benn's retreat. Stansgate has provided a holiday home for three generations of a family who have served in the cabinets of all five Labour Prime Ministers: William Wedgwood Benn in those of Ramsay MacDonald and Clement Attlee; Tony Benn those of Harold Wilson and James Callaghan; and his son Hilary in that of Tony Blair.

Gazetteer

ASHDON, Essex. The village was the scene of a ferocious agricultural-labourers strike in June 1914. Un-unionised labour was brought in and met resistance from the Ashdon workers. Sixty constables were drafted in. 'When the police began breaking up the mass marches on the farms, the Ashdon men regrouped their forces into mobile bands of pickets who moved swiftly and unexpectedly, and ranged far and wide across the countryside.' Eight Ashdon men appeared at Saffron Walden police court, and two hundred strikers from neighbouring villages assembled in Ashdon and marched to Saffron Walden with union banners, red flags and hefty sticks. The trouble attracted outside support and George Lansbury, Ben Tillett and Sylvia Pankhurst all visited the area to give their support. As war approached, and men volunteered for military service, the farmers were obliged to accept the union's demands.

AYOT ST LAWRENCE, Hertfordshire. Shaw's Corner, now a National Trust property, was the home of George Bernard Shaw (1856-1950), Fabian essayist, playwright and lifelong socialist. It houses an excellent museum dedicated to the memory of G.B.S., with numerous personal effects. It has on display his membership card for the Cyclists' Touring Club. Shaw's body was cremated and his ashes were scattered in the garden.

BRADWELL-ON-SEA. Bradwell Lodge. A fine Adam house. Home of Tom Driberg, MP, journalist, socialite and predatory homosexual, from 1939 to 1971 when obsessive extravagance forced him to sell it for £26,000. 'Peed under the ilex tree and tried to feed the ducks,' was his last entry in his own Visitors Book.

BRESSINGHAM, Norfolk. In the years after the Napoleonic wars, hunger and despair stalked the East Anglian countryside. This village was the scene of the destruction of farm machinery that led to the hanging of George Fortis and Noah Peake on Castle Hill, Norwich in April 1822.

BURSTON, Norfolk. Strike School. In 1914, the teacher of the village school, Kitty Higdon, and her husband, Tom, incurred the wrath of the Rector and the leading farmers of the village. They were socialists and Tom was the local secretary of the Union of Agricultural Workers. The Higdons were sacked, but the great majority of the children, with parental support, refused to recognise the dismissal and went on strike. The Higdons continued to teach their pupils on the village green. Local and national trades unions supported them and, war notwithstanding, funds were gathered for the building of a new school. The people and institutions – unions, branches of the Independent Labour Party and individuals such as Leo Tolstoy – who contributed are commemorated on the outside of the building, which was formally opened by George Lansbury in 1917. The strike continued to 1939, 'the longest strike in history'. The Strike School is now a museum, with a mission statement: 'to be a centre of rural democracy and a memorial to the villagers' fight for freedom.' The strike is annually celebrated, on the first Sunday of September, with a rally and a march round the village. At one recent rally, a later rector has apologised for the behaviour of his predecessor.

BURY ST EDMUNDS, Suffolk. Abbey. In the fourteenth century, the Abbey was prosperous and controlled much of the economy of the city. Franciscan friars, by contrast, showed sympathy with the poor. In 1327, an alliance of friars and citizens led to a revolt that looted the Abbey, beat up the prior and controlled the town for most of the year. The authorities, after some months, regained power and rebels were arrested. Thirty carts were needed to carry the arrested people to royal courts in Norwich. All were convicted and imprisoned. The Abbey became a target in the Peasants' Revolt of 1381.

CAMBRIDGE. 54 Bateman Street. First home of Labour historians and activists Raymond

Postgate (1896-1971) and his sister Margaret Cole (1893-1980), who thought it an 'uglyish house'. She much preferred Cambridge to Oxford, where she lived briefly with her husband, G. D. H. Cole, and rather than live in Oxford, chose committee work and life in north London. She wrote her own memoirs, *Growing up into Revolution* (1949), describing her Cambridge childhood. Raymond was also a Labour historian and wrote a biography of his father-in-law, George Lansbury. His last decades were devoted to improving the nation's eating habits. He was the founder and editor of *The Good Food Guide*.

CAMBRIDGE. Girton College. Margaret Postgate (later Mrs G. D. H. Cole), Labour historian, went to Girton after a miserable time at Roedean. The College transformed her, in her own words, from 'an unpresentable tadpole into a moderately decent sort of frog'.

CAMBRIDGE. King's College. In spite of, or perhaps because of, an association with Eton College, King's College has long had a reputation for unorthodoxy. It nurtured Hugh Dalton and Tam Dalyell (Old Etonians both), Peter Shore and Charles Clarke. Eric Hobsbawm and Nicholas Kaldor taught there. E. M. Forster was a Fellow. While at Cambridge, Tam Dalyell was President of the Cambridge University Conservative Association. He later became a Labour MP, from 1962 to 2005, Father of the House, and thorn in the flesh of Margaret Thatcher and Tony Blair. In the 1870s, two undergraduates, Henry Salt and J. L. Joynes, became pioneer members of the Social Democratic Federation. They had 'kicked against the pricks of authority, their major exploit being to release a mole to desecrate the sanctity of the Senior Fellows' lawn.' They went on to teach at Eton.

CAMBRIDGE. Trinity College. The largest College has numbered among its alumni Labour's first Minister of Agriculture, Noel Buxton; Labour's first Minister of Education (or President of the Board of Education) Charles Trevelyan; as well as H. M. Hyndman.

CARDINGTON, Bedfordshire. From the airport, in October 1930, the British airship R101 set off with the Labour Secretary of State for Air, Lord Thomson, on board. The airship crashed at Beauvais in northern France in a fierce storm and was destroyed in an inferno, killing 46 crew and passengers, including Lord Thomson. It was from a Bedfordshire airfield that Glenn Miller also set off on his final fatal flight.

CLARE, Suffolk. One mile to the north is a chapel converted to a house. This was the home of the communist historian A. L. Morton (1903-86).

COGGESHALL, Essex. Paycockes. A wool merchant's house dating to the sixteenth century, home of Conrad Noel, Christian Socialist, who rented it from his cousin, Noel Buxton, who bought it in about 1900 for £500. It had been the home of his sixteenth- and seventeenth-century Buxton ancestors, but had degenerated into a tumble-down row of cottages.

FRAMLINGHAM, Suffolk. St Michael's Church. In the church-yard is buried John Goodwyn Barmby, 1820-81, Unitarian, poet (*The Return of the Swallow, and other Poems*, 1864, and other volumes) and radical, said to have coined the word 'communism' and who, in 1841, founded the Communist Propaganda Society.

FRISTON, Suffolk. The Chequers Inn. A rural Chartist meeting place.

GAINSBOROUGH, Lincolnshire. Thomas Cooper (1805-92), the Chartist poet, spent his child-hood, youth and early manhood here. He attended the Free School and lived in Sailor's Alley (since demolished, but a reminder that Gainsborough was an inland port), and became a shoemaker, when he undertook a masochistic course of self-instruction, 'seldom later in bed than three or four in the morning.'

GREAT DUNMOW, Essex. Bigods Hall. Two miles to the north of the town this is now an electronics factory. In 1897, under the inspiration of the Countess of Warwick, the socialist aristocrat who lived at nearby Easton Lodge, a coedu-cational agricultural boarding school was in operation. It was in partnership with the Essex County Council and was, as a former chairman of the Education Committee said, twenty years ahead of its time.

GREENSTEAD-JUXTA-ONGAR, Essex. Ivy Cottage. In 1838, after appeals and agitation, the Tolpuddle Martyrs, who had been transported to Australia, for trade union activity, were brought back and lived here until a reactionary parson had their lease cancelled. Formerly Repentance Cottage, the house, with Gothicesque windows, faces the village pond.

GRIMSBY, Lincolnshire. For nearly 20 years the Labour MP was Anthony Crosland. He had been a major intellectual and his book *The Future of Socialism* (1956), had an influence on the Labour governments of the 1960s. Crosland was a militant advocate of comprehensive education as Secretary of State for Education from 1965 to 1967. He ended up as James Callaghan's Secretary of State for Foreign Affairs 1976-77, dying in office (and in Oxford). His ashes were scattered from a boat, *Brenda Fisher*, off Grimsby, although an obstinate gale blew the grey sooty ashes back at his widow, Susan. Instead of decorously scattering the ashes over the waters, 'I flung the box with the remaining ashes as far as I could.'

HALESWORTH, Suffolk. 14 The Thoroughfare. Birthplace of George Lansbury (1859-1940), though he believed he was born at a toll house at nearby Wenhaston. His father was employed on the railways.

HARLOW, Essex. The Leah Manning Centre: The Centre commemorates the contribution of a woman who was Labour MP for East Islington, and later, Epping, and president of the National Union of Teachers. The Centre is 'the focal point of Harlow Council's care and provision for the town's older residents. While other council-run facilities provide sheltered accommodation, the Leah Manning Centre offers senior citizens of Harlow a place to relax, meet other people, seek advice or receive a good meal, hair cut or chiropody service.'

HERTFORD. Port Vale. Site of

the Victorian church, Christ Church, which was demolished in the 1960s. In the 1930s, Eric Heffer, born and brought up here, was thrown out from service as a choirboy in the church. 'When I joined the Christ Church choir I thought we sang because of our love of the church and its teachings, but I soon discovered that we were also paid. The choirboys felt the payment was too small. They discussed it and said we should ask for more money. I was deputed to lead the delegation and we threatened not to sing at the Easter Services. We won the increase but then the choirmaster said my voice was breaking and I would have to leave.' A block of flats has replaced the church, which stood in front of a primary school.

HERTFORD GREEN, Hertfordshire. Haileybury Public School. The school attended by Clement Attlee. Eric Heffer (1922-91), left-wing Labour MP, was brought up in Hertford and, as a teenager, worked as a delivery boy. On one occasion he surprised MPs by saying he had gone to a public school. 'Which one?' Conservative MPs asked. 'Haileybury, I used to deliver meat there on a Saturday morning.' He was later invited to the school to talk to the boys. 'I referred in my speech to Attlee and my friend Sir Geoffrey de Freitas having been old Haileyburians. I told the boys that I did not know what their future held, but had they gone to Longmore Senior School in Hertford [Heffer's old school], they might become well-known MPs. It went down well; much better than my quotes from R. H. Tawney on public schools.'

HOGSTHORPE, Lincolnshire. On a farm in this village was born Christopher Addison, who was the first Labour politician to be made a Knight of the Garter. He was a medical doctor, the very first Minister of Health – in Lloyd George's Coalition government, joined the Labour Party and took demotion and became a Parliamentary Secretary for Agriculture in Ramsay MacDonald's first government. He served with Attlee ending up as an 82-year-old Leader of the House of Lords. Is this a twentieth-century record for being a Cabinet minister?

HOLLESLEY BAY, Suffolk. George Lansbury, busy in the East End of London, organised a colony here for training out-of-work men to grow food. Lansbury received support – as did other Lefties at the time – from an American millionaire, Joseph Fels, who 'acquired a large set of buildings (once used as an Agricultural Training College) for the Central Unemployment Committee . . . The former college had accommodation for 335 men, together with residences for farmers. There were 30 cottages, four sets of farm buildings and an open-air swimming bath. It had workshops, a wharf, a warehouse on the river front, and a light tramway connecting the wharf to the farmers' gardens. There were eight glasshouses and two hundred acres of gardens. George Lansbury . . . used to come down every week-end to organize classes and recreation.'

IPSWICH, Suffolk. 4 St Margaret's Street. Site of former pub, the Admiral's Head, Chartist meeting place.

IPSWICH, Suffolk. 19 Lower Brook Street. William King (1786-1865) was born in this house. His father was Master of Ipswich School. William became a physician and worked in Brighton. He was a pioneer of Co-operative democracy, founding a Co-operative Benefit Fund and a Co-operative Trading Association, and inspiring the 'Rochdale Pioneers' of 1844.

IPSWICH, Suffolk. North Bank, Belstead Road. Place of death of George Hines (1839-1914) who served in the Royal Navy in the Crimean War, lived in Ipswich and was active in the Co-operative movement; founder member of the Ipswich ILP and author of *Co-operative Fairy Tales.*

IPSWICH, Suffolk. St Mary-le-Tower Church. Claude Stuart Smith, organiser of the Church Socialist League, became curate here after the First World War. Despite pain and ill-health, he was the inspiration for spreading a social gospel, the influence of which, Conservative businessmen in Ipswich had no doubt, led to the growth of socialist opinion in Ipswich and the return as Labour MP in 1922 of Robert Jackson, stonemason, trade unionist and Christian Socialist. Smith died in 1924. The streets of Ipswich were lined by working men and women for the funeral. The unemployed of the town provided a guard of honour, with scarlet banners of socialism and trade unionism.

KENNINGHALL, Norfolk. White Horse Inn. A plaque inside the pub records the demonstration, in February 1836, of desperate farm labourers who stormed a meeting of the Poor Law Guardians in the inn, 'armed with bludgeons and other weapons.' They were protesting against the new Poor Law: 'We came here for bread, and bread or blood we will have.' The forces of order prevailed and the men were sentenced to up to twelve months in prison.

LAINDON, Essex. Sumpners Farm. George Lansbury established a farm colony here in the 1890s. In March 1904, an American supporter of British socialism, Joseph Fels, provided the Poplar Guardians with this hundred-acre farm, to be worked by the able-bodied unemployed under their charge. One hundred men went there from the workhouse, and lived in corrugated iron buildings on the estate. Small gangs carried out different tasks to avoid the monotony that would arise from sticking an eight-inch fork into a hard-clay soil, week after week. It is not clear where the farm was. Laindon has been much built over in the last century.

LEISTON, Suffolk. Summerhill School. The most liberal school in Britain, founded and led by A. S. Neill (1883-1973), and after that by his daughter. Discipline and coercion were banished. A child, it was thought, should grow up without fear. A. L. Morton (1903-86), communist historian, taught there.

LITTLE EASTON, Essex. Easton Lodge. The ancestral home of Frances Evelyn Maynard who, on marriage, became the Countess of Warwick. She was seriously rich, more than a friend of King Edward VII when he was Prince of Wales, and became an ardent socialist, thanks to the persuasive powers of Robert Blatchford. A member of the Social Democratic Federation and then the Labour Party, she entertained lavishly at the Lodge, especially during the first Labour government of 1924, when Easton Lodge became a Labour 'Chequers'. The Lodge was offered to both the Labour Party and the TUC, but neither took up the offer. There were also proposals to turn it into a Labour College, with G. D. H. Cole as Principal. Lady Warwick died in 1938, and the house was pulled down, as too expensive to maintain, in 1950. The west wing, where Lady Warwick lived, survives. A small museum in the dovecote has a panel recording her socialist activities. The once-magnificent gardens are open to the public during summer weekends and are slowly and imaginatively being restored.

LITTLE EASTON, Essex. The Glebe. Formerly the old parsonage, and to the east of the Lodge, this house was the home from 1911 to 1927 of H. G. Wells, who rented it from the Countess of Warwick. His novel *Mr Britling Sees it Through* was based on life in Little Easton during the First World War. He entertained writers and Lefties here, including Sidney and Beatrice Webb and Harold Laski, as well as Charlie Chaplin.

LITTLE EASTON, Essex. St Mary's Church. In the Maynard chapel there is a bust of the Countess of Warwick, although she is not buried with her own ancestors, but with those of her husband, at Warwick.

NORWICH, Norfolk. Described by the painter Amelia Opie as 'that city of sedition'. For William Morris, Norwich seemed 'as likely a place as any in England for the spread of socialism.' Morris inaugurated the local branch of the Socialist League in March 1886, a meeting attended by up to two thousand.

NORWICH, Norfolk. Castle. Robert Kett's rebellion against enclosures in 1549 failed. After confronting, successively, two government armies, Robert Kett was caught, tried and sentenced to death. He was strung up outside the main entrance to the castle, as a plaque on the site contritely records.

NORWICH, Norfolk. Cathedral. In 1892, the Trades Union Congress met in Norwich. Some delegates, including Keir Hardie, wandered off to look at the cathedral. Outside they watched the sun go down and the twinkling of lights coming from the many windows. 'Suddenly,' recalled one who was there, 'the voice of old Hardie rose through the stillness, giving vocal expression to the Twenty-third Psalm, and we all joined – Christians and agnostics – blending our voices, not so much in any devotional spirit as out of deference to the influence of the place.' Old Hardie was then actually 36.

NORWICH, Norfolk. Keir Hardie Hall, St Gregory's Alley. Now a Working Men's Club with programmes of Eastern art and salsa dancing, this was the office of the Independent Labour Party and, in 1923, was the union headquarters for the agricultural workers' strike of 1923, the aim of which was 'not a tick of the clock over fifty hours and not a penny less than 26 shillings a week.' Was this developed into the slicker slogan of the miners in the approach to the General Strike in 1926, 'Not a penny off the pay, not a second on the day.'?

NORWICH, Norfolk. Market Place. In January 1887, there was a demonstration of the unemployed seeking assistance from the local council. The Mayor rebuffed them offensively and they looted nearby food shops. The police arrived to see foodstuffs being passed over the heads of the crowd. 'I saw a ham run over the people's head,' one of the constables said in court later. Thereafter, the events of the day were known as The Battle of Ham Run. Charlie Mowbray and Fred Henderson (who lived on to the 1950s) of the Socialist League were imprisoned as a result and were the last to be put on a treadmill in Norwich.

NORWICH, Norfolk. Friars Quay. Plaque to Mark Wilks (1748-1819), Baptist Minister. Mark Wilks of Wheelers' Chapel was an ardent reformer. The Norwich weavers were Radicals, and were in close touch with the main centre of contemporary Leftie-ism, the London Corresponding Society, whose leading democrat, Thomas Hardy, was tried for sedition in 1794. Leftie England anxiously awaited the verdict. A delegate from the Norwich Corresponding Society, called Davey, attended the trial and travelled night and day to bring the news to Norwich. He reached the Meeting House while Wilks was in the pulpit. 'What news, brother?' Wilks asked. 'Not guilty,' came the reply. 'Then let us sing, "Praise God from Whom all blessings flow."'

NORWICH, Norfolk. Mousehold Heath. Robert Kett led twenty thousand villagers in protest against enclosures in 1549. They camped on the heath before facing two successive armies sent out by the government.

OXBURGH, Norfolk. Old Rectory. H. M. Hyndman (1842-1921) was privately educated here by the Rector, Alexander Thurtell. Hyndman always regarded the two and a half years at Oxburgh as the most useful part of his educational life, riding regularly to hounds and playing cricket, but also working hard at mathematics and reading widely. He always retained his toffish airs, even when he became Britain's most prominent socialist and founder of the Social Democratic Federation.

ST FAITH'S, Norfolk. Village Green. The Socialist League had weekly meetings here in the 1880s, alarming the vicar, who warned: 'Beware of these men! They revile the Queen, calling her a German pauper.' St Faith's long had a reputation as a Leftie centre, though it is now a comfortable dormitory village on the outskirts of Norwich.

SOUTHWOLD, Suffolk. 3 Queen Street. Home, from the 1920s, of George Orwell's family, and his base after his return from Burma and before living in London. He also lived at Montague House, High Street, where there is a plaque.

SKEGNESS, Lincolnshire. Jubilee Clock Tower. Skegness grew up as a seaside resort thanks to the railway. It was particularly popular with people from the Midlands, and, in the early days of seaside resorts for the masses, special trains came from Leicester. To make these Midlanders feel at home, the Clock Tower was built, it has been claimed, with the clock tower in the centre of Leicester in mind.

STEEPLE, Essex. Stansgate. This house on the Blackwater was built by Tony Benn's grandfather in 1899. The house was sold off and reacquired by Tony Benn's father, William Wedgwood Benn (1877-1960), in 1926 and it became the family retreat and holiday home of the whole family. From the house, William Wedgwood Benn took the hereditary title Viscount Stansgate in 1941. His eldest son, Michael, was consulted and was willing to succeed to the title. But Michael was killed in action in 1944, and Tony, who wanted a political career, was less willing to inherit the title and exile to the House of Lords. William died in 1960. The lawyers argued that a hereditary peerage could not be disclaimed. Tony Benn's constituency was declared without a Member of Parliament. At the by-election, Benn stood and was elected, but was formally disbarred from entering the House of Commons. It took another two years to change the law and allow hereditary peers to disclaim their titles. Among the first to take advantage of the change of law, apart from the second Viscount Stansgate, were Viscount Hailsham, who reverted to being Quintin Hogg for seven years, and the Earl of Home (Sir Alec Douglas-Home). Both were vying to succeed Harold Macmillan as Prime Minister in 1963 – not quite what Tony Benn had in mind. The heir to the Stansgate title now is Hilary Benn's elder brother. But hereditary peers can now sit in the House of Commons.

STOWMARKET, Suffolk. Town Hall. In December 1840, the High Sheriff of Suffolk summoned a meeting to congratulate Queen Victoria on the birth of a daughter. When the High Sheriff and six other gentlemen appeared on a balcony, they saw beneath them several hundred hostile Stowmarket workers, led by local Chartists. The High Sheriff moved a Loyal Address, whereupon the workers submitted a pro-Chartist addendum, with the observation that childbirth was somewhat more comfortable in a palace than a workhouse. The Sheriff declined the addendum. The crowd refused to vote on the Loyal Address, but when the local Chartist leader put the addendum as a motion it was carried with Three Cheers for the Charter.

THAXTED, Essex. Church. The living was in the hands of the nearby chatelaine of Easton Lodge, the socialist Countess of Warwick. She appointed Conrad Noel, who saw himself as a catholic communist. He was vicar from 1910 to his death in 1942. On his arrival, angry crowds lined the pavements, and there were loud and provocative catcalls. In 1914, he displayed the flags of all allied nations in the church and included the Red Flag of the Internationale which had on it the words, 'He hath made of one blood all nations.' In 1921, during the miners' strike, someone objected to the Red Flag and removed it. Conrad Noel replaced it. It was pulled down again by students from Cambridge. He put up another, higher in the church, and had it guarded night and day. But later, a Consistory Court ordered its removal. He then said, defiantly from the pulpit, 'That flag has been removed but the preaching will go on.' With the support of Gustav Holst, a Thaxted resident, he introduced colourful processions accompanied by music, choir, organ and orchestra. The chapel above the north porch is dedicated to the Blessed John Ball, a preacher during the Peasants' Revolt. The chapel is closed, alas, on the advice of the insurers. On the door are the words from John Ball, 'Good people, things will never go well in England so long as goods be not in common.' A succession of curates went on to spread Noel's ideas – 'the Thaxted movement' – around the country. Conrad Noel is buried here, and an inscription to his memory is on the outside wall to the east of the high altar. He has a bust in the nave. His son-in-law, Jack Putterill – Father Jack – continued the socialist and musical tradition, and became the chairman of the local branch of the National Union of Agricultural Workers. He is buried in the north chapel.

THETFORD, Norfolk. Thomas Paine Hotel, White Hart Road. Site of the birthplace of Thomas Paine (1737-1809), author of *The Rights of Man*, an inspiration for democrats all over the world, or, in the words of the *Dictionary of National Biography*, 'a sort of text-book for the extreme radical party in England'. The hotel serves an excellent Sunday roast with a discount for senior citizens – very appropriate in the birthplace of a pioneer advocate of old-age pensions.

THETFORD, Norfolk. Thomas Paine Statue. The burgesses of Thetford were long embarrassed at the memory of their most famous son, seeing him as a seditious radical (true), and there was no public memorial to him. He was also an inspiration to democrats in the United States, where he died, and Americans were appalled at the absence of a statue. The American Thomas Paine Foundation provided the gold-painted statue for Thetford in 1964, which was graciously accepted.

THETFORD, Norfolk. Grammar School. Thomas Paine's alma mater.

THETFORD, Norfolk. Ancient House Museum. There is a section dedicated to Thetford's (and Norfolk's) most famous son, Thomas Paine.

TILTY, Essex. Church. The Countess of Warwick owned the living of this tiny village and made the first of her socialist appointments here when George Maxted became Rector in 1907.

UPSHIRE, Essex. Church. Grave of Noel Buxton (1869-1948), first Labour Minister of Agriculture, 1924 and again 1929-30, who introduced the Agricultural Wages (Regulation) Act, which established a Wages Board. Although limited, it did raise the minimum rate of agricultural labourers throughout the country. Noel Buxton was from high-minded Norfolk liberal-aristocratic stock, and was one of the Liberal MPs who shifted to Labour in 1919. His interests were mainly overseas, and especially the Balkans, though he always had a concern for agricultural labourers, and was a friend of George Edwards. Noel Buxton lived at the Warlies, a hideous nineteenth-century building down the road from the church.

WALLINGTON, Herts. Kit's Lane. A cottage in Kit's Lane, in this deeply rural village, was where George Orwell (1903-50), writer, lived from 1936 to 1940, incompetently running a shop and slipping away to pay homage to Catalonia. He kept a goat and hens and dug up the garden, coming across twelve discarded boots in two days. He wrote *The Road to Wigan Pier* (1937) here.

WYMONDHAM, Norfolk. Both Robert Kett (1492-1549), leader of the Rebellion against enclosures, and Edwin Gooch (1850-1930), leader of the National Union of Agricultural Workers, son of a blacksmith, were both born here.

WYMONDHAM, Norfolk. Kett's Oak. In 1549, a movement to enclose common land swept East Anglia. Peasants used common land for the grazing of their beasts, collecting fuels and using herbs for their pharmacopeia. A major rebellion was led by Robert Kett, a Wymondham landowner. He commanded twenty thousand peasants in armed revolt against the government. This tree, carefully preserved, is on the Norwich road, one mile from Wymondham, and was the rallying point for the rebels.

WYMONDHAM, Norfolk. Abbey. William Kett, Robert's brother, who also took part in the revolt, was hanged from the tower in 1549.

Hayfield
Blackwell
Millthorpe
Chesterfield
Harriseahead
Clay Cross
Stoke-on-Trent
Pentrich
Burslem
Keele
Bucknall
Hucknall Torkard
Basford
Bulwell
Newcastle-Under-Lyme
Barlaston
Derby
Nottingham
Beeston
Repton
Ruddington
Wem
Sawley
Loughborough
Wellington
Anstey
Leicester
Walsall
Wednesbury
Sutton Coldfield
Handsworth
Birmingham
Stourbridge
Oundle
Coventry
Bewdley
Rugby
Kenilworth
Old Milverton
Warwick
Leamington Spa
Raunds
Barford
Northampton
Almeley
Fownhope
Ross-on-Wye

5.

The Midlands

Mark Allen

The Midlands is a region inextricably linked to the Industrial Revolution. Both Leicestershire and Northamptonshire have associations with the shoemaking trades, and Nottinghamshire's textiles – lace in particular – are very well-known. Recently, both Derbyshire and Nottinghamshire have been major coalmining areas, and parts of Staffordshire became so associated with a particular industry that the area gained the name, 'Potteries'. On a demographic level, in the nineteenth century the industrial parish of Birmingham became more populous than the small county of Rutland. Given the working man's ascendancy in the region, it is hardly surprising that many a Leftie can claim links to the Midlands.

Having said that, the Midlands is still a curate's egg of Leftie-ism. The southern and western parts of the region around Shropshire, Herefordshire and Worcestershire remain *relatively* untouched by industrialism. Just as Wollaton near Nottingham, had been the site of the first recorded 'rail road' in 1609, so Hereford was the last city in the country to be connected to the railway network in the 1850s.

So some parts of the Midlands feature more than others here. That makes them no less important, of course, as anyone who is familiar with the writings of William Hazlitt (who lived in Wem, Shropshire) will know. The growth of manufacturing industries has meant that some features of pre-industrial protest movements have been erased from the modern landscape. So the lead-mining Levellers of

Nottingham Arboretum

Derbyshire are not included, as very little remains as a memorial to them – although a case could be made for including the historian G. E. Aylmer, who wrote authoritatively about them and was born in Shropshire and buried in Herefordshire. The gazetteer for the Midlands concentrates primarily on those Lefties who have been involved in protests (be they Luddite, Chartist, suffragist and others), trade unionism and Labour representation. I have also looked at some of the prominent Lefties who have passed through the various educational institutions of the region, and a few significant people who are in some way connected with the area, but who are not easily pigeon-holed into neat categories.

Large-scale factory work started in Derbyshire. The resentment at unemployment caused by factories like Arkwright's in Cromford led to a series of countrywide protests and riots in the early 1800s. Midlands action centred around the framework knitters of Derbyshire, Leicestershire and Nottinghamshire, and were popularised through the figure of Ned Ludd, a mysterious individual who was probably an amalgam of several agitators. However, he is reputed to be from Anstey in Leicestershire and there are several sites connected with Luddites in the gazetteer. Luddite disturbances were most violent in 1811 and 1816-17. Two sites of protest against specific hosiers are included in Bulwell and Loughborough, as is the burial place of Lord Byron, who expressed sympathy with the protesters' plight in the House of Lords.

The attack on the Heathcoat and Boden factory in Loughborough, one of the last Luddite attacks, illustrates the strength of support for the Luddites. E. P. Thompson, in *The Making of the English Working Class*, states that London magistrates, who went to Nottingham on behalf of the government to assess the Luddite situation, reported that 'almost every creature of the lower order both in town & country are on their side.' This attack was directed against the factory of one man, John Heathcoat, who was said to be developing efficient new forms of lacemaking machines. Unlike most cases of Luddite activity, the violence was directed against the machines and against individuals. One man was shot, and the protesters spent most of the time disabling the machines. Their leader, James Towle, was tried in Leicester and, in spite of the support of over 50 witnesses, who gave him an alibi, was convicted and hanged. Other men were also later tried, and, when six of them were hanged in Leicester, the *Leicester Journal* reported that a crowd of some fifteen thousand people gathered to sing hymns with them. Towle's burial in Basford also brought the crowds out. But the use of capital punishment on protesters, as against transportation for many earlier miscreants, seems to have put an end to further major disturbances.

The end of the Napoleonic Wars brought about as much hardship for iron and textile producers as increased mechanisation did. The consequent excessive demands on the Poor Law caused many to call for reform. Some demanded the overthrow of the government. A heritage trail now outlines the route followed by the group of three hundred men who set out from Pentrich in Derbyshire on 9 June 1817, with the aim of achieving just that. They made for Nottingham but were easily apprehended thanks to William Oliver, a government spy. Their leaders, the so-called Pentrich Martyrs – Jeremiah Brandreth (who E. P. Thompson notes may have been a Luddite), William Turner and Isaac Ludlam – were arrested and charged with high treason. They were found guilty and have the dubious honour of being among the last people in the country to be hanged, drawn and quartered. This took place at Derby Gaol, now a museum and, curiously, 'ye olde pie shoppe'. Both the Gaol and the eighteenth-century house on the site of near-by Nottingham Castle were attacked in 1831, when the parliamentary movement for reform seemed to be faltering.

Whether or not the Chartists embodied early socialism in Britain, they were certainly a movement of the people – they did, after all, launch a 'People's Charter'. For this reason, Chartism's strong links with the Midlands are included here. The Birmingham Political Union was important in the early days of the movement, and, later, the National Chartist Church continued to form a focus of activity – at least in the Birmingham area. Of greater national significance is Feargus O'Connor, one of the major figures of the movement, who became the only Chartist MP. He is remembered in his constituency of Nottingham by a statue in the city's Arboretum. A number of radicals who supported Chartist calls for franchise reform, if not other aspects of the campaign – for example, John Biggs and Anthony Mundella – have associations with both Nottingham and Leicester. Leicester was the birthplace, and, intermittent home of Thomas Cooper, the leader of that city's Chartists who was a radical, writer and religious lecturer. Originally a Methodist he became, in later life, a Baptist.

Religious Nonconformity was especially strong in Staffordshire and Derbyshire. John Clifford was also a Baptist minister and avowed pacifist, who was vociferous in his opposition to the Boer War. Born in Sawley in Derbyshire, there is a chapel dedicated to his memory in nearby Beeston, just over the Nottinghamshire border. Later in life, he joined the Labour Party, and he is included here for his dedication to social reform.

The Primitive Methodist movement, which grew out of the Wesleyans, had many working-class supporters. It is not hard to see why. They were formed around Burslem in the Potteries by Hugh Bourne and William Clowes, and while support for the 'Prims' was widespread, the Potteries and parts of Derbyshire remained particular areas of strength. They differed from the Wesleyans in that they eschewed what they saw as the increasingly hierarchical church, and preferred open-air meetings and a more 'democratic' organisation. Attitudes towards female preachers were less hostile than elsewhere, and support among ordinary people grew in a church where education was seen as less important than religious conviction. Open-air meetings also meant that it was possible to gather in any open space. The Prims' supporters were drawn from many agricultural trades and mining, with a particularly high proportion of labourers represented. Mow Cop, where the movement started, as well as places associated with Hugh Bourne and William Clowes in

North Staffordshire, are in the gazetteer. A visit to the excellent museum of Primitive Methodism at Englesea Brook, just over the border in Cheshire, is also recommended.

Barford in Warwickshire was the birthplace and burial place of Joseph Arch. He, too, was a Primitive Methodist preacher, but he became a vigorous campaigner for the rights of fellow agricultural labourers. His campaigns took him into the trade union movement. He was the first President of the National Agricultural Labourers' Union and was keen for ordinary men to become involved in parliamentary politics. By the mid 1880s, he was an MP who, though he sat on the Liberal benches, was effectively a radical member who fought for the interests of Labour.

The industrial heritage of the Midlands has been noted. It is hardly surprising, therefore, to find several places, such as the Oddfellows' Hall in Birmingham, that have links to the early years of the Trades Union Congress. Many more such places have not survived. However, the TUC can boast three distinctive leaders who came from this region – George Potter (a journalist and unsuccessful parliamentary candidate, but the president of the TUC in 1871 who galvanised the Reform League in its campaign to extend the franchise), Sir Arthur Pugh (chairman during the 1926 General Strike) and Len Murray (general secretary of the TUC during the 1978-79 'winter of discontent' and the early years of Margaret Thatcher's governments. The Transport and General Workers Union must also thank the Midlands for two notable leaders – Arthur Deakin from Sutton Coldfield (another Primitive Methodist) and Frank Cousins from Bulwell. Whereas Deakin was a key figure in supporting the moderate Hugh Gaitskell, a more radical union figure is found in Coventry nearby: Tom Mann. Mann, like the early Marxist Ernest Belfort Bax, was a both a native of Warwickshire and a guiding light for more radical Lefties. Mann was active in the British Socialist Party

– a forerunner of the Communist Party of Great Britain – and had been prominent in the late-nineteenth-century industrial disputes that led to New Unionism. Bax and the more unconventional Edward Carpenter – who settled at Milnthorpe, Derbyshire – were founding members of the Social Democratic Federation, which was to the left of the fledgling Labour Party.

The Labour Party has had a presence in the Midlands – and not least in the Derby area – from its earliest days. Richard Bell, another chairman of the TUC, was one of two working-class MPs returned in the General Election of 1900. Unlike the other member, James Keir Hardie, Bell was happy to sit on the Liberal benches. The seat was again in Labour hands with J. H. ('Jimmy') Thomas, who sat in Ramsay MacDonald's Labour Cabinets, both before and after MacDonald's break with Labour. William George Glenvil Hall, from Almeley in Herefordshire – a county with few Leftie associations – was a member of the Independent Labour Party, and then a Labour MP. Although a personal friend of MacDonald, he opposed MacDonald's National government of 1931. Another member of the first Labour Cabinet of 1924 was Josiah Wedgwood, from the Staffordshire pottery family.

The Derbyshire Labour tradition was carried on by Tom Williams, Minister of Agriculture in Clement Attlee's government; but today, Labour's best known representative is Dennis Skinner, MP for Bolsover. He is only the second man to represent the constituency since 1945 – the other being Harold Neil, also an ex-miner. Skinner has been a backbencher for 35 years, but has become a master in parliamentary procedure and the down-putting one-liner. He is typical of what many may now regard as the traditional, and increasingly uncommon, Labour man. His uncompromising socialist views and incorruptibility have seen him at odds with both the Conservative Party and the Labour leadership. He refuses overseas trips and any suggestion of improper influence. He is assiduous in his attendance in the House of Commons, and his mordant wit makes him a popular MP; a parliamentarian pursuing unswervingly the interests of his Derbyshire constituents.

The cause of women's emancipation has long been associated with Lefties (although there have been exceptions – Ernest Belfort Bax opposed the extension of the franchise to women). Vera Brittain, lifelong campaigner for peace and women's rights, prolific writer, founder of the Campaign for Nuclear Disarmament, and the mother of Shirley Williams, comes from Newcastle-under-Lyme and is buried at Old Milverton in Warwickshire.

The educational institutions of the Midlands – of all types and levels – have produced, and continue to produce, their fair share of Lefties. The veteran socialist campaigner Ken Coates was educated at the University of Nottingham and became a Lecturer in Adult Education. He has had considerable influence on the Labour Left on issues of peace and industrial democracy. Never a Westminster MP, he was elected a Member of the European Parliament in 1989. The University College of North Staffordshire (later the University of Keele) had a number of Lefties among its founding fathers – its first Principal was A. D. Lindsay, who had the support of local councillor, and the Vicar of Etruria, the Reverend Thomas Horwood. Nor are the independent schools without Leftie links. The publisher of the 1930s Left Book Club Victor Gollancz used to teach at Repton, and the socialist historian R. H. Tawney was a pupil at Rugby. Marcia Williams and Bernard Donoughue, both in Harold Wilson's 'kitchen Cabinet', were at Northampton state schools. Dennis Howell, the country's first Sports Minister and a former professional football referee, went to Handsworth Grammar School. And while we are on football, Eric Varley, who was in James Callaghan's cabinet, when young, played for a season or two with Chesterfield Football Club.

Some Lefties linked to the Midlands belong to a tradition that goes beyond the radical/trade union/Leftie movement. Religion and public service have provided a fulfilling role. Frank Cousins' deputy in the Ministry of Technology in the mid 1960s was C. P. Snow, a Leicester lad who also achieved distinction as scientist, civil servant and novelist. Bewdley was the birthplace of the Conservative Prime Minister Stanley Baldwin. But his son, Oliver, became a Labour MP, a writer, playwright, soldier, journalist and, after succeeding his father to be second Earl Baldwin of Bewdley, Governor of the Leeward Islands.

Gazetteer

ALMELEY, Herefordshire. Spearmarsh Villa was the birthplace of William George Glenvil Hall (1887-1962), who joined the Independent Labour party in 1905 and became the first Labour Member of Parliament for Portsmouth Central, from 1929 to 1931, returning as MP for Colne Valley in 1939. He was Financial Secretary to the Treasury, 1945-50, and chairman of the parliamentary Labour Party, 1950-51. He remained an MP to his death, and was among those petitioning the Home Secretary for a reprieve for Derek Bentley, hanged in 1952 for a murder he did not commit.

ANSTEY, Leicestershire. Reputed birthplace of Ned Ludd, who gave his name to the Luddite movement, a militant protest against the new machinery of the Industrial Revolution that either made people redundant or depressed their wages and living standards. The movement spread throughout the Midlands and parts of Yorkshire in 1811 and 1812. The caricature of Ludd is as a kind of village idiot, but very little is actually known about him.

BARFORD, Warwickshire. Joseph Arch Public House, Bridge Street. The pub is named to commemorate the birth in Barford of Joseph Arch (1826-1919), in a cottage opposite the church, in the churchyard of which he is buried. Arch started work as a bird scarer on a local farm at the age of nine, and went on to became a Primitive Methodist preacher, a Radical, the first president of the National Agricultural Labourers' Union, campaigner for the extension of the franchise, and Liberal MP for North West Norfolk, 1885-86 and 1892-1902.

BARLASTON, Staffordshire. Cemetery. Grave of Josiah Wedgwood (1872-1943) who was born in the village. A scion of the pottery family he was MP for Newcastle-under-Lyme from

1906 to 1942 when he became the first Baron Wedgwood of Barlaston. He was a radical Liberal MP at first, but switched to Labour immediately after the First World War, and was Chancellor of the Duchy of Lancaster in Ramsay MacDonald's first Labour government. Never a team man, he was a militant supporter of Jewish claims to Palestine, and devoted his latter years to the History of Parliament.

BASFORD, Nottinghamshire. St Leodegarius' Church. In the churchyard is the grave of James Towle, executed for participation in Luddite riots and buried on 21 November 1816. Several thousand spectators attended the funeral.

BEESTON, Nottinghamshire. The John Clifford Memorial Baptist Church. Named after John Clifford (1836-1923), born in Sawley, Derbyshire, social reformer, Baptist and campaigner against the Boer War.

BEWDLEY, Worcestershire. Astley Hall. Birthplace of Oliver Baldwin (1899-1958), son of the Conservative Prime Minister, Stanley Baldwin. Oliver was an author, journalist, playwright, politician, soldier and Governor of the Leeward Islands. A colourful and forthright personality, he joined the Social Democratic Federation and was MP for Dudley, 1929-31. In February 1931, he joined Oswald Mosley's 'New Party' for one day. He succeeded his father, on the latter's death in 1947, as Earl Baldwin of Bewdley. Charismatic, homosexual and headstrong, his family regarded him as rather a black sheep.

BIRMINGHAM. The city has a strong Radical heritage, going back to the English Civil War in the seventeenth century, when most of the Parliamentarians' weaponry was supplied from Brum. Some early Chartist groups emerged here, for example, The Birmingham Political Union and, later, the Birmingham Chartist Church, established by Arthur O'Neil. Among the many Brummie Lefties is John Golding (1931-99) who made a speech lasting eleven and a quarter hours about the proposed privatisation of British Telecom.

BIRMINGHAM. The Oddfellows'

Hall, Upper Temple Street. The venue for the second Trades Union Congress, 23-28 August 1869, the first for which substantial records survive.

BIRMINGHAM. King Edward VI Grammar School. Dave Hill (1948-), Tony Blair's second communications manager, succeeding Alastair Campbell in 2003, was a pupil here. Thirty years earlier he was responsible for polishing Roy Hattersley's image.

BIRMINGHAM. St Paul's Grammar School. Clare Short (1946-), one of seven children, spent her secondary education here, remembered as the most confident girl in her class.

BLACKWELL, Derbyshire. Birthplace of Tom Williams (1888-1967), described by Clement Attlee as the greatest Minister of Agriculture of all time. He was also responsible, during the Second World War, for the 'Dig for Victory' campaign.

BUCKNALL, Staffordshire. Ford Hayes Farm, Hayes Lane. Birthplace of Hugh Bourne (1772-1852), founder, with William Clowes, of the Primitive Methodist movement. Whereas the Wesleyan Methodists at the time were middle-class people addressing the working-class and telling them to behave, the Primitive Methodists had working-class people preaching to other working-class folk, and women preachers too. The movement provided the background to many nineteenth-century trade unionists. Jabez Bunting, a leading early-nineteenth-century Wesleyan Methodist, claimed to oppose democracy as one opposes sin. The 'Prims', by contrast, had a social message of improving both public morality and the welfare conditions of the working class. Bourne was an advocate of education for the poor, and temperance.

BULWELL, Nottinghamshire. Forest just outside the old village. Here, on 4 November 1811, led by 'Ned Ludd', up to 70 villagers gathered and attacked the machines of the hosier, Edward Hollingsworth. 'Luddite' disturbances continued for over a year in the neighbourhood. 28 Minerva Street is the birthplace of Frank Cousins (1904-86), general secretary of the Transport and General Workers Union 1956-64 and 1966-69. Between 1964 and 1966 he was Minister of Technology in Harold Wilson's first government, having as his ministerial deputy the novelist C. P. Snow.

BURSLEM, Staffordshire. William Clowes Street. Named after the co-founder (with Hugh Bourne) of the Primitive Methodist movement. Professionally he was a potter, and before he saw the light, thanks to Bourne, he had been a drinker and a gambler.

CHESTERFIELD, Derbyshire. Chesterfield Football Club. Eric Varley (1932-) played for the Spireites, as the team is nicknamed, coupling it with an apprenticeship as a mining electrician. He became the nominee of the National Union of Mineworkers for the Chesterfield parliamentary seat, which he held until 1984. He was Secretary of State for Energy in 1974 on the team under the skippership of Harold Wilson, and was transferred to Industry the following year, a position he held when James Callaghan took over the captaincy. He became a strong campaigner for the market economy, thus moving politically from inside left to outside right. He is now Lord Varley of Chesterfield. He was followed as MP by Tony Benn. Barbara Castle was born and Frank Cousins died in Chesterfield, 1910 and 1986 respectively.

CLAY CROSS, Derbyshire. Tupton Hall Grammar School. School of Dennis Skinner MP (1930-), the 'Beast of Bolsover'. Many know Clay Cross as Skinnerville. In his youth he used to imitate Al Jolson and Johnny Ray in working men's clubs. One of the best-known backbenchers, he is seen as a man of sea-green incorruptibility. He indulges in few of the privileges of MPs, has no passport and so does not take trips abroad. A teetotaller, he does not drink with journalists or Tories. Witty and ever an espouser of all Leftie issues, he has also been a keen athlete and cyclist. Dennis's brother was one of the Clay Cross councillors imprisoned for resisting rate capping in the local government sector.

COVENTRY, Warwickshire. Bell

Green Farm, Foleshill. Birthplace of Tom Mann (1856-1941), a trade unionist who gained fame for his support of the London match girls in their dispute with Bryant and May in 1888, and his leadership of the London Dock Strike of 1889. He also set up the British Socialist party during the First World War. Mo Mowlam was born in Coventry.

DERBY. 'Derby is true to Jimmy.' With these triumphalist, if trite, words J. H. ('Jimmy') Thomas greeted his narrow election victory in 1931, after abandoning the Labour Party to follow Ramsay MacDonald into the National government. A larger-than-life railway trade union leader, he was in all Ramsay MacDonald's governments, and loved the London social life so much that he was dubbed by the cartoonist Low, 'the Right Honourable Dress Suit'. Thomas replaced the more conservative Richard Bell as Labour MP in 1910. Bell had been, with James Keir Hardie, one of the two MPs elected under the Labour Representation Committee banner in 1900.

DERBY. Gaol and Ye Olde Pie Shoppe. Opened in 1756, Derby Gaol was Derby's second gaol, and the Borough Gaol until 1840. Among those imprisoned and executed there were Jeremiah Brandreth, one of the leaders of starving framework knitters who, in 1817, took up arms to march on Nottingham. With two others, he was one of the last people in Britain to be hanged, drawn and quartered. In 1831, protesters angry at the failure of the parliamentary reform movement stormed the gaol.

DERBY. Grammar School. J. A. Hobson (1858-1940), anti-imperialist theoretician, journalist and Fabian, attended this school.

FOWNHOPE, Herefordshire. Lower House. Birthplace of the social reformer, feminist and sometime Labour politician Edith Picton-Turbervill (1872-1960). An active Christian and proponent of a greater role for women within the Church of England, Edith Picton-Turbervill was active in public life for over 60 years. Missionary work in India was followed by involvement in the non-militant suffragist campaign. By 1919, she had joined the Labour Party, becoming one of fourteen female MPs when she was elected to represent The Wrekin in 1929. She supported a campaign to prevent pregnant women being hanged, but was defeated by a 'National' candidate in the 1931 General Election. She remained active in women's movements for the rest of her life.

HANDSWORTH, Warwickshire. Grammar School. The alma mater of Denis Howell (1923-98) who was the first Sports Minister, having earlier worked at the Hercules bicycle factory, and been a qualified football referee. He was MP for Small Heath for over 30 years. In 1976, the Labour Prime Minister Harold Wilson gave him responsibility for dealing with severe drought. Heavy rains followed almost immediately and he was given the sobriquet the Minister of Floods. The title of his autobiography, *Made in Birmingham*, speaks volumes.

HARRISEAHEAD, Staffordshire. School Farm, Mow Cop. The location of the all-day, open-air religious meeting in 1807, consisting of prayers, singing and sermons, that led to the organisers, Hugh Bourne and William Clowes, setting up the Primitive Methodist movement, which had a distinctly working-class identity, and provided many Chartists and nineteenth-century trade unionists. The Primitive Methodists were merged with the main Wesleyan body in 1932. Across the border, at Englesea Brook Chapel in Cheshire, is an excellent small museum, in an old 'Prim' chapel, illustrating the history of the movement.

HAYFIELD, Derbyshire. Recreation Ground. On 24 April 1932, the British Workers Sports Federation organised a mass trespass of Kinder Scout, setting out from here. Four or five hundred ramblers walked over private land in order to publicise the importance of access to the hills. There were tussles with gamekeepers, and six men were detained by the police. The act was symbolic but drew attention to the private ownership of areas of great natural beauty. It created the climate for the development of National Parks. The demonstrators sang *The Red Flag* as they set off from Hayfield. Hiking and the active enjoyment of the countryside has been a Leftie thing from Hugh Dalton to Chris Smith (who was, at one stage of his career, warden of a remote Youth Hostel in Wester Ross).

HUCKNALL TORKARD, Nottinghamshire. St Mary Magdalene Church. Here lies the poet Lord Byron (1788-1824) who, in a celebrated speech in the House of Lords in 1812, expressed a passionate sympathy for the Luddites. The government proposed a Bill making frame-breaking – already punishable by fourteen years' transportation – a capital offence. 'Suppose it passed,' he said of the Bill. 'Suppose one of these men, as I have seen them – meagre with famine, sullen with despair, careless of a life which your lordships are about to value at something less than the price of a stocking-frame – suppose this man (and there are a thousand such from whom you may select your victims) dragged into court to be tried for this new offence by this new law, still there are two things wanting to convict and condemn him: and these are, in my opinion, twelve butchers for a jury and a Jeffreys for a judge.'

KEELE, Staffordshire. University. Founded as the University College of North Staffordshire in 1950, its inspiration and first principal was Lord Lindsay (1879-1952), formerly Master of Balliol College, Oxford and anti-Chamberlain candidate in the 1938 Oxford 'Munich' by-election. One of the main local supporters was the Reverend Thomas Horwood, Vicar of Etruria, socialist and City of Stoke-on-Trent councillor. With these godfathers, the university became known in the 1950s as 'Kremlin on the Hill'. Among its graduates are John Golding (1931-99), described as 'a master of every trick in the political trade', who became the local MP; and Alun Michael (1943-). Clare Short (1946-) spent a year here. Her child, conceived here, was given up for adoption, but mother and son were joyously reunited in 1996.

KENILWORTH, Warwickshire. George Potter (1832-93) attended a Dame school here before going on to be a carpenter and trade union activist, and president, in 1871, of the Trades Union Congress. A popular man, his newspaper *Bee-Hive* bankrupted him. He failed repeatedly to get into Parliament.

LEAMINGTON, Warwickshire. 27 Clarendon Square. The birthplace of Ernest Belfort Bax (1854-1926), a rebellious lad from a middle-class Quaker family, who thought of becoming a composer but instead became a reporter for the *Evening Standard*. He was influenced by reading Karl Marx's work, and was responsible for introducing Marx's work to the English-speaking world. A friend of William Morris and George Bernard Shaw, he was a leading member of the Social Democratic Federation and a prolific writer on socialism, history and aspects of the Reformation in Europe. A barrister by profession, he was not popular with suffragists, whose cause he opposed. He was an uncle of Arnold Bax, the composer.

LEICESTER. 11 Churchgate. An early eighteenth century house, that was used as a coffee shop by Thomas Cooper (1805-92) who was born nearby and lived in Sailors Alley Yard. Cooper, a self-educated journalist reported on, and then joined and led, the Chartist movement in Leicester, bringing their numbers up to 2,500. Implicated in the Plug Riots in 1842, he was sent to prison for two years, after which he eschewed the violent methods he had once embraced. He wrote an epic poem, *Purgatory of Suicides*, not much read these days, and a much more lively autobiography. After an escape from a railway accident he became a born-again Christian and Baptist minister.

LEICESTER. Welford Place. A Grade II listed statue of John Biggs (1801-71) is to be found here. Biggs, a native of Leicester, was three-times Mayor of the City, an MP and hosier who formed a radical group to campaign for franchise reform, splitting the local Liberals in the process. He left politics in the 1860s, after a Conservative victory, and was forced to sell his business and his house. He lived his remaining years in West Street, where he died.

LOUGHBOROUGH, Leicestershire. Mill Street, between the Market Place and Ashby Road. The site of Heathcote and Boden's lace factory, which was attacked by Luddites on 28 June 1816, a Friday night. The owners were offered compensation of £10,000 but refused to take the money and moved to Tiverton, Devon, instead.

MILLTHORPE, Derbyshire. Millthorpe Cottage. Edward Carpenter (1844-1929) resigned his comfortable living as curate of St Edward's Church, Cambridge, under Frederick Denison Maurice, Christian Socialist, and, after a spell as teacher and then living with a labourer in Sheffield, bought a farm in Millthorpe in 1883, opting for the simple life. It was to remain his home for nearly 40 years. He worked the land and lived in an openly homosexual relationship – a brave (and illegal) thing to do at that time – with a working-class lover. Carpenter was a founding member of the Social Democratic Federation, a writer, and poet, who penned *Towards Democracy* and the hymn, *England Arise!* He was a proponent of many, then unfashionable, causes, such as sandal making, vegetarianism, nudism and communism. He campaigned against air pollution and was curious about Eastern religions. A pacifist, he opposed both the Boer War and the First World War. He had an influence on E. M. Forster and D. H. Lawrence. George Orwell may have had him in mind when, in *The Road to Wigan Pier,* he railed against 'every fruit-juice drinker, nudist, sandal wearer and sex maniac' in the Labour Party.

NEWCASTLE-UNDER-LYME, Staffordshire. The birthplace of Vera Brittain (1893-1970), the daughter of a paper manufacturer, who became an author, poet, feminist and journalist. In the First World War she lost a brother and also a fiancé, and recalled her misery in *Testament of Youth* (1933). In it, she gives a feminine perspective on the 'lost generation'. She spent the war as a Volunteer Aid Detachment nurse. In the Second World War, she was a pacifist and a critic of aerial bombing in German towns. She was an active member, in the early days, of the Campaign for Nuclear Disarmament; and the editor of this volume remembers meeting her selling *Peace News* in Trafalgar Square in 1961. Vera Brittain was the mother of Shirley Williams, Cabinet minister in the governments of Harold Wilson, 1974-76, and James Callaghan, 1976-79. She was one of the founders of the Social Democratic Party and, later, Leader of the Liberal Democrats in the House of Lords.

NORTHAMPTON. Grammar School. Attended by Bernard Donoughue (1934-), a man who, according to his autobiography, *The Heat of the Kitchen*, rose from a slum background to be Senior Lecturer in Politics at the London School of Economics, senior policy adviser to Harold Wilson and James Callaghan when they were Prime Ministers and, as Lord Donoughue, junior minister in Tony Blair's first government.

NORTHAMPTON. High School. Marcia Williams (1932-) – later Baroness Falkender – attended this school before going on to Queen Mary College, University of London, and to work in the Labour Party headquarters. At school she organised protests against the Head, whom she accused of bullying another pupil. She developed a close and confidential relationship with Harold Wilson during his years as leader of the Labour Party, and, indeed, for the rest of his life. With Lady Wilson, she was present at his death. She had a prickly relationship with those who worked with her, but probably added a humanity to Wilson's austere intellectualism.

NOTTINGHAM. Arboretum. Here one can find the Grade II listed statue of Feargus O'Connor (1795-1855), the Chartist leader who became the Chartists' one and only MP when he gained the seat for Nottingham in July 1847. Early in his career he was regarded as somewhat reckless, but he was largely responsible for avoiding confrontation at the Chartists' Kennington rally of 1848. A frequent contributor to *Northern Star,* he died in 1855 after suffering mental illness, probably as a result of syphilis.

NOTTINGHAM. St Mary's Church. Gravener Henson (1785-1852), a Nottingham native, married here, although he himself was a Wesleyan. Involved in the Framework Knitters' Committee, he was closely associated with the Luddites, and, in the eyes of some, was even believed to be General Ludd himself. In later life, he moderated his views somewhat and became an accountant. He used to frequent the Isaac Newton pub and died, an asthmatic, in Broad Street. Neither the pub nor the house in Broad Street survive.

NOTTINGHAM. Castle. The castle was a symbol of authority and, conversely, a target of radical reformers in the early years of the nineteenth century, and especially on 10 October 1831. Instigated by the rejection by the House of Lords of a parliamentary Reform Bill, rioting broke out in Nottingham and lasted a number of days. Mills and property were destroyed in a vague echo of the Luddite insurgency fifteen years earlier. The eighteenth-century castle building was set alight, looted and remained roofless and in a ruinous condition until it became England's first municipal museum. It is still open to the public as a museum.

NOTTINGHAM. Nottingham High School. Among the school's alumni are Geoff Hoon (1953-) and Ed Balls (1967-). Hoon went on to Jesus College, Cambridge to study Law, lectured in Law at the University of Leeds, was a Member of the European Parliament from 1984 to 1994, and MP for Ashfield from 1992. He rose rapidly in the Blair governments to become a luckless Secretary of State for Defence. Balls was Chief Economic Adviser to Chancellor of the Exchequer Gordon Brown, before fighting Normanton at the 2005 General Election. He first came to prominence when Michael Heseltine commented on the econo-speak of a Gordon Brown speech, stated, 'It's not Brown's, its Balls'!'

NOTTINGHAM. University of Nottingham. Ken Coates (1930-) was Professor in the Department of Adult Education. A former miner, and Chairman of the Bertrand Russell Peace Foundation, he has written extensively on human rights issues, poverty, democracy, socialism and disarmament. One of the University's forerunners was the Nottingham Peoples' College, where Anthony Mundella (1825-97) served on the Board. Mundella, a former Chartist and Liberal MP, who was supportive of trade union recognition and education reform, is buried in St Mary's churchyard.

OLD MILVERTON, Warwickshire. St James Church. The ashes of Vera Brittain (1893-1970) lie in the churchyard.

OUNDLE, Rutland. Oundle School. One Old Boy was Kenneth Robinson (1911-96) who was Minister of Health – as a boy he had wanted to be a doctor, but circumstances obliged him to be a clerk at Lloyds – and afterwards Minister of Land and Planning in Harold Wilson's first governments. He was also the author of a standard biography of Wilkie Collins.

PENTRICH, Derbyshire. The Pentrich Revolution Heritage Trail is a four-mile walk around the village that was at the centre of the Pentrich Rebellion of 1817. Ten plaques commemorate parts of the village associated with the Rebellion, including Ashfields Farm, St Matthew's Church and the old Pentrich Mill. Thirty five armed men, the 'Pentrich martyrs', marched towards Nottingham to be part of a national uprising to overthrow the government. Led by Jeremiah Brandreth, they scattered on the appearance of the military. They were rounded up, imprisoned and tried in Derby for treason.

RAUNDS, Northamptonshire. Raunds in the nineteenth century was a bootmaking town, specialising in footwear for the army. But in 1905, the War Office were tight-fisted in their payments. A strike of those making boots for the army in Raunds did not seem to be getting anywhere and so, on 8 May, a leading light of the local branch of the National Union of Boot and Shoe Operatives James Gribble, himself a former soldier, organised 115 men in a march to London. Keir Hardie spoke at a rally in Trafalgar Square, and the government acknowledged that the strikers had a case. After an official inquiry, a standard rate was set for future contracts and an arbitration board was established.

REPTON, Derbyshire. Unfit to serve in the First World War, Victor Gollancz (1893-1967) taught at Repton Public School. Later he was introduced to publishing by William Wedgwood Benn (father of Tony) and his brother, Ernest Benn, and became the most successful and influential Leftie publisher in the middle years of the twentieth century. He published the Left Book Club and was first publisher of *Tribune*. He was also an activist, supporting Jewish refugees coming out of Germany, and being one of the founders of the Campaign for Nuclear Disarmament. Gollancz persuaded H. G. Wells and E. Nesbit to work for him. He also published Fenner Brockway and G. D. H. Cole. One of his most famous publications was George Orwell's *The Road to Wigan Pier*. Another was Kingsley Amis' *Lucky Jim*.

ROSS-ON-WYE, Herefordshire. Birthplace of Sir Arthur Pugh (1870-1955), known primarily as the chairman of the TUC during the General Strike of 1926. He served on the general council of the TUC until 1936 and was actively involved in the steel unions: the British Steel Smelters' Association, the Iron and Steel Trades Confederation and the British Iron, Steel and Kindred Trades Association all benefited from his input. He wrote *Men of Steel*, a history of the metal unions.

RUDDINGTON, Nottinghamshire. Framework Knitters, Chapel Street. A working museum that shows life in the textile towns in the nineteenth century.

RUGBY, Warwickshire. Rugby School. The alma mater of Richard Acland (1906-90) and R. H. Tawney (1880-1962). Acland was a Christian Socialist who created the Commonwealth Party to break up the wartime by-election truce, eventually joining the Labour Party after 1945. 'Do not ask, "Is it expedient?" Simply ask "Is it right?"' was his philosophy. He resigned from the Labour Party over its nuclear policy and became a founder of the Campaign for Nuclear Disarmament. Tawney was also a Christian Socialist, an economic historian and an ethical writer on equality and politics. He taught at the London School of Economics and was active in the Workers' Educational Association.

SAWLEY, Derbyshire. 52 Wilne Road. A plaque commemorates John Clifford (1836-1923), born in Sawley, a Baptist minister and, for most of his life, a Liberal supporter. He was an advocate of free adult education and women's rights, and a supporter of many strikes against harsh conditions in the 1880s and 1890s. He led passive resistance to the 1902 Education Act and campaigned against the Boer War. By 1918, he was a Christian Socialist and a supporter of the Labour Party. The local Baptist church, erected in 1800, is a few doors away from Clifford's birthplace.

STOKE-ON-TRENT, Staffordshire. North Stafford Hotel. Between the hotel and the railway station is a statue of Josiah Wedgwood, the eighteenth-century potter. In 1906, his descendant, another Josiah, won Newcastle-under-Lyme in the General Election. He and his brother, Ralph (father of the historian C. V. Wedgwood), 'celebrated at midnight by climbing the statue of Josiah Wedgwood outside Stoke Station and decorating it with the blue ribbons of the Liberal Party – which were removed next morning by Cecil, the head of the family.'

STOURBRIDGE, Worcestershire. Wollescote. Birthplace of Joseph Westwood (1884-1948), though he moved with his family to Scotland when he was three years old. He was Secretary of State for Scotland in Clement Attlee's government, but his service was cut short when he and his wife were killed in a car crash.

SUTTON COLDFIELD, Warwickshire. Birthplace of Arthur Deakin (1890-1955), General Secretary of the Transport and General Workers Union after Ernest Bevin. The son of a cobbler, he ruled the Union with a rod of iron, and threw his block vote to the Right, and against causes espoused by Aneurin Bevan and his allies, and became crucial in the rise to the leadership of Hugh Gaitskell in 1955.

WALSALL, Staffordshire. Queen Mary's Grammar School. David Ennals (1922-95), one of three brothers who emerged from a Dissenting tradition to work in radical international politics, attended this school. John became secretary general of the World Federation of United Nations Associations and of the UK Immigration Advisory Service. Martin became secretary general of the National Council for Civil Liberties and of Amnesty International, and a founder of International Alert. David became a politician, working as the secretary to the International Department of the Labour Party and then MP, first for Dover and later for Norwich South. He was a Minister of State in the Foreign and Commonwealth Office in Harold Wilson's 1974 government, and Secretary of State for Social Security in James Callaghan's government.

WARWICK. Warwick Castle. Home of the Countess of Warwick, who wrote its history. She was the Labour candidate in a by-election in 1923, merged, because of the dissolution of Parliament, into the General Election. Her Conservative opponent was Anthony Eden (later Prime Minister), whose sister was married to Guy, son of Lady Warwick. Eden was also engaged to Beatrice Beckett, both stepdaughter and niece of Lady Warwick's daughter, Marjorie. Eden won.

WEDNESBURY, Staffordshire. Wednesbury High School. Peter Archer, later Lord Archer of Sandwell (1926-), went to this school. He was a long-serving Labour politician whose notable achievements include helping to form 'Labour First', a group that attempted to keep the Labour Party together in the difficult days of the 1980s. He was also responsible for the final abolition of the death penalty from the Statute book. It had been abolished for murder in the 1960s but had been retained for high treason, piracy on the high seas and arson in Her Majesty's dockyards. All this went as a result of an amendment proposed by Peter Archer – rather what one would expect from a good Methodist.

WELLINGTON, Shropshire. Grammar School. The school's most celebrated Leftie Old Boy was Len Murray (1922-2004), general secretary of the Trades Union Congress from 1973 to 1984. He was the son of a Shropshire farm labourer, won a scholarship to New College and ended up as the Right Honourable Lord Murray of Epping Forest OBE.

WEM, Shropshire. Noble Street. The childhood home of William Hazlitt (1778-1830), radical essayist and critic. Hazlitt did not support the French wars, was a critic of political corruption, which he viewed as rife, and called for the reform of the voting system. Popular in the Victorian period, his works fell out of fashion in the early twentieth century, although Michael Foot has latterly restored interest in him.

Prestatyn
St Asaph's
Aberffraw
Bethesda
Caernarfon
Snowdon
Penmachno
Wrexham
Llanystumdwy
Criccieth
Pwllheli
Penhros
Penrhyndeudraeth
Glyndyfrdwy
Llyn Celyn
Bala
Llanuwchllyn
Llanelltyd
Sycharth
Abergynolwen
Machynlleth
Newtown
Ceri Goetre
Aberystwyth
Pantycelyn
Llanidloes
Llangeitho
Tregaron
Llangranog
Llwynrhydowen
Cilmery
Llangammarch Wells
Fishguard
Penboyr
Rhydcymerau
Mynachlog-ddu
Bwlchyriw
Gwernogle
Efailwen
Trefeca
Talgarth
Whitland
Camarthen
Narberth
Llanddowror
Ferryside
Merthyr Tydfil
Coed Grwyne
Hirwaun
Monmouth
Aberdare
Tredegar
Blaina
Maerdy
Aberfan
Trellech
Cwmafan
Abersychan
Llantrisant
Aberavon
Trehafod
Llanvaches
Senghenydd
Llangeinor
Pontypridd
Glyntaff
Llanwern
Llangwm Uchaf
Tonypandy
St Fagans
Newport
Penarth
Cardiff

6.

Wales

Joe Hillaby and Caroline Hillaby

Welsh identity has been forged through relations with the English. This is celebrated in the earliest Welsh poetry which is, 'next to Greek and Latin, the oldest in Europe'. In the late sixth century, Taliesin, in his 'Death Song for Owain, son of Urien', described how

> Sleepeth the wide host of England
>   With light in their eyes,
> And those that had not fled
>   Were braver than were wise.
>
> Owain dealt them doom
>   As the wolves devour sheep;
> That warrior, bright of harness,
>   Gave stallions for the bard.

In the ninth-century *englyn*, stanzas of three or four lines, an anonymous poet looks back to the sixth century. Heledd laments the death of her brother, Cynddylan, ruler of Pengwern, in battle, possibly defending Trenn – Tern in Shropshire:

Dark is Cynddylan's hall tonight
With no fire, no songs.
My cheek's worn out with tears.

Dark of roof is Cynddylan's hall
After the English destroyed
Cynddylan and Elfan of Powys.
Cynddylan's Hall

Eagle of Eli that watches the seas,
In the estuaries fishes no longer.
In the blood of men it calls its feast.

Grey-capped eagle of Pengwern, tonight
Is its claw aloft,
Greedy for the flesh I love.
The Eagle of Eli

The antiquity and continuity of Welsh poetry have been an inspiration to the national movement ever since. The *englyn*, the oldest recorded metrical form, has remained popular to the present day. In 1936, after the Penrhos trial, Waldo Williams used it to reproach fellow members of Plaid Cymru:

Inside and not a soul – to hear
The heroes brave,
O God you will explain,
Are three the bloody Blaid?

Although the Welsh were divided, Offa (King of Mercia, 757-96) felt it necessary to build a 167-mile dyke, with a 30-foot wide bank and a twelve-foot ditch, from Llanfynydd near Mold to Rushock Hill in

Herefordshire. Rhodri Mawr (ruled 844-77) united Gwynedd, Powys and Seisyllwg. His grandson, Hywel Dda (c900-50), united Seisyllwg with Gwynedd, Powys and Deheubarth, a kingdom extending from St Asaph's to St David's and Kidwelly, and in 914 sought to codify their laws and customs at his manor of Whitland. But these unions were brief.

Border, and internecine, warfare continued until William the Conqueror achieved a brief accommodation with Rhys ap Tewdwr. But during his son's reign, the Anglo-Norman barons of the march

The Bevan Stones

unleashed an onslaught against Wales. By 1100, all land west of the Conway was conquered: the Earl of Shrewsbury had advanced from Montgomery as far as Cardigan Bay and what is now 'Little England beyond Wales', Pembroke. In the south Builth, Brecon and Glamorgan fell. The ambush and death of Richard fitz Gilbert, at Coed Grwynne in 1136, after Stephen's accession, heralded a Welsh national revival. It was short-lived, but for a century the threat of alliances between rebel barons and the Welsh remained a feature of English politics.

The end of an independent Wales came when Llywelyn, the last native prince, was killed at Cilmeri in 1282, and Edward's ring of castles was completed around the north. Llywelyn's principality became the appanage of the heir to the English throne. The Statute of Wales, proclaimed by Edward at Rhuddlan, divided Llywelyn's principality administratively into six counties, but the marcher barons retained their lordships. At Lincoln, in 1301, Edward 'of Caernarvon' was invested as first English Prince of Wales. Such investitures lapsed in the reign of King Henry VIII, but were revived by Lloyd George in 1911. Subsequently, the only serious challenge to the English came with the Owain Glyn Dwr revolt, 1400-13.

In the late fifteenth and early sixteenth century, Wales's splintered judicial administration provided a ripe environment for lawbreakers, and handsome opportunities for personal gain for law officers. The Council of the Welsh Marches, based in Ludlow, was incapable of resolving this problem. Henry VIII's answer was the 1536 Act of Union, by which the Westminster Parliament enacted that 'the country or dominion of Wales shall be, stand and continue forever incorporated united and annexed with (the) realm of England . . . To reduce (the Welsh) to perfect order . . . utterly to extirp all and singular the sinister usages and customs of the same . . . the laws, ordinances and statutes of England shall be used, practised and exercised in the said country.' The ancient marcher lordships, retained by the Statute of Wales, were now replaced by seven new counties – Denbigh, Montgomery, Radnor, Brecon, Monmouth, Glamorgan and Pembroke – in addition to the six counties established in 1284. Law was to be administered by county courts, within four circuits of the Great Sessions, the only specifically Welsh administrative institution, held at Caernarfon, Carmarthen, Denbigh and Brecon. Each served three counties. Monmouth, however, had to look to Westminster. The four Sessions towns became Wales's main urban centres. Carmarthen, the largest, had a population, in about 1560, of merely two thousand. Furthermore, each shire was to send one knight, and each county town – except for Merioneth – one burgess, to the English Parliament. The beneficiaries were pre-eminently the bilingual gentry and the merchant class, both becoming integrated into the English ruling classes.

While Welshmen and Englishmen were held to be equal before the law, all court business was to be conducted 'in the English tongue', and 'no person that used the Welsh speech shall enjoy any office or fees within the (joint) realms.' At a stroke, Welsh was reduced to the language of an underclass, for monoglot Welsh speakers, the vast majority, were unable to follow any legal process. Four and a half centuries passed before parity between the two languages was achieved. In 1971, the Archbishop of Wales and others vainly demanded that 'any laws that violate the principle of equal linguistic rights in Wales be repealed – so that Welsh-speaking Welshmen shall not be treated in their own country as though they were aliens speaking a foreign tongue.' Only by the Welsh Language Society's 20-year campaign of civil disobedience was parity achieved, in the 1980s.

The English Reformation had little impact on Wales until 1587 when John Penry's *Humble Supplication* was presented to Parliament. This drew attention to the parlous condition of the Welsh church, whose people 'were perishing for lack of food', the saving knowledge of the gospel, a necessity for salvation. Its priests were 'dumb and greedy dogs . . . adulterers, drunkards, thieves, roisterers and most abominable swearers.' Even members of the clergy accepted they were 'like bells without clappers'. In the St David's diocese, there were only fourteen preachers; in Bangor, more concubines than preachers. For Penry, as for other early reformers, the pattern of church life was to be the spontaneous outpouring of the Holy Spirit, as laid down in the New Testament: 'If any thing be revealed to another that sitteth by, let the first hold his peace. For ye may all prophesy one by one, that all may learn, and all may be comforted.' Every member was to participate in church government. Such a view had profound political implications. In 1593, Penry was tried for sedition. On hearing sentence of death, he told his judges that 'imprisonment, judgments, yea, death itself are not meet weapons to convince men's consciences, grounded on the word of God.' Wales had had three Marian martyrs, but Penry was its only Elizabethan martyr.

Ironically, Penry's sharp criticisms of the Welsh church probably persuaded Archbishop Whitgift to support the translation into Welsh of the full Bible by William Morgan, Vicar of Llanraeadr-yn-Mochnant and later Bishop of St Asaph's; a task completed in 1588, when Welsh bishops were ordered to ensure that their clergy had, and used, Welsh Bibles. For Glanmor Williams, the translation is 'an incomparable masterpiece' which 'saved the linguistic and cultural heritage of Wales'. Its 'majestic and dignified renderings, nevertheless beautifully lucid and intelligible, combine the strength and purity of the ancient language with a flexibility and modernity that enabled Welsh to measure up to the new demands being placed on it.' For Sir Ifor Williams, it was 'the greatest gift the Welsh people ever had'.

Close to his end, Penry spoke of his dear and native country. 'I come, with a rope about my neck, to save you. However it goeth with me, I labour that you may have the Gospel preached among you. Though it cost my life, I think it well bestowed.' However it was some 40 years before 'gathered churches' began to appear in Wales. Such churches were 'constituted and gathered . . . by a free mutual consent of believers joining and covenanting to live as members of a holy Society.' In Wales, the first evidence for preaching the gospel came with the opening of Archbishop Laud's campaign against 'Inconformity' in 1633. At St Mary's Cardiff, in 1638, William Erbery had to resign; at Llanfaches, William Wroth, Rector, was ejected. Three men became the dominant force in Welsh religious life until 1660 – Cradoc, of nearby Llangwm, and his converts Morgan Llwyd of Wrexham and Vavasor Powell of Knucklas. In 1639, Cradoc, Llwyd and Powell are found at Llanfaches – joining Mr Wroth at his first 'gathered church' there.

On the outbreak of the Civil War, all four fled, first to Bristol and then to London. After the Commons' victory, its Committee for Plundered Ministers sent Cradoc, Llwyd and Powell as itinerant preachers to Wales. In response to Penry's *Humble Supplication* came the 1650 Act for the Propagation of the Gospel in Wales to establish some one hundred preaching ministries. When Puritanism broke into sects, Congregationalists and Baptists were strongest in Wales. Powell and Llwyd, now Fifth Monarch Men, awaited Christ's imminent arrival. Outraged at Cromwell's Protectorship in 1653, Powell denounced him as 'the dissemblingest perjured villain in the world', but most Welsh Puritans, including Llwyd, followed Cradoc in supporting Cromwell.

At the Restoration of Charles II, two of Wales' three regicides were executed: Major General Thomas Harrison and Llwyd's patron, Colonel John Jones. The third, Thomas Wogan, somehow escaped from the Tower of London and fled to Holland. Retribution was sought not only for Charles the Martyr, but for the Anglican church. Ninety-three Welsh ministers were ejected before the Cavalier Parliament imposed its new Act of Uniformity in 1662. This sought 'the peace and honour of religion' by the imposition of a new, more anti-Calvinistic Book of Common Prayer, with the sacraments, rights and ceremonies of the Church of England. Already, the 1661 Corporation Act had introduced oaths of allegiance and supremacy. This was supplemented by the 1673 Test Act, which excluded from public office any who refused the Anglican sacrament. These acts, which remained in force until 1828, destroyed any chance of a comprehensive church. They were the foundation of Nonconformity – Dissent. Charles's attempt to use his dispensing powers led, in 1664, to an Act to Suppress Religious Conventicles, which prohibited unlawful religious meetings of more than five persons, outside the family. Even before 1660, where no church or house was available, religious meetings had been held in the open countryside – a tradition maintained by the Methodists. Now such meetings became the rule. At Bwlchyrhiw, services were held in a cave, on nearby Craig yr Eglwys. The Five Mile Act, 1655, excluded Dissenting ministers and teachers from residing within five miles of any corporate borough.

The Quakers, steadfastly refusing to compromise over matters of conscience, suffered most, a persecution calmly recorded in their *Sufferings of the Friends*. The Lord, however, opened a 'door of mercy'. In 1681, some thirty thousand acres – Haverford, Radnor and Merion counties – were bought in Pennsylvania. Welsh Baptist emigration had begun earlier. John Miles, founder of their first church, at Ilston in Gower, in about 1649, crossed the Atlantic in 1663. Welsh Baptists spread across the south. The American Revolution provided Wales with a flood of material for radicals and reformers. In 1688, the Whigs rewarded the Dissenters with a Toleration Act. All taking the oath of allegiance and supremacy, except Catholics and anti-Trinitarians, were granted freedom of worship – so long as Meeting House doors were not 'locked, barred or bolted'; but the profound social division had been created between church and chapel, which in Wales was to lead, after the Second Reform Act, 1867, to the triumph of the chapel. Yet the passage of the bill to disestablish the Church of Wales came only in September 1914, and its implementation on 1 April 1920.

University entrance being restricted to those subscribing to the Anglican Articles of Faith, Welsh Nonconformist academies were founded to prepare men for the ministry. Samuel Jones, Fellow of Jesus College and Vicar of Llangynwyd, Glamorgan, who lost his living under the Act of Uniformity, established the first 'university' for Dissenting ministers at Brynllywarch. After 1700, such academies flourished throughout Wales. Untrammelled by the restrictions suffered at Oxford and Cambridge, many fostered a critical spirit, Carmarthen being the most outstanding. Here lay the roots of Welsh Unitarianism: the move from Calvinism, through Arminianism, rejection of predestination, and Arianism, to rejection of the Trinity. Jenkin Jones, educated at Carmarthen under Thomas Perrot, maintained that Jesus died for all, and not merely the elect, and that divine sovereignty was compatible with free will. He founded Wales' first Arminian chapel, at Llwynrhydowen, near Llandysul, in 1733. By 1742, there were six other Arminian chapels on this tract of the Teifi, the Black Spot of Calvinistic demonology. Arianism, the belief that Christ was not consubstantial with the Father, but created by Him, the denial of Christ's true divinity, was being espoused at Lammas Street chapel, Carmarthen, in about 1750. The county claimed Wales's first Unitarian chapel, at Cwm Cothi, near Gwernogle, in about 1794.

Wales's first primary schools were Anglican, with instruction in English. To further his evangelical missions, Griffith Jones, Rector of Llandowror, 1716-61, established a network of circulating schools, with instruction in Welsh. By 1761, 3,300 schools had been set up in 1,600 locations, taking literacy, and love and respect for the native language, to half the population. Catherine the Great commissioned a report on his work. Welsh Methodism, which flourished in the soil tilled by Griffith Jones, dates from the meeting of Howel Harris and Daniel Rowland in 1737. William Williams Pantycelyn, the third leader, was Wales's greatest hymn writer, a major poet, author and profound thinker. Welsh Methodism was quite distinct from English. Founded before John Wesley's conversion in 1738, its first Association took place in 1743, before Wesley's first Conference. Critically, Welsh Methodism was Calvinistic; Wesleyan Arminian, opposing predestinarianism with free will. Yet, operating as a church within a church, Welsh Methodism strongly opposed separation from the Anglicans. Thomas Charles carried the Methodist revival into North Wales. A lifelong opponent of separation, he had to accept formal severance from the Anglicans in 1811. The gradual fusion of New and Old Dissent had profound political consequences: the hegemony of Welsh liberalism and Nonconformity, which lasted until 1920.

As Baptists, Quakers and Independents all had settlements there, the American Revolution brought political awareness to Wales. Richard Price, who anticipated Kant's basic views on ethics in *Principal Questions in Morals* (1757), lifted the American colonists' claims from narrow legality to universal moral right in *Observation on the Nature of Civil Liberty and the Principles of Government* (1776). Price and Washington were granted Yale University's only honorary doctorates of law in 1781. Price's *Importance of the American Revolution* (1784) influenced the constitution makers. Sections of his *Love for our Country* were read to the French National Assembly, 'Tremble, oppressors of the world . . . you cannot keep the world in darkness.' His insistence that governments held power only as a trust from the people provoked Burke's *Reflections on the French Revolution*, to which Tom Paine responded with *The Rights of Man*. Price's death in 1791 was a national day of mourning in France. Jacobinism spread through the Welsh towns. The works of the Old Dissent, of Ebery, Cradoc, Powell and Llwyd, were now revisited. Those of Price and David Williams, founder, with Franklin, of the Deist 'Thirteen Club', had not to wait so long. Their political heirs were to be found in the new industrial areas of Wales, among the members of Working Men's Associations and the Chartists; but in much of rural Wales, especially the north, deference and submission remained deeply embedded. Only the 1867 Reform Act and the 1872 Ballot Act emancipated Williams' 'oppressed and degraded peasantry' from its 'feudal ideas and habits'.

In 1770, almost all Wales was dependent, directly or indirectly, on agriculture. By 1851, it was only a third, for the late eighteenth and early nineteenth century witnessed the massive industrialisation of Wales's economy. Coal production rose 50-fold, from 2 per cent to 11 per cent of British output, between 1750-55 and 1831-35. Rich veins of anthracite, dry, and then smokeless, steam, and finally bituminous coal, stretched from Kidwelly and the valley of the Gwendraeth Fawr in the west as far as Blaenavon and Pontypool, beyond the Ebbw, in the east. Coal was also mined in Flint and Denbigh. Iron production rose from 5000 tons in 1720 to 525,000 tons in 1840, over a hundred-fold. By 1860, when production was 969,000 tons, iron gave way to steel – produced from Spanish non-phosphoric ore. Copper and tin smelting were centred on Neath and Swansea, supplied, after 1768, by Welsh copper, predominantly from Mynydd Parys in Anglesea. Pontypool, under the Hanburys, concentrated on tin plate and japanning. North Cardiganshire was especially rich in lead. At Penrhyn, where Richard Pennant revolutionised slate production, output rose from 1000 to 20,000 tons between 1782 and 1808, and a good quarryman's pay by one third, between 1843 and 1865.

Industrialisation was accompanied by massive population growth, from 590,000 in 1801 to 1.2 million in 1851, and then to 2.7 million in 1921, when the post-war depression brought it to a sudden halt. While Ireland suffered large scale emigration, Wales experienced only internal migration. In 1801, one fifth, in 1851, one third, and in 1911, about two thirds of its population was concentrated in Glamorgan and Monmouthshire. Urban growth was also spectacular between 1801 and 1861: in Merthyr, from 7,700 to 46,000; Swansea from 7000 to 34,000; Cardiff from 2000 to 33,000; and Newport from 1,500 to 25,000. After the opening of the Bute West Dock in 1839, and Bute East in 1854, Cardiff pulled ahead rapidly. In 1841, the Taff Vale Railway transported 41,000 tons of coal; by 1860, it was 2.3 million. South Wales was supplying almost a third of the world export of coal. Considerable immigration from England in the late nineteenth century had a profound impact on the Welsh language.

From the 1820s, increasingly violent public protest characterised south and central Wales: strikes and lockouts, Chartist demands for political reform, and action against enclosures, turnpike tollgates, tithes, the end of out-relief and the building of workhouses. Economic depression – the aftermath of the Napoleonic wars – witnessed the beginnings of trade unionism among Monmouthshire's coalminers, and with it the so-called 'Scotch Cattle' who, like opponents of enclosure, Rebecca's Children, and turnpike rioters, operated as secret societies. Their customs, such as *ceffyl pren*, a wooden horse like the English skimmington ride, were drawn from rural life. Members usually wore women's clothes and had blackened faces. After the Monmouthshire miners' strike failed, the Scotch Cattle terrorised opponents, night and night again. In spite of a heavy military presence – some 1,300 troops – only one of the Cattle was apprehended. For his part in a Scotching at Argoed, Edward Morgan was hanged on the roof of Monmouth Gaol in 1835, despite the jury's appeal for clemency.

The greatest popular rising was at Merthyr in 1831. The Unitarians had provided a strong radical tradition, but agitation for parliamentary reform, wage reductions due to overproduction, and relentless pursuit of minor debt by the Court of Requests created an explosive situation. The result was a mass uprising. At least sixteen people were shot dead, and many more wounded. Throughout Carmarthenshire, parts of Cardigan and Pembrokeshire, especially the Towy and Teifi valleys, grievances about enclosure, tithes and the new Poor Law led to violent social unrest. At Narberth in January 1839, five months before the first of the turnpike riots, an attempt was made to burn down the workhouse. Similar incidents occurred later at Haverfordwest, Llanelli and Aberaeron. At Newcastle Emlyn, a letter entitled 'Vengeance in Blood', in red ink, promised to 'take care of' the master if he did not flee, forthwith.

The flannel towns of Newtown and Llanidloes were early centres of factory production and Chartism. Robert Owen's Grand National Consolidated Trade Union, which published Wales's first working-class newspaper, the bilingual *Y-Gweithiwr*, 'The Worker', came to nought as a result of the verdict against the Tolpuddle Martyrs, but his belief in co-operation was amply vindicated. In Wales, the first break with the Chartist policy of change by peaceful means, 'moral force' not 'physical force', came at Llanidloes, with a five-day riot in 1839. At Newport, when some five thousand Chartists marched on the Westgate Hotel, a fusillade killed 20. The demonstrators fled. John Frost, Zephaniah Williams and William Jones were arrested and dispatched to Monmouth Gaol.

The 'leading figure of Welsh Chartism', Hugh Williams, a Carmarthen solicitor, who defended both Chartist and Rebecca rioters, was so feared that all his mail was monitored at Carmarthen and London. When Henry Hetherington, an author of 'The People's Charter', was arrested in 1841, Williams provided the cash to buy, and thus safeguard, his business. The full force of rural unrest came late, in 1842. *The Times* correspondent wrote of the 'boldness of enterprise, rapidity of movement, unity of purpose, dexterity of execution and celerity of retreat of these Cambrian Cossacks'. In June 1843, some four hundred mounted Rebeccans galloped into Carmarthen in full daylight, launching a mass attack on the workhouse. They were dislodged only by the dragoons, one of whose horses, spurred on to cover fourteen miles in 80 minutes, dropped dead on the spot, and another died the next day. Strenuous military repression paid off, but victory lay with Rebecca. Major changes in turnpike law and administration were implemented in July 1844. Rebecca's name, and techniques, were adopted in 1856 by protesters in the Carmarthenshire uplands destroying enclosure fences, and in 1869 by others fighting poaching wars on the upper Wye.

The Welsh cultural revival of the late eighteenth and early nineteenth centuries began with the Welsh societies in London: the Cymmrodorion, founded in 1751; the Gwyneddigion, 1770; and the Cymreigyddion, 1794. The second, with people from North Wales, played the major role. All members had to speak fluent Welsh and be devoted to the music of the harp. It published the poems of Dafydd ap Gwilym in 1789, and three volumes of *Myvrian Archaeology*, 1801-07, major early-literary texts. It supported *Cylchgraw*, one of Wales's earliest journals, which included articles on the French Revolution, slavery, prison conditions and the legendary twelfth-century Madoc. The Cymreigyddion revived eisteddfodau, previously held only in taverns. The Cymmrodorion helped to found the National Eisteddfod in the 1860s, and published the *Dictionary of Welsh Biography* (1959 and 1970).

Iolo Morgannwg, born Edward Williams, father of Druidism and the Welsh antiquarian revival, and author of the *Myvrian Archaeology*, insinuated his own fabrications into Dafydd ap Gwilym's poems. Stonemason, and laudanum addict, he sought continuity for the Welsh cultural tradition from the era when the Celtic Druids had defended Britain. His means was the Gorsedd Beirdd, the Assembly of Bards, which first met on Primrose Hill in London in 1792, and had its first Welsh meeting, on the top of Stalling Down, east of Cowbridge, in 1795. At the 1819 Carmarthen Eisteddfod, Iolo built a stone circle on the Ivy Bush Hotel lawn, but permanent stone circles were only introduced at the National Eisteddfod in 1888. At the Pontypridd circle, a major centre for radical mass meetings, Evan James and his son James, author and composer respectively of *Hen Wlad fy Nhadau*, 'Old Land of my Fathers', were admitted to the Gorsedd in 1850. Although Griffith John Williams revealed Iolo's fraud and forgery, he remained convinced that Iolo was a brilliant scholar and the most charming of romantic poets. Iolo's Romantic Movement became 'the symbol of Welsh nationality, guaranteeing its continuity', doing for poetry and music what Morgan's Bible and Penry's *Humble Supplication* had done, through the work of the leaders of the Old and New Dissent, for the Welsh language and gospel.

Dr William Price of Llantrisant (1800-93), a devoted follower of Iolo Morgannwg, combined the roles of renowned healer, Chartist leader, self-proclaimed Druid and greatest of Welsh eccentrics. Besides deriding his own profession and established religion, he was one of the very few who derided the law and its practitioners. At the Glamorgan assizes, 1853, the 'learned counsel' for his defence was his seventeen-year-old daughter, Gwenllian Harnes, 'Countess of Glamorgan'. His acquittal, after sixteen hours, was greeted with ecstatic cheers. The discovery of fine dust, burnt bones and bronze buttons, during the 1830 excavation of the Bronze Age barrow on Pontypridd Common, probably inspired 84-year-old Price's public cremation, over half a century later, of the body of his infant, Iesu Grist. The failure of his trial established the legality of cremation.

The report of the 1847 Commission on Education described the Welsh language as 'a vast drawback'. For *The Times*, 'ignorance of English excluded the Welsh from the civilisation of their English neighbours'. This 'Treason of the Bluebooks' branded the Welsh people as dirty, lazy, ignorant, superstitious, deceitful and promiscuous. At a stroke it brought language and national issues to the forefront. Conflict between the Anglican National Society, and the Nonconformist, non-sectarian British and Foreign Society became intense. Fierce battles for control of the elective School Boards, established by Forster's Education Act of 1870, fuelled demands for the disestablishment of the Church.

The Second Reform Act of 1867 increased Merthyr's electorate from some 1,400 to 14,600, and gave the borough a second MP. Here, in 1868, Henry Richard, supported by miners and Nonconformists, triumphed. Thomas Edward Ellis, openly advocating Home Rule for Wales, was elected for Merioneth. Believing Ireland an example for Wales, he voted, with seventeen other Welsh MPs, for Gladstone's disestablishment of the minority Irish Church. Welsh disestablishment came 50 years later. In Wales, Liberal Nonconformist predominance was ensured by the 1872 Ballot Act, for Henry Richard ending 'feudalism'. The 1888 Local Government Act extended Nonconformist predominance to county government. It failed, however, to secure the Welsh radicals' aim of Home Rule and disestablishment, or even protection of the 90 per cent of the Welsh farmers who were tenants. In the 1880s, 100,000 Welsh people left the land.

In 1868 Henry Richard asked, 'The people who speak this language [Welsh], who read this literature, who own this history, who inherit these traditions – have they not a right to say, "We are the Welsh nation?"' *Cymdeithas yr Iaith Gymraeg*, the first Welsh Language Society, established in 1885, campaigned for Welsh as a medium of instruction in schools, and as a language studied in its own right. The Cross Commission of 1886 accepted that Welsh should be a grant-earning subject like other languages. Inspired by 'Young Ireland', *Cymru Fydd*, 'Wales of the Future', founded in 1886, sought to create Welsh as a 'nationality of the spirit as well as the letter'. As an independent Welsh party, it failed due to the hostility of the South Wales Liberal Federation. One of the founders, O. M. Edwards, Fellow of Lincoln College, Oxford, devoted his life to fostering national consciousness of, and pride in, Welsh history, literature and culture, by writing popular works for adults and children, publishing journals offering outlets to young writers, and editing Welsh classics. Abandoning Oxford to become Chief Inspector of Schools, he promoted Welsh as a part of the curriculum. However, by 1891, 69 per cent of the population spoke English; only 54 per cent spoke Welsh. In 1901, the figures were 85 per cent and 43 per cent respectively; in 1911, 92 per cent and 43 per cent respectively, a reflection of the industrialisation, and thus demographic predominance, of Monmouthshire and Glamorgan, which accounted for over half Wales's population. Welsh language and literature seemed doomed.

William Abraham, 'apostle of industrial peace', and secretary of the Rhondda-based Cambrian Miners' Association, sought stability by co-operation with the employers, linking wages to prices and profits. Elected miners' MP for Rhondda in 1885, he shamed members in the House of Commons who laughed at his Welsh by explaining that it was the Lord's Prayer. Overproduction and downward adjustment of wages, with many miners facing starvation, led to the 1898 strike. Its collapse heralded victory for Mabon's young rivals, William Brace and Tom Richards, and their policies of a minimum wage and a comprehensive union. Within a year, the South Wales Miners Federation (SWMF) had more than

100,000 members. The strike opened the coalfield to Christian Socialism. The miners' weekly, *Tarian y Gweithiur*, 'the Workers' Shield', became an organ of the Independent Labour Party (ILP). Keir Hardie's election, as the ILP member for Merthyr, underlined the great divide between Monmouthshire and Glamorgan, and virtually the rest of Wales, except the iron and coal areas of Flint and Denbigh, and the slate quarries around Snowdonia. The great Penrhyn lockout of slate quarrymen, 1900-03, hardened attitudes.

Noah Ablett, Arthur Cook, James Griffiths, Frank Hodges and Arthur Horner were all deeply aroused by the religious revival of 1904-06, led by the young miner, Evan Roberts of Loughor, with its mystic doctrine of salvation by personal experience, not dissimilar to that of such preachers of the Old Dissent as Walter Cradoc and Vavasor Powell. For Griffiths, the revival and the ILP were complementary, and one of Roberts' lieutenants, the minister J. H. Howard, stood as an ILP parliamentary candidate.

However, under Ablett, Roberts' new social vision was soon transformed into a search for revolutionary ideologies. Arthur Cook, Aneurin Bevan and others studied Marxist economics at the London Central Labour College, which, with the Plebs League's tutorial classes and the *Plebs Magazine*, disseminated syndicalist and Marxist ideology. In 1910, 12,000 miners joined the Cambrian Combine Strike. When 9000 marched on Llwynypia, 'rioters were struck down like logs, with broken skulls, and left on the ground'. The *Rhondda Socialist: the BOMB of the Rhondda Workers*, first published in 1911, publicised Sorel on workers' syndicates, and such evangelists of socialism as Tom Mann and the American miners' leader, Big Bill Haywood. *The Miners' Next Step* (1912) advocated pithead democracy and syndicalism. Cook, imprisoned for anti-war activity in 1918, was elected to the SWMF Executive in 1919 and the executive of the Mining Federation of Great Britain in

1921. Cook's obduracy for 'not a penny off the pay, not a second on the day', in the face of the post-war collapse of the Welsh coal industry, led to falling membership and rival unions. Before his death in 1931 he even flirted with Oswald Mosley's New Party.

Markets lost in 1914-18, cheap German and American imports, and the decline in coal-burning vessels brought a severe crisis to Wales's coal industry. Some 80,000 miners were unemployed by February 1921. For the rest, wages had been cut and hours increased. Between 1920 and 1929, mining jobs fell 40 per cent, from 275,000 to 165,000, and by 1930, the South Wales steel and iron industry was in trouble. In 1932, official unemployment was 43 per cent in Wales, as compared to 27 per cent in Britain as a whole. By 1935, almost 15 per cent of children in Rhondda were suffering from malnutrition. In 1937, its general mortality rate was higher than in Stepney, and in 1938, 62 per cent of the unemployed had been without work for three years. Almost half a million people emigrated from Wales between 1921 and 1939.

Arthur Horner collaborated closely with Cook, but their paths diverged. Like Cook, he opposed war in 1914, believing coal owners and government were enemies nearer home than the Kaiser. Fleeing to Ireland, he joined Connolly's Citizens Army 'to vest ownership of Ireland in its people'. After the 1917 Swansea riots, inspired by the Petrograd soviet, he was sentenced to two years' hard labour for sedition. A hunger strike led to his release under the 1913 Cat and Mouse Act. A founder member of the Communist Party, at Maerdy he became 'the Tribune of Little Moscow'. After the Communists broke with Labour in 1927, he stood against Labour at Merthyr in 1931 and 1933. First communist president of the SWMF in 1936, he destroyed the Industrial (Company's) Union. In 1939, ignoring Comintern policy, he welcomed the war against Fascism. After the SWMF joined the

National Union of Mineworkers (NUM), Horner drafted the Miners' Charter with Emanuel Shinwell, and supported Clement Attlee in the 1948-50 wage freeze and devaluation crisis. In 1959 he was elected General Secretary of the NUM.

Attlee's government inaugurated central planning on an unparalleled scale, with nationalisation of the coal, and iron and steel industries, but massive investment and concentration of resources failed to save either industry. By 1981, the number of Welsh miners had fallen from 130,000 to 25,000, a process the 1984 strike failed to halt. By 1990, only 4000 miners remained. Despite concentration of the steel industry at Port Talbot, Ebbw Vale, Shotton and Llanwern, its workforce fell from 63,000 to 19,000 between 1973 and 1983. Extraction was replaced by such new industries as British Nylon Spinners at Pontypool, Hoover at Merthyr, Rover at Cardiff, Ford and Prestcold at Swansea, the Royal Mint at Llantrisant, Firestone and British Celanese at Wrexham, and Hotpoint at Llandudno. Newtown's population rose from 5,500 to 13,000 with new-town status. Industrial collapse left 11,600 acres of derelict land in Glamorgan and Monmouthshire by 1964. After the trauma of the 1966 Aberfan disaster, transformation began, from 1975 under the Welsh Development Agency.

With the triumph of Nonconformity, after 1868 Wales gained a sense of identity such as had not been enjoyed since the Act of Union; but the jingoism which swept the country in 1914 utterly dispelled any desire for Home Rule. The creation by Woodrow Wilson and Lloyd George, at the Versailles settlement, of nation states, not only for Hungarians and Poles but also for the one million Estonians, together with Britain's acceptance of an Irish Free State, encouraged the small group of Welsh nationalists. Founded in 1925 at the Pwllheli National Eisteddfod, the Welsh National Party, *Plaid Gendlaithol Cymru*, later *Plaid Cymru*, the

Welsh Party, stood for Welsh as the only official language and the medium for all education, and the sustaining of Welsh culture. Saunders Lewis, elected President at the 1926 Machynlleth summer school, retained office until 1939. In 1930, the need to press the party's case in English speaking Wales led to the dilution of his 'Welsh-only-Wales' policy to 'recognition and official protection' of the Welsh language, culture and traditions.

The turning point in the party's history came with the burning of buildings on the site of the Royal Air Force's Pen-y-Berth 'bombing school' on the quatercentenary of the Act of Union, and the subsequent trials of Saunders Lewis, Rev Lewis Valentine and D. J. Williams. At the first trial, at Caernarfon in October 1936, the jury could not agree. The trial was transferred to London, to ensure a jury 'without bias', provoking Lloyd George's vitriolic comment, 'This is the first government that has tried Wales at the Old Bailey.' All three refused to give evidence other than in Welsh, but only Williams was allowed to plead, as it could not be proved he spoke English. All three were sentenced to nine months' imprisonment. At Wormwood Scrubs, Lewis listened to his radio play *Buchedd Garmon*, 'Heritage of St Germanus'.

> My country of Wales is a vineyard, given into my keeping
> To be handed down to my children and my children's children
> As an inheritance for all time.
> And look, the pigs are rushing in to despoil it.

On regaining their freedom, *Y Tri Lanc*, 'The Three in the Fiery Furnace', were welcomed with unbounded enthusiasm. Their actions were 'to form an essential strand in the moral and national consciousness of generations of Welsh-speaking intellectuals'. Williams returned to his school, Valentine to his chapel. But

Saunders Lewis was dismissed from his lecturership in Welsh at Swansea, even before the verdict was given.

With gathering clouds of war and its outbreak in 1939, Plaid Cymru's policy was one of neutrality, encouraging conscientious objection. Iorwerth Peate, pacifist, poet and author of *The Welsh House* (1940), 'a silver key to the whole tradition of Welsh buildings', a 'book of moral value', was dismissed from the National Museum. From Waldo Williams, Quaker and nationalist, the war brought forth a number of remarkable poems:

Rose-red sky above the snow
   Where bombed Swansea is alight,
Full of my father and mother I go,
   I walk home in the night.
They are blest beyond hearing,
Peacemakers, children of God.

What is their estate tonight,
   Tonight, with the world ablaze?
Truth is with my father yet,
   Mother with forgiveness stays.
The age will be blest that hears them,
Peacemakers, children of God.

Y Tangnefeddwyr/The Peacemakers

After 1945, Plaid Cymru, under Gwynfor Evans' leadership, opposed conscription and the armed forces' confiscation of land in the Preselis, and at Tregaron, and the drowning of another remote Welsh village at Trawsfynydd, home of the 'shepherd poet', E. H. Evans. Waldo responded to the threat of Preselis' desecration by a 16,000-acre artillery range, which could have encompassed half of Mynachlog-ddu, with:

My Wales, brotherhood's country, my cry, my creed,
Only balm to the world, its mission, its challenge,
Pearl of the infinite hour that time gives as pledge,
Hope of the tedious race on the short winding way.

It was my window, the harvest and the shearing.
I glimpsed order in my palace there.
There's a roar, there's a ravening through the windowless forests.
Keep the wall from the brute, keep the spring clear of filth.

Preselau/Preseli

Of his nature language he writes:

We that perceive her rank, through the mist of her troubles,
Let's raise here the old, indestructible stones.

The 1961 census showed that, since 1891, the number of Welsh speakers had halved, from 54 per cent to 27 per cent. Saunders Lewis, frustrated by the drift and fragmentation of Plaid Cymru, brought the Welsh language issue to the forefront of the nationalist agenda with his 1962 BBC Wales lecture *Tynged yr Iaith*, 'The fate of the language'. 'The conduct of local and central government', he insisted, 'should be made impossible without using Welsh'. His blunt statement, 'the language is more important than self-government', led to the foundation of the Welsh Language Society at Plaid Cymru's 1962 summer school. Its objective was to achieve, as far as possible by non-violent means, equal status for Welsh, and its use by official bodies throughout Wales. In February 1963, members blocked the Trefachan bridge, Aberystwyth. The same year, the Hughes-Parry Committee recommended that 'Equal Validity be adopted as the basic principle', but the failure of the 1967 Welsh Language Act to bind ministers or local authorities led to the 'green paint' campaign on offending road signs. George Thomas, Secretary of State for Wales, apparently ignorant of Belgian, Swiss and South African practice, asserted that bilingual signs would be too expensive, confusing and dangerous; but the Welsh Office gave way after a year's 'truce' was called in 1969.

Plaid Cymru was also successful in these years. Megan Lloyd George, founder of the 'Parliament for Wales Group' in 1950, and an active member of the Welsh Language Society, including its Treweryn Defence Campaign, died in 1966. In the ensuing Carmarthen by-election, Gwynfor Evans' victory over Labour, by more than 1,500 votes, provided Plaid Cymru with an enormous boost. It was a triumph for the Language Society when he took his oath as an MP in Welsh. The party won an even higher proportion of the vote in by-elections. In 1969, more than a thousand supporters of the Society gathered at Cilmeri by the monument of Llywelyn, *Ein Llyw Olaf*, 'our last prince', to protest against the insult of investing an Englishman as Prince of Wales. When Dafydd Iwan, architect student, folk singer and chairman of the Society 1968-71, recorded 'Carlo' and young members wore badges 'No Englishman for Prince of Wales', much of the response was unsympathetic. Deep public shock at the many explosions attributed to *Mudiad Amddiffyn Cymru*, Movement for the Defence of Wales, and the death of the two men apparently planting explosives at Abergele on the investiture morning, may have cost Gwynfor Evans his Carmarthen seat at the 1970 General Election.

In that year, however, when Dafydd Iwan was imprisoned for refusal to pay a fine, 21 Welsh JPs clubbed together to pay it. In court the Language Society adopted Waldo's *Cymru a Cymraeg*:

> And she is danger's daughter. Her path the wind whips . . .
> Till now she has seen her way clearer than prophets.
> She'll be as young as ever, as full of mischief.
>
> *Cymru a Chymraeg/Welsh and Wales*

As has been pointed out, Waldo gave the youthful members of the new second language society 'the joyousness of the apocalyptic struggle, in which passive resistance on behalf of the language was linked to anti-imperialism and the campaign for peace'. The 1971 language census brought disastrous news in respect of the Society's long term aim. Welsh speakers were now a mere 20 per cent of the population. The inauguration in 1982 of the BBC's *Sianel Pedwar Cymru, S4C,* however, marked success in terms of its immediate aims.

By 1964, despite Aneurin Bevan's determined opposition, a Secretary of State for Wales had been appointed, controlling local government, planning, housing and roads. Further devolved government foundered on Labour's belief that it would prejudice the centralised control essential for a planned and integrated economy, and a fear of any further growth in the power of the nationalists. In 1974, Labour polled only 47 per cent of the Welsh vote. At Westminster, dependent on Ulster Unionists, the Scottish Nationalist Party and Plaid Cymru support, it accepted devolution as an item on the agenda. A referendum, mandatory under the 1978 Wales Act, could hardly have been held at a worse time. Having already experienced the complex carve-up of the 1974 Local Government Act and a winter of industrial discontent, over 46 per cent of the electorate voted against, fewer than 12 per cent for devolution, in 1979. This probably reflected what Gwyn Williams described as the 'denial of Welshness to the English-speaking Welsh' and 'a bitter self-exclusion of the English-speaking Welsh from the Welsh people and nation.'

Nevertheless, change came rapidly in the 1990s. The 1993 Welsh Language Act established a board 'to promote and facilitate' Welsh, including grants to the National Eisteddfod, *Urdd*, Welsh nursery schools and the Welsh Books Council. In May 1997, the

Conservatives lost their remaining Welsh MPs, and Ron Davies, as Secretary of State, arranged a referendum on Welsh devolution for September. With a mere 50 per cent turnout, the majority for a Welsh Assembly was 6,721, 0.6 per cent. Its powers included development and funding of the National Health Service, developing education, integrated transport, housing, information and commercial technology, Welsh cultural heritage, and the administration of European Union and local authority funding.

A growing sense of unity and identity may explain the dramatic shift between the 1979 and 1997 results. In a National Labour Force Survey of 2001, only 33 per cent of the population over fifteen regarded themselves as 'not Welsh'; another 7 per cent had a sense of joint identity. Furthermore, the English-speaking majority were increasingly confident that their lives had not been adversely affected by the 1993 Language Act. The 2001 Census shows the first increase in Welsh speakers, from 19 per cent to 21 per cent, largely associated with the schools' language teaching programme. Thirty-nine per cent of ten to fifteen-year-olds claimed ability in speaking, reading and writing Welsh. In 2004, the Patagonian-born Veronica Jones de Kiff was the first person to make her naturalisation oath in Welsh. The future of the Welsh language, however, will be secure only if it returns to the home, and if it continues as a literary force.

We never noticed her. She was like light, she had no colour.
We never noticed. She was the air, took smell
To our nostrils. Was water on our lips, the light of taste.
We were not conscious of her arms around the land.
No danger then. Now it's where larks
Do not climb back to heaven.
Some unwished yesterday has parted them.
This is a nation's winter – the cold heart
Does not know its five joys are lost.

Yr Heniaith/The Old Language

Poetry extracts come from *The Peacemakers* (1997) and *Welsh Verse* (repr 2003), both translated by Tony Conran. The former includes a helpful 'Note on Translations'.

Gazetteer

It is assumed that the majority of readers will be non-Welsh speaking. Place-names have first been given in their most commonly known form, followed by the Welsh. They are located by their unitary authority, whether County, City or County Borough.

ABERAVON / Aberafan, Neath Port Talbot. St Mary's Churchyard. Grave of 'Dic Penderyn', Richard Lewis, hanged after the Merthyr Tydfil rising in 1831. Thousands attended his coffin on its journey from the gallows in Cardiff. In the 1960s, steel workers from Port Talbot paid for the headstone.

ABERDARE / Aberdâr, Rhondda Cynon Taff. Hen-dy-cwrdd, Trecynon. The Old Meeting House where Thomas Evans (1764-1833), otherwise Tomos Glyn Cothi, founder of Wales' first Unitarian chapel, and Radical poet, preached 1811-33, and was buried. When his daughter was interred alongside him, his body was found upside down, indicating that he was buried alive. After that, family physicians were enjoined to administer the needle test to ensure the departure of life.

ABERDARE / Aberdâr, Rhondda Cynon Taff. Victoria Square. A standing stone commemorates James James, composer of the Welsh national anthem, buried in the cemetery. The first Welsh Language Society, Cymdeithas Iaith Gymraeg, was founded at the 1885 Aberdare National Eisteddfod.

ABERFAN, Merthyr Tydfil. Memorial Gardens. At 9.15 a.m. on Friday, 21 October 1966, a 30-foot-high wave of slurry, weighing thousands of tons, swept from Tip 7 down Mynydd Merthyr with a jet-like roar, engulfing part of Pantglas Junior School, cottages and terraced houses. A hundred and forty-four lost their lives, including 115 children and five teachers at the school. Many others were injured. Nobody was found alive. A Tribunal found 'a total abstinence of tipping policy was the basic cause of the disaster' and the National Coal Board at fault. In the cemetery, where about half the victims are buried, is a columned monument.

ABERFFRAW, Isle of Anglesey / Sir Ynys Môn. Anglesey Countryside Centre. Y Tywysogion, 'The Princes' Monument. Aberffraw was the principal court of Rhodri Mawr (844-77), who united Gwynedd with Powys and Seisyllwg, and the later princes of Gwynedd. The blood of Rhodri remained the prime qualification to rule Wales until the death, in 1282, of Llywelyn the Last, lamented as 'the oaken door of Aberffraw'. The site then became a symbol of Welsh identity and independence.

ABERGYNOLWEN, Gwynedd. Pont Ty'n-y-fach. A pink granite obelisk commemorates Mari Jones (1784-1866), who, aged sixteen, walked forty miles barefoot over Cader Idris to Bala to buy a Welsh Bible from Thomas Charles. Having none to spare, he gave her his own. Her example inspired the foundation, in 1804, of the Bible Society, in whose London offices her Bible now rests.

ABERSYCHAN, Torfaen. Secondary School. In the twentieth century there were two main routes into the House of Commons for Labour: the trade union movement and the universities. The quality of the Welsh secondary school system is reflected in the names of some who took the latter route. From the Grammar School at Abersychan, Roy Jenkins departed for Balliol College, Oxford; from Llanelli, Elwyn Jones went to Gonville and Caius and the presidency of the Cambridge Union; from Pontypridd, Brynmor John to University College, London; from Tonypandy, George Thomas to University College, Southampton and ultimately the Speakership; from Lewis School, Pengam, Neil Kinnock went on to University College, Cardiff. Jenkins and Kinnock were miners' sons, but, by 1966, some half, and by 1970, three quarters, of Welsh Labour MPs came from a professional background: able men; but they 'had not been in the oven.'

ABERYSTWYTH, Ceredigion. Trefachan Bridge. The present Welsh Language Society, founded in 1962 in response to Saunders Lewis' historic BBC Wales lecture, *Tynged yr Iaith*, 'The Fate of the Language', demanded equal status for Welsh. In February 1963, demonstrators, mostly students, blocked the bridge over the Rheidol, closing the A47 coast road. Summonses, they insisted, should be in Welsh. Their leader was Edward Millward, who later tutored the Prince of Wales in Welsh, enabling him to turn the tables on the Society's 1969 anti-investiture campaign.

ABERYSTWYTH, Ceredigion. University College. Hugh Owen Building. By his *Open Letter to the Welsh People* on day schools, in 1843, Hugh Owen (1804-81) placed primary education firmly on Wales's political agenda. Instrumental in founding Normal Schools at Bangor (1858) and, for women, at Swansea (1871), he began the struggle for a Welsh university in 1854. Despite government support being withheld, a degree-awarding college was established when the Castle Hotel Aberystwyth, built for £80,000, was acquired for £10,000 in 1872. To meet mounting costs, Owen organised a house-to-house collection throughout Wales for the People's University. Over 100,000 contributions – mostly under two shillings (10 pence) – came from chapels, slate-miners' groups and individuals. After 1962, Aberystwyth students were the force driving the Welsh Language Society.

BALA, Gwynedd. High Street. Statue of Thomas Edward Ellis (1858-99). A graduate of Aberystwyth and New College, Oxford, Ellis came under the influence of Michael Daniel Jones, 'the Parnell of Wales'. A founder of Cymru Fydd, he was elected MP for Merioneth in 1886. His uncle, and M. D. Jones' widowed mother had been among the many tenants evicted by Tory landowner William Watkin Edward Wynne, for voting Liberal in 1859. Ellis 'transformed the injustice of a class into the indictment of a nation', and advocated Welsh Home Rule, rural rent tribunals, land nationalisation and the disestablishment of the Church in Wales. For him, as for Robert Owen, Wales was a land of individualism but also of *cyfraith, cyfnawdd, cymorthau, cymanfaoedd*, social co-operation and associative effort. Ellis was an inspiration for the founders of Plaid Cymru in their struggle for self-government and the preservation of Welsh identity.

BALA, Gwynedd. Tegid Street. Marble statue outside the Calvinistic Methodist Church of Thomas Charles (1755-1814). A student at Llandowror School, Carmarthen Academy and Jesus College, Oxford, he was the leader of the second generation of Welsh Methodists. Long an opponent of separation, he accepted severance from the Church and ordination of ministers only in 1811. Charles placed Welsh Sunday Schools, for children and adults, on sound foundations, with instruction in Welsh, oral and written examinations, and book prizes. He is buried at Llanycil, Bala's original parish church.

BETHESDA, Gwynedd. Streic Fawr Monument. When in November 1900, Lord Penrhyn, owner of the slate quarries, refused to recognise a committee representing slate quarrymen, 2,800 men were locked out. Of these, 1,600 left Bethesda, a thousand of them never to return. The quarries reopened in June 1901, but the *cynffonau*, blacklegs, were given a sharp welcome by the 3000 demonstrators, and driven out of town by the strikers' notices, 'There is no traitor in this house'. Chief Constable Ruck brought 100 infantry and 30 dragoons into Bethesda, and 200 infantry and 60 cavalry into Bangor. All the local councils protested against his unauthorised use of troops. News of the small remote community fighting for its identity against the arrogant wealthy proprietor roused support throughout Britain. But the quarrymen had to return on Penrhyn's terms in November 1903. 'We are still here', the monument records.

BLAINA, Blaenau Gwent. Council Offices: 1935 Riot Memorial. In 1839, Zephaniah Williams, landlord of the Royal Oak, the site of many important Chartist meetings, led his contingent to the Newport rising from nearby Nant-y-glo. Almost a century later, on 21 March

1935, a march of the unemployed, led by Communist Councillor Phil Abrahams, was met in Blaina by a police charge with drawn batons. Two hundred civilians and seven police were injured, and eighteen demonstrators were charged with unlawful assembly and riot. The sentencing of eleven, to from four- to nine-months' imprisonment, 'roused the whole of south Wales': the trial was 'not a criminal proceeding but a political prosecution', denying workers' rights to demonstrate.

BWLCHYRHIW, Carmarthenshire. Chapel site. Baptists and Independents held services here from 1662, first in a cave on nearby Craig yr Eglwys, and then in the smithy. The Independents left in 1688 and the Baptists built the first chapel, in 1717. Their baptismal pool can be seen in the stream. Bwlchyrhiw's narrow valleys inspired one of William Williams' hymns.

CAERNARFON, Gwynedd. Castle. Here, in 1911, the future King Edward VIII was invested as Prince of Wales. James Keir Hardie, Labour MP for Merthyr Tydfil, castigated the ceremony, masterminded by David Lloyd George, where 'every flunkey in Wales, Liberal and Tory alike, grovelled on his hands and knees to take part', a scene to 'make every patriotic Welshman blush with shame'. In this constituency, in 1929, Lewis Valentine, Plaid Cymru's President and one of the Penrhos three, gained 609 gallant votes, fighting Lloyd George, and in 1974, Dafydd Wigley won Plaid's first seat.

CAERNARFON, Gwynedd. Castle Square. Statues of David Lloyd George, local MP, 1890-1945, and of Hugh Owen, father of Welsh university education, born at Langeinwen, across the straits from Caernarfon.

CARDIFF / Caerdydd. Queen Street. Statue of Aneurin Bevan (1897-1960), Member of Parliament for Ebbw Vale from 1929 to his death, unveiled in 1987 by Michael Foot. It was a bad image for a forward-looking city and a waste of public money (£16,000), claimed Cardiff North's Conservative MP.

CARDIFF / Caerdydd. Gorsedd

Gardens. The national monument to David Lloyd George, erstwhile radical, 'funded from the pence of pensioners as well as the pounds of the better off', was unveiled by Harold Macmillan, Conservative Prime Minister, in 1960.

CARDIFF / Caerdydd. Site of the Old County Gaol. A plaque commemorates Dic Penderyn, hanged after the 1831 Merthyr Tidfil riots, now considered innocent. The Labour government has refused a posthumous pardon, but an annual rally continues to be held here on 13 August.

CARDIFF / Caerdydd. Alexandra Gardens. Memorial to the Welsh Volunteers in the Spanish Civil War. A large block of granite with two bronze plaques. On one, an olive tree grows from the International Brigade emblem with a dove of peace in flight. Below are the farewell words of Dolores Ibárruri Gómez, 'La Pasionaria', to the Brigaders in Barcelona, departing for home, October 1938. It bears the Welsh inscription of the poet, pacifist and the Independent Labour Party's 'most eloquent spokesman' in Welsh, T. E. Nicholas, 'That the earth might be free'. Out of the 169 Welsh volunteers who served, 33 lost their lives.

CARMARTHEN / Caerfyrddin, Carmarthenshire. Presbyterian Academy, Priory Street. As Nonconformists were barred from the universities of Oxford and Cambridge, the Presbyterian and Congregational Fund Boards established a Welsh Academy in the 1660s. The Academy was in Priory Street by 1710, when Carmarthen was probably Wales's largest town. The curriculum was broad: not only the Greek Testament, the Hebrew Psalter and Ecclesiastical history, but also astronomy, conic sections, trigonometry, fluxions (Newtonian calculus) and philosophy, including Locke, the Scottish School and Kant. It was the seedbed from which radical Unitarianism played a major role.

CERI GOETRE, nr. Newtown, Powys. 'The house i' the wood' of Vavasor Powell (1617-70). Converted by Walter Cradoc, Powell became a radical itinerant preacher, being frequently arrested. A judge at Radnor

Assizes, finding him not guilty, invited him to dinner. Powell's grace was 'the best he had ever heard', but for Powell, all lawyers were 'thieves and pick-purses'. He trained other itinerant preachers and was an exponent of *cymanfr*, the large open-air preachings that were to feature prominently in Welsh history. Sessions could last seven hours, but thousands flocked great distances to hear him. At the Restoration of King Charles II, he was arrested at Goetre, near the river Mule, where he had 'room for 12 in his beds, 100 in his barns and 1,000 in his heart'. Most of his last ten years he spent in gaol, where he wrote *The Bird in His Cage Chirping*. Powell ended his days in the Fleet, preaching to prisoners and visitors.

CILMERY, Powys. Memorial stone to Llywelyn, Ein Llyw Olaf, 'our last prince'. Llywelyn (1258-82) was killed by the bridge over the Irfon. His head was cut off, taken to King Edward I and later displayed in London. He still holds a unique position in Wales's history as 'sponsor of the first experiment in Welsh statehood', acknowledging his role in building 'the enduring fabric of Welsh nationality'. Over a thousand supporters of the Welsh Language Society gathered at Cilmery to protest against the investiture of an English Prince of Wales.

COED GRWYNE, Monmouthshire. A wooded valley, on the A40 west of Abergavenny, marks the beginning of the Welsh national revival. King Henry I's death in 1135, and a contested succession, provided the opportunity to push back the Anglo-Norman invaders. Their mightiest warlord in western Wales, Richard fitz Gilbert, disregarding caution, rode through the valley in 1136, bidding his fiddler sing and play. Ambushed, all were killed. Owain and Cadwalder of Gwynedd invaded Ceredigion.

CRICCIETH / Cricieth, Gwynedd. Cemetery, the Lloyd George family vault. Megan Lloyd George, a Liberal MP for Anglesey, was the first woman in the 'macho, chauvinistic politics' of Wales. She initiated the first House of Commons 'Welsh Day' and founded the 'Parliament for Wales Group' in

1950, but lost her seat the following year. Joining Labour, she became MP for Carmarthen at a by-election in 1957. She advocated a Welsh Secretary of State, was active in the Welsh Language Society and gave the Sugar Loaf, near Abergavenny, to the National Trust. She died at Brynawelon, her Criccieth home. The vault records 'Lady Megan Lloyd George CH MP 1902-1966'.

CWMAFAN, Neath Port Talbot. Tabernacl Methodist Chapel. Here, aged fourteen, William Abraham, 'Mabon' (1842-1922), became leader of the Band of Hope, conducting the choir at sixteen, and, shortly afterwards, instructing the Sunday School. 'What I am today, I owe to the Sunday School, the Band of Hope and the Eisteddfod.' Failing to find employment in Chile's copper mines, Mabon returned to Wales and worked in the Waunarlwydd coalmine at Gowerton. As trade union conciliator and arbitrator in the Rhondda, he negotiated the 'sliding scale' and later 'Mabon's Monday', a monthly miners' holiday to regulate output. He was MP for Rhondda 1885-1918 and Rhondda West 1918-22, Liberal to 1908, and, thereafter, Labour.

CWMAFAN, Neath Port Talbot. Welsh Miners Museum. Much information and evidence about the Senghenydd and other mining disasters, and of prevalent miners' diseases such as pneumoconiosis.

EFAILWEN, Carmarthenshire. Y Becca on the A478. Here, on 13 May 1839, the first Welsh tollgate was destroyed. An upright stone with a bronze plaque depicts men on horseback attacking the tollgate. 'Through these beginnings the roads of the country became free.'

FERRYSIDE, Carmarthenshire. St Ishmael's Church. Grave of Hugh Williams (1796-1874). A Carmarthen solicitor, who defended the Llanidloes and Rebecca rioters 1839-41, he was traditionally held the 'real Rebecca'. A disciple of Robert Owen, Williams was the leading Welsh Chartist, founding Wales's first Working Men's Association, at Carmarthen. With Richard Cobden, his brother-in-law, he met Abraham Lincoln. His first wife, 25 years his senior, had property at St

Clear. Two months after her death, aged 90, Williams married Elizabeth Anthony, 39 years his junior. He died at Cobden Villas, Ferryside.

FISHGUARD / Abergwaun, Pembrokeshire. West Street. Memorial to D. J. Williams (1885-1970), *Llenor* (literary man), *Cenedlgarwr* (nation lover), also schoolmaster, founder and early leader of Plaid Cymru.

FISHGUARD / Abergwaun, Pembrokeshire. Midland Bank. Monument to Waldo Williams (1904-71), poet, pacifist and nationalist.

GLYNDYFRDWY, Denbighshire. Owain Glyn Dwr's manor. Here, on 16 September 1400, he was proclaimed Prince of Wales, immediately raising the standard of revolt. When Monmouth-born Prince Harry, Henry IV's son, was invested Prince of Wales in 1399, Iolo Goch lamented in a poem addressed to Glyn Dwr, 'where once there were Britons the English now hold sway. What a daily tragedy for Welshmen.' Here, Owain opened his thirteen-year campaign, the last rising against the English, attacking Ruthin, Denbigh, Rhuddlan, Flint, Holt, Oswestry and Welshpool.

GLYNTAFF, Pontypridd, Rhondda Cynon Taff. Wales's first crematorium. William Price of Llantrisant (1800-93), greatest of Welsh eccentrics, aged 84, publicly cremated the body of his infant, Iesu Grist, believing he followed Celtic ritual. An unsuccessful prosecution established the legality of cremation. His own cremation was attended by an estimated 20,000 people. Between Y Garreg Siglo and the crematorium are the two roundhouses built by Price as an entrance to his intended new mansion.

GWERNOGLE, Carmarthenshire. Capel Sant Silyn. A plaque marks the birthplace of Thomas Evans (1764-1833), 'Tomos Glyn Cothi', weaver, Unitarian and poet. Nearby are the ruins of his Unitarian chapel, T Cwrdd Cwm Cothi, the first in Wales. He suffered two years in Carmarthen gaol and two sessions in the pillory for singing in public his Song of Liberty:

And when upon the British shore
The thundering guns of France shall roar,
Vile George shall trembling stand,
Or flee his native land,
With terror and appal;
Dance Carmagnole, dance Carmagnole.

In gaol he wrote his Welsh-English dictionary.

HIRWAUN, Rhondda Cynon Taff. Tower Colliery. Wales's only remaining deep mine, opened in 1864, employed a thousand miners as late as 1962, when nine were killed by a firedamp explosion. In 1994, British Coal decided on closure, but 239 miners organised a buyout, each contributing £8,000 from their redundancy packets. Reopened in January 1995 as Goitre Tower Anthracite, in its first year the pit made a profit of £4 million.

LLANDDOWROR, Carmarthenshire. Church. Tomb of, and monument to, Griffith Jones (1683-1761), a shepherd boy, who after an intense religious experience, determined to become a clergyman. A brilliant preacher, he was 'hated by his jealous clerical brethren'. Denied their pulpits, he preached from tombstones and mountains, attracting thousands. He founded the Circulating School movement, training his teachers at Yr Hen Coleg, The Old College, Llanddowror.

LLANELLTYD, Gwynedd. Churchyard. Tomb of Frances Power Cobbe (1822-1904), social writer, theist, suffragette and anti-vivisectionist. Cobbe struggled for reform of the law concerning divorce and women's rights. She founded the Antivivisection Society in 1875, and published *The Duties of Women* in 1881. Her gravestone is inscribed, 'Bless her for her noble and unselfish life – as a writer on religious and moral subjects and a valiant champion of the oppressed both man and beast.'

LLANGAMARCH WELLS, Powys. Two miles south west lies Cefn-brith, birthplace of John Penry (1563-93), Wales's first puritan martyr. The Welsh clergy 'knowing not what preaching meaneth', he made his Humble Supplication to Parliament in 1587 for a Welsh

Bible and a preaching ministry. Wrongly suspected of authorship of *The Marprelate Tracts,* which excoriated the bishops, Penry was betrayed and charged with 'inciting rebellion'. Hanged, leaving four daughters – Deliverance, Comfort, Safety and Sure Hope – he died for the sovereignty of the individual conscience.

LLANGEINOR, Bridgend. Tynton. Birthplace of Richard Price (1723-91), theologian, actuary, philosopher and 'first citizen of the world'. When his father, a morose and bigoted Calvinist, found him reading a volume by Arian, denying Christ's divinity, he burned the book. Price studied at Carmarthen Academy, wrote on population and life assurance, and co-founded the Unitarian Society. His actuarial tables are still in use. Tyn-ton continues to deteriorate, and his memorial stone was removed to Rollins College, Florida, but railings at the A4093/A4064 junction commemorate Price, in English and French, not in Welsh.

LLANGEITHO, Ceredigion. Statue and burial place of Daniel Rowland (1713-90). Born at Pantybeudy, Nantcwnlle, Rowland became his brother's curate at Llangeitho. Converted by Griffith Jones, he thundered against people's sins, becoming joint Methodist leader with Harris. Llangeitho became the cockpit of Methodism, crowds flocking to hear 'the greatest preacher in Europe'.

LLANGRANNOG, Ceredigion. Urdd Gobaith Cymru, 'League of the Hope of Wales', camp. Founded by Ifan ab Owen Edwards (1895-1970) in 1922, with uniforms, camps, *eisteddfodau* and *mabolgampau*, games, by 1934, Urdd had 50,000 members. A permanent camp was established in 1932 at Llangrannog, now a residential activity centre for 350 children.

LLANGWM UCHAF, Monmouthshire. Church. Walter Cradoc (c1610-59), father of Welsh independency and preacher, with a 'wonderful faculty of coming down and bringing with him the things of God to the meanest of his Auditors', was vicar here, 1655-59. An approver under the Propagation of the Gospel Act, he supported Cromwell's assumption of the

Protectorship. All trace of his tomb in the chancel has gone, but a wall plaque does commemorate his son-in-law Richard Creed, Admiral Blake's secretary.

LLANIDLOES, Powys. Trewythen Arms Inn. A strong Dissenting town, and, with a depressed textile industry in the 1830s, it became a Chartist centre in April/May 1839, witnessing the collapse of the Chartist policy of change by peaceful means. Magistrates, fearing trouble, lodged three metropolitan and two local policemen here, and swore in special constables. The following morning, the crowd forced its way into the Trewythen Arms, released three passers-by who had been arrested, and dragged the Mayor and two policemen out from under a bed. Chartists took over the town. Five days later the twelfth regiment from Ireland, having marched over Plynlymon, with foot soldiers from Brecon, Montgomeryshire and South Shropshire Yeomanry Cavalry, came to 'restore order'. Thirty-two people were arrested. Thomas Powell, who had pacified the crowd and released the police, was jailed for a year, and a Llanidloes man transported for fifteen years. The arrest of the popular Chartist leader Henry Vincent spread the revolt to the South Wales mining districts.

LLANTRISANT, Monmouthshire. Bull Ring. Monument to William Price (1800-93), doctor, Chartist and eccentric. Noted for his druidic dress – white tunic, scarlet waistcoat and green trousers with a fox's pelt on his head – Price was a qualified surgeon, vegetarian, anti-vivisectionist and advocate of herbal medicine, who rejected vaccination and denied treatment to smokers. A Chartist leader, after the Newport Rising he fled to Paris, where he met Heine. He refused nomination as Chartist candidate for Merthyr Tydfil in 1841. An exponent of republicanism, co-operatives, miners' organisations, and of free love, his permanent legacy was the right to cremate.

LLANUWCHLLYN, Gwynedd. Statues of Owen Morgan Edwards (1858-1920) and Ifan ab Owen Edwards, father and son. O. M. attended Llanuwchllyn National School; 'but for Welsh Sunday School I should be illiterate today'. Fellow of Lincoln College, Oxford, his contribution to the revival of Welsh as a literary language was outstanding. As a founder of *Cymru Fydd* ('Wales of the Future') he believed 'all is sacred – every hill and valley. Our country . . . is not a dead grave. Every hill has its history, every neighbourhood its romance . . . Efforts of our fathers have consecrated every field. The country's muse has sanctified every mountain.' From 1907, as Chief Inspector of Welsh schools, O. M. revolutionised Welsh language teaching.

LLANUWCHLLYN, Gwynedd. Near Bryngwyn. Old Chapel. The Manse and graveyard are birth and burial places of Michael Daniel Jones (1822-98), 'the Parnell of Wales'. He trained for the ministry at Carmarthen, but emigrated to the United States and founded the Brython Association to assist Welsh immigrants in Ohio and Pennsylvania. Returning to Wales in 1850, he succeeded his father as Principal of Bala Independent College. A stout opponent of English landlordism and capitalism, he established Y Wladfa as an independent Welsh homeland in Patagonia in 1865. 'There is no consistency,' he said, 'in advocating personal liberty while opposing liberty for nations.' The first official British visit to Y Wladfa was made by the Welsh Assembly's Minister for Culture and Language in 2004.

LLANVACHES / Lanfaches, Newport. St Dyfrig's and Tabernacle Reform Churches. For 40 years, William Wroth (c1576-1641), Rector of St Dyfrig's, devoted himself to converting his folk from 'their sinful courses'. Accused of 'leading away many simple people', Wroth appeared before Laud's Court of High Commission. In 1639, he founded the first 'gathered church' in Wales, in 'the New England Way', assisted by Cradoc, Powell and Llwyd. Wroth is commemorated as 'apostle of Wales' on the Memorial Hall, his 'gathered church' on the 1924 chapel.

LLANWERN, Monmouthshire. St Mary's Church. Memorial to Margaret Haig Thomas, Viscountess Rhondda (1888-

1958), daughter of D. A. Thomas, head of the Cambrian (mine owners') Combine, and minister in Lloyd George's wartime government. A militant suffragette, Margaret organised the movement's first meeting in Newport. Imprisoned for attempting to bomb a letter-box, she was released after five days' hunger strike. As she returned on the *Lusitania* from an official trip to the United States with her father, the boat was torpedoed and she spent three hours in a lifejacket before being rescued. In 1917, she founded the Women's Royal Air Force. She inherited her father's business interests and Llanwern Park in 1918, becoming Viscountess Rhondda, but was excluded from the House of Lords. George Bernard Shaw commented that she would have shown up 'the business ignorance and general imbecility of the male sex as never before'. Margaret devoted the rest of her life and £250,000 to *Time and Tide*, a magazine with a strong women's interest ('Time and tide wait for no man.'), to which Shaw, Virginia Woolf, D. H. Lawrence and Rebecca West were among the contributors.

LLANYSTUMDWY, Gwynedd. Lloyd George Museum. Born in Manchester, David (1863-1945) was brought up here from the age of four. Following his request, his grave, above the Dwyfor valley, is marked by a simple boulder; but two lordly sets of wrought-iron gates, one surmounted by flambeaux and drapery, the other by elephants, stand at the entrance to the museum and grave.

LLYN CELYN, Ceredigion. Reservoir and Tryweryn Dam. When, in 1957, the City of Liverpool proposed a Bill for a reservoir that would drown the valley, with all its farms, cottages, chapel, school and shop, every Welsh MP, including the anti-nationalist Ness Edwards, voted against the destruction of an ancient Welsh community of some 70 people. This was the land of the *penillion telyn*, stanzas sung to the harp reflecting rural life, whose interests were the weather and the seasons, festivals and fairs, love and courting, satire and humour, 'passionate yearnings and heartfelt sadness'. Feeling was so strong that Henry Brooke, the minister responsible for the decision to support the scheme, was the only person in that office not to be invited to the National Eisteddfod. As a gesture of atonement, Liverpool built a chapel, memorial gardens and a cemetery, now sadly neglected, incorporating masonry from Celyn's drowned chapel. A nearby tablet records Hafod Fadog Farm, meeting place of Celyn's Quakers, some of whom emigrated to Pennsylvania, and their burial ground.

LLWYNRHYDOWEN, Dyfedd. Chapels. Wales's first Arminian chapel was built on the crossroads site by Jenkin Jones (c1700-42), the 'apostle of Arminianism' and a student of Carmarthen Academy. His rejection of predestination was warmly received. By 1742, the area had become the Black Spot of Calvinist demonology, with six other Arminian chapels in the Teifi valley. The 'Old Chapel' replaced Jones's chapel. Another Carmarthen student, William Thomas, 'Gwilym Marles', (1834-79), a Glasgow graduate, was Unitarian minister 1860-79. Influenced by the American theologian and social reformer, Theodore Parker Thomas campaigned enthusiastically for the Liberals in the hotly contested 1868 Cardiganshire election, where a Vaughan of Trawsgoed was defeated. Many tenant farmers who failed to vote for their landlords were evicted. The Alltyrodin Estate withdrew the Chapel's 99-year lease on the pretext that it was used 'other than for the worship of God'. The Chapel thus joined some two hundred tenants who were evicted for voting Liberal. Nationwide contributions paid for the New Chapel, opened 1879, half a mile to the west, where William Thomas is buried.

MACHYNLLETH, Powys. Senedd-dy-Owain Glyn Dwr (Owain Glyn Dwr's Parliament House). The present sixteenth-century building is on the site where, in 1404, Owain Glyn Dwr, following the example of Hywel Dda, called four men from each commote to the *Senedd*. Here, in 1926, was held Plaid Cymru's first summer school, when Saunders Lewis was elected President.

MAERDY, Rhondda Cynon Taff. The Park. A green and black, laden coal dram commemorates the closure of the last of Rhondda's 53 major collieries. Maerdy was dubbed 'Little Moscow' for the militant socialism of its miners. Noel Ablett (1883-1935), a member of the executive council from 1911, persuaded the South Wales Miners' Federation to transfer its scholarships from Ruskin College, Oxford to the Central Labour College, London. After the failure of the 1911 miners' strike, Ablett contributed to *The Miners' Next Step*, advocating pithead democracy and syndicalism. When the Rhondda became the cockpit of the class war in 1917, Maerdy's pits flew the Red Flag. On Ablett's initiative, Arthur Horner (1894-1968) was elected checkweighman at Maerdy. A founder of the Communist Party, Horner became the 'Tribune of Little Moscow'. Maerdy's miners were the last to return to work after the 1926 General Strike. In 1927, Horner led Wales's first hunger march, from Maerdy. Such were the economic conditions here, that average house prices fell from £350 in 1920 to £50 in 1935. Of the Rhondda's 25 pits in 1947, only Maerdy, reconstructed in the early 1950s, remained in 1969. There was not one Maerdy blackleg during the 1984-85 Miners' strike, but the pit was closed in 1990.

MERTHYR TYDFIL / Tudful. Central Library. Plaque to Richard Lewis. In 1977, Len Murray, General Secretary of the Trades Union Congress, unveiled a memorial plaque to Richard Lewis, reading

> To Dic Penderyn, born 1808 at Aberavon
> Hanged 13 August 1831 at Cardiff
> Martyr of the Welsh Working Class

Unitarian democrats controlled Wales's most populous town by 1831 when, on 3 June, a crowd of some ten thousand confronted 80 Argyll and Sutherland Highlanders outside the Castle Hotel, demolished in the 1960s. The Red Flag was raised for the first time in Britain, but the outcome was 'the most ferocious and bloody event in British industrial history'. More civilians were killed here than at Peterloo.

MERTHYR TYDFIL / Tudful. Civic Centre, bust of James Keir Hardie (1856-1915). Merthyr remained radical throughout the nineteenth century. In 1868, Henry Richard, 'MP for Wales', represented its miners and Nonconformists. In 1900, Keir Hardie, founder of the Independent Labour Party, became Wales's first Labour MP. Advocate of Welsh Home Rule, he retained Merthyr until his death. His bust, outside the Town Hall, was removed to the Civic Centre when the Town Hall was sold for redevelopment – an ironic fate for the man who held that the Welsh, 'like all Celts, are socialist by instinct'.

MONMOUTH / Trefynwy, Monmouthshire. Shire Hall Courtroom. Here, in November 1839, the Chartists John Frost, Zephaniah Williams and William Jones, leaders of the Newport Rising, heard their sentence: to be 'drawn on a hurdle to the place of execution . . . hanged by the neck until dead; afterwards the head of each to be severed from its body, and the body, divided into four quarters, disposed of as Her Majesty thinks fit'.

MONMOUTH / Trefynwy, Monmouthshire. County Gaol, Hereford Road. Frost, Williams and Jones were housed here and heard gallows being hammered together above their heads. Queen and Cabinet had unanimously supported the sentence but the Lord Chief Justice raising a technicality at the last minute, the sentence was commuted to transportation. The Chartist journal, *Western Vindicator*, was edited 'by Henry Vincent, now resident in Monmouth Gaol'. And here William Edwards penned his *Address to the People*. The Gatehouse is all that is left of the gaol.

MYNACHLOG-DDU, Pembrokeshire. Monument to Waldo Williams (1904-71), pacifist, nationalist and 'most astonishingly original' Welsh language poet of the twentieth century. Part mystic, part saint, Waldo was born in Haverfordwest, only learning Welsh after his move to Mynachlogddu, under Preseli's brow, at the age of seven. Wales, its land and language were his spur. He started writing Welsh poetry as a student of English Romanticism at Aberystwyth. During the Second World War, he was head of Puncheston (Casmael) Primary School.

I'll walk once more on Weun Cas' Mael –
And bushes of gorse tell the tale,
Sick withered winter without fail
 Is losing the day.
'Our kindly sky will be blue in a while,'
 Flaming, they say.

The horrors of the atomic bomb caused him great anguish, and he suffered gaol twice, for refusing to pay taxes during the Korean War.

NARBERTH / Arberth, Pembrokeshire. Former workhouse, Tenby Road. Narberth Poor Law Union was founded in 1837 to serve the town and 48 other parishes and townships. In 1839, crowds tried to burn the yet unfinished workhouse. It was threatened with a second attack in 1843 if the inmates' food was not improved. The workhouse has been converted into holiday accommodation as part of Allensbank Holiday Park.

NEWPORT / Casnewydd. Westgate Hotel, rebuilt 1884-46. At Nant-y-glo, in October 1839, the Chartist leaders, former Newport mayor John Frost, Zephaniah Williams and William Jones, debated freeing Henry Vincent from Monmouth Gaol, even creating a 'Silurian Republic'. In vain, Frost counselled calm. Later he informed Dr William Price, who promised seven cannons, of a vast march on Newport on 4 November. Frost led the Blackwood contingent, and Williams that from Ebbw Vale. Despite the absence of Jones and most of his Pontypool men, some five thousand Chartists marched on the hotel, where the Mayor of Newport had stationed 30 soldiers. After a fusillade killed 20, the demonstrators fled. Frost, Williams and Jones were arrested and dispatched to Monmouth Gaol. In 1991, a three-part bronze by Christopher Kelly, representing 'Apotheosis', 'Still Life' and 'Ideal City', was unveiled outside the hotel to mark the sesquicentennial of the rising.

NEWPORT / Casnewydd. John Frost Square. Kenneth Budd's lively Chartist Mosaic, 1978, colourfully portrays the soldiers' murderous fire from the Westgate Hotel on the Chartists, with their banners and motley collection of weapons. Their banners proclaim their aims: 'Secret Ballot'; 'A Vote for

All Men over 21'; 'A Wage for Members of Parliament'; 'Elections to Parliament Every Year'; 'Equal Electoral Districts'; 'Abolish Property Qualifications for Members of Parliament'.

NEWTOWN / Y Drenewydd, Powys. Memorial Museum, birthplace of Robert Owen (1771-1858), pioneer of factory reform, and father of co-operation and nursery schools. Son of a saddler and ironmonger, he left Newtown at the age of ten to serve as a draper's apprentice in Manchester. Founder of New Lanark and author of *A New View of Society*, Owen returned to Newtown in 1858 and died here on 17 November.

NEWTOWN / Y Drenewydd, Powys. Robert Owen's tomb. This lies by the churchyard wall of the abandoned thirteenth-century St Mary's parish church. It is now surrounded by remarkable Art Nouveau railings, with a relief of workers receiving justice at Owen's hand, inscribed 'Each for All', and a full-face portrait of him above.

NEWTOWN / Y Drenewydd, Powys. The Free Library, Broad Street. A Robert Owen wing was added in 1903 by the Co-operative Union.

NEWTOWN / Y Drenewydd, Powys. Memorial to Thomas Powell (1802-62) in St Mary's churchyard. A Chartist 'moral force' leader, disciple of Robert Owen and friend of Henry Hetherington, Powell was rewarded for restoring order during the Llanidloes riot of 1839 by imprisonment.

NEWTOWN / Y Drenewydd, Powys. Short Bridge Street. Statue of Robert Owen, erected in 1956 by the Co-operative movement.

PANTYCELYN, Carmarthenshire. Home of William Williams (1717-91), most gifted of Welsh hymn writers, 'major author and profound thinker'. Converted by Howel Harris, he was one of early Methodism's three leaders. Pantycelyn is still in the family's hands.

PENARTH, Vale of Glamorgan. Cemetery. Tomb of Saunders Lewis (1893-1985), who spent his last 28 years in Penarth. Scholar and creative writer, he contributed more than anyone to the preservation of Welsh as a living language.

PENBOYR, Carmarthenshire. Pant-yr-efel, between Cwmhiraeth and Felindre. A footbridge over a stream leads you up a track to the birthplace of Griffith Jones (1683-1761), rector of Llanddowror, founder of the Welsh Circulating Schools and arguably the 'greatest Welshman of the eighteenth century'.

PENMACHNO, Conwy. Ty Mawr, birthplace of William Morgan (c1544-1604), first translator of the complete Bible into Welsh. His 1588 Bible combines 'the vigour and purity of the medieval classics with a new flexibility and wider range of expression.' This is the 'beginnings of the literature of modern Wales', a literary canon when, after the Act of Union, the gentry were becoming Anglicised, the bards silent and Welsh as a written language was in peril. In Puritan and Nonconformist hands, Morgan's Bible became a powerful weapon in the challenge to the Anglican church in Wales, a challenge ultimately leading to disestablishment. Now National Trust property, Ty Mawr, in the remote Wybrnant valley, houses a collection of Welsh Bibles.

PENRHOS, Gwynedd. Illustrated metal plaque commemorating Penyberth. Construction of a Royal Air Force bombing school was moved to Penrhos after two English sites were rejected on environmental grounds. All protest at this further encroachment on traditional Welsh society proving fruitless, in 1936, Saunders Lewis, Lewis Valentine and D. J. Williams set fire to the premises and surrendered to the police. Their trial was removed from Caernarfon to the Old Bailey, London, to ensure a jury 'without bias', and provoked Lloyd George's comment, 'This is the first government that has tried Wales at the Old Bailey.' Refusing to give evidence other than in Welsh, the three were sentenced to nine months' imprisonment. Waldo Williams bemoaned, 'Are three the bloody Blaid?' but their impact on Welsh-speaking intellectuals was profound.

PENRHYNDEUDRAETH, Gwynedd. Plas Penrhyn. Home

of Bertrand Russell (1872-1970). Born in Wales, at Trellech, he spent his last ten years at Penrhyndeudraeth, above Portmeirion, with the Glaslyn estuary and Snowdonian mountains to the north, and Morfa, Harlech and the castle to the south. From here, Russell continued his vigorous political career. He publicly destroyed his Labour Party membership card. A founder of the Campaign for Nuclear Disarmament, at the age of 89 he was imprisoned for his activities with the Committee of one hundred. The only Welshman to be awarded the Nobel Prize for Literature, Russell died here. His body was taken, in a plain coffin, to Colwyn Crematorium, and his ashes were scattered over the bay.

PONTYPRIDD, Rhondda Cynon Taff. The Rocking Stone, Y Garreg Siglo. The earliest evolutionary example of a Gorsedd circle symbolises the relationship between bardic and Labour movements. The Bronze-Age mound, encircled by a bank, ditch and stones, became a focal point for Iolo Morgannwg's ceremonies in about 1800. Excavated in 1830, it was later extended, including the bardic serpent. Chartists assembled here, and in 1893 over ten thousand heard Morgan Thomas denounce the demoralising impact of the Sliding Scale and demand a 20 per cent rise. Not hussars, dragoons or infantry, but ineffective organisation killed the strike, yet the meeting heralded a movement that led to the South Wales Miners' Federation.

PONTYPRIDD, Rhondda Cynon Taff. Miners' Memorial. A large iron sheave and small winding house enclosed by a brick wall, erected by the South Wales Area Executive of the National Union of Mineworkers, commemorating the men, women and children killed or injured in the South Wales coalmines, was unveiled by Neil Kinnock in 1991.

PONTYPRIDD, Rhondda Cynon Taff. Ynysangharad Park. Memorial commemorating Evan and James James, composers of the Welsh National Anthem. Evan (1809-78) wrote 'Hen Wlad fy Nhadau' at his Mill Street home; his son, James (1832-1902) composed the music.

PRESTATYN, Denbighshire. 10 North Avenue. Birthplace of John Prescott (1938-), National Union of Seamen leader, one of the 'tightly-knit group of politically motivated men' behind the seamen's strike of 1966 who were denounced by the then Labour Prime Minister, Harold Wilson. MP for a Hull constituency, Prescott became Deputy Prime Minister in 1997.

PWLLHELI, Gwynedd. Maesgwyn Temperance Hotel. Here Plaid Cymru was founded in August 1925, a merging of The Welsh Movement, Y Mudiad Cymreig, mostly cosmopolitan intellectuals, some influenced by *Action Française*, and the Welsh Home Rule Army, Byddin Ymreolwyr Cymru, predominantly Nonconformist Home Rulers, many pacifists. The executive included the Penrhos three. Plaid's concern was primarily cultural rather than political, the defence of the Welsh language. At Senedd-dy-Owain Glyn Dwr, Machynlleth, in 1926, Saunders Lewis was elected president, holding office until 1939.

RHYDCYMERAU, Carmarthenshire. Chapel. Grave of David John Williams (1885-1970), writer, schoolmaster and founder and early leader of Plaid Cymru, one of the Penrhos three. Born at Penrhiw-fawr, Rhydcymerau, Williams worked for five years in the mines before going to University College, Aberystwyth, and on to Jesus College, Cambridge. His autobiographical *The Old Farmhouse*, translated with EEC support by his friend Waldo Williams, and *Twenty-Six Years Old* reveal his detestation of English desecration – the army and Air Force's weapons ranges, and the Forestry Commission's vast, dead lands of conifers.

ST ASAPH'S, Denbighshire. Cathedral. The Bible Translators' Memorial carries statues of William Morgan, his predecessors and collaborators.

ST FAGANS, Cardiff. Folk Museum, Maestir Schoolhouse. The Commission on Education in Wales's 1847 Blue books pronounced Welsh as a 'manifold barrier to the people's moral progress and commercial prosperity', and imposed a wholly English educational system.

Children who spoke Welsh were obliged to wear a placard, 'Welsh Not'. O. M. Edwards described this 'damnable system . . . Every day it found its way around my neck. I spoke one language, the mistress another – I learned nothing.' This, with the acid comments on Welsh society, united Old and New Dissent to form a Welsh-speaking Nonconformity that was to dominate Welsh politics for most of the next two centuries. The museum illustrates much of this link between language and Nonconformity, both religious and political.

SENGHENYDD, Caerphilly. Memorial to Britain's worst coal mining disaster, 1913. In 1901, eighteen months after production began at the Universal Pit, explosions had killed 81 men and boys. Consequent safety recommendations were not implemented. In 1913, when miners were working in more confined spaces, another explosion occurred: 439 miners, including 63 teenagers, died. Charges against the owners were dropped and the manager was fined just £24. An appeal resulted in the owners being fined £10 with five guineas costs. The memorial was erected only in 1981.

SNOWDON, Gwynedd. The Gladstone Rock. In 1892, the octogenarian W. E. Gladstone opened Watkins Path to the summit and addressed thousands on 'Justice for Wales'. Relying on his personal following, Welsh Liberals had fought the 1886 election on the 'Gladstone ticket'. Next year, 60 trains took fifty thousand people to Swansea to hear him and to take part in a march past that took over four hours. For Kenneth Morgan, Gladstone raised Wales's people 'from relative obscurity into a continuity and tradition of their own.'

SYCHARTH, Powys. Five miles west-south-west of Oswestry, Glyn Dwr's principal manor, linked by Fford Owain Glyn Dwr across the Berwyns to Glyndyfrdwy, and immortalised in Iolo Goch's highly descriptive poem. Recent work confirms much of his praise: a circle of water within an embankment; court with bridge and gateway; hall on motte, with lofts where the bards slept; nine storehouses 'stocked as full as [London's] Cheapside'; lawns for peacocks, heronry, orchard, vineyard, dovecote; fishponds stocked with pike and salmon. All this Prince Harry destroyed in 1403.

TALGARTH, Powys. St Gwendoline's. Burial place of Howel Harris, Methodist leader and later advocate of the communal life. Here, before the altar, he experienced conversion in 1735. From his father's still legible tombstone in the graveyard, Harris held open-air prayer meetings.

TONYPANDY, Rhondda Cynon Taff. Pandy Square and Llwynypia. Sites of the most extensive riots after the Merthyr and Newport Risings. In 1910, twelve thousand Cambrian miners were on strike; all pits closed except Llwynypia, defended by Chief Constable Lindsay with his '99'. Their violent baton charges dispersed the strikers attacking its power station. It took 50 Cardiff constables an hour to clear Pandy Square where they reassembled. Lindsay called for military support, but Home Secretary Winston Churchill halted the train at Swindon. Next afternoon, nine thousand men marched on Llwynypia. Rioters, struck down 'like logs', were left on the ground. Samuel Rays was killed. *The Times* likened the scene to the streets of Odessa and Sebastopol in the winter of 1904, but Churchill established Home Office control over the police in industrial disputes. The strike continued till September 1911.

TREDEGAR, Blaenau Gwent. The Aneurin Bevan Trail. Cardiff has Bevan's statue, but Tredegar was his home. In the 2005 General Election, Blaenau Gwent showed its mettle, rejecting the Labour Party headquarters' imposed woman candidate with a mere 32.3 per cent of the vote. Peter Law, educated at Nant-y-glo, an Open University graduate and expelled after 40 years as a member of the Labour Party, won the seat as an Independent.

TREDEGAR, Blaenau Gwent. Maes-y-Berwin Residential Home, Charles Street. The site of number 32, birthplace of Aneurin Bevan. The family later moved to number 7, now a wilderness.

TREDEGAR, Blaenau Gwent. 2 Queen Street. Home of Aneurin Bevan's mother. Formerly part of the workhouse, it became Nye's constituency base.

TREDEGAR, Blaenau Gwent. Masonic Hall. Nye Bevan's youthful debating society used to meet here.

TREDEGAR, Blaenau Gwent. The Circle. The clock tower, a gigantic cast-iron Tuscan column of 1858, dedicated to the Duke of Wellington, 'Our Hero', is now surrounded by four roundels in tribute to Aneurin Bevan. 'I never used to regard myself so much as a politician as a projectile discharged from the Welsh valleys. When I listen to the cacophony of harsh voices trying to intimidate I close my eyes and listen to the silent voices of the poor.' His wife, Jennie Lee, said that 'going round with Nye was like surf-riding on the Niagara Falls – at times you had to be agile or you would be drowned in the sparkling tireless movement and ebullience.'

TREDEGAR, Blaenau Gwent. 10 Morgan Street. A plaque proclaims, 'Michael Foot, Labour MP Ebbw Vale 1960-83, Blaenau Gwent 1983-92, lived here.' Michael Foot was Bevan's friend and biographer, as well as his constituency successor.

TREDEGAR, Blaenau Gwent. LCT Laboratories, between Sirhowy and Bryn Serth roundabouts. Formerly, Sirhowy Elementary School, attended by Aneurin Bevan.

TREDEGAR, Blaenau Gwent. The Bevan Memorial Stones. This is where Bevan's ashes were scattered, and later those of his widow, Jennie Lee. Devised by Michael Foot and others, and unveiled by Foot in 1972, they are reminiscent of the Bronze Age and bardic circle above Pontypridd. The largest stone represents Nye, the others his constituency: Ebbw Vale, Tredegar and Rhymney. As architect of the National Health Service, Bevan failed to negotiate a unified system: boards were responsible for hospitals; medical councils for doctors and local authorities for caring services. But universal access to the best care, free at the point of delivery, continues. Although Bevan was a non-believer, the scattering was marked by a sermon by Donald Soper, the Methodist socialist pacifist. For many, as for John Davies, after Nye Bevan there has been 'no charismatic figure in the Labour Party in Wales – nor in Britain generally.'

TREFECA, Powys. Coleg Trefeca and Museum. Here, in 1752, Howel Harris, influenced by the Moravians of Fulneck, brought together his extended family. His vast energy had profoundly influenced Welsh Methodism. Joint leader with Daniel Rowland, Harris was expelled in 1750, primarily for his relationship with Madam Griffiths rather than on theological grounds. On her death in 1752, he gave away his horse and founded Coleg Trefeca. One hundred men, women and children, with others on neighbouring farms, shared their lives, holding property in common. Quarrying stone and felling trees, they rebuilt Trefecca in the Strawberry Hill Gothic style. Self-sufficient in agriculture and building works, including masonry, plastering, joinery, carpentry and even making furniture and clocks, members of the community produced flax and wool for their clothing and built a printing press, producing 50 books in as many years. This communal life of the *Teulu*, family, is illustrated in the museum.

TREGARON, Ceredigion. Statue of Henry Richard (1812-88), pacifist and propagandist. Born at Prospect House, he was ordained Congregational Minister in 1835. He became secretary of the Peace Society in 1848, arguing for the settlement of international disputes by arbitration. Supported by the 'Nonconformist Election Committee' and the mining community, Richard triumphed at Merthyr Tydfil in 1868. One of the earliest campaigners for a Welsh education system, the Welsh language, the resolution of the land question and the disestablishment of the Anglican church, he rapidly became 'MP for Wales' and had a profound influence on Gladstone. This opened a new phase in parliamentary politics.

TREHAFOD, Rhondda Cynon Taff. Lewis Merthyr Colliery. Arthur Cook (1883-1931), originally from Somerset, entered this colliery aged nineteen. Like Noah Ablett and Arthur Horner he was aroused by the great religious revival of 1904-06, but soon moved to revolutionary ideologies, being a contributor to *The Miners' Next Step*. Imprisoned in 1918 for anti-war activity, like Arthur Horner, Cook was a founding member of the Communist Party as 'a humble follower of Lenin', but he resigned in 1921. He joined the executive of the Miners' Federation of Great Britain that year, becoming National Secretary in 1924, when one hundred thousand miners were unemployed, thirty thousand in South Wales. His was the cry, 'Not a minute on the day, not a penny off the pay.' In Moscow, in 1926, he was welcomed enthusiastically, becoming an honorary member of the City Soviet and honorary student of the Mining Academy. He was stripped of both honours in 1929. Shortly before his death, he flirted briefly with Oswald Mosley's New Party. Lewis Merthyr, closed in 1983, is now the Rhondda Heritage Park.

TRELLECH, Rhondda Cynon Taff. Cleddon Hall. Formerly Ravenscroft, the birthplace of Bertrand Russell (1872-1970), philosopher, mathematician, educationalist, advocate of free love, and political activist. He was the third child of Lord Amberley, eldest son of the former Prime Minister, Lord John Russell. John Stuart Mill was his godfather. In 1874 his mother and sister both died of diphtheria. Aged three, he was taken to his father's deathbed and committed to the austere care of his grandmother at Richmond Lodge, Queen Victoria's gift to his grandfather. 'To prevent scandal', a veil was drawn over his mother's relationship with the family tutor, and thus his Ravenscroft years. His grandmother's puritanical tutelage, intended to prepare the child to follow in his grandfather's footsteps and maintain the sacred work of Reform, produced instead the 'ardent young communist sent down from Oxford for atheism . . . and preaching free love', who, later, was to lose his Trinity College, Cambridge lecturership. Russell was imprisoned in 1918, and again at the age of 89 – after direct action in protest against Britain's nuclear weapons policy.

WHITLAND, Carmarthenshire. Canolfan Hywel Dda. In 914, Hywel Dda, 'the Good', grandson of Rhodri Mawr, united Wales, except Morgannwg and Gwent. From each cantref, he summoned six men to his white house on the Taff, Ty Gwyn ar Daf. Here they codified their customs under six headings: king and court, society and status, crime and tort, women, contract, and property, represented at Whitland by six gardens. Land was to be divided equally between sons, *cyfran*. After seven years a wife could claim half the family property, and responsibility for children was shared. There was no 'chasm between legitimate and illegitimate children'.

WREXHAM. Rhos Ddu Dissenters Burial Ground. Monument to Morgan Llwyd (1619-59). As mystic, and forerunner of the Quakers, he held that God spoke to every man and all he had to do was to listen and obey. As a writer, 'at its best, his prose is unequalled in Welsh'. Llwyd was converted by Cradoc while at Wrexham Grammar School. In 1642, with Cradoc and Powell, he fled from Llanfaches to London, where they were regarded the 'most fearless asserters of civil and religious liberty'. As Chaplain to the Parliamentary Army, he attacked tithes, 'the landed Titan' and 'the shameless depredations of lawyers'. In 1656, he settled at Bryn-y-ffynnon, the Wrexham house of Colonel John Jones, Cromwell's regicide brother-in-law, where he became convinced of the imminence of Christ's personal reign in accordance with the seventh chapter of the Book of Daniel and the twentieth chapter of Revelations. In 1661 a cavalier, 'in great rage and malice', thrust his sword as far as it would go into Llwyd's grave. His tomb is lost, but in 1912 Dame Margaret Lloyd George unveiled a monument to Morgan Llwyd, which today guards a sad little park.

Heysham
Middleton
Blackpool
Newchurch-in-Pendle
Burnley
Preston
Blackburn
Haslingden
Blackstone Edge
Ramsbottom
Rochdale
Bolton
Wigan
Bury
Westhoughton
Oldham
Manchester
Liverpool
Salford
Ashton-Under-Lyne
Droylsden
Stalybridge
Birkenhead
Raby Mere
Bucklow Hill

7.

Lancashire and Cheshire

John Belchem

The banners and symbols of the Labour movement are as integral to 'Lowryscape' images of the North as are the bracing moors, plain-speaking, commonsensical down-to-earth folk and hard, honest graft. Since the Industrial Revolution, when the 'machinofacture' of the Lancashire cotton industry set the pace, the North West has been at the forefront of Radical and Labour movements. Until the late nineteenth century, the initiative lay in the provinces, not in the metropolis, with industrial Lancashire leading the way, the advance guard of Labour and the Left. During the 'Luddite' disturbances in the middle of the Napoleonic wars, when protesters in other textile regions (the East Midlands hosiery districts, the Yorkshire wool and worsted areas) persisted with the old non-political backward-looking ways and means, Lancashire workers were to add a new political dimension. Alongside machine-breaking and other time-honoured means of 'collective bargaining by riot', which sought to recall local authorities and employers to uphold the hallowed (and doubtless mythologised) customs of the past (a 'moral economy' of fair prices, just wages, honest measures and decent, unadulterated quality), Lancashire Luddites demanded parliamentary reform and an end to the hated 'war system'. This 'politicisation of discontent' was taken a stage further amid the distress accompanying the transition to peace without plenty after Waterloo. Impoverished by the lack of work, and the hefty regressive burden of indirect taxation required to finance 'Old Corruption', Lancashire workers meeting at Middleton, home town of the radical weaver poet Samuel Bamford, pledged themselves to a forward-looking radical programme of universal manhood suffrage, annual Parliaments and the ballot. Politics, they had come to understand, was the key to amelioration, protection and justice for the working class:

> They must seek a Power in the Constitution . . . a Power that will curtail luxury – by diminishing Taxation, and will enable the people to buy shoes, stockings, shirts, coats, hats, etc. and then there will be a demand for labour . . . suffrage commensurate with *direct* Taxation, seems to grant, that property only ought to be represented; whereas, labour makes property, and therefore in the name of common sense ought to be represented.

A remarkable campaign of mass meetings followed, defiantly disciplined and peaceable demonstrations of ever-growing strength, in marked contrast to the riotousness of the eighteenth-century crowd. The highlight of these great carnival gatherings, popular outings for whole families, trades and communities, was the arrival of the local female union or reform society, dressed in best white attire, to present to the chairman, as at Blackburn on 5 July 1819, an elaborate cap of liberty 'made of scarlet silk or satin, lined with green, with a serpentine gold lace, terminating with a rich gold tassel.' With its multivocal constitutional and republican meanings, the cap of liberty was well chosen as the rallying symbol of the 1819 campaign: the Roman badge of freedom, it was an ancient and revered emblem which had adorned Britannia's spear and the coinage of the realm until the 1790s when it acquired revolutionary connotations as the livery of French anarchy and Jacobin terror. In a co-ordinated campaign of overwhelming 'pressure from without', local meetings led to a series of huge demonstrations, of which, that planned for St Peter's Fields, Manchester, in August, was to be the

The Free Trade Hall

largest yet, 'rather a meeting of the County of *Lancashire* etc than of Manchester alone'. Nonplussed by the government's legal scruples and apparent inability to crush this 'mass platform', the Manchester magistrates decided to 'bring the matter to issue'. 'If the agitators of the country determine to persevere in their meeting', the stipendiary magistrate announced, 'it will necessarily prove a trial of strength and there must be a conflict.' On 16 August 1819, the magistrates gained their bloody victory. At least eleven people were killed and many hundreds injured when the magistrates sent in the inebriated publicans, butchers and shopkeepers of the local yeomanry to arrest Henry Hunt and other leaders on the platform, and then ordered in the fifteenth Hussars to disperse the peaceable crowd. After this, the 'Peterloo' massacre, open protest gave way to insurrectionary planning, at which point the initiative passed from Lancashire to the West Riding, a transpennine pattern to be repeated after the failure and defeat of the great mass-petitioning campaigns of the Chartist challenges in the 1830s and 1840s.

The high point of Lancashire Chartism was the 'general strike' of 1842, now commemorated at several sites across the North West. In the middle of the worst depression of the century, wage disputes soon escalated into a general turnout for the Charter, a political strike ratified and legitimised by a rapidly and democratically convened trades conference in Manchester. Most delegates were cotton-factory workers (spinners, power-loom weavers, calico printers, dressers and dyers) or members of the engineering and metal-working trades, the supposed beneficiaries of industrial change, but who had yet to acquire the 'aristocratic' status and security they were to enjoy in mid-Victorian decades. Artisan trades were also well represented, particularly in the less secure clothing and building sectors, and there was also a small number of distressed textile outworkers, mainly silk-weavers and fustian cutters. By historical coincidence, the executive of the National Charter Association assembled in Manchester at this point in August, the anniversary of Peterloo, having come to unveil the memorial to Henry Hunt at Ancoats (alas, long since demolished). Although the strike involved up to half a million workers from the Scottish coalfields to South Wales and Cornwall, the Chartist executive was well aware that support was patchy and uneven outside the cotton districts. Fearful of partial and incomplete insurgency, they refused to assume command. Over 1,100 people were tried in connection with the turnouts, after troops and special constables were called in to quash the strike. In 1842, indeed, more people were arrested and sentenced for public order offences than in any other year in the nineteenth century.

The final defeat of Chartism marked a decisive watershed in working-class endeavour, with 'advanced' Lancashire again pointing the 'new model' way forward. For the increasing numbers of mid-Victorian workers who could afford regular subscriptions (and no credit), dividend-paying co-operative societies (based on the Rochdale Pioneers), affiliated friendly societies (such as the Manchester Unity of Oddfellows) and amalgamated trades unions (subsequently brought together in Manchester as the Trades Union Congress) offered respectability, security and all the other benefits of collective mutuality. The dire distress of the cotton famine, however, following the Federal blockade of Confederate ports during the United States Civil War in the 1860s, imposed a severe strain on the savings and resources of the collective self-help institutions, by which 'Rochdale Man' maintained working-class pride and respectability. In the circumstances, the forbearance of the cotton workers, their refusal to despair, riot or condemn the American North, was remarkable, reviving middle-class confidence in the innate liberalism of the working class. It was this behaviour, indeed, that prompted Gladstone's conversion to reform, as he considered it, 'a shame and a scandal that bodies of men such as these should be excluded from the parliamentary franchise'. As 'Lib-Labism' subsequently flourished, radical history was revisited and rehabilitated to suit Liberal taste: free trade, respectability and 'improvement' inform the iconography and inscriptions on display at key sites of memory and remembrance throughout the Lancashire coalfield (a bastion of Lib-Labism), the cotton districts and other parts of the industrial North West.

Tensions and strains soon developed within Lib-Labism, but the impetus towards political independence – 'Labour's turning point' –

came from the other side of the Pennines, premised on Yorkshire pragmatism. Founded in Bradford in 1893, the Independent Labour Party (ILP) was committed 'to secure the collective ownership of the means of production, distribution and exchange', but the term socialist was not to appear in the party's title, nor in its manifesto, a programme of reforms little in advance of progressive Liberalism. Here the important practical consideration was not to offend the recently much-expanded trades unions (now extended to the 'semi-skilled' and 'general' workers), whose support was indispensable if Independent Labour parliamentary representation, the desideratum of the ILP, was to be achieved at the earliest opportunity. A short cut to political effectiveness, this 'Labour alliance' was pursued with single minded instrumentalism. Alternative strategies were squeezed out of consideration, much to the chagrin of Robert Blatchford (a timekeeper on the Weaver Navigation at Northwich, prior to discovering his vocation in political journalism and the *Clarion* movement) and the Lancashire socialists, advocates of a United Socialist Party, a fusion of groups including the ILP and the Social Democratic Federation, shorn of its initial (London-based) sectarianism.

The North West, then, occupies a proud and prominent position in the narrative of Labour history; indeed, in some studies it stands as proxy for the nation. However, there are a number of regional 'peculiarities', which demand attention. First, an important structural factor. In the scale and size of its workplace units, '*factory*' Lancashire was ahead of the rest of Britain, 'the *workshop* of the world'. As Karl Marx appreciated, large factories aided the process of worker combination and organisation, but they also provided the context for successful exercises in employer paternalism. The appeal of 'clog Toryism' in urban Lancashire demonstrated the powerful purchase of paternalism and employer influence when extended to the 'manly' idioms of popular culture. Masters of the common style, Tory employers championed the working-man's right to his glass of beer and idle pastimes, defending good old-fashioned fun against the 'improving' interventionism of the Liberals. There was no condescension or moral preaching in the manful paternalism of 'Sir Harry' Hornby, the latest 'gamecock' of the Hornby dynasty, a family of squire-employers, whose Tory politics were proudly followed by their loyal and devoted Blackburn workers. Whether Tory or Liberal, paternalist employers were generally reluctant to concede recognition, amend labour law and submit to collective bargaining. Robert Platt, a cotton manufacturer and leading light of the Stalybridge Liberals, offered trips and treats in order to 'beat all trade unions out of court'. In keynote speeches at Platt's various functions, Dan Lynne, a long-serving employee and 'trusted servant' underlined the message of deference and non-unionism, drawing upon populist suspicion of paid officials: 'They wanted no third party to interfere between them and their employer: they acknowledged no paid secretary or committee in a back room, drinking brandy and water, and smoking cigars at the expense of the public.' A later generation of 'progressive' industrialists, such as Lever (whose Port Sunlight 'model' village merits a visit) and Brunner (whose chemical works led the way to a 'second' Industrial Revolution in the North West), introduced a 'new Liberal' approach based on conciliation, collectivism and distributive justice. Amplified through the journalism of C. P. Scott of the *Manchester Guardian*, 'progressivism' – a limited force elsewhere in the country – attracted considerable popular electoral support in Edwardian Lancashire, convincing some historians that the Liberal Party, having adjusted to 'class politics' and working-class needs, stood in better long-term shape (but for the First World War) than the fledgling Labour Party.

A second significant factor is geographical. Given its proximity to Ireland, the North West experienced high levels of in-migration from across the Irish Sea. The Irish contributed much to the Labour movement in the North West: to take just one example, John Doherty, the great trade union leader of the 1820s and 1830s, pioneer advocate of a general union, first of all spinners, then of all trades, hailed from Buncrana, County Donegal. However, the presence of the Irish throughout the North West enabled the Tories, defenders of the faith as well as guardians of popular culture, to play the ethno-sectarian card. Popular Toryism flourished as the volume of anti-Irish, anti-Catholic propaganda increased, rallying freeborn Englishmen to protect the Protestant constitution from the enemy within. The pattern of sectarian politics was most pronounced in Liverpool, the main port of entry, where the Irish who stayed put were denigrated as a kind of underclass; unable, unwilling or unsuited to take advantage of opportunities elsewhere in Britain or the New World. Liverpool was a Tory town, proud of its 'Tory democracy' and pioneer municipal collectivism, projects which served to protect the 'marginal privilege' of the Protestant worker. Local notables continued to monopolise political positions, but, as need arose, Tory dignitaries were able to mingle at ease within a network of overlapping associations (party, sectarian and popular), displaying the common touch which soon became a distinguishing (and essential) characteristic of local Tory leadership – a style perfected in Archibald Salvidge's electoral machine, perhaps the most remarkable example of British 'boss politics'. When its lesser counterweight, the Irish National Party, passed into the hands of second-generation (i.e. Liverpool born) Irish, it displayed less interest in the fate of Ireland than in the immediate needs of the local Catholic community in housing and employment. As a cross-class formation, this 'Nat-Labism' proved more resonant and enduring than conventional Lib-Labism elsewhere: the Scotland Division was to be T. P. O'Connor's parliamentary fiefdom for over four decades, complemented by the American-style machine politics of local Irish-national councillors. While the extent of political patronage and welfare benefits at the disposal of these Orange and Green sectarian machines is open to question, both reached deep into their respective constituencies (further down than skilled male workers who dominated organised labour), assisted by pub- and parish-based networks of associational culture and collective mutuality. Despite valiant efforts to provide a vibrant, non-sectarian counter-culture, socialists secured little influence. 'Liverpool is rotten,' Ramsay MacDonald declared in 1910, 'and we had better recognise it.' Indeed, there was little advance for independent Labour in Liverpool until interwar slum clearance gradually destroyed the community base of the old sectarian politics, the transfer of the 'Catholic' machine into Labour, keeping the party to the Right. It was not until 1955 that Labour gained control of the municipal council, a generation later than equivalent triumphs in other major conurbations. Reduced to an empty shell by further slum clearance of the inner-city Catholic wards, the moribund party machine subsequently fell into the hands of Militant activists. By operating municipal politics in typical Liverpool 'Tammany' style – Chicago rather than Petrograd on the Mersey – Militant failed to offer a more inclusive Labour politics open to the ethnic, gender, special-interest and other working-class groups who had taken to the streets in 1981 to protest against their marginalised status.

At odds with its backward role in Labour history, Liverpool's reputation for militancy needs to be placed in historical perspective. It should also be assessed in the context of the city's distinctive pattern of industrial relations. When the organised Labour movement eventually established itself in the diffuse maritime, dockland and casual labour markets, amid the fervour of the 'new unionism' of the late nineteenth century, it (maybe necessarily) took the form of big bureaucratic unions, a structure which quickly provoked a militant 'rank and file' reaction. Casual labourers lacked the guaranteed time, relevant experience or financial resources for regular involvement and subscription. Full-time officials perforce dominated their unions, bureaucrats who sought union incorporation in national agreements with employers, to which end they were prepared both to discipline and decasualise the membership. In so doing, they offended the independence and pride of the Liverpool labourer. For all its ills, casualism was a cherished symbol of independence, the best guarantee of freedom from irksome work-discipline, from the tyranny of the factory bell – one of many ways in which Liverpool, a city apart, sought to distance itself from adjacent 'industrial' Lancashire (with its much higher female employment). In protesting against decasualisation, the workers were championed by syndicalist advocates of direct action, but the incidence of subsequent rank and file militancy seems to have been determined less by theory and praxis than by specific grievances and traditional attitudes. Long after the decline of the docks, shipping and casualism, Liverpool workers continued to protest against workplace impositions and innovations – national agreements, bureaucratic structures and new work practices – which denied their residual independence and democratic local autonomy. Workers in the new industrial plants of the Merseyside Development Area, a belated and unhappy attempt at industrial diversification, gained a reputation for antipathy to factory discipline and managerial prerogatives. This prompted some observers to trace a 'masculinist' cultural continuity back to the old traditions of waterside casualism and seafaring independence; the legacy of dockers who offered themselves for employment when they wished, and of seamen who were able to pick and choose their ships. Liverpudlian militancy, however, was by no means restricted to men at work. The militant *suffragette* tactics of the Women's Social and

Political Union proved particularly popular in Liverpool, attracting new supporters to the cause. Elsewhere in Lancashire, most working-class women, dismayed by the increasing distance of the WSPU from its local socialist roots, transferred their energies into peaceable, radical *suffragist* organisations.

With its nineteenth-century focus and its attention to Liverpool (*in* the industrial North West but not *of* it) this brief introduction to the region reflects my own enthusiasms. In the best traditions of the Left, a number of colleagues have given freely of their knowledge and advice to help me compile a list of entries extending beyond mere personal preference. Pride of place here must be accorded to Paul Salveson, whose pioneer study *The People's Monuments: A Guide to Sites and Memorials in North West England*, published by the Workers' Educational Association in 1987, has been my *vade mecum*. John Walton guided me towards a wider Lancastrian perspective, while Terry Wyke offered his unrivalled expertise on Greater Manchester. Several others kindly provided help with individual entries, including Nick Mansfield, Jim Garrets, Jonathan Pepler, Michael Huggins, Alan Rice and Ann Dennison. And, as I was concluding my list of entries, an interesting article by Bob Hayes on 'Heritage, Commemoration and Interpretation: Labour and Radical Movements and the Built Environment' appeared in the 2004 issue of the *North West Labour History Journal*. My apologies to the inhabitants of Cheshire and Wirral for the paucity of entries from their areas, but not all of the North West, it would seem, is the territory of the Left.

Gazetteer

ASHTON-UNDER-LYNE, Cheshire. 43 Elizabeth Street. In a commendable commitment to history from below, Tameside Metropolitan Borough Council has placed a celebratory blue plaque here, the home from 1900 to 1910 of Hannah Maria Mitchell. A working-class campaigner for female suffrage and labour interests, she strove always to integrate socialist and feminist beliefs. Ignored by the Pankhursts, when overwork as a paid organiser for the Women's Social and Political Union led to a nervous breakdown, Hannah turned to other groups to pursue suffrage, pacifist and labour causes, issues she continued to champion as a City of Manchester councillor. As she poignantly observed in her posthumously published autobiography, *The Hard Way Up*, 'most of us who were married had to work with one hand tied behind us.'

BIRKENHEAD, Cheshire. Birkenhead Park. Opened in 1847 as the first publicly funded park, Birkenhead Park was designed by Joseph Paxton in what was to be a forerunner of Olmstead's design for Central Park, New York. In September 1932, during the 'devil's decade' of the 1930s, the park gates were an assembly point for demonstrations of the unemployed, organised by the National Unemployed Workers Movement, in protest against the means test and in demand for increases in relief. Some demonstrations led to violent clashes with the unrestrained police. The park was used for schemes of unemployment relief during the 1920s and 1930s.

BLACKBURN, Lancashire. Darwen Street. A plaque commemorates the 1842 strike of cotton operatives, the 'Plug Riots'.

BLACKPOOL, Lancashire. The Lancashire and Cheshire Miners' Federation Convalescent Home. This is one of the few buildings linked to the Labour Movement judged of sufficient architectural merit to gain inclusion in Nikolaus Pevsner's *Buildings of England*. It is recorded as being 'much better architecturally' than adjacent North Shore hotels.

BLACKSTONE EDGE, Lancashire. A dramatic natural amphitheatre high in the Pennines, this was a superb venue for great Chartist regional meetings, linking the Lancashire Chartists with their comrades in the West Riding. In August 1846, Ernest Jones, the last of the gentlemen leaders, rose to prominence after his 'maiden speech to his new allies' – an event he later recollected in an eponymous poem.

BOLTON, Lancashire. 16 Wood Street. The Bolton Socialist Club is one of the oldest independent socialist clubs, being founded in 1888. Originally based in Back-Cheapside, it moved to 13 Lorne Street, before being sited here in 1905. It has served as the venue not only of the Bolton Socialist Party, but also for a plethora of political and cultural activities. Distinguished visitors in its early days included Mrs Pankhurst, Eleanor Marx, James Connolly, Tom Mann and Ben Tillett. In later years, its range and reputation declined into a drinking dive, prompting a successful relaunch on May Day 1984, led by striking miners and nursery nurses. In 2005 its future is precarious.

BOLTON, Lancashire. John Fielding Monument, Queen's Park. Positioned next to Benjamin Disraeli, the lifesize, rather stiff statue of John Fielding (rendered doll-like by its massive pedestal) indicates the esteem formerly accorded to trade union leaders for whom, as the inscription attests, 'unity and equity were the guiding principles of life'. Instrumental in uniting spinners' organisations into one union in Bolton, 'second to none in the kingdom for wealth and power', Fielding, who was secretary of the local trades' council, was one of the first trade union leaders to be appointed to the magisterial bench. Tens of thousands of workers attended the unveiling ceremony in 1896, at which speakers condemned 'sweating' processes and 'sweated' cloth.

BUCKLOW HILL, Cheshire. A well-heeled village with some surprising Leftie connections. As an escape from observation of the condition of the working class, Friedrich Engels took much enjoyment in riding to hounds from here with the Cheshire Hunt, spending seven hours in the saddle on 31 December 1857. At the end of the nineteenth century, the Clarion Club rented a house, 'Acropolis', to establish 'the first Socialist Guest House' for 'the refreshment, recreation and accommodation at reasonable cost' of Clarionettes from Bolton, Liverpool, Manchester and industrial Lancashire. A lively socialist counter-culture developed with 'the utter absence of Sabbatarianism, class distinction and moth-eaten convention', prompting the alarmed landlord, Lord Egerton of nearby Tatton Hall, to refuse to renew the five-year lease.

BURNLEY, Lancashire. Manchester Road.The founder and leader of the Social Democratic Foundation, H. M. Hyndman (1842-1921), was based in London, but in the 1890s came to Burnley and stood for Parliament in 1895. In his memoirs he recalls how, on his first visit 'in quest of a little fresh air, I walked up to the top of Manchester Road and looked down upon Burnley from the hill-top. There it lay in the hollow, one hideous Malebolge of carbon-laden fog and smoke, the factory chimneys rising up above the mass of thick cloud like stakes upon which, as I said to my companion, successive generations of the workers and their families had been impaled. When I took [William] Morris up to the same spot later, and we looked down together upon this infernal pit of human degradation, his language of denunciation of the system, and the classes who engendered and maintained such horrors, was nothing short of apocalyptic in its fury.'

BURY, Lancashire. Textile Hall, on the corner of Manchester Road and Silver Street. This was opened in 1894 as the physical embodiment of the local spinning, carding and weaving unions. These trades are depicted in the magnificent semicircular panel above the central doorway. Where previously they had met in pubs and hired rooms, trade unions throughout the late Victorian and Edwardian high point of 'textile Lancashire' proudly constructed their own premises, in the case of Bury, in the town's most prestigious street. Later industrial decline obliged the unions to sell the building in the 1970s.

DROYLSDEN, Lancashire. Library. While all the other plaques in Tameside are conventional heritage blue, the one affixed to Droylsden Library, acknowledging the birth of Harry Pollitt (1890-1960) in the town is appropriately and defiantly red. As general secretary and chairman of the Communist Party of Great Britain, Pollitt, the 'true son of the British working class', linked what has been the open socialist culture of the industrial Britain of his youth (into which he was inducted by his mother, an active member of the Independent Labour Party) with the harsher disciplines of international communism. Until he died, Pollitt loyally kept a portrait of Stalin on display in his living room.

HASLINGDEN, Lancashire. Irish Democratic League Club, Michael Davitt branch, George Street. Michael Davitt (1846-1906), Irish nationalist and labour leader, was brought up in the weaving town of Haslingden, his family having been evicted from County Mayo in 1850. Davitt suffered a major industrial injury at the age of ten, when his right arm was amputated by unguarded machinery. Having served several years imprisonment in Dartmoor on a Fenian arms charge, he became a leading force in the Land League, promoting the 'new departure' in Irish nationalism, while also developing close ties with British labour leaders, including H. M. Hyndman and James Keir Hardie. There is a public monument opposite the Club, and also memorial tablets in St Mary's Church and in the Church of the Immaculate Conception.

HEYSHAM, Lancashire. 'Sambo's Grave'. At the mouth of the Lune Estuary, near Sunderland Point, lies an isolated but poignant reminder of North West England's involvement in the slave trade. 'Sambo's Grave' is the burial place of an anonymous black adolescent in unconsecrated ground in the 1730s. The location subsequently became an important marker for those opposed to the slave trade, and continues to attract visits and tributes as a key site of memory (the politically incorrect name notwithstanding) for the history of the black Atlantic.

LIVERPOOL. Anglican Cathedral. Funded to a large extent by the city's merchant class, Sir Giles Gilbert Scott's magnificent Anglican Cathedral has two claims on the attention of the Leftie tourist. Fred Bower worked on the construction of the cathedral in the early years of the twentieth century. In his autobiography, *Rolling Stonemason*, he records 'the secret of the foundation stone'. Wrapped between copies of *Clarion and Labour Leader* (provided by his schoolboy sparring partner, James Larkin) Bower placed a socialist address:

> To the Finders, Hail!
> We, the wage slaves employed on the erection of this cathedral, to be dedicated to the worship of the unemployed Jewish carpenter, hail ye! Within a stone's throw from here, human beings are housed in slums not fit for swine. This message, written on trust-produced paper with trust-produced ink, is to tell ye how we of today are at the mercy of trusts. Building fabrics, clothing, food, fuel, transport, are all in the hands of money-mad, soul-destroying trusts. We can only sell our labour, as wage slaves, on their terms. The money trusts today own us. In your own day, you will, thanks to the efforts of past and present agitators for economic freedom, own the trusts. Yours will indeed, compared to ours of today, be a happier existence. See to it, therefore, that ye, too, work for the betterment of all, and so justify your existence by leaving the world better for your having lived in it. Thus and thus only shall come about the Kingdom of 'God' or 'Good' on Earth. Hail, Comrades, and – Farewell.

The Lady Chapel was the first part of the cathedral to be completed. Dedicated to famous Christian women, including Josephine Butler (1828-1906), social reformer and one of Liverpool's pioneer suffrage campaigners, it provided the perfect setting for the more daring and militant actions of local suffragists. In January

1914, suffragists were manhandled and knocked to the (sanctified) ground, after one unfurled a banner proclaiming 'I came not to send peace, but a sword.' A contingent of police was drafted in the following week, but failed to keep women away from Evensong.

LIVERPOOL. St George's Plateau. Liverpool's great space for civic ceremonial in front of St George's Hall has been the site of many demonstrations and confrontations, including 'Red Sunday', when, on 13 August 1911, eighty thousand assembled to support striking transport workers. According to the police, violence broke out in a side street, initiated not by strikers, but by elements, variously described as 'idle', 'Irish' and 'hooligan'. As 'trouble' spread, troops and police reinforcements from Birmingham and Leeds were sent in to clear the plateau with ill-disciplined baton charges, injuring hundreds – hence 'Red Sunday' is also known as 'Bloody Sunday'. While looting and sectarian violence continued overnight, Bloody Sunday brought new unity and resolve to Liverpool workers, marshalled by the syndicalist Tom Mann for a general strike, which, for a few days at least, brought the city 'near to revolution', prompting the government to despatch a gunboat to the Mersey.

LIVERPOOL. Unity Theatre, Hope Place. Located in a former synagogue, this base for professional touring theatre has links going back to the thriving socialist culture of the 1930s, the days of the Unity Theatre movement and the Left Book Club Theatre Guild. From the start, the Merseyside Left Theatre, renamed Merseyside Unity Theatre in 1944, was radical and experimental. Its unlicensed production of *Waiting for Leftie*, performed in Chester, led to questions in Parliament. Unlike most other Unity Theatres, however, the group staged classics alongside contemporary left-wing theatre, doing much to make theatre accessible to the working class. Ironically, the abolition of censorship in the 1960s weakened the Unity Theatre movement, as mainstream theatre, with its greater resources, was able thenceforth to offer radical fare. Merseyside Unity Theatre managed to survive into the early

1980s, one of its last initiatives being to acquire the premises in Hope Place, where the spirit lives on, providing a venue for writers, actors and companies committed to radical and accessible theatre.

LIVERPOOL. Newz Bar and Brasserie, Water Street. The former New Zealand House has been transformed into a trendy bar with a radical difference. A place of pilgrimage and refreshment for Lefties, its walls are adorned by eight magnificent murals, the work of David Jacques, celebrating 'Some Liverpool Radicals'. The depictions, embracing Liverpool's Celtic, cosmopolitan and maritime past, include: New Unionism; the Fabian Jeannie Mole and other pioneer socialist women and trade union organisers; Big Jim Larkin and the Anarcho-Syndicalists; the 1911 General Transport Strike Committee; the National Union of Ships' Stewards, Cooks, Butchers and Bakers; Conscientious Objectors in Walton Gaol during the First World War, including the Welsh-speaking pacifist George Davies; the Kirkdale branch of the Ancient Order of Hibernians; and the Merseyside Volunteers in the International Brigade 1936.

LIVERPOOL. Liverpool Royal Infirmary, Pembroke Place. A plaque has recently been placed on this building, currently occupied by the Brownlow Group Medical Practice, to commemorate Robert Noonan, formerly Croker, and better known by his pseudonym Robert Tressell (1870-1911), author of the great proletarian novel, based on the Edwardian building trade, *The Ragged Trousered Philanthropists*, published posthumously in abridged form, 1914, the full version not appearing until 1954. Taken ill en route for a new life in Canada, the penniless Tressell spent some time in the Liverpool Workhouse before his death in the Royal Infirmary in February 1911, and subsequent consignment to a pauper's grave in Walton Park Cemetery.

MANCHESTER. Town Hall, Albert Square. A marble bust of Abel Heywood, defiant campaigner against 'taxes on knowledge', who subsequently displayed considerable radical enterprise in his commitment to cheap publications for the working class, can be found in the sculpture hall next to a memorial to the International Brigade. As agent of the unstamped *Poor Man's Guardian,* he was imprisoned in Salford New Bailey in 1831, and fined on several occasions. When the Stamp Duty was reduced, he built up a core business through the sale and distribution of radical newspapers – he was selling eighteen thousand copies of the Chartist *Northern Star* in 1838. Thereafter, he expanded his activities to become the largest wholesale newsagency in the country. At the same time, he moved into Liberal politics, being twice mayor of Manchester, and, as befitted his continuing concern for the condition of the poor, he chaired the Paving, Sewering and Highways Committee for 47 years.

MANCHESTER. Balloon Street. In front of the complex of buildings attesting to the financial strength of the Co-operative Bank is a statue of Robert Owen (1771-1854) – an exact replica of that in his birthplace, Newtown – installed in 1994 as part of the 150th anniversary celebrations of the birth of the modern co-operative retail and banking movement, otherwise divorced from Owen's vision of a new moral world of communitarian socialism. At the unveiling ceremony, Owen was hailed as 'an economic and social guru for the twenty-first century when the extremes of Adam Smith to the right and Karl Marx to the left have lost much of their appeal'.

MANCHESTER. Chetham's Library, Long Millgate. The most complete late medieval residential complex to survive in North West England, Chetham's houses a famous library, founded in 1653, the oldest public library in the English-speaking world, much appreciated by Karl Marx on his visits to his colleague and collaborator Friedrich Engels, resident in Manchester on business. Engels' first posting in Manchester, 1842-44, resulted in his researching and writing one of the most original studies on the new industrial society, *The Condition of the Working-Class in England in 1844,* published in 1845. He returned in 1850 and remained until 1870, during which Marx visited him on at least 25 occasions. They often went to Chetham's together, reading at the four-sided desk in the alcove, consulting publications which Marx found difficulty in obtaining in London.

MANCHESTER. Martyrs' Memorial, St Joseph's Cemetery, Moston. A much defiled and vandalised Celtic cross erected in memory of William Allen, Michael Larkin and Michael O'Brien, executed on insecure and unsafe evidence for the murder of a Manchester policeman, Sergeant Brett, in 1867, at the height of anti-Irish feelings, the Fenian scare. Established by the Irish in Britain as a hallowed site of memory in the Gaelic Revival at the end of the nineteenth century, the monument (designed by the Bootle nationalist and monumental mason, John Geraghty) to the victims of a British miscarriage of justice has subsequently served as the focus of anti-Irish demonstrations, particularly during periods of IRA activity.

MANCHESTER. Mechanics' Institute, 103 Princess Street. Opened in 1857, this Italian palazzo building is redolent with Labour history, hosting what was, in effect, the first Trades Union Congress, in May 1868. Having gone through a variety of educational and other uses, the building became the home of the National Museum of Labour History, opened by Jack Jones on May Day 1990. In May 1994, public galleries were opened at the Pump House in Bridge Street, while the Princess Street site still houses museum stores and offices, the Textile Conservation Studio and the Labour History Archive and Study Centre. In line with the vocabulary favoured by New Labour, the museum decided to use one name to embrace the whole organisation in 2001, namely the People's History Museum.

MANCHESTER. Pankhurst Centre, 60-62 Nelson Street, Chorlton-on-Medlock. After the death of her beloved husband Richard, a fellow ILP activist, the financially straitened Emmeline Pankhurst (1858-1928) and her daughters moved into this modest Georgian townhouse in Chorlton, where she took the post of Registrar of Births and Deaths. Although founded in this house in 1903, the Women's Social and Political Union really came to public notice with the militant intervention of Annie Kenney of Saddleworth and Christabel Pankhurst, at the Free Trade Hall, Manchester in 1905. Dominated thereafter by the autocratic Christabel, the WSPU abandoned links with the ILP and mounted a militant but socially conservative campaign of middle-class womanhood, to coerce the political establishment into conceding 'Votes for Ladies'. Opened by Barbara Castle in 1987, the house is now a women's centre – 'a unique environment in which women can learn together, work on projects and socialise' – and a heritage project, incorporating an exhibition room and a parlour recreated as it might have been when the Pankhurst women lived there, 1898-1907.

MANCHESTER. Peterloo, St Peter's Fields. The derisive sobriquet 'Peterloo', coined in bitter mockery of the recent Battle of Waterloo, expressed public outrage at the 'massacre' on St Peter's Fields, Manchester, 16 August 1819. A crowd, estimated at sixty thousand, assembled in a disciplined manner to attend a radical mass meeting calling for universal manhood suffrage. The Manchester magistrates, however, dismayed by the government's refusal to introduce special legislation to ban such monster gatherings and much alarmed by reports of preparatory midnight drilling on the moors, decided to take matters into their own hands and ordered the arrest of Henry 'Orator' Hunt, the star speaker on the platform. Inexperienced in crowd control – and allegedly inebriated – the publicans and shopkeepers of the Manchester and Salford Yeomanry rode roughshod through the assembly, seizing radical banners and flailing their sabres. At least eleven people were killed and many hundreds injured. The area was finally cleared by the fifteenth Hussars. The Manchester magistrates were officially thanked for their decisive action, but the government took the utmost care to ensure against any repetition of their bloody deeds. Much of the open space of St Peter's Fields has been built over, but parts – the area between the GMEX Arena, the Midland Hotel and the Radisson Edwardian Free Trade Hall Hotel – remains open and accessible. Inside the hotel is the misleading record, 'The site of St Peter's Fields where on 16th August 1819 HENRY HUNT RADICAL ORATOR addressed an assembly of about 60,000 people. Their subsequent dispersal by the military is remembered as PETERLOO.'

MANCHESTER. Free Trade Hall. In an early indication of the Liberal appropriation of the Radical tradition, the Anti-Corn Law League built free trade halls on the site of Peterloo to accommodate its ticket-entry political meetings. Opened in 1856, the third such hall was an architectural tour de force in Lombardo-Venetian style. The most important public meeting hall in North West England, the Manchester Free Trade Hall was the venue chosen by Annie Kenney of Saddleworth and Christabel Pankhurst, in October 1905, for the dramatic intervention of suffragette militancy. They asked the Liberal speaker if an incoming Liberal government would give votes to women. Thrown out without answer, they continued their protest, were arrested and imprisoned in Strangeways Gaol. A plaque marking this event is now displayed near the foyer of the luxury hotel that occupies the building.

MANCHESTER. Town Hall. The Sculpture Hall houses a wooden low relief carving by Sol Garson, unveiled in 1983, in somewhat belated honour of the men and women from Greater Manchester who served in the International Brigades fighting Fascism in the Spanish Civil War, 1936-39. The inscription bears the words of Dolores Ibárruri, 'La Pasionaria', acknowledging Spain as 'the cause of all advanced and progressive mankind'.

MIDDLETON, Lancashire. Cemetery behind St Leonard's Church. A great obelisk memorial to Samuel Bamford (1788-1872), weaver, radical, poet and antiquarian. A gifted organiser and activist in the heroic days of early nineteenth century radicalism, Bamford led the Middleton contingent to the ill-fated meeting at St Peter's Fields in August 1819, for which he was sentenced to one year's imprisonment. He was less prominent thereafter, the

Peterloo massacre having served to underline the superior physical power of the state. Although he continued to support legal and political reforms, and to believe in a self-educated and self-disciplined working-class movement, independent of the middle class, he appeared as something of an apostate, patronised by liberals for his strictures on Chartist physical force bluster and demagogic leadership. The obelisk, recently renovated to remove traces of vandalism, symbolises the mid-Victorian liberal appropriation of the radical tradition with its bronze portrait medallion of Bamford as sage old man, its paean to free trade and the eulogy by John Bright.

NEWCHURCH-IN-PENDLE, Lancashire. Clarion House, Jinny Lane. A delightful socialist haven set amid magnificent scenery, a reminder of the fellowship and co-operation embodied in the Clarion movement and the Independent Labour Party. Sponsored by Robert Blatchford (1851-1943), the Clarion Cycling Club took the late-Victorian urban working class out into the country, where healthy exercise was combined with political propaganda. Members dismounted to distribute socialist literature and to hold impromptu meetings, disturbing the 'Sabbath quiet' of remote country villages. Built in 1912 with a loan of £350 from the Nelson Weavers Association, this last surviving Clarion House under the direction of the Trustees of the Nelson ILP Land Society is still open every Sunday to welcome cyclists, walkers, ramblers and fellow socialists with tea and good cheer. A gem.

OLDHAM, Lancashire. Lees Brook Mill, Lees. A blue plaque honours Annie Kenney, a pioneer of suffragette militant tactics, joining Christabel Pankhurst as the first to interrupt a political meeting in the Free Trade Hall, Manchester in 1905. Having acquired notoriety through such means, the Women's Social and Political Union shifted from its Lancashire working-class and socialist roots, as personified by Kenney, prompting many working-class women to align with the adult suffragists and non-militant female suffragists. Kenney, however, remained loyal to the Pankhursts, for whom she served as an invaluable symbol of working-class support for the militant suffragette cause.

OLDHAM, Lancashire. Alexandra Park. Robert Ashcroft Memorial. A bronze statue on a granite pedestal was erected in 1903 by public subscription – and unveiled by the town's leading cotton trade unionist – in memory of 'The Workers' Friend', Robert Ashcroft. Legal adviser to the Association of Operative Cotton Spinners, Ashcroft, briefly a Conservative Member of Parliament for Oldham before his unexpected death in 1899, was a leading campaigner for better working conditions. A skilled conciliator, he ensured that the Brooklands agreement emerged out of the bitter trade dispute of 1892-93, a measure which placed industrial relations in the cotton industry on a new footing.

PRESTON, Lancashire. Lune Street. 1842 Massacre Statue. The work of Gordon Young, and inspired by Goya's painting 'The Execution of 3 May', this is an impressive memorial to the five striking cotton workers killed by the military (the 72nd Highlanders) during the early days of the great 1842 turnout. Outraged by progressive wage cuts amid the most severe distress of the nineteenth century, workers united in an early form of 'general strike', an exercise in economic and political pressure based upon community support and participation, seeking not just the restoration of wage rates, but also parliamentary reform – the implementation of the People's Charter – their only guarantee of 'a fair day's wage for a fair day's work'. The massacre occurred as crowds marched through the town, having left a mass meeting at Chadwick's Orchard (now the site of Preston's Covered Market), the hallowed venue of radical and Chartist meetings in the town, favoured by Henry 'Orator' Hunt for his election meetings, during his brief period as MP for the borough, 1830-32.

RABY MERE, Cheshire. A Wirral beauty spot, which witnessed an important 'public access' demonstration, organised by the socialists of the Liverpool Clarion Club in 1912, to protest at the action of Sir William Lever in enclosing the Eastham footpath with six-foot-high corrugated-iron fencing, and in preventing cottagers at Raby Mere from supplying refreshments to visitors on Sundays. Despite his credentials as a progressive model employer at Port Sunlight, Lever was condemned for a 'new landlordism' far worse than 'old Toryism', which made it 'impossible for the working men and working women of Liverpool to enjoy sunshine and fresh air in that part of Wirral as they had done in the past.'

RAMSBOTTOM, Lancashire. 238 Bolton Road. Although recently moved to allow for alterations, a valuable early record of female radicalism can still be seen on the front elevation of this house, in the form of a stone above the door, bearing the inscription 'Female Union Society, Holcombe-brook, 1824'. A prominent feature of radical protest in the Peterloo period, female reform societies (basing themselves on the rules of the two largest societies, the Blackburn Female Union Society and the Female Union Society of Stockport) were established across the cotton district to emphasise the extent of community involvement with its great mass meetings, carnival outings for whole families, trades and communities.

ROCHDALE, Lancashire. Toad Lane. One of the best-known heritage sites of the 'new model' Labour movement of the mid nineteenth century, based on the premises of the Rochdale Pioneers, the originators of the 'dividend' in 1844 – the division of profits among members in proportion to the amount spent. Previously associated with Robert Owen's utopian socialism and communitarian projects, co-operation was henceforth concerned with shopkeeping and manufacturing, providing members with decent unadulterated goods and an automatic savings bank, advantages restricted to better-paid workers, as most societies refused to allow credit, thereby excluding the poor from access to collective self-help. The virtues were much appreciated by the female clientele, but the complex organisational and committee structure tended to be a male preserve.

SALFORD, Lancashire. Jubilee House, 51 The Crescent. The Working Class Movement Library is a great treasure house of the Left, containing a unique collection of books, pamphlets, banners, badges and other artifacts from the 1760s to the present, built up through the dedication, enthusiasm and intense political awareness of two activists of the Labour movement, Edmund Frow (1906-97) and his wife, Ruth. Having all but taken over every inch of space in their Old Trafford house, this magnificent collection moved to its current premises (the former Salford Royal Nurses Home) in 1987, aided by financial support – now under budgetary threat – from Salford City Council.

STALYBRIDGE, Cheshire. Joseph Rayner Stephens Memorial, Stamford Park. A magnificent granite obelisk funded by workers' subscriptions to honour J. R. Stephens (1805-79), a former Wesleyan Methodist minister and 'revolutionary Tory', unrestrained in condemnation of the horrors of the Poor Law and the 'factory system', but less vehement in support of manhood suffrage. On the anti-Poor-Law platform in the 1830s, Stephens deliberately courted arrest, so that the legality of the 'fiend-begotten, coarser food, new Poor Law' could be tested in court. He introduced himself as 'a revolutionist by fire, he was a revolutionist by blood, to the knife, to the death.'

STALYBRIDGE, Cheshire. Town Hall, Waterloo Road. There are two plaques on the frontage. One commemorates J. R. Stephens. The other lays claim to the town's pioneering role in the general strike of 1842, also known as the 'Plug Riots'. Strictly speaking, the familiar tactics of the 'Plug Plots' – the drawing of plugs from boilers to prevent engines from resuming work, as strikers marched from one establishment to the next, encouraging workers to join the turnout – were first put into effect by striking Staffordshire miners in July 1842. In August, the initiative passed to Stalybridge and the cotton districts before spreading across the land. At its height, the strike involved some half a million workers from Dundee and the Scottish coalfields to South Wales and Cornwall. Hence the inscription that calls it 'the biggest single exercise in working class strength in nineteenth century Britain.'

WESTHOUGHTON, Lancashire. The Wagon and Horses Public House, Wingates. Stained-glass windows in the front bay of the smoke room commemorate the Luddite attack in April 1812 on the Wray and Duncroft steam power loom, Westhoughton, when the owners had recently upgraded their machinery, thereby further undermining the customs, practices and 'moral economy' of the local hand-loom weavers. In the temporary absence of the military, the mill was totally destroyed by fire, for which retribution was severe at the Lancaster Special Commission in June, when four Westhoughton Luddites, including a 12-year-old boy, were hanged, after being convicted on the evidence of paid spies.

WESTHOUGHTON, Lancashire. St Bartholomew's Church. In the churchyard is a monument commemorating the Pretoria Pit Disaster, when, on 21 December 1910, over 340 miners were killed in one of the worst pit disasters in British history. The colliery was owned by the Hulton family, descendants of William Hulton, the infamous magistrate who ordered in the Yeomanry at the Peterloo massacre in Manchester in 1819.

WIGAN, Lancashire. Office Building, Wigan Cemetery. Nestling beneath a tree is an impressive monument to William Pickard, the Wigan Miners' leader and founder member of the Lancashire and Cheshire Permanent Relief Society in 1872. Committed to arbitration rather than militancy, he was castigated by Liberal friends for splitting the Radical vote by standing as a Labour candidate, sponsored by the Amalgamated Association of Miners in the General Election of 1874. The inscription, now difficult to read because of weathering, is an eloquent reminder of the strength of collective mutuality and of the former importance of coal mining, now vanished from these parts of Lancashire, as elsewhere in Britain. 'Erected by the voluntary contributions of 35,000 workers in the collieries of this district in recognition of distinguished services for a quarter of a century towards the amelioration of the condition of the mining population of this kingdom.' An authentic memorial to the Labour movement in contrast to the heritage pastiche of Wigan Pier.

Hubberholme
Scarborough
Ripon
Brimham Rocks
Dacre
Colne Valley
Ickornshaw
Bridlington
York
Keighley
Bradford
Pudsey
Leeds
Todmorden
Halifax
Kippax
Mirfield
Normanton
Huddersfield
Dewsbury
Hull
Marsden
Holmfirth
Barnsley
Worsborough Dale
Orgreave
Sheffield

8.

YORKSHIRE

Keith Laybourn

Yorkshire, as much as any English county, can lay claim to a long and continuing history of dissent, left-wing agitation and political initiative. In the eighteenth century, the expansion of the factory system led to strikes and conflict, and the consequent displacement of working groups, producing one version of the Luddism of the early nineteenth century, led by George Mellor the Huddersfield cropper. He, and two of his accomplices, were hanged at York for the murder of William Horsfall, a merchant and manufacturer of Huddersfield. There was also a considerable outburst of Chartism in Bradford, Leeds and Sheffield, led by radical figures such as Feargus O'Connor and Peter Bussey. Bradford and Huddersfield were the centres of the Short Time or Factory Movement led by Richard Oastler, and Bradford, Huddersfield and Todmorden were centres of agitation against the New Poor Law. In the 1860s, the demand to widen the franchise was dominated by the National Reform Union, which organised demonstrations on Woodhouse Moor, Leeds, and to a lesser extent by the National Reform League. Above all,

Bradford was the centre of Independent Labour Party activity and, more than 40 years ago, E. P. Thompson noted that the ILP was the first provincially-based socialist society in Britain. In the twentieth century many leading political figures, such as Harold Wilson, Labour Prime Minister 1964–70 and 1974–76, came from Huddersfield. Almost continuously then, for more than two hundred years, Yorkshire has been one of the foremost counties in the history of the British Left. Unfortunately, the physical evidence of their activities does not always survive, even though the archive offices are packed with the surviving records of their activities. However, occasionally plaques or their equivalent have been placed on the spots where particular buildings once stood or events took place, and some of these appear in the gazetteer.

The Woollen and Worsted Industries and Luddism

The Industrial Revolution of the late eighteenth and early nineteenth centuries is the turning point for any study of Labour history in Yorkshire. Without the rapid economic and social change it brought and the new machinery it introduced, and the hardening of relations between masters and workmen, there would have been little possibility of either an organised or unorganised response from the working classes. The first major evidence of conflict between master and workman comes with the activities of the Worsted Committee, formed in 1777, to ensure that masters involved in 'putting out' wool to be spun and yarn to be woven were not robbed by those they hired. This led to conflict, but there is little in terms of physical evidence of survivals of the new machinery and new techniques of industrial organisation. There were major problems in the Yorkshire woollen and worsted industries. Factories emerged in the late eighteenth and early nineteenth centuries containing more than four handlooms, or equivalent equipment, thereby breaking customary law. This was one reason why the workers of the West Yorkshire textile district burned down Benjamin Gott's Bean Ing Mills in Leeds – on the site of what is now the Yorkshire Post building in Leeds – in the 1790s, and Bradley Mills near Huddersfield in 1818. However, the Luddism of the 1812-13 period offered the most important

Hubberholme Church

example of worker protest against the new machinery. Although Luddism varied from area to area in the West Riding textile district of Yorkshire it had much to do with the displacement of the croppers, who cropped the wool with cropping shears. New machinery, such as the gig mills which were originally in effect sets of shears on a frame, threatened to replace many of these workers, and they, with the support of many handloom weavers, petitioned Parliament for the enforcement of old laws. However, the Report on the State of the Woollen Manufacture of 1806 decided that the new machinery was not a threat to jobs and that the old laws could be withdrawn. However, within six years the majority of Yorkshire croppers had lost their jobs, and they attacked mills and mill owners. On 11 April 1812 an attack on Rawfolds Mill, near Huddersfield, led to two Luddites being killed by the military who were defending it. The Yorkshire movement was eventually suppressed in early 1813, following the trial and execution, at York, of George Mellor, William Thorpe and Thomas Smith for the murder of William Horsfall on Crosland Moor outside Huddersfield. There followed a period of political repression under the Tory government of Lord Liverpool, which made it very difficult for workers and trade unionists to operate other than in secret.

Trade Unions

The repeal of the Combination Acts in 1824, and the subsequent amendment in 1825, temporarily released working men from economic and political suppression. There was a rapid growth in trade unionism nationally, as well as in Yorkshire, but this met a setback with the failure of the Grand National Consolidated Trade Union and the prosecution of the Tolpuddle Martyrs in 1834. The Yorkshire trade unionists had, in any case, not lasted long, either in Saddleworth in the late 1820s or following the Bradford wool-combers' and weavers' strike of 1825. At this stage the radical politics of the Short-Time movement and the Anti-Poor-Law League took over. However, by the 1850s, some trade unionism was re-emerging in Yorkshire, mainly in the engineering and craft trades. The most significant development was the formation of the South Yorkshire and West Yorkshire miners' unions, both formed in 1858, though they amalgamated in 1881. The South Yorkshire miners were based at an 'Arthurian' building at 1–2 Huddersfield Road, Barnsley, constructed under the leadership of John Normansell who, in 1872, was the first working man to become a member of a borough council – in this case Barnsley. The Huddersfield Road building was, in the 1970s and 1980s, the headquarters from where Arthur Scargill ran the Yorkshire miners and the National Union of Mineworkers. It contains an impressive assembly hall, which, as a result of the decline of the Yorkshire NUM, is now practically defunct.

The light-metal and cutlery trades of the Sheffield area were particularly active in the 1860s. Organised on a craft basis they resorted to the sabotage of equipment and to intimidation, and the events of the 1860s provide some of the stronger evidence of the way in which trades unions were prepared to be aggressive in their pursuit of control of the labour market. The Sheffield Outrages of 1866, which culminated in a Royal Commission and a Report in 1867, reflect the willingness of trades unions to use intimidation. 'Rattening', the practice of removing wheel bands from grinding machines to dangerous effect, was a common method of disciplining workmen, and sometimes workers' houses were blown up, as in the case of the Hereford Street outrage of 8 October 1866.

Yorkshire trade unionism really took off in the late 1880s in the woollen and worsted industries as well as in mining, and continued to develop apace until the late twentieth century, when Margaret Thatcher's period as Prime Minister (1979-90) saw national trade union membership fall from over thirteen million to just over eight million. There are no obvious physical locations for trade unionism that would attract the attention of the Leftie tourist however, though there is a wealth of trade union archive material available. The only significant building is John Lister's Manningham Mills, Bradford, where, in 1890-91, a small number of textile union leaders, and particularly W. H. Drew, led a workforce of about five thousand out on strike. The massive building, however, was central to the development of the Independent Labour Party in Bradford.

The Factory Movement

Fortunately, given the comparative weakness of Yorkshire trade unionism in the nineteenth century, working-class protest and demands for social and political justice took many forms in Yorkshire.

Richard Oastler, for example, led the Factory, or Short-Time, movement. This began when Oastler, the Land Agent at Fixby Hall near Huddersfield, wrote a number of letters to the *Leeds Mercury* and *Leeds Intelligencer* complaining of child labour. As a result some Huddersfield textile workers met at Fixby Hall in 1831 and formed the 'Fixby Hall Compact', encouraging workers to organise Short-Time committees committed to 'ten hours a day and a time book'. Fixby Hall survives as the base of a golf course. Oastler gained support for his movement throughout the region, and particularly in Huddersfield and Bradford. The Whig government set up a commission to investigate child labour, a commission that included Edwin Chadwick, the social reformer. Among the places they stayed was the George Hotel, Huddersfield, which was then on its original spot near the Market Cross. Here demonstrations were held to influence them, most obviously from the Short-Time committee which felt no need for legislation other than the enforcement of maximum hours. In addition there was much fiery oratory from the Reverend George ('Parson') Bull, whose chapel still survives at Bradford. The movement was eventually successful, being most active in the early 1830s and the early and mid 1840s. Oastler was not always able to lead the movement and was imprisoned for a time at the Fleet debtors prison from where he issued his *Fleet Papers*. He eventually retired to Leeds and died in August 1861, and is buried at St Stephen's (Church of England) Church near Kirkstall.

Anti-Poor Law Agitation

Faced with the rising cost of Poor Law relief in the late eighteenth and early nineteenth centuries, pressure was applied on the government to examine ways of reducing the cost of the Poor Law. A Whig government set up a Royal Commission on the Poor Laws in February 1831 which produced its Report in 1834. It was largely the work of Nassau Senior, the *laissez-faire* economist, and Edwin Chadwick, and formed the basis of the Poor Law Amendment Act of 1834, which established the principle of 'less eligibility', the workhouse test and the bureaucratic demand for administrative centralisation and uniformity. Although the workhouse test became the focus of much contemporary criticism, it is clear that it only served to act as a mechanism to establish less eligibility, the central tenet of 1834. In good Benthamite fashion it suggested that if the allowance system were removed, the idle pauper would be forced to seek comfort through work. Therefore, the standard of relief offered by the Poor Law had to be below, not above, the wages of the industrious worker. The workhouse test was simply a way of putting the less-eligibility principle into practice. It was also considered necessary since it would end outdoor relief, remove the poor from subsidy by the Poor Law, and restore the principle of work.

The Poor Law Amendment Act was passed in August 1834 with only limited opposition from William Cobbett and *The Times*. Under the Act, parishes had to be regrouped into Poor Law unions and the principle of less eligibility and the workhouse test applied. By and large rural counties and some industrial areas, such as the North East, accepted the Act without significant opposition. However, the textile belt of the West Riding of Yorkshire – and particularly Todmorden, Huddersfield and Bradford – as well as many areas in Lancashire, offered serious opposition. Richard Oastler, the leader of the Factory movement, carried this support into the anti-Poor-Law movements in the Huddersfield area, where he attacked the new

Poor Law as the 'catechism of Hell'. Peter Bussey and Rev George Bull did much the same in Bradford. The result was some anti-Poor-Law agitation and rioting in the three towns in 1837 and 1838. There were riots in Bradford in 1837, a refusal to appoint a clerk to the Guardians in Huddersfield and riots by local taxpayers in Todmorden. There was also much opposition in areas where the issue was less emotive. In Halifax, for instance, the *Halifax Guardian* opposed the new Poor Law as 'un-English, pernicious and wicked', encouraged the mass meetings of resistance held on Hartshead Moor and published accounts of the ill-treatment, separation and starvation imposed by the new Poor Law. It encouraged general opposition to the new Law, to Mott, the Assistant Commissioner for the district, and to any suggestion of the construction of a new workhouse. Eventually, the new Poor Law adapted to the new circumstances, permitting outdoor relief to be paid, until the Goschen Minute of 1869 proposed that philanthropic bodies be responsible for outdoor relief, and that Poor Law unions gradually cease such provision. Evidence of these developments and the physical conditions endured by the poor can be found in the Workhouse of the Poor at Ripon.

Chartism

The popular protests of the anti-Poor-Law agitation and the Short-Time movement were then overtaken by the emerging Chartist movement. Leeds was a centre of such activity. Feargus O'Connor's *Northern Star* was produced from there for a time, and much of the textile district of the West Riding witnessed Chartist disturbances in the 1840s with meetings at Peep Green near Hartshead Moor. There were Plug Plot marches in Bingley, Bradford and Halifax in 1842, when Chartists marched around the district to ensure that plugs were pulled from the boilers of the steam engines, in the hope that mill textile production would be curtailed and that unemployment among weavers and croppers reduced. There was a hope that much of the new textile machinery, which was reducing the demand for older craftsmen, would be removed. This was particularly the case in 1847 and 1848 in Bradford where many Chartist supporters were wool-combers threatened by the new machinery. Indeed, there were very serious disturbances in Bradford: inns, such as Jacob's Well, were the focus of Chartist agitation and, in early 1848, Bradford saw many disturbances connected with the wool combers and the Irish community. Many 'physical force' Chartists were working men who had lost their jobs and were hoping that Chartism would provide them with employment, an erroneous view since the Charter was about political reform such as manhood suffrage and annual Parliaments.

The Independent Labour Party

Chartism gradually expired after 1848 with Parliament's failure to respond to the third great Chartist petition, but its support flowed into other great movements. In the 1860s it flowed into the National Reform Union, organised in Bradford and Manchester. The Union demanded a widening of the property franchise to include more working men. Organised by millionaires such as Titus Salt the philanthropist and founder of Saltaire, the movement exerted considerable impact in the West Riding of Yorkshire. It often joined forces with the more working-class-based National Reform League which sought manhood suffrage. Together they mounted considerable agitation such as the march to a meeting at Woodhouse Moor in Leeds in 1867, in anticipation of the 1867 Reform Act which did extend the property franchise. Nonetheless, the most important heir to the Chartist tradition, although there were few surviving Chartists to support it, was the Independent Labour Party (ILP).

The ILP emerged as a national organisation in January 1893 after meetings at the Labour Institute, Peckover Street, and at St George's Hall, a famous concert hall built in 1853. The ILP arose out of numerous small socialist societies and Labour unions formed in the early 1890s to represent the political interests of the working classes. The Manningham Mills strike of 1890-91 was a catalyst in the emergence of this new movement. Samuel Cunliffe Lister, the main owner of Manningham Mills, imposed wage reductions of from 17 to 33 per cent on the workforce and was faced with a strike by his five thousand workers, though some were locked out. After a dispute lasting nineteen weeks, the defeated strikers returned to work. However, by that time the dispute had rallied the workers of Yorkshire behind the Manningham strikers; the manufacturers and middle classes of Bradford had alienated the workers by their actions. During the dispute, the Bradford Watch Committee threatened to revoke the licence of the Star Music Hall (now the Star) for allowing it to be a venue for strikers. Indeed, the issue of 'free speech' led to further conflict when, on 12 April 1891, the strikers held a meeting at St George's Hall at which Ben Tillett, one of the leaders of the 1889 London Dock Strike, was billed to speak. The authorities banned an outdoor overflow meeting in Dockers' Square (now known as Norfolk Gardens) which led to frayed tempers, and the following day thousands of workers attempted to assert their right to 'free speech' by holding an outdoor meeting. It eventually led to violence and the reading of the Riot Act. The strikers were forced back to work less than a week later but, by that time, some workers had decided on political action. After some preliminary meetings, the Bradford Labour Union (later the ILP) was formed on 21 May 1891 at Firth's (formerly Laycock's) Temperance Hotel in East Parade. This fulfilled the hopes of Charlie Glyde, a Labour leader, who in the middle of April 1891, had stated that 'we have had two parties in the past: the can'ts and the won'ts, and it's time we had a party that will.'

The 'party that will' spread rapidly, with the Colne Valley Labour Union being formed on 21 July 1891, the Huddersfield Labour Union on 14 September 1891, the Halifax Labour Union in July 1892, the Keighley Labour Union in October 1892 and the Leeds Labour Union in November 1892. These, and others, helped to form the national Independent Labour Party at Bradford in January 1893.

The new organisation drew upon wide support. Textile workers were attracted in large numbers, as well as a socialist poet called Tom Maguire who lived in Leeds and wrote extensively about the economic exploitation of the factory workers. However, it was not only workers who were drawn to it. A small number of the middle classes and landed gentry were also attracted. John Lister, owner of the Shibden Hall estate in Halifax, became Treasurer and entertained James Keir Hardie and other Labour leaders at his residence.

The ILP was a significant political force in the West Riding of Yorkshire, exerting its greatest influence in Bradford and Halifax, where it won parliamentary seats in 1906 – returning Fred Jowett for Bradford West and James Parker for Halifax. It also won the Colne Valley by-election with Victor Grayson in 1907. Grayson had been training to be a Dissenting minister, but gave this up to enter politics, claiming, much to the annoyance of Keir Hardie, to be the first socialist in the House of Commons.

There was also a cultural side to the new movement which organised itself in clubs, and associated itself with Clarion Glee Clubs, choirs and groups such as the Labour Church and socialist Sunday schools. Frequently, the ILP branches or associated organisations would visit the moors or Brimham Rocks for healthy walks and singsongs. The Bradford ILP had a cinema and a hall, Jowett Hall, where it held meetings and put on plays and shows. Jowett Hall was burned down, but was on the site now occupied by the present Bradford Playhouse, off the Leeds Road.

The ILP helped to form the Labour Representation Committee in 1900 – following a meeting with the TUC in Doncaster in 1899. This developed into the Labour Party in 1906 and was a training ground for many later Labour leaders. It attracted Philip Snowden, born at Ickornshaw in Cowling near Keighley, Chancellor of the Exchequer in the Labour governments of 1924 and 1929–31; and Frank Betts, a tax officer, and the father of Barbara Castle.

Out of this fertile political environment emerged a number of political leaders of the twentieth century. Harold Wilson, Labour Prime Minister, 1964-70 and 1974-76, was born near Huddersfield. Other Labour leaders represented Yorkshire constituencies, most notably Hugh Gaitskell, but also Arthur Greenwood, Ellen Wilkinson and Denis Healey. Betty Boothroyd was born at Wakefield, Roy Hattersley and David Blunkett in Sheffield. Although not a political figure, and Liberal rather than Labour, J. B. Priestley represented the radical and leftward attitudes of progressive Labour Bradford, and is honoured in a statue standing in front of the National Museum of Film and Photography.

Yorkshire was often the venue of Labour Party conferences, one of the most important being at Scarborough in 1960. This was the occasion when the leader of the party, Hugh Gaitskell, resolved to 'fight and fight and fight again' against the Conference decision to support unilateral, rather than multilateral, disarmament.

Industrial Labour and the General Strike

The Manningham Mills strike was one of the first major strikes in Yorkshire, which had not been a particularly powerful trade union area in the nineteenth century. The textile industries of the West Riding were weak until well into the twentieth century, although the light-metal and cutlery trades of Sheffield and the miners of South Yorkshire were much more effectively organised. Indeed, the coalminers were organised as the West Yorkshire Mining Association and the South Yorkshire Mining Association in 1858, before amalgamating as the Yorkshire Miners' Association in 1881. They were involved in a major national miners' strike in 1893 and, on the death of their Liberal leader, Ben Pickard, they abandoned the Liberal cause and, with the Miners' Federation of Great Britain, joining the Labour Party on 1 January 1909.

Major and, indeed, continuing industrial conflict had helped to force the coalminers and most other industrial groups, to support the Labour Party, which had come to rely heavily on the trade unions in the early twentieth century. Although the Labour Party did not always reciprocate fully with the trade unions, a policy of separate spheres seems to have operated between the unions and the party in the twentieth century, there was considerable mutual support during the General Strike of 1926. Nationally, this saw 1.75 million strikers come out in support of a million or so coal miners who were being threatened with reductions of about 10 per cent of their wage rates, as well as extended hours of work and the loss of national negotiations. Herbert Smith, secretary of the Yorkshire miners and president of the Miners' Federation of Great Britain, was a Yorkshire man, famed for his blunt manner and known as 'the man in the cloth cap'. As well as occupying the Arthurian headquarters of the Yorkshire miners at Barnsley, he was also a pub landlord, running the Woodman Inn, Smithies, just to the north of Barnsley. (This, incidentally, was the pub whose team Tommy Taylor played for as a teenager; he went on to play for Barnsley and Manchester United. A working-class lad, he was the first player to be worth almost £30,000.)

The collapse of the General Strike and the defeat of the miners left deep resentment within the mining community of Yorkshire. This persisted through to the major coal disputes of 1972, 1973-74 and

1984-85. During these years, Arthur Scargill, one time pensions officer for the Yorkshire miners and later president of the National Union of Mineworkers, argued that the class war was still being fought and that the miners must fight to gain revenge for 1926. While the miners were successful in the disputes of the 1970s, the year-long coalminers' strike of 1984-85 saw the defeat of the miners and the large-scale closure of mines. This has meant that by the beginning of the twenty-first century, the British coal industry is barely employing thirty thousand people. The 1984-85 dispute was the cause of many industrial confrontations, one of the most famous being the deployment of over eight thousand police to prevent mass picketing at the Orgreave coke depot near Sheffield. Several hundred miners were arrested and hundreds of police and miners injured in what became a watershed in mass picketing. The practice declined afterwards.

The Trades Union Congress has held many important meetings in Yorkshire. The 1899 meeting at Doncaster has been already mentioned. At Bridlington in 1939, the TUC issued the 'Bridlington Agreement' whereby unions agreed not to poach members from other unions.

Marxism and the Communist Party of Great Britain

Although they have played a relatively small part in the history of Labour in Yorkshire, Marxism and the Communist Party have left their mark on the historical map. Marxist organisations joined with others in Leeds in 1917 to form the Workers' and Soldiers' Council. Philip Snowden was the chairman at the Leeds Convention which hailed the (pre-Bolshevik) Russian Revolution and demanded a general plan for peace. It did not develop any further, but at the beginning of 1921 Leeds provided the venue for a conference to reform the Communist Party of Great Britain. Otherwise, communist influence was relatively limited, though there was a violent march of communists in Leeds during the General Strike of 1926. Some prominent communists lived in Yorkshire, such as the historian, E. P. Thompson, who lived in Halifax; he left the party in 1956.

Conclusion

Yorkshire has a rich tapestry of Labour history. There have been industrial conflicts on a grand scale, popular movements and significant political breakthroughs. Much of this survives in the written record, in oral history and in memory. Relatively little, beyond obvious natural and urban landscapes, survives in a literal sense. Nonetheless, there is ample to divert the Leftie tourist.

Gazetteer

BARNSLEY. 1-2 Huddersfield Road. The headquarters of the Yorkshire District of the National Union of Mineworkers, a fine building which has a roof that looks like the towers in the castles of Arthurian legend. Not surprisingly, the building was referred to locally as 'King Arthur's Castle', partly out of reference to Arthur Scargill, the Yorkshire and national miners' leader. Inside the building, apart from the offices, is a superbly ornate hall where the Yorkshire District held its conferences and delegate meetings.

BRADFORD. Bierley Chapel, next to the Bradford Ring Road. This was the scene of many fiery speeches opposing the long hours of child labour made by the Reverend George ('Parson') Bull who played a major role, alongside Richard Oastler (1789-1861), in the Factory movement of the 1830s and 1840s.

BRADFORD. Jacob's Well. A public house in the centre of Bradford is reputed to have been a meeting place for Chartists. It is close to the Irish/Chartist stronghold of 1840s Bradford.

BRADFORD. Manchester Road, a few hundred yards from Jacob's Well. The site of running battles between Chartists, the police and the soldiery in April 1848 when the authorities tried to arrest some leading Chartists, and in particular Isaac Jefferson, better known as 'Wat Tyler'.

BRADFORD. Bradford Playhouse, off Leeds Road. In the area of 'Little Germany' this is on the site of Jowett Hall, destroyed by fire, but named after Fred Jowett (1864-1944), the first socialist on Bradford Town Council, which was the first council to provide free school meals. Jowett became MP for West Bradford and First Commissioner for Works in Ramsay MacDonald's first Labour government of 1924. At the end of July and the beginning of August 1932, this was the meeting place for the Special Conference of the Independent Labour Party (ILP) which resulted in the ILP disaffiliating from the Labour Party.

BRADFORD. Mamma Mia's Eating Parlour, in a narrow alleyway off East Parade. Formerly Laycock's (also known as Firth's) Temperance Hotel, and in the 1960s, the Golden Lion Chinese Restaurant. In 1891 this was the birthplace of the Bradford Labour Union, which was soon to become the Bradford Independent Labour Party. It became a famous meeting place and saw many literary meetings attended by J. B. Priestley.

BRADFORD. Manningham Mills. The site of a nineteen-week conflict, between December 1890 and April 1891. Five thousand workers came out on strike – though some were locked out – against wage reductions of between 17 and 33 per cent. The mills covered fifteen acres and were built in 1873 to replace former mills that had been burnt down. They were owned by Samuel Cunliffe Lister, later Lord Masham. He sold half off in 1889 for over £1 million which he used to buy the Swinton and Rievaulx estates. The United States imposed the heavily protective McKinley tariff in 1890. To offset the impact of this tariff Lister worked his mills hard and imposed swingeing wage cuts. The conflict was bitter and divided the whole of Bradford, brought in national leaders such as Ben Tillett and Tom Mann, and culminated in disturbances in the centre of Bradford, leading to the reading of the Riot Act. The strikers were eventually defeated and forced back to work. However, the Bradford Labour Union, which became the Bradford Independent Labour Party, was formed in the wake of the defeat and became the basis of the movement that led to the creation of the Labour Party.

BRADFORD. Norfolk Gardens, between the Town Hall and St George's Hall. Originally known as Dockers' Square, it was the scene in April 1891 of violence between the authorities and the Manningham Mills strikers.

BRADFORD. Statue of J. B. Priestley, outside the National

Museum of Film and Photography. Although essentially a Liberal rather than a Labour figure, J. B. Priestley (1894-1984) admired the progressive politics that the Independent Labour Party brought to Bradford. He was influenced partly by his father, Jonathan, a schoolmaster, one of the four headmasters who in the autumn of 1907 dished out food at the first serving of the free municipal-school meals.

BRADFORD. The Black Bull public house, Ivegate. The meeting place of a Republican Club formed in 1872. Here republicans and socialists met to exchange ideas. Prince Kropotkin, the anarchist, spoke at the club in the late 1870s.

BRADFORD. The Labour Institute, Peckover Street. A former Methodist Chapel located in what is known as 'Little Germany' at the bottom of Leeds Road, this was converted into the headquarters of the Bradford Independent Labour Party in the early 1890s. Here, and at St George's Hall, a national conference met to form the Independent Labour Party in January 1893. To commemorate the centenary a mural was painted on a wall to the side, claiming that it was the site of the foundation of the ILP. It is on the wrong building. The correct building, the Labour Institute, is next door.

BRADFORD. The Star public house. Formerly the Star Music Hall, it was the meeting place of the Manningham Mills strikers until the authorities restricted their rights.

BRADFORD. St George's Hall. Built as a new concert hall in 1853, it was the scene of a meeting addressed by Ben Tillett in April 1891, which partly provoked the riots during the Manningham Mills strike in Bradford. It was also the venue for one meeting connected with the formation of the ILP in January 1893, and the scene for the 'coming of age' conference of the ILP held at Easter 1914.

BRADFORD. Undercliffe Cemetery. Bradford contains the remains of the employer class rather than of many Labour leaders. The most obvious is the Egyptian tomb of Alfred Illingworth, MP for Knaresborough and for

Bradford between 1880 and 1895; he was a great opponent of independent Labour interests in Bradford from 1890 until his death in 1907.

BRIDLINGTON. The location for the Trades Union Congress of 1939 which saw the passing of the 'Bridlington Agreement' resolution in which it was agreed that trades unions would not poach the membership of other unions.

BRIMHAM ROCKS. The scene in the 1890s of socialist Sunday school outings, meetings of socialist choirs, Clarion Club activities and other socialist trips.

COLNE VALLEY. Victor Grayson (1881-1922/41?) was elected MP for the constituency at a parliamentary by-election in 1907. He was strongly supported by Anglican priests and Nonconformist ministers, and fought the by-election against the wishes of the Labour Party leadership. He then claimed to be the first socialist in Parliament, and pressed for a Right to Work Bill. He lost his seat at the General Election of January 1910, but continued to work for a party of socialist unity, the British Socialist Party, before disappearing from the scene in 1922. It has been suggested that he went to Australia and New Zealand and returned to Britain before being killed in the Blitz.

DACRE, near Harrogate. Birthplace of Alfred Richard Orage (1873-1934), who became an elementary teacher for the Leeds School Board in the 1890s and joined the Independent Labour Party. He moved to London and edited *New Age* from 1907 to 1922, making it an anti-statist paper, espousing the idea of a craftsman-based society of guild socialism.

DEWSBURY. Dewsbury Technical College. Betty Boothroyd (1929-), born in Dewsbury, attended this College at the age of seventeen, having spent the last years of the war as a singer and dancer, touring the country with the Swing Stars Band. She became Labour MP for West Bromwich in 1973 and the first woman to be Speaker of the House of Commons in 1992.

HALIFAX. The North Bridge. The original bridge was the scene of minor disturbances connected with the Plug Plots of 1842, when textile workers marched between Bradford and Halifax and forced the closure of mills by pulling out the plugs from the boilers of steam engines.

HALIFAX. Shibden Hall. The home of John Lister, the first treasurer of the Independent Labour Party. Lister switched from the Liberal Party to the ILP/Labour and also from the Church of England to Roman Catholicism. Educated at the University of Oxford where he heard the lectures of William Morris, he inherited Shibden Hall and its estates. An environmentalist, Lister was concerned about the quality of life of the working classes and stood unsuccessfully for Parliament for the Halifax Labour Union/ILP in 1892 and 1895, attended the first National Conference of the ILP in Bradford in January 1893, and financed the activities of both the national ILP and the Halifax ILP. In the 1890s and early twentieth century Shibden Hall was the venue for sporting, swimming and gala events of the ILP. Lister offered accommodation at the Hall for leading Labour figures who came to Halifax. Keir Hardie stayed several times and, in his newspaper, The Labour Leader, reflected that 'all the gangral elements of the Labour movement descend upon Shibden Hall, much to the disgust of the butler.' Lister was also a poet and echoed a perennial gripe at Labour leadership:

> Anything! Anything! Just to get in
> Any tale! Any tale! So you may win
> All the false lying spirits unchain,
> Barter your soul, man, your voter to claim.

Shibden Hall has been under local-government management since the 1920s, and is now open to the public as a museum.

HALIFAX. Edward P. Thompson (1924-93), the historian of Labour, was raised and lived in Halifax. He was a member of the Communist Party until November 1956, when the Soviet invasion of Hungary led to his resignation, although he was heading for a break in editing *The Reasoner*, a journal that was calling for inner-party democracy within the essentially Stalinist leadership of the party.

HOLMFIRTH. Cemetery. William (Bill) Owen, actor and strong Labour Party supporter, who starred in the television series, *The Last of the Summer Wine*, is buried here. Holmfirth is also the birthplace of Ben Turner (1863-1942) who held many positions in the Yorkshire woollen and worsted textile industry, was Labour MP for Batley and Morley (1922-24 and 1929-31) and president of the Trades Union Congress in the late 1920s. He gave his name to the modestly successful Mond-Turner talks, after the General Strike of 1926, held between the Federation of British Industries and the TUC, aimed at producing an agreement to work together to put pressure on the government on economic policy.

HUBBERHOLME. St Michael and All Angels Church. The ashes of J. B. Priestley (1894-1984) are buried in the churchyard, here in the North Yorkshire Dales.

HUDDERSFIELD. Fixby Hall. Richard Oastler (1789-1861) was Steward for the Thornhill Estate at Fixby from 1820, when he succeeded his father, to 1838, when he was dismissed. He was the leader of the Short-Time, or Ten-Hour movement and began the demand for shorter hours of work for children and women with a famous letter he wrote to the *Leeds Mercury*, criticising child labour. At Fixby in 1831, he met a group of textile workers who agreed to campaign for a ten-hour day and a time book, the latter removing the need for state inspection by getting the workers to sign in before working ten hours and then signing out. Oastler stood, unsuccessfully, for Parliament in Huddersfield. He became a debtor and was committed to Fleet prison where he produced *Fleet Papers*.

HUDDERSFIELD. 4 Warneford Road, Cowersley, one mile from Milnsbridge. This small terraced house was the birthplace, on 11 March 1916, of Harold Wilson (1916-95).

HUDDERSFIELD. Railway Station. Outside is a statue, erected in 2001, of Harold

Wilson (1916-95), leader of the Labour Party 1963-76 and the third Labour Prime Minister, 1964-70 and 1974-76. A brilliant student and economist at Oxford, he claims that the term, 'desiccated calculating machine' allegedly used by Aneurin Bevan about Hugh Gaitskell, was really meant for him. He ended up as Lord Wilson of Rievaulx KG.

HUDDERSFIELD, Crosland Moor. In 1812 William Horsfall of Ottiwells near Huddersfield, a woollen-textile manufacturer, was murdered here by George Mellor, a cropper from Longroyd Bridge. Mellor and his Luddite accomplices were arrested, tried at York in January 1813, and hanged.

HUDDERSFIELD. Market Cross, between McDonald's and a pizza restaurant. The site of the George Hotel. Demonstrations took place here in 1833 when Edwin Chadwick and other Factory commissioners were gathering evidence about child labour. Four years later it was also the scene of riots and disturbances against Alfred Power who was attempting to impose the New Poor Law in Huddersfield. In the late 1840s the hotel was removed in order to build John William Street and to give access to the newly built railway station. The hotel was reconstructed on a side street where it stands today.

HULL. Birthplace of Robert Applegarth (1834-1924), general secretary of the Amalgamated Society of Carpenters and Joiners, 1862-71. A key figure of the 'Junta', the group of leading trade union secretaries behind the launch of the Trades Union Congress. A leading light in the Manhood Suffrage movement, he helped to organise the visit of Garibaldi to England in 1864.

HULL. The Docks. The scene of many strikes, including the unofficial strike of 1954 when four thousand dockers refused to unload more than 60 ships because of the continuance of hand techniques.

ICKORNSHAW. Just outside Cowling, the moor contains a nine-foot-high cairn erected in 1938 in honour of Philip Snowden (1864-1937), Chancellor of the Exchequer in the Labour governments of

Ramsay MacDonald, 1924 and 1929-31. Born in the hamlet of Ickornshaw, he became an ILP pioneer. He was MP for Blackburn, 1906-18, and for Colne Valley, 1922-31. A cripple and an austere teetotaller, he was an inspirational orator and an opponent of the First World War. He was briefly in MacDonald's National government when he turned bitterly on his former colleagues. He was cremated and his ashes were scattered across Ickornshaw Moor. His wife, Ethel, who died in 1951 is also honoured.

KEIGHLEY. Philip Snowden (1864-1937) was active in the Keighley Labour Church in the 1890s. Denis Healey (1917-) lived in Keighley from the age of five to the age of eight: his father was Principal of Keighley Technical School. At the Cosy Corner Picture House his life-long fascination with films was born.

KIPPAX. Birthplace of Herbert Smith (1862-1938), president of the Miners Federation of Great Britain, 1922-29, and a prominent member of the TUC. Known as 'the man in the cloth cap', he was famed for his blunt comments, such as – after the TUC called off the General Strike on 12 May 1926 – 'There's more diarrhoea inside Transport House than outside.'

LEEDS. Beckett Street Cemetery. The Leeds socialist and poet of Irish origin Tom Maguire (1866-95) is buried here. His epitaph reads: 'Socialist, bold, cautious, true and loving comrade.'

LEEDS. Bus Station. Near the toilets is a plaque dedicated to Tom Maguire (1866-95). Born in the Bank District of East Leeds into a working-class Irish-immigrant family, Maguire formed the Leeds branch of the Social Democratic Federation in September 1884 and helped to reorganise it as the Leeds branch of the Socialist League six months later. He was a committed poet, writing poems such as 'Mammon Land', 'The Coming of Democracy', 'To the Wage Slave' and 'A Victim' which starts

> O! I am tired of factory toil.

His poetry can be found in *Tom Maguire: A Remembrance*

edited by Alf Mattison and Isabella Ford, and in his *Machine Room Chants*.

LEEDS. Parkinson Building, University of Leeds. Museum of the History of Education, which has school desks and the equipment of yesteryear alongside log books and other manuscript sources.

LEEDS. University. Attended by Arthur Greenwood (1880-1954), born in Hunslett. He was Minister of Health in Ramsay MacDonald's second government, 1929-31. It was to Greenwood that L. S. Amery said, 'Speak for England, Arthur', in the House of Commons debate in September 1939 when, in the absence due to illness of Clement Attlee, he was about to speak on behalf of the Labour Party in response to a feeble speech from Neville Chamberlain.

LEEDS. Hugh Gaitskell Community Centre. Leeds South was represented by Hugh Gaitskell (1906-63) from 1945 to his death. After Winchester and New College, Oxford, he was a Workers' Educational Association tutor in his early twenties and produced a short history of Chartism. He was Chancellor of the Exchequer in 1950 in the last year of Clement Attlee's government and leader of the Labour Party from 1955 to his death.

LEEDS. St Stephen's Church, Kirkstall. The grave of Richard Oastler (1789-1861) can be seen through a grille from outside the church, positioned underneath the altar. He had been the leader of the Ten-Hour movement and a campaigner against child labour.

LEEDS. York Road. The scene of conflict between communists, largely from Castleford, and the authorities during the General Strike of May 1926. In 1921, the one-year-old Communist Party had a convention aimed at reorganising the party. A picture of the delegates sitting in front of the market beneath a sign on a stall, 'Harry Verity, These Prime Bullocks and Heffers', can be found in *Under the Red Flag* by Keith Laybourn and Dylan Murphy. Leeds had also been prominent in greeting the first Russian (Menshevik) Revolution on 3 June 1917. About 1,150 delegates attended the Conference and passed resolutions, hailing the Russian revolution, aspiring for a general peace based on the rights of nations to decide on their own affairs and demanding the creation of a charter of liberties by the British government. They called for a Council of Workers and Soldiers' Delegates in every town and every urban and rural district. Philip Snowden, who fourteen years later denounced the 1931 Labour manifesto as 'Bolshevism run mad', was responsible for the latter and talked of painting Britain red.

MARSDEN. In this community large iron sledges were made, known as 'Enochs'. In the Luddite period in the early 1810s, 'Enochs were used to break down doors and smash sharing frames. The Luddite cry was 'Enoch made them, Enoch shall break them.'

MIRFIELD. Community of the Resurrection. The quarry at this Anglican monastery was used for Labour and suffragette meetings in the early twentieth century. Keir Hardie spoke in this natural amphitheatre, as did Emmeline Pankhurst, leader of the Women's Social and Political Union. In the early twentieth century the community was run by Father Bull who was sympathetic to the early socialists and organised a message of congratulations from Yorkshire religious leaders to the Labour Party after its parliamentary successes in the 1906 General Election. The community was for some years the home base of Father Trevor Hudelstone, tireless campaigner against South African apartheid.

NORMANTON. Normanton Girls' Grammar School. Originally a mining village near Leeds, Alice Bacon (1909-93) was born here, the daughter of a mining family, and attended this school, going on to be a teacher, MP for Leeds, a Gaitskell loyalist and a minister in the governments of Harold Wilson between 1964 and 1970.

ORGREAVE. Coke Depot. The depot was the scene of violent confrontation between miners and pickets in May and June 1984 during the Miners' Strike of 1984-85. Over eight thousand police prevented mass picketing by more than 32,500 pickets during which 273 were arrested and hundreds of police and miners injured. 'The Battle of Orgreave' proved to be a turning point in the strike, and mass picketing by the miners tailed off significantly thereafter. The plant has now gone and a plaque marks the area of conflict, although it may have been put in the wrong place.

PUDSEY. Moravian School, Fulneck. Richard Oastler (1789-1861), the leader of the campaign against child labour, attended this school. In 1945 Denis Healey failed to win the constituency of Pudsey and Otley in the General Election.

RIPON. The Workhouse Museum of the Poor. The museum illustrates the conditions faced by the poor, who were forced into the workhouse in the eighteenth and nineteenth centuries.

SCARBOROUGH. The Spa Theatre. The scene of the Labour Party Conference in 1960, when the conference voted for unilateral disarmament by 3.3 million to 2.9 million votes. This provoked the pledge of the party leader, Hugh Gaitskell, to overturn the vote, saying he would 'fight and fight and fight again to save the party we love'. More recently, Scarborough was the scene of the last significant Social Democratic Party Conference in 1989. The party had survived two years after most of the SDP had merged with the Liberals. The conference came to a halt before the party leader, David Owen, gave his speech. He had therefore to give a speech from a makeshift platform in what became known as 'The Speech on the Beach'. The party expired soon afterwards.

SHEFFIELD. Manchester Road School for the Blind. Attended by David Blunkett (1947-), Labour MP for Sheffield Brightside, Secretary of State for Education and Skills 1997-2001 and Home Secretary, 2001-04. Blind from birth, he became a dynamic and determined political leader of Sheffield City Council.

SHEFFIELD, City Grammar School. Alma mater of Roy Hattersley (1932-), Birmingham MP and minister in Labour governments from 1964 to 1970 and 1974 to 1979. Hattersley became Deputy Leader of the Labour Party from 1983 to 1992, since when he has busied himself as writer, novelist, historian and *Guardian* columnist.

SHEFFIELD. Hereford Street. On 8 October 1866 the house here of Thomas Fearnehough was blown up. This was one of the outrages organised by members of the Light Metal Trade and Cutlery Union who sought to enforce their control over the labour market. Only the offer of indemnity from prosecution to those who were guilty of this, and other offences, revealed the extent to which William Broadhead of the Grinders' Union, was prepared to go to enforce the Union's will. Broadhead had employed Samuel Crooks to enforce the union's power on several occasions for the sum of £15 – 'that was about the regular sum'.

TODMORDEN. Town Hall. Built by John Fielden, a factory master who lived at Todmorden and wrote *The Curse of the Factory System* (1836), in support of the Ten-Hour movement. He also opposed the introduction of the New Poor Law.

WORSBOROUGH DALE. Birthplace of Arthur Scargill (1938-), President of the National Union of Mineworkers from 1982 to 2003, particularly associated with the NUM national strike 1984-85.

YORK. Gaol. Now part of York Museum. Here George Mellor, cropper and Luddite leader, was held and hanged for murder with two of his co-conspirators in January 1813. Feargus O'Connor, Chartist leader, also did time here.

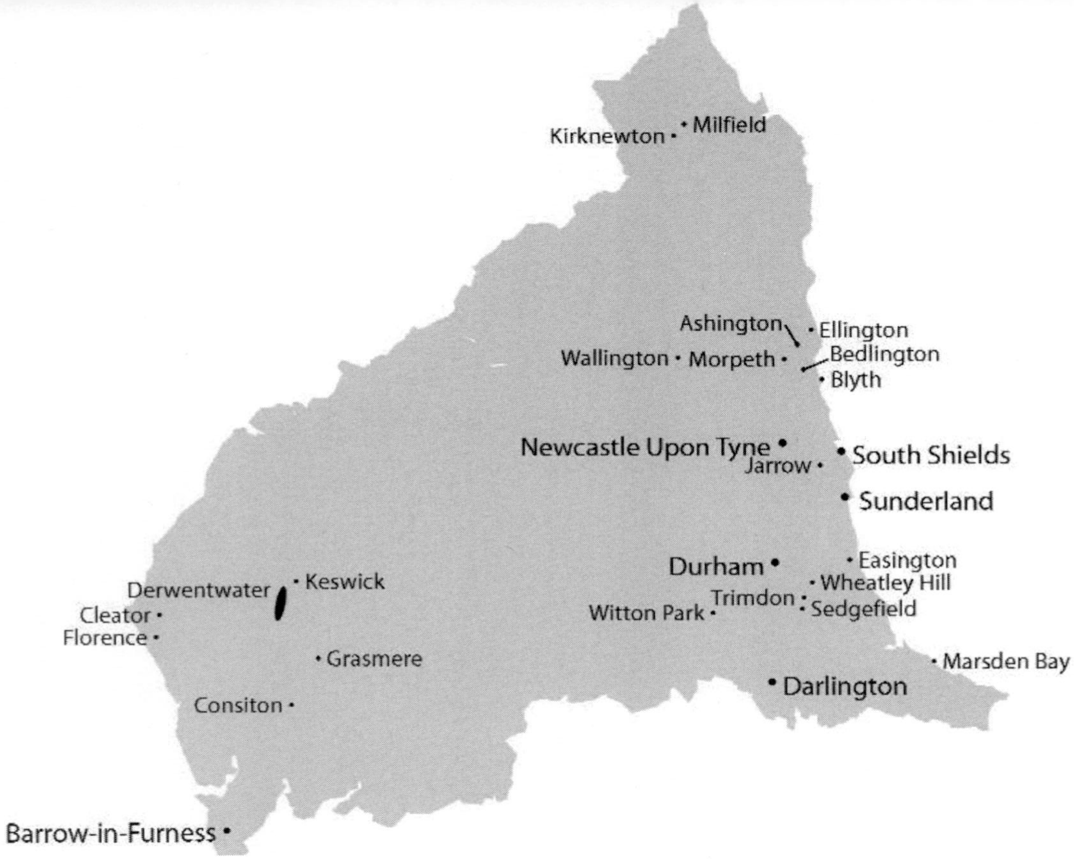
Kirknewton
Milfield
Ashington
Ellington
Wallington
Morpeth
Bedlington
Blyth
Newcastle Upon Tyne
Jarrow
South Shields
Sunderland
Durham
Easington
Wheatley Hill
Trimdon
Sedgefield
Witton Park
Marsden Bay
Darlington
Derwentwater
Keswick
Cleator
Florence
Grasmere
Consiton
Barrow-in-Furness

9.

THE NORTH

Paul Routledge

It was once the ancient kingdom of Northumbria, home to invading Viking kings. Something of the spirit remains, for the North East has been a defiant breeding ground of trade union and political militancy for almost two centuries. Composed these days of the counties of Durham, Tyne and Wear, and Northumberland, the region is a rich seam in the history of the Left. The industrial analogy is apt, because coalminers formed the backbone of the Labour movement from the early nineteenth century to the present day. They handed down a fighting tradition, a pantheon of heroes (with the occasional villain) and monuments in stone and steel to eras of struggle and radicalism.

The present generation does not always appreciate what is rapidly disappearing. New Labour figures like Tony Blair, Alan Milburn and Stephen Byers, who profited greatly from their links with the region, rarely exhibit respect for its Left heritage: Tony Blair has for years ignored invitations to the Durham Miners' Gala, the premier event in the Northern Labour movement's calendar, even though it takes place a few miles from his constituency home. They are the worse for their loss, and so are we. But at least we can see what they are missing.

Perhaps the first port of call for the political traveller, and certainly the last, is the Market Tavern in Durham's tiny cobbled Market Square. This real-ale pub, the last in the square, adjoins the warren of a covered market, more like a souk than a traditional northern open-air fair. The Market has thrived since the city council announced in 1853 that the local water was unfit for human consumption. The thirst of market-goers 'could only be quenched by ales from this house', announces a plaque, which also states that the Durham Miners' Association (DMA) was founded in this pub in 1871. This is incorrect. The union was established here in 1869, by pioneers determined to end the wage slavery of the colliers and their families.

From the Market Square, walk down Silver to Red Hill, the majestic brick and stone offices of the Durham Mineworkers' Union built in 1915 to replace earlier premises opened in North Road in 1875. Set amid spacious grounds, Red Hill is a testimony to the sense of permanence that the miners felt in that era. 'We are here to stay', states this building. Alas, all that is left of the Durham mining industry is this stately edifice. All the pits, which at their height employed 110,000 men, have closed, the last in the 1990s. Despite the coalfield's reputation for moderation in post-war years, a reputation buttressed by the Union's wily general secretary, Sam Watson (1898-1967), a fixer in the mould of Peter Mandelson's grandfather, Herbert Morrison, miners in Durham were among the first out in the Great Strike of 1984 and among the last to return to work in 1985. Their militancy was rewarded with an accelerated closure programme which saw the pits shut down like dominoes.

In the grounds of Red Hill, four large statues stand as guardians of the Union's past, eternal reminders of John Forman (1822/23-1900), Alexander Macdonald (1821-81), William Patterson (1847-96) and John Wilson (1837-1915). Of these, Wilson was the most prominent. Born in Greatham, the son of a quarryman, Wilson worked down the pit as a young man. His life changed at the age of 30, when he converted to Primitive Methodism, giving up gambling and drinking, a rite of passage not unusual among miners' leaders in

Brantwood

Victorian times. Wilson travelled to the United States, experiencing conditions in the mines of Pennsylvania and Illinois, and worked at Wheatley Hill colliery on his return. Sacked for being an 'agitator' – strike leader – he refused to leave the village and set up a stationery shop. In 1869, he was one of the founders of the DMA and rose to become its general secretary in 1895. Wilson became Liberal MP for Houghton-le-Spring, 1885-86 and for Mid-Durham in 1890, when he beat the Conservative coal owner Vane Tempest.

William Patterson, another quarryman's son, and a Methodist New Connection lay preacher and Freemason, was born in Durham and at the age of eighteen persuaded men at Hesworth colliery to form a Union lodge. At the age of 21 he was one of the founders of the DMA and became a full-time agent in South Durham. He was renowned as a rescuer during pit disasters, but his greatest legacy was the Union's 455-page rule book which governed, as best the officials could, behaviour at sometimes rowdy lodge meetings. Patterson, a radical with scholarly aspirations, was dismissed as a 'persistent plodder' but died loaded with praise.

Macdonald is the odd man out in the group. Born in Lanarkshire, he went down the mines at the age of eight, but at 25 paid his way through Glasgow University by working underground during the summer. He qualified as a mine manager and became the Scottish miners' leader, serving also from 1874 as Liberal MP for Stafford. He was accused of 'currying favour' with the Conservative leader Benjamin Disraeli, in his declining years.

John Forman, another founder of the DMA, lived to the relatively old age – for a miner – of 77. He chaired the first Big Meeting – the present-day gala – in 1872, heaping scorn on the fear expressed in local newspapers that the gathering was for the instigation of a general strike of pitmen. He 'apologised' for giving 'great alarm to the delicate citizens of Durham'.

The constituency of Labour's fifth Prime Minister, Tony Blair, Sedgefield, has some modern (naturally) exhibits in the Leftie show. The village of Sedgefield itself straggles down both sides of a green and tries to be more county than Durham but does not quite pull it off. Kids with mobile phones infest the streets at night, forcing people to take refuge in the Dun Cow pub. A couple of miles up the road is the Trimdon Labour Club, of which Tony Blair is a member. The inside, if you can talk your way in for a pint of Federation, is much like any other working-men's club, only posher.

Far more rewarding is the journey a few miles north to Wheatley Hill, last resting place of the legendary Peter Lee (1864-1935), after whom the nearby new town of Peterlee is named. Lee had worked in fifteen pits by the age of 21, and was notoriously one of the lads, hard-drinking, blaspheming and fist-fighting until he saw the light in the Lanky House pub in Wingate close by, joining the Primitive Methodists. He gave up dissolution, learned to read and write, and travelled as a miner to the United States (Ohio, Pennsylvania and Kentucky) and later to South Africa, returning to become check-weighman at Wheatley Hill colliery. He rose to become President of the DMA and of the National Miners' Federation. He was an early advocate of national pay agreements in the industry and a preacher 'in the ranting tradition'. He was also chairman of Durham County Council (in 1919), the first Labour Chairman of any County Council in Britain.

To the south west is regenerated Witton Park. Then you pass through Shildon, pausing if you wish to see the plethora of railway museums which tell you much about a way of life that has virtually disappeared. Rail pioneers George Stephenson and Timothy Hackworth are strongly associated with the neighbourhood. Darlington, at the end of the Durham trail, once housed the massive North Road locomotive works, today an unkempt industrial 'park'.

There is yet another rail museum at North Road station, small but well-furnished with memories of a railway town. The West Cemetery contains the grave of, among thousands of others, Arthur Henderson (1863-1935), leader of the Labour Party, 1931-32, and previously Home Secretary (1924) and Foreign Secretary (1929-31).

Another grave in the same cemetery is that of John Hyslop Bell, who was born in Dumfriesshire and moved to London to be a civil servant. He came to the North East in his twenties to prosper as the region's most famous journalist. He was invited by Darlington's Liberal establishment to found the radical *Northern Echo* in 1870, but perhaps his greatest contribution was the appointment, a year later, of William Thomas Stead (1849-1912) as editor. Stead, a native of Embleton, Northumberland, was only 22 and had no newspaper experience, but he was a naturally brilliant campaigner. His paper was instrumental in returning thirteen Liberal MPs from the county in the 1874 General Election, the 'Durham 13', as they were known. Stead was educated at home by his father, a Congregational Minister, and first tasted controversy as the clerk and speech writer – spin doctor, as we would say today – of a prominent Newcastle councillor. He began writing articles for local papers, until catapulted by Bell into the *Echo* editorial chair. He achieved national fame with a campaign over the Bulgarian atrocities committed by the Turks in 1876. In 1880 he became editor of the *Pall Mall Gazette*, where he continued his ground-breaking work in investigative journalism, campaigning and typographical reform. In 1912, against the advice of a clairvoyant, he sailed for the United States on the *Titanic*, and went down with the ship playing bridge.

Northumberland advertises itself as 'England's Border County' and there is a strong feel of Scotland about the place. Squat, single-storey stone houses with massive chimneys are common to both. Sparsely populated in the north, Northumberland shares with the coalmining traditions of Durham, though the 'howkies' of the county – men who howked the coal out of the ground – always maintained a fierce independence from their brothers across the Tyne.

However, this county also gave birth to pioneering women: Christian reformer Josephine Butler, and Emily Wilding Davison, the suffragette who died under the hooves of the King's horse at Epsom for her cause. Butler was born at Milfield Hill and is buried at Kirknewton. Emily Davison was brought up in Longhorsley and is buried in Morpeth.

To the south is Ashington, which has been described as 'the biggest pit village in England'. Originally composed of eleven terraces, of which fewer than half survive, Ashington exploded in the middle of the nineteenth century when fine workable seams were tapped. Ashington is now more famous for its footballers – Jack and Bobby Charlton, and the legendary 'Wor' Jackie Milburn who won 263 caps for England and whom Tony Blair imagined he saw playing. A statue of Milburn trapping the ball (with his left foot, naturally) graces the town.

South of Ashington lies the old town of Bedlington, a farming neighbourhood that was hustled into the coal era. Dr James Trotter came here as a doctor in 1864 and worked to put Northumberland's first working man into Parliament: Thomas Burt.

North Shields, at the mouth of the Tyne, still echoes to the mournful cries of the seagulls, which in past days found more sustenance from the fishing fleet. The port once had a wooden dolly, set up in 1774, reputedly the figurehead of a ship. She was Everyfishwife, 'no slim, simpering Goddess-like creature, but a bluff, saucy, hearty-looking hussy with a full-floating petticoat, something in the style of Good Queen Bess.' Fishermen would break off bits for good luck as they sailed, and several versions graced the fish quay, which still functions and is crowded at weekends with local people buying fish suppers. I recommend the Waterfront Chippy, at £3 for fish and chips. A fine new bronze fishwife, a creel upon her back, has taken the place of Bess, in a rose garden outside the library in Northumberland Square, a Georgian remnant of old North Shields.

Across the river in South Shields they have their wooden dollies too, now replaced by a statue of Dolly Peel, a real life 'fishwife' of the 1800s who eventually went to sea herself as a nurse. The statue shows her laughing, with fish at her feet.

Unsurprisingly, South Shields is also the home of the lifeboat. It was invented here in 1790, after the wreck of the *Adventure* the previous year, watched by helpless townsfolk who were unable to rescue the crew. A reward of two guineas was offered to build a vessel to save mariners' lives, and a huge sandstone monument on the seafront on the road south of the town recalls the historical argument over who actually invented the modern lifeboat. The palm is usually given to William Wouldhave, parish clerk to nearby St Hilda's church, but this has been claimed by another local man, Henry Greathead. Both are commemorated on the pinnacle, which sits alongside an actual lifeboat, *Tyne*, credited with saving 1,028 lives.

If you have overdosed on monuments, a pleasurable surprise awaits a few miles further on in Marsden Bay, at the Grotto. And inland lies the home of the Venerable Bede, the town of Jarrow, 'the town that was murdered', and from where, in October 1936, two hundred men marched to London and stirred the conscience of the nation. Four out of five men in the town were unemployed.

To the west, adjacent to County Durham and Northumberland and sharing the region's geology, Cumbria exhibits similar traditions of political activity, with one notable exception. To the south and east, the Lake District has nurtured and attracted poets, painters, thinkers and craftsmen, and continues to do so. To the west, the coal, ironmaking and shipbuilding industries of the coastal belt spawned unions and political awakening. A fault line between the two runs practically through the middle, roughly consistent with the old boundaries of Cumberland and Westmorland. The two co-exist uneasily, with the county town of Carlisle, a railway centre, forming a separate political entity to the north.

Cumbria may not boast the sheer size of the North East's political tradition, but it is still worthy of investigation. Monuments of the past, from the half-hidden St Mary's Grotto at Cleator Moor to the glories of Brantwood, John Ruskin's home by Coniston Water, bear ample testament to a distinctive history of Leftie endeavour. The region's radical history is probably best surveyed by a route round the once great industrial periphery, beginning in Millom, and concluding in Grasmere, the last resting place of William Wordsworth. His early years as a sympathiser with the French Revolution claim him for the Left, even though he degenerated into a reactionary in his years as Poet Laureate. He was one of ours before he was one of theirs: sadly, an odyssey all too familiar.

From the M6, the road to south Lakelands twists below hills towards the river Duddon. If time is not of the essence, a side-trip will take you down the Furness peninsula to Barrow, which I have always found to be a grim little town, the home of Britain's nuclear Polaris and Trident submarine building. It was here that Albert Booth MP, the least known Labour Employment Secretary of modern times, committed political hara-kiri by leading a march of the Campaign for Nuclear Disarmament through the streets. He lost the constituency in the Falklands War General Election of 1983, but it later reverted into safe Labour hands. Today, without a trace of irony, Barrow markets itself as 'one of the best kept secrets of Britain', a Victorian town seen best in the Dock Museum.

But for the real feel of the Industrial Revolution I prefer Millom, where ghostly ironmasters seem to lurk at every corner. The road snakes down the beautiful Duddon estuary to the former iron-ore mining town, where pride of place in the market square is given to an evocative sculpture of a worker at the last mine, Hodbarrow, closed in 1968. He stands by an ore wagon, and you can almost smell the red dust. The statue is also dedicated to Millom's first freeman, the poet Norman Nicholson (1914-87). A small museum at the railway station, open from Easter to October, celebrates the region's attractions. On the December day I was there, it was too cold even to take down the details of the exhibits inside.

The winding coastal road takes you north from Millom, with the Irish Sea to your left and brooding hills like the 1,070 feet Black Combe to the right, past the improbable battlements of Muncaster Castle and the baleful presence of Sellafield Nuclear Power Station (Visitor Centre) to the Florence Mine just off the ring road around the attractive town of Egremont. Florence Mine houses an excellent 'heritage centre' which illustrates the life and working of the last deep working iron ore mine in western Europe.

Further north at Cleator is a shrine built by victims of the Depression, inspired by a caring priest.

Skirting the hills, the A5068 brings us to Cockermouth, the birthplace of honorary Leftie Fletcher Christian, the mutineer on the *Bounty*. He was born in Moorland Close in 1764, and educated at the town's Free Grammar School. He went to sea in 1783, and first served under Captain Bligh three years later on the *Britannia*, when the two became friends. It was not to last, for Christian led the Navy's most famous mutiny on the *Bounty* during her voyage to Tahiti in 1789, finally settling on the Pitcairn Islands with eight shipmates and a group of captive Polynesian natives. His exploits are commemorated on story boards outside a pub named after him in the High Street. Christian would no doubt have approved, but the despotic Bligh, who survived being set adrift in mid-Pacific by the mutineers, would probably turn up his nose at this hostelry.

Practically opposite the pub is the house where William Wordsworth (1770-1850) was born. This is now a museum. The poet, a youthful revolutionary, is buried at Grasmere to the east.

A few miles south west on the A593 brings the radical traveller to Coniston, a place of pilgrimage for one of the Left's great intellectual figures, John Ruskin (1819-1900), who, as art critic, artist, writer, philosopher and social revolutionary, was one of the Victorian giants. As a socialist he bequeathed Ruskin College Oxford, where thousands of working men have gained the university education denied to them by the class system. Born in London, the son of a prosperous wine merchant, his first contact with Cumbria was at the tender age of five, when his family visited Keswick. 'The first thing I remember,' he wrote later, 'as an event in life was being taken by my nurse to the brow of Friar's Crag on Derwentwater. It was the creation of the world for me.'

The family returned to the Lake District twice more over the next few years, and at the age of eleven, Ruskin wrote a 2,310 word poem to describe his formative experiences. After studying at Oxford, Ruskin leapt to fame with his championship of J. M. W. Turner and the Pre-Raphaelites, and became a leading cultural icon. In the 1850s, he became involved in Radical politics, teaching at the Working Men's College in London and fashioning his own brand of Christian Socialism. Ruskin continued to visit Cumbria and, after the death of his father made him a wealthy man, he bought the country residence of Brantwood from W. J. Linton, a wood carver and revolutionary.

Ruskin consistently attacked the idea of 'economic man', and as a thinker he was hailed by prophets as diverse as Mahatma Gandhi who confessed that his work 'transformed my life' and Tolstoy who described Ruskin as 'one of those rare men who think with their hearts'. Thought is not enough, of course, and Ruskin College Oxford, a testament to the practical necessity of education and political organisation, is perhaps his greatest political legacy to men like the iron and coal miners who sweated for their wages not 20 miles from Brantwood.

Cumbria, Northumberland and Durham were never revolutionary in the way that, say, Red Clydeside was. The miners were early to politics, but took decades to shake off Liberalism and espouse an independent Labour Party. These counties are quintessentially English, and, contemptible though the word is, *moderate* in their reforming zeal. However, in their hills and along their industrially desecrated coastlines, the men and women of these counties nurtured the Left in a steady, loyal, accumulative fashion, so that they remained strongholds of the Labour Party in its darkest hours. The downside was the creation of one-party politics in some areas, notably Durham and Newcastle upon Tyne, which corrupted local politicians. That tradition, albeit diluted, allowed a Blair project to find a firm base in this region. It is unlikely that the writer of a similar guide book in a hundred years' time will find visible traces of that generation, as may be found of the pioneers remembered in these pages.

Gazetteer

ASHINGTON,
Northumberland. Woodhord colliery. A Museum of Mining, 'Gannin doon the pit' (temporarily closed but expected to reopen in 2006), replaces the colliery site. It houses a showcase for the pitmen painters who formed the increasingly well-known Ashington School. The men drew and painted in a hut behind the local cinema, drawing on memory for their real-life mining-community pictures.

BARROW-IN-FURNESS,
Cumbria. Dock Museum. Here, in the town's old graving dock, you can study the Vickers photographic archive, explore a Second World War submarine and take a virtual tour of the 1950s liner, *Oriana*. The social and industrial history of a shipbuilding community is also on display.

BEDLINGTON,
Northumberland. Front Street, Memorial to Dr James Trotter. Front Street is an agreeable jumble of buildings set back from the road. The sandstone memorial which bears more than a slight resemblance to the Albert Memorial, is to Dr James Trotter, a Scots medical practitioner who came here in 1864. He fought to improve the town's water and sanitation. He also wrote books and verse, but he is best remembered for putting Northumberland's first working man into Parliament: the miners' leader Thomas Burt (1837-1922). Trotter resisted pressure to stand himself, and acted as agent for Burt instead. Burt, the son of a miner, was born in nearby Murton Row (now gone from the map) and went down the pit at the age of ten. He educated himself in the English classics, economics and politics and was elected secretary of the Northumberland Mineworkers' Association in 1863. After the 1867 Reform Act, he stood (at Trotter's urging) as Radical

Labour candidate at Morpeth in the 1874 General Election. He joined Alexander Macdonald, the Scots miners' leader, as one of the first two working men to enter Parliament and remained at Westminster for 44 years, holding office under Gladstone at the Board of Trade. But Burt had no truck with the Independent Labour Party, founded in 1893, and died four years after retiring from the House of Commons at the age of 80. J. R. Clynes described Burt as 'the forlorn hope of the mighty British army of workers who flung open the gates of St Stephen's.' He would not have made it but for the self-effacing Dr Trotter.

BLYTH, Northumberland. Princess Louise Secondary School. Ted Short (1912-), elected deputy leader of the Labour Party from 1972 to 1976, was headmaster of this school. A gritty loyal man, he was Secretary of State for Education from 1968 to 1970, having been an uncorrupt leader of the Newcastle upon Tyne City Council.

CLEATOR, Cumbria. St Mary's Catholic Church. In a small park by the church lies a unique memorial of the Depression, the grotto of Our Lady of Lourdes, built by unemployed men 'inspired by a priest for the care of his people'. Father F. C. Clayton organised jobless men to construct the shrine some forty feet high with stone from local pit slag heaps. They benefited from a 'Clog Fund' which gave vouchers for clothing and footwear. It was opened by the Abbot of Douai Abbey, and rededicated by Cardinal Basil Hume in 1980. Not even its most religious admirer would call the rough-hewn grotto beautiful, but as Marc Almond wrote in *Enchanted Britain*, 'there is an atmosphere of peace surrounding it', and pilgrims still come to this lonely setting, created by anonymous labourers three generations ago.

CONISTON, Cumbria. Brantwood. The home, from 1871 to his death, of John Ruskin (1819-1900). He bought the property after the death of his father made him a wealthy man. Here he was visited by many eminent Victorians, including Charles Darwin, Holman Hunt and Kate Greenaway. From here he issued forth *Fors Clavigera: Letters to the Workmen and Labourers of Great Britain,* in which he challenged 'supporters and apologists for a capitalist economy' and strongly influenced the nascent trade union movement and early leaders such as Tom Mann (1856-1941) and Ben Tillett (1860-1943). Ruskin retired here in 1884 and stopped writing five years later, after which he rarely spoke. He died in 1900, leaving a rich political and cultural inheritance. Brantwood is filled with the great man's drawings and watercolours, together with some of his original furniture, books and lares et penates. A video presentation explores his work and life in a Victorian country house. There are special events, and regular readings from Ruskin's words in the study. Brantwood has over 250 acres of woodland gardens, lakeshore meadows and moorland hilltop.

CONISTON, Cumbria. St Andrew's Church. Although he is commemorated in Poets' Corner, Westminster Abbey, the grave of John Ruskin (1819-1900) lies here beneath a memorial cross sculpted by W. G. Collingwood.

DARLINGTON, County Durham. North Road Station. A railway museum is sited near an industrial park that once housed the massive North Road locomotive works.

DARLINGTON, County Durham. West Cemetery. Grave of Arthur Henderson (1863-1935). Henderson was leader of the Labour Party from 1931, after the defection of Ramsay MacDonald, to 1932, when he was supplanted by George Lansbury. Born in Glasgow, Henderson was brought up in Newcastle upon Tyne, where he became a foundryman and active trade unionist. A Wesleyan Methodist, he had a chequered political career, in and out of Parliament as a Labour MP for a variety of constituencies around the country. Known as 'Uncle Arthur', he was Home Secretary in Ramsay MacDonald's first Labour government of 1924 and Foreign Secretary in his second,

1929-31. He was awarded the Nobel Peace Prize in 1934 for his disarmament diplomacy. He lived at various addresses in Darlington, latterly in Windsor Terrace.

DARLINGTON, County Durham. Priestgate. A small plaque on the rusting door of the offices of the *Northern Echo* commemorates the editorship of the radical campaigning journalist, W. T. Stead (1849-1912). On the opposite side of the road, outside the public library, is a striking memorial in the shape of an iron ring set in a heavy granite block. This is the stone to which Stead tethered his dogs and pony when he lived at Grainey Hall. An inscription records that 'the boulder is an enduring symbol of his indomitable courage and strength of character and may keep green the memory of one of England's greatest men. His body perished in the *Titanic* as she sank on 15 April 1912. His spirit still lives.' This should be a place of pilgrimage for all journalists.

DERWENTWATER, Cumbria. Friar's Crag. A memorial erected by Canon Hardwicke Rawnsley marks the spot where John Ruskin, (1819-1900), at the age of five, beheld the beauty of the Lake District: 'It was the creation of the world for me,' he subsequently wrote. From here you can take in a vista from the Irish Sea to Helvellyn.

DURHAM. County Hotel. From the balcony, generations of Labour leaders before Tony Blair, have 'taken the salute' at the annual Durham Miners' Gala. This is held on a Saturday in July and is known as The Big Meeting. From early morning, the miners (once a miner, always a miner: they would not welcome the term 'former') and their families assemble in Market Square behind the glorious banners of their pits. These are perhaps the Labour movement's greatest works of art, immortalised in John Gorman's book *Banner Bright*. With highly stylised scenes of industrial, union and domestic activity, portraits of union leaders and slogans such as 'Educate, Organise, Agitate', they are a pictorial history of a way of life fixed in bright colours on silk.

Punctuated by brass and silver bands, the procession winds its way down the twisting street to Elvet Bridge, across the river Wear and on to a nearby park for uplifting speeches. Nowhere else, not even at the TUC's Tolpuddle Martyrs' Rally, is the soul of Labour so honestly – and noisily – on show.

DURHAM. Market Tavern, Market Square. In 1869 (and not, as a plaque states, 1871) the Durham Miners' Association was founded here – the forerunners of the Durham branch of the National Union of Mineworkers.

DURHAM. Red Hill. The offices of the Durham Mineworkers' Union, built in 1915. In the grounds can be seen statues of Victorian Durham miners' leaders John Forman (1822/23-1900), Alexander Macdonald (1821-81), William Patterson (1847-96) and John Wilson (1837-1915).

EASINGTON, County Durham. Colliery. This colliery was the last mine in County Durham to close – in 1993. It once employed more than two thousand men, working in seams far out to sea. In the Great Strike of 1984-85, Easington was a bastion of defiance to the Conservatives. The colliery village is separate from the old village, which boasts a church with a Norman tower. Its fame (or infamy) is more recent. On 29 May 1951, 81 miners and two rescuers were killed by an explosion in the pit. They are remembered in a memorial avenue of trees, one for each death, and on a plaque mounted on a slab of rock from the pit bottom. The panel records that the men died *together*, a reaffirmation of the solidarity of miners. 'To honour the memory of those who lost their lives,' it states, 'let Passers-By Do Likewise. Get Understanding and Promote Goodwill in all Things.' The sorrows of the past seem to hang over the village. Two big brick schools are boarded up, for sale. The largest building still in use is the Social Welfare Centre, formerly the Miners' Institute and Hall, but some of the pit rows have been brightened up, and people here are plainly determined not to have a sentence of community death carried out.

ELLINGTON, Northumberland. A pit here, employing three hundred men, was the last remaining colliery in Northumberland, servicing a power station for the Lynemouth aluminium smelter. Its closure was announced in January 2005, although there are three hundred million tonnes of recoverable coal still underground. Ellington still has the feel of an authentic mining community, with the pit site beside the social centre, where girls go for dance classes of a Saturday morning. On the beach are lovingly cared-for huts, reminiscent of the workers' dachas of Russia.

FLORENCE, Cumbria. Heritage Centre. In spite of its infuriating name, this is an excellent place to visit. It is based on the last deep working iron ore mine in western Europe. Here, you can take an underground tour of the mine, emerging covered with the distinctive red dust of hematite ore. Florence, named after the Chairman of the mining company, was opened in 1914 to meet the needs of Millom's pig iron trade. Its output was later used at the Workington steel railway line manufacturers, on whose products the world travels. The present shaft was sunk in 1940, and is being extended to Ullcoats mines, where visitors are taken. These days, the ore is chiefly employed in the castings trade, but can also be found in the pigments industry, being used for paints and cosmetics. On the mine surface, an exhibition, simple but sympathetically laid out, tells the story of the miners, their industry and their way of life. These men, like John Cairns, winner of the Edward Medal ('the Miners' VC') for life-saving equipment during disasters, stare down powerfully from photographs, as real as if they were in your living room. Here are their boots, their detonator boxes, their iron 'prickers', their helmets, their tokens and the records of their sick fund societies. I defy anyone to see all this and not feel moved.

GRASMERE, Cumbria. St Oswald's Church. In the churchyard lies the body of William Wordsworth (1770-1850), an early example of one who moved from Left to Right as he became older and more prosperous. Some idea of his relatively straitened origins and early view of life may be gleaned from an inscription on the gingerbread shop by the burial ground, which records that this was the village school for more than two hundred years from its opening in 1630. The Lakeland bard 'who believed that universal education was the way for children to escape from poverty, taught here.' Wordsworth spent some time in revolutionary France in 1791, befriending Michel de Beaupuy, an aristocratic adherent of the revolutionary cause, and even proposed marriage to Annette Villon, who bore his daughter Caroline. Lack of money obliged him to return home, but he maintained his devotion to the Revolution until it started to devour its children, and he found literary and financial success after the publication of *Literary Ballads* in 1798. Twenty years later Keats found him campaigning with the Tory Lord Lonsdale in the General Election. Wordsworth is buried in a private family plot hard by the river Rothay, under the shadow of a yew tree, one of eight he planted himself. Elsewhere in the graveyard is buried Dr William Spooner, the begetter of spoonerisms, which I suppose are an early form of Leftieness, having at their heart a subversive nature.

JARROW, Tyne and Wear. Town Hall. A plaque commemorates the Jarrow Hunger March of October 1936. Jarrow was, in the words of its Labour MP, Ellen ('Red Ellen') Wilkinson, the 'town that was murdered'. In the 1930s eight out of every ten men were unemployed. It was from here that the Hunger March set out, when two hundred men walked to London to demand jobs for a town that once thrived on shipbuilding, coal and the steel industry. Their untriumphal progress to the capital awakened the conscience of the nation, but not of the National government. Prime Minister Stanley Baldwin, who had recently succeeded the renegade Labour leader Ramsay MacDonald, refused to meet the marchers. They were pelted with bread rolls by diners on the steps of the Reform Club as they made their way to a rally in Hyde Park, organised by the Unemployed Workers' Movement led by the communist Wal Hannington. The dejected demonstrators returned home empty-handed, but their contribution to Labour history has never been forgotten. The familiar black and white images of the thin-faced, cloth-capped men of the Jarrow Crusade winding their way through villages, caped against the rain, the front ranks playing mouth organs, have stirred emotions for generations. The last marcher died in October 2003.

JARROW, Tyne and Wear. Morrison's supermarket. Outside the store is a monument commemorating the Jarrow marchers of October 1936.

JARROW, Tyne and Wear. 66 Albert Street. Birthplace of John S Clarke (1885-1959), Labour MP and lion tamer. He worked as a young man in the circus and engaged in revolutionary politics, hobnobbing with Lenin in Moscow. He was a political poet. For example:

> The landlord calls it rent and winks the other eye,
> The merchant calls it profit and he heaves a heavy sigh,
> The banker calls it interest and puts it in the bag,
> But our honest friend the burglar simply calls it swag.

KESWICK, Cumbria. Mining Museum. The museum covers all aspects of Cumbria's long and often painful history of digging up lead, copper, graphite, coal, slate, iron and gypsum.

KIRKNEWTON, Northumberland. St Gregory's Church. Josephine Butler (1828-1906), women's rights campaigner, is buried modestly at the back, by the heating boiler. A cruciform memorial, raised barely a foot above the burial slab, records this as the family grave. The inscription is overgrown with lichen, whose growth is also progressively obscuring a much later modest slate plaque which reads simply, 'Josephine Butler 1828-1906'. This windswept resting place under lowering, thousand-foot Yeavering Bell, is a place for reflection.

MARSDEN BAY, County Durham. The Grotto. Originally carved out in 1782 by a local quarryman, Jack the Blaster, it was used in the 1950s by a group of Leftie writers, artists and politicians. Thereafter, the Grotto became a place of resort, and still is, reached by a convenient lift at the cliff edge. Nowadays it is a bistro, but tea for two may be enjoyed for £2 while the waves pound the shore only yards away.

MILFIELD, Northumberland. Birthplace of Josephine Butler (1828-1906), campaigner for women's rights. She was the daughter of John Grey, a cousin of 'Lord Grey of the Reform Bill' and of Hannah Annett, whose family was of Huguenot descent. The father was deeply religious and hostile to the slave trade. Josephine, as a child, was 'haunted by the problems which present themselves to every thoughtful mind'. In 1852 she married an Oxford don, George Butler, moving eventually to Liverpool in 1866 where she began campaigning generally to improve women's education, and specifically to improve the desperate plight of prostitutes, setting up a rest house for them in the city. In 1868 she published *The Education and Employment of Women*, calling for women's suffrage. In her battle against child prostitution she exposed the case of the thirteen-year-old daughter of a chimney sweep bought for £5 by a woman working for a London brothel. As a result of her campaign, the age of consent for sex was raised from thirteen to sixteen. She remained a suffragette supporter to her death.

MORPETH, Northumberland. St Mary the Virgin's Church. The grave of Emily Wilding Davison lies in the graveyard. It is reached by going through the lychgate on the Great North Road, round the church, turning sharp right and then left uphill among the trees to a commanding site, where a granite obelisk records her burial in June 1913. An inscription from the Gospel of St John reads, 'Greater love hath no man than this, that a man lay down his life for his friends.' Below is inscribed, 'Deeds Not Words.' Elsewhere in the churchyard lie fallen Polish servicemen of the Second World War, a reminder that 'greater love' did not die with her. Davison threw herself under the King's horse, Anmer, at the

Derby at Epsom in June 1913, and died of her injuries a few days later. Historians and feminists alike have since disputed whether she intended to pin the colours of the Women's Political and Social Union to the horse, or to commit suicide. The anti-suicide camp cites Emily's purchase of a return ticket to Epsom and the lack of any suicide note. Whatever her intentions, her death stirred the public imagination as none of her sisterhood had before. Davison was brought up in Longhorsley where her mother kept a confectionery shop. She took first class honours in a university extension course and became a tutor, in the manner of the day. With her fiery red hair, green eyes and tall and slender build, she was no less striking in appearance than in her feminist views. In 1911, she was jailed for the arson of a postbox, and endured the humiliation of being forcibly fed. Davison threw herself from the prison landing and was saved only by the protective wire netting. Described as 'one of the most daring and reckless of militants', she was involved in many other escapades before the fateful day at Epsom. It is claimed that she believed that the deliberate giving of a woman's life would create the atmosphere necessary to win victory and bring the sufferings of all militants to an end. What was initially criticised – if not condemned – as self-willed, unofficial action quickly metamorphosed into heroism when public sympathy exploded in her favour. Fifty thousand people followed her cortège from London Victoria to King's Cross, and another twenty thousand waited at Morpeth – five times the town's entire population. Little girls carried lilies, and members of the Women's Political and Social Union held banners carrying Emily's cry, 'Fight on! God will give you victory!' As she was lowered into her grave, a purple cloth was thrown over her coffin, embroidered with the words, 'Welcome, Northumbrian Hunger-Striker!'

NEWCASTLE UPON TYNE, Tyne and Wear. Jesmond Cemetery. Beneath a majestic monument lies the remains of Thomas Burt (1837-1922), one of the first working men to be elected to Parliament. A miner from the age of ten and an autodidact, he was secretary of the Northumberland Mineworkers' Association in 1863.

SEDGEFIELD, County Durham. Dun Cow Public House. In November 2003, Tony Blair brought President George W. Bush for a drink here. The beer is good but no better than the pub next door, where it is cheaper.

SOUTH SHIELDS, Tyne and Wear. Seafarer Statue. A bronze statue erected in 1990, the inspiration of Jim Slater, a native of the town who became general secretary of the National Union of Seamen. Slater was one of Harold Wilson's famous (or notorious) 'tightly-knit group of politically motivated men' in the 1966 national seamen's strike. He persuaded the Countess of Mountbatten to unveil the larger-than-life sculpture of a seaman at the wheel of a heaving deck. He knew about such things, having served in wartime Atlantic convoys to Murmansk.

SUNDERLAND, Tyne and Wear. Sunderland Football Club. Sid Weighell (1922-), railwayman, supplemented his fireman's wages by playing in the Club's reserves.

TRIMDON, County Durham. Trimdon Labour Club. A pan-tiled red-brick building which witnessed the coronation of Tony Blair, the local MP, as leader of the Labour Party in 1994. He did a triumphant walkabout on the green outside, first punching the air.

WALLINGTON, Northumberland. The home for 50 years of the baronet Sir Charles Trevelyan (1870-1958) who was President of the Board of Education in the first Labour government of Ramsay MacDonald, 1924. Elder brother of the historian, G. M., he was a Liberal MP from 1906 and became Under-Secretary at the Board of Education in the government of H. H. Asquith, but resigned over the government's ultimatum in 1914 that led to Britain's involvement in the First World War. He was President of the Board of Education in the second Labour government and tried to raise the school leaving age to fifteen and to provide limited education grants for low-income families. Frustrated by Ramsay MacDonald's timidity he resigned in 1931. He was an enlightened squire of Wallington from 1904, providing all employees with a week's paid holiday and, from the 1920s, paying child allowances to every family on the estate. He gave the property to the National Trust in 1941, continuing to reside there as a tenant. As Lord Lieutenant of Northumberland he made the magistracy more representative of all sections of society.

WHEATLEY HILL, County Durham. Cemetery. The grave of Peter Lee, a simple stone on an earth-filled square, can easily be missed in its modest plot not a hundred yards from the entrance on the right. Peter Lee (1864-1935) was President of the Durham Miners' Association and of the Miners' Federation, the first Labour leader of Durham County Council (and of any county council). The new town of Peterlee is named in his honour.

WITTON PARK, County Durham. There is not much to see, but much to marvel at here. Witton Park was invented for industrial revolution, to serve the Mary Ann, Jane and George collieries and Bolchow and Vaughan's blast-furnaces, which employed a thousand men. Peopled largely by migrant Welsh and Irish labour, Witton Park once had fourteen pubs (and four policemen to keep order). In the First World War, it was a place of refuge for Belgians. After the Second World War planners sought to wipe it off the map by slum clearance and the refusal of planning permission for new homes. This was 'the village that refused to die' after being condemned by county hall planners as a 'Category D' settlement in the 1960s, when the rundown of the coal industry was at its height. A local Labour grandee likened it to a gangrenous limb, an unplanned place 'to suit the capitalist class'. Happily, the human spirit is stronger than the planner's slide rule. With a lead from the local church, St Paul's, an unassuming stone building with a wooden bell tower, Witton Park survived and now flourishes. After the execution order was lifted in the 1980s, the Bishop of Jarrow blessed the first house to be built. Some of the old terraces around the Green are partly intact and the beautiful Victorian station, on the Weardale heritage railway, is being restored. The stunning views have always been there. Witton Park is zeal at its best.

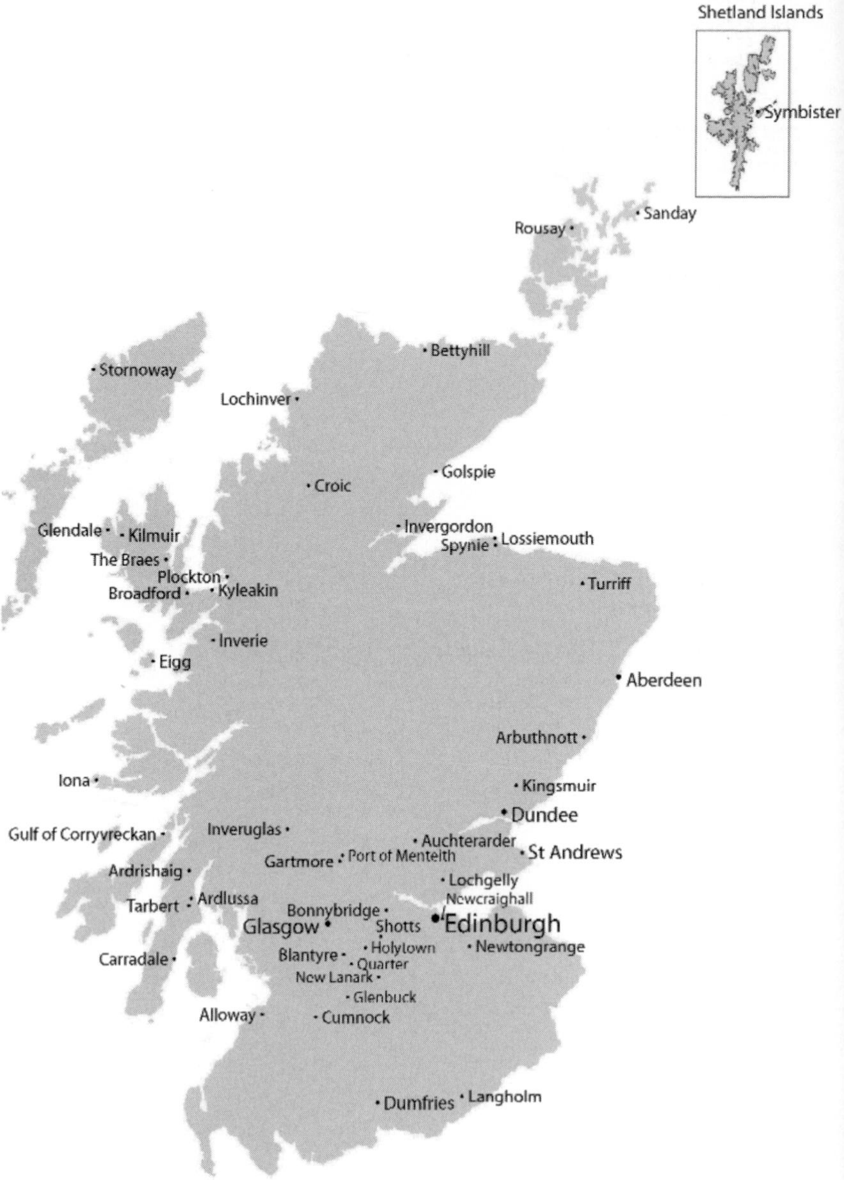
Shetland Islands
Symbister
Sanday
Rousay
Bettyhill
Stornoway
Lochinver
Golspie
Croic
Invergordon
Spynie
Lossiemouth
Glendale
Kilmuir
The Braes
Plockton
Broadford
Kyleakin
Turriff
Inverie
Eigg
Aberdeen
Arbuthnott
Iona
Kingsmuir
Dundee
Gulf of Corryvreckan
Inveruglas
Auchterarder
St Andrews
Gartmore
Port of Menteith
Ardrishaig
Lochgelly
Newcraighall
Tarbert
Ardlussa
Bonnybridge
Glasgow
Shotts
Edinburgh
Holytown
Newtongrange
Carradale
Blantyre
Quarter
New Lanark
Glenbuck
Alloway
Cumnock
Dumfries
Langholm

10.

Scotland

Alan Campbell

> Country: Scotland. Whit like is it? . . .
> It depends. It depends . . .
> Ah dinna ken whit like your Scotland is. Here's mine.
> National flower: the thistle.
> National pastime: nostalgia.
> National weather: smirr, haar, drizzle, snow.
> National bird: the crow, the corbie, le corbeau, moi!

That is the way the Chorus ('La Corbie', the Crow) introduces Liz Lochhead's *Mary Queen of Scots Got Her Head Chopped Off*, a play that appeared in 1987, the depths of the Thatcher years, when Scotland had more or less declared itself a Tory Free Zone but was still ruled from London by a Conservative government. The democratic deficit was obvious, and there was clear resentment about that state of affairs. But it also led to a vivacious sense of defiance. Liz Lochhead's play was written in Scots dialect and put on stage by the effervescent Communicado Theatre Company.

The spectacle was a celebration of confident creativity.

There was a lot of that (the creativity business) going on at the time. It was as if the unfairness of the political set-up encouraged all sorts of talent to flourish in the spirit of: 'Well to hell with all that. Look what we can do in spite of it.' Scottish music, painting, theatre, poetry, novels, historiography, were all thriving.

It is that aspect of creativity that I most like to introduce Leftie friends to. When I invite them on a journey round Scotland, they will notice that my landmarks are biased towards literary figures since I know more about them than I do about politicians. I would expect Leftie interest to gravitate naturally towards artists, poets, bohemians, and all those who like to say 'No' (or in Scotland 'Naah') to authority, just as the redoubtable Ian Hamilton Findlay created a garden called 'Little Sparta' at Stonypath, Dunsyre, which includes poetry, sculpture and other art installations. He was in a state of minor insurrection against the authorities for a number of years. Creative efforts like his thrive in being defiant.

The Declaration of Arbroath and why we don't really hate the English

'Defiance' would be the national spirit of *my* Scotland. As you look back through the centuries, its most obvious expression is the anti-English nationalism that has been a defining feature of Scottish identity since the days of Wallace and Bruce, and the Wars of Independence:

> For as long as a hundred of us are left alive, we will yield in no least way to English dominion. We fight not for glory nor for wealth or honours; but only and alone we fight for freedom which no good man surrenders but with his life.

That is one translation of the most famous passage in the 'Declaration of Arbroath', a letter sent to Pope John XXII in 1320 by the earls and barons of Scotland asking him to stop supporting King Edward II's claims to Scotland. (After all, 'proud Edward's armies' had

John Smith's Grave

been soundly beaten at Bannockburn in 1314 and he had been 'sent homeward to think again' – the words of 'Flower of Scotland', that dirge which is dutifully droned out when Scotland plays a game of rugby these days.) The original letter to the Pope was in Latin, but all the translations capture an astonishing outspokenness and obstinacy:

> He Who Knows All [i e God, not the Pope] knows that if the King of the English would leave us in peace, we and our own Lord King would go joyfully thither . . . But if too readily, or insincerely, you put your faith in what the English have told you, and continue to favour them to our confounding, then indeed shall the slaying of bodies, yea and of souls, and all those evils which they shall do to us, or we to them, be charged to your account by the Most High.

'So there ye are, Mr Pope!' you might feel like adding.

Anti-English defiance is not xenophobic. It is a function, on the one hand, of an anxiety about being oppressed. Scotland to England is five million to 50 million people. 'We're small. They're big. They've taken us over.' On the other hand, the positive side would add, '*But we can still do better!*' That is the enduring sense of self-worth that survives whatever might befall, and from which emerges the periodic surges of creativity that Scotland produces.

James Maxton, one of the best of the Red Clydesiders, put it beautifully in a powerful speech during the 1924 debate on the Home Rule Bill. He was uncomfortable about the national exclusiveness implied by anti-English sentiment and made it clear that he had no quarrel with the English. But he was convinced that Scotland could make a better go of things on its own.

> Give us our Parliament in Scotland. Set it up next year. We will start with no traditions. We will start with ideals. We will start with purpose, with courage. We will start with the aim and object that there will be 134 men and women, pledged to 134 Scottish constituencies, to spend their whole energy, their whole brain power, their whole courage, and their whole soul, in making Scotland into a country in which we can take people from all the nations of the earth and say: 'This is our land, this is our Scotland, these are our people, these are our men, our works, our women and children: can you beat it?'

It is that kind of promise that is at the heart of my Scotland.

The Democratic Disposition

There is another point in the Declaration of Arbroath that is worth looking at. The section immediately preceding the best known passage states that should Robert the Bruce, the victor of Bannockburn, sell out to the English, then . . .

> . . . we should cast [him] out as the enemy of us all, as subverter of our rights and of his own, and should choose another king to defend our freedom. For so long as a hundred of us is alive . . .

That is astonishing for 1320. The idea appeared again in 1579 when George Buchanan, James VI's tutor and one of the founding fathers of Presbyterianism, published *The Law of Government among the Scots*. He said that the people were always more powerful than their rulers and had the right, indeed the sacred duty, to remove them if they turned tyrannical. Arthur Herman, in *The Scottish Enlightenment*, points out that this view is conventionally ascribed to John Locke when in fact it belongs to 'a Presbyterian Scot from Stirlingshire writing more than a hundred years earlier'. Yes, but the earls and barons were on to it 250 years before that.

The Kirk

The Scottish Kirk was a bundle of explosive contradictions. From the start it was anti-establishment and democratic. Its office bearers were called 'elders' following the New Testament word *presbyter* (*presbys* meaning 'old', *presbytes*, 'an old man'), and they were elected. Bishops, in 'episcopacy', were not. Scottish Presbyterianism was in one sense then, a people's religion. Authority came directly from God, and nothing on earth was superior to Him, kings and aristocrats included. To that extent, it appeared to be a religion that allowed traditional forms of authority to be challenged.

But we associate 'democratic institutions' with habits of tolerance, fairness, and openness to diversity of opinion. The Kirk was certainly not in that kind of business. From its early personification in John Knox, through the Covenanters of the seventeenth century, it presents a picture of fanatical zealots bent on destroying anything that did not conform to their strictures. No more cakes and ale. Nor dancing, nor carnivals, nor anything enjoyable on the grim Sabbath Day. The magnificent beauties of monasteries and cathedrals were seen as idolatrous and were destroyed. 'Obscene and degrading punishments,' wrote the historian John Prebble, 'were imposed in the righteous belief that they were necessary for the salvation of the sinner, and were accepted in the spirit of a people at war who will endure indignities and privations that would be insufferable in peace.'

Yet from this dour, unforgiving dogmatism came one enormous social benefit – literacy. The Schools Act of 1696 led to the establishment of schools in every parish, the idea being that everybody should be able to read Holy Scripture. Once everyone could read, books were everywhere, both religious and secular. Scottish historians claim that the country became Europe's first modern literate society. England did not catch up until the 1880s.

Scottish education went its way differently from the rest of the United Kingdom and always claimed superiority. The issue was put in sharp political focus when George Davie published *The Democratic Intellect* in 1961. Alas, all such efforts to make us aware of the strengths of our past have had little impact on the growing list of ignorant and damaging educational policies that various governments have produced since then. I have included in the gazetteer landmark references to the eccentric edges of Scotland's contribution to education in the person of A. S. Neill.

The Scottish Enlightenment 1730-90

It could be argued (and many would insist) that the Scottish Enlightenment is not at all 'Leftie'. Many of its leading figures were, in terms of their social outlook, deeply reactionary. But it was a huge achievement that rises above the politics of Left and Right. It is a gift of 'enlightenment' to humanity as a whole and it is something the country is justly proud of. Articles showing that David Hume was 'racist' are trivial and do nothing to assess the impact of his philosophy. More seriously, the appropriation of Adam Smith as an icon for the worst and wildest extremes of 'neo-liberalism' is a scandalous oversimplification which assaults us daily. It is not a joke – like Bill Herbert's wonderful poem, 'Why the Elgin Marbles must be returned to Elgin' – to say that we should rescue Adam Smith from the Adam Smith Institute.

A minimal list for the 1730-90 period would start with Francis Hutcheson, who taught philosophy at Glasgow University and go on to include David Hume (philosophy and history), Adam Smith (economics), Adam Ferguson (sociology), Thomas Reid ('common sense' philosophy), William Robertson (history), James Hutton (geology), Joseph Black (chemistry), William Cullen (clinical medicine), Hugh Blair (rhetoric and language), Henry Home, Lord Kames, James Burnett, Lord Monboddo (legal philosophy and anthropology), and Dugald Stewart (philosophy and economics).

On the more practical side, Edinburgh was at that time one of the foremost medical centres in the western world. Robert Sibbald had founded the Royal College of Physicians, and Alexander Munro established a dynasty of professors of anatomy. Robert and James Adam (architecture), and Allan Ramsay and Henry Raeburn (painting) had international reputations. And William Smellie produced the first Encyclopaedia Britannica in a narrow close off Edinburgh's High Street.

Edinburgh

Hutcheson was associated with Glasgow and Thomas Reid with Aberdeen, but the Enlightenment was overwhelmingly an

Edinburgh phenomenon. Adam Smith eventually settled in Edinburgh, and his memorials can be included in a Leftie walk up Edinburgh's 'Royal Mile'.

Thinking back to the Enlightenment we have a picture of these comfortable gentlemen in their Edinburgh taverns and clubs. But the times were turbulent. In the west of the country the rapid industrialisation of Glasgow was to lead to the event where the Leftie tradition in Scotland begins: the Calton Weavers' Strike of 1787. Edinburgh itself, right in the middle of Enlightenment creativity, felt the full force of the 'Forty-five' – the Jacobite rebellion of 1745 when Bonnie Prince Charlie led his Highland army all the way to Derby, shaking the foundations of the Hanoverian dynasty. William Robertson, the historian, was a young volunteer in the militia that tried, unsuccessfully, to save Edinburgh from the Highland horde. These Gaelic speaking Highlanders came from a different world – a way of life that saw its end on Culloden Moor in 1746 when the Prince's army was finally destroyed by the Duke of Cumberland. The brutality of the repression which followed marked the onset of long-standing, melancholy times. (It is best to say 'GAH-lick' for the language in Scotland. 'GAY-lick' is appropriate for Ireland.)

The Highlands and Islands

My Scotland wants to bring the Highlands and Islands into firmer focus. Just as English people (in general) have limited perspectives of Scotland, so those from Scotland's heavily-populated 'Central Belt' (in general) have little awareness of life beyond the Highland Line, that geological fault running roughly on a diagonal from Dumbarton to Stonehaven.

Land was the main issue in the Highlands – landownership; the landlords; the factors (agents who run the estates); the rents; who and what is the land for? It remains so today. Year after year, Scottish agricultural agencies and government bodies churn out volumes of statistical data on farming and land use, and set out acres of rules, regulations and initiatives. But nothing, ever, appears on the question of land ownership. John McEwen produced his pioneering *Who Owns Scotland* (without a question mark) in 1977, and in 1996 Andy Wightman issued his updated version. But they have to work against the grain, like guerrilla fighters or *franc-tireurs*. www.whoownsscotland.org.uk is now Andy Wightman's online location for the struggle.

All these issues of landlords, factors, rents, and right to the land come together in the tragic and dramatic context of 'The Highland Clearances'. Three aspects of the Clearances are worth emphasising. First, it is as well to know by name which estates were involved and which areas were cleared. I have summarised this as best I can in the gazetter showing how far the evictions were scattered over the Highlands and Islands. Secondly, having appreciated where the events took place, one will be more aware of where they did not. Time and again visitors pass through deserted glens, see the remains of abandoned houses, crofts, and steadings, and wrongly assume they are looking at an area that was 'cleared'. That leads to the third point: that most of the depopulation of the Highlands and Islands was due to voluntary migration. From the 1760s onwards, people left for the cities and for the colonies to escape economic hardship and seek the promise of a better life elsewhere. The Clearances took place within that much wider context of migration and depopulation. That does not present what happened in a more acceptable light. On the contrary, it shows more clearly how casual and capricious the cruelty of the Clearances was.

Lowland Scots think of Highlanders in enduring stereotypes. The 'teuchter' is a country bumpkin sort of character, as the comedian Andy Stewart liked to present in his song 'Donald, whaur's yer troosers?' – rather simple, rather slow, rather unsophisticated, and someone to be lightly patronised. Even Frank Fraser Darling, who did invaluable pioneering work on the ecology of the area, could write in 1947 that 'Donald is indifferent on the whole, not consciously indifferent, but unconscious of ultimate consequences, and he always desires to please.'

But it was the same Donald and Donaldinas (yes, women took prominent parts in the resistance) who showed so much mettle during the Highland Land Wars of the 1880s that armed police, marines, and gunboats became common features of the government's response to local unrest. Ian Carter, who at one time taught history at the University of Aberdeen, has written:

> Highland crofters' stubborn refusal to acquiesce in their own liquidation has kept alive an account of Highland history that differs markedly from the account usually provided by sleek academic commentators. The crofter's version of history is a story of class oppression, of the depredations suffered by peasant farmers at the hands of the landlords and capitalist farmers . . . It is in the crofting counties, alone of the Scottish regions, that land ownership is a vital political issue.

The Land Wars time was a counter-offensive against 'capitalist' agriculture and resulted in a remarkable success – the Napier Commission set up by the government to look into the question of land in the so-called 'crofting counties', which resulted in large scale reform.

As a contrast, in North East Scotland (another self-contained region of Scotland, little appreciated by those in the 'Central Belt') in the relatively rich agricultural hinterland around Aberdeen, where the questions and reforms of the Napier Commission did not apply, 'capitalist' agriculture won the day, as illustrated in the Turra Coo incident described in the gazetteer under Turriff.

Red Clydeside and John Maclean

It is not such a long road from the Turra Coo to Red Clydeside. They are the same era; Lloyd George figures prominently in both stories. It is difficult, though, to appreciate the conditions people lived through then. Those days are nearly a century away and barely within living memory. In Glasgow so much has vanished: the Calton, the Gorbals, Anderston, and the other famous districts have all been largely cleared. The grim tenements and 'backlands' with the 'room-and-kitchen' and 'single-end' dwellings hung on till the 1950s, but have now vanished. There was 'The Forge' in Bridgeton, the huge engineering works where Davie Kirkwood was the leading shop steward. There was St Enoch's Station, from where, in 1922, the Red Clydeside MPs left in triumph for Westminster. Both are now shopping malls.

To look back at those times in Glasgow is both an enduring source of inspiration and a useful perspective to qualify today's received ideas – those comfortable assumptions that make up 'the enormous condescension of posterity'. There is a current mantra in political commentary that 'socialism has failed; capitalism has won' – as empty an idea as Thatcher's 'There's no such thing as society.' Vacancies like these show how modern affluence relaxes into impoverished social views. By contrast, the sheer vivacity of the guiding ideas and moral vision followed by those who took part in the Red Clydeside story represent the most profound values that human beings have ever tried to express.

The people involved pursued their struggles with extraordinary courage, sometimes in conditions of poverty that seem hardly bearable. 'In May 1923 my wife and I were evicted,' wrote Harry McShane who lived until 1988,

> We had been living on 15s a week from the labour exchange, and our rent in Thistle Street, Gorbals, was 6s. All we had to live on was 9s a week. It was a very cautious time for us, a very tough time. We lived on toast; my wife said her stomach was all scratched from toast with nothing on it. There were many others in just the same situation.

'A cautious time', says Harry McShane, the old communist. His account is one of the best – vivid and good humoured – but I am sure many of his assessments would be queried by others.

Willie Ross said that the Scots were a 'disputatious people' and Red Clydeside is a good example of how Scottish disputes are triggered. Two questions that cause controversy are: How red was Red Clydeside? And: How important was John Maclean?

The basic events are not disputed. There was 'unrest' on the Clyde between June 1915 and March 1916. Two parallel disputes were going on. One was the 'dilution strike' where engineers (skilled craftsmen) organised by the Amalgamated Society of Engineers and the Clyde Workers Committee (CWC) were resisting government proposals to introduce unskilled labour and women into the engineering works to boost output for the war effort. As a result of this dispute David Kirkwood, the shop steward at Parkhead Forge, and other members of the CWC were arrested under the Defence of the Realm Act, convicted, and 'deported' to Edinburgh.

Alongside this was a rent strike triggered by an attempt by landlords to implement rent increases. The 'Glasgow Women's Housing Association' emerged. Helen Crawfurd, Mary Barbour, and Agnes Dollan were prominent figures. With the help of John Wheatley and the Independent Labour Party (the ILP founded by Keir Hardie in 1893), they organised mass demonstrations and resistance to evictions. The protests resulted in the '1915 Rent Restriction Act', which, in various forms, remained in force till the days of Margaret Thatcher. As the historian of the Clydesiders, Iain McLean wrote:

> No government of any party found it possible to remove rent control until the Housing Acts 1980 and 1988. Nor did any find it possible to force local authorities to charge market rents, or rents which covered costs, on council housing. Thus the two cardinal features of British housing policy from 1919 to 1979 were laid down in Red Clydeside.

The Clyde Workers' Committee appeared again as principal organiser of the '40 Hour Week' strike that resulted in 'Bloody Friday', the Battle of George Square, on 31 January 1919. As a result of this Emanuel ('Mannie') Shinwell, William ('Willie') Gallacher and others went to jail for incitement and rioting.

In May 1918 John Maclean went to jail (for the third time), sentenced to five years penal servitude for sedition, and was sent to Peterhead Prison. Such was the intensity of feeling shown in the marches and demonstrations on his behalf in the following months that the government decided to have him released less than seven months into his sentence. He returned to Glasgow on 3 December 1918 to a huge reception at Buchanan Street Station where the crowds sang revolutionary songs and chanted slogans. 'Great John Maclean had come hame tae the Clyde.'

Finally, on 20 November 1922, following the General Election, eighteen of the new MPs from Scotland and the West of Scotland, the 'Red Clydesiders', left in triumph on the night mail train for Westminster. The crowd of between fifty thousand and a hundred thousand sang 'The Red Flag', 'Jerusalem', and the 124th Psalm. Gordon Brown has written that this moment 'still ranks as the Scottish Labour Movement's finest hour'.

So, was there a 'revolutionary situation' on the Clyde? The 1915-16 unrest was clearly no such thing. The moment, if there was one, was Bloody Friday in January 1919. Certainly, when Gallacher and Kirkwood emerged from the City Chambers to try to control the crowd, they were pretty shaken, and appeared unlikely revolutionary leaders. But what made the events look revolutionary was the reaction of the government in London. Cabinet papers reported that: 'The Secretary for Scotland [Robert Munro] said that, in his opinion, it was more clear than ever that it was a misnomer to call the situation in Glasgow a strike – it was a Bolshevist rising.' Munro duly sent up soldiers, six tanks, and a hundred motor lorries that night by train. There were Scottish soldiers in the Maryhill Barracks but it was thought safer to send English soldiers. Nothing much happened. The strike petered out in early February. If Munro thought there was a Bolshevist rising in progress, Harry McShane, who would later join the Communist party, did not: 'We regarded the 40-hour strike not as a revolution but as a beginning. Other things could follow: it was the first rank-and-file agitation to be led by socialists after the war.'

Perhaps Arthur Woodburn was right when he said, 50 years after the events, that 'the most revolutionary thing that ever happened in Scotland at that time was when J. S. Clarke's wife made Davie Kirkwood wash the dishes – which he'd never done before.'

If anything, Bloody Friday damped down any enthusiasm for revolution and strengthened the ILP in its efforts to get activists into Parliament. The 1922 triumph for the ILP marked a victory for *anti*-revolutionary politics which accepted the path of parliamentary activity. How far did they get with that?

Since 1914, John Wheatley and Tom Johnston (editor of *Forward*) had been campaigning for Wheatley's '£8 cottage scheme' to solve Glasgow's awful housing problem. Wheatley was also instrumental in the success of the Rent Strike of 1915. He became a government minister after the ILP success and his 1924 Housing Act became the basis for all future house-building and planning programmes. Wheatley is therefore quite properly seen as the ILP's highest achiever, and housing reform as the ILP's greatest success.

James Maxton was the other ILP star. Gordon Brown's assessment is that, even though he never held office, even though the ILP eventually faded away, even though Maxton himself was 'belittled and dismissed as "a beloved rebel"', nevertheless:

> . . . at the height of his powers, in the 1920s, he threatened to change the whole course of politics by offering British socialism a third way between Labour gradualism and Communism.

The revolutionary situation was not to be found in the events of the streets but in people's 'hearts and minds'. This is why John Maclean was one of the most inspirational figures of his time. Thousands protested against his sentence in 1918. Thousands welcomed him 'hame tae the Clyde' when he was released that December. Thousands lined the streets and followed his funeral the four miles from Eglinton Toll to Eastwood Cemetery when he died in 1923.

He did not lead an influential political party. In pre-war debates with Tom Johnston in *Forward* he argued that the Labour Party was 'a miserable caricature of Marxism'. He kept out of the ILP and later refused to join the Communist Party (although Lenin had made him Russian Consul in Glasgow after October 1917). In conventional political terms he was powerless, yet Basil Thompson, head of British Military Intelligence at the time, believed Maclean to be the most dangerous man in Britain. He represented a different kind of power.

John Maclean was convinced that if the working class were properly educated in Marxist economics then the organised forces of capitalism could be defeated. He set up the Scottish Labour

College and from the start several hundred attended at Central Halls every Sunday afternoon. Harry McShane said Maclean's classes were 'the most attractive feature of the Glasgow movement before the First World War.'

> [For John Maclean] . . . the problem of the seizure of power didn't arise – somehow or other the class struggle was going to bring about socialism and that was that . . . It wasn't just his oratory that influenced people but the feeling that he was a man who could be trusted, a man of integrity . . . He was always deadly serious, but he could cause excitement by the things he said. He was a schoolteacher and he loved teaching.

Maclean's detractors query what he 'achieved'. But when you are a teacher you cannot measure or count or appraise how much you may have inspired people, although the thousands who turned out for Maclean is a measure in itself of what he meant to people. Those who have written most eloquently about Maclean were themselves teachers (and poets): Sorley MacLean, Morris Blythman, Hamish Henderson, Hugh MacDiarmid. His was an inspiration that transcended politics.

Gazetteer

ABERDEEN. Summerhill Academy, on the Lang Stracht, going west out of Aberdeen. Now an administrative base for Aberdeen City Council's Education Department, it was an academy where R. F. Mackenzie was appointed headmaster in 1968. His educational ideas had been profoundly influenced by A. S. Neill's child-centred practices at Summerhill School, Leiston. (The fact that the Academy was also named Summerhill is purely coincidental.) Neill's school was independent but Mackenzie had constant battles with an education system based on rules and discipline, demanding obedience to authority. He insisted that children should be allowed freedom to grow in understanding, and was casual about authority, discipline and, above all, exams. Parents and half the staff complained to the Education Authority about Mackenzie's 'unusual and particularly permissive philosophy'. Finally, in 1974, after an inquiry that amounted to a trial, Mackenzie was suspended and his teaching career came to an end. Pupils went on strike. Many parents and supportive staff felt betrayed. Although his view about examinations has not won through, his opposition to corporal punishment has. He wrote an account of his Summerhill years, *The Unbowed Head* (1976). That, and his other works, remain to this day a source of inspiration and hope for all interested in education.

ALLOWAY, South Ayrshire. Burns's Birthplace. Robert Burns (1759-96) was born in a cottar house.

ARBUTHNOTT, Kincardineshire. The Lewis Grassic Gibbon Centre. This centre is next to the village hall in sight of Arbuthnott School attended by James Leslie Mitchell (1901-35), alias Lewis Grassic Gibbon, who was born at the farm of

Hillhead of Seggat near Turriff, Aberdeenshire. When he was eight, the family moved to the farm of Bloomfield near Arbuthnott. He went on to Mackie Academy Stonehaven, then worked as a journalist in Aberdeen and Glasgow. From 1919 to 1929 he served in the RASC and in the RAF as a clerk. He settled, improbably, in Welwyn Garden City in 1931, where he died. He was a prolific writer – novels, stories, essays, commentaries, and a biography of Mungo Park. He collaborated with Hugh MacDiarmid on a collection of essays. But his outstanding achievement was the trilogy, *A Scots Quair*, about a woman who grows up in a rural farming community and moves to the town and later a city. The trilogy is constructed against the background of the Great War and the Depression. It experiments with Scots speech – Lallans or the Doric. Gibbon is said to represent a 'romantic' communism, though it is difficult to see what a decent or plausible 'unromantic' communism would have looked like in those times.

ARDLUSSA, Isle of Jura, Argyll and Bute. Barnhill. A house four miles to the north of the village, this was the home of George Orwell (1903-50) from 1946 to 1950. Here he worked on a book with the working title *The Last Man in Europe*, which he completed in 1948. The final title reversed the digits of the date: *1984*. Orwell was already ill with tuberculosis when he arrived and was obliged to return to London where he died. In spite of illness he relished the remoteness of this challenging place.

ARDRISHAIG, Argyll and Bute. Memorial to John Smith (1938-94), leader of the Labour Party, 1992-94, who was born in the village. His father was headmaster of the primary school in St Clair Road, now converted into houses. The memorial is on the seafront beside the car park.

AUCHTERARDER, Perth and Kinross. St Mungo's Chapel, Gleneagles House. South of the hotel. Gleneagles has nothing to do with eagles. 'Eaglais' is the Gaelic for church and refers to this chapel that was renovated in 1929. Outside is a four-sided obelisk commemorating the four children of Robert Haldane: R. B.,

Elizabeth, Sir William and J. S. R. B., first Viscount Haldane (1856-1928), who became Lord Chancellor in Ramsay MacDonald's first Labour government of 1924. Elizabeth (1862-1937) was the first woman Justice of the Peace in Scotland. J. S. was a physiologist and father of J. B. S. Haldane (1892-1964), scientist and on the editorial board of the Communist Party newspaper, *Daily Worker*, and of Naomi Mitchison (1897-1999), socialist, novelist and feminist.

BETTYHILL, Sutherland, Highland. In 1883, Angus Mackay of Farr gave testimony to the Napier Commission, investigating crofters' grievances. 'The land our forefathers lived upon so happy and prosperous,' he told them, 'is now under deer and sheep, and turning into moss and bog, which is not profitable to man nor beast, while we are huddled together in small townships on the sea shore, exposed to all the fury of the wild sea breezes, which generally carry away the little corn we have. We want more land, security against eviction, compensation for improvements, and fair rent.'

BLANTYRE, North Lanarkshire. Baptist Church,163 Auchinraith Road. Outside the church is a monument commemorating two mining disasters. The first took place on 22 October 1877 when about 210 men died. It was Scotland's worst mining disaster. 'The Blantyre Explosion' became a well known folk song:

> The explosion was heard, all the women and children
> Wi' pale anxious faces they haste tae the mine
> When the news was made heard the hills rang with their mourning
> Twa hundred and seven young miners were slain.

Two years later there was another explosion: 28 men died.

BONNYBRIDGE, Falkirk. Radical Pend. A rusting plaque records:

THE RADICAL PEND
NAMED TO COMMEMORATE
THE BATTLE OF BONNYMUIR
APRIL 5TH 1820

In April 1820 during the hardship following the Napoleonic Wars, placards appeared in

Glasgow calling for a general strike. 'Scotland Free or a Desert' was the slogan. A group of weavers from Glasgow marched towards Falkirk heading for the Carron Ironworks where armaments were manufactured. They were attacked by troops at the 'Battle' of Bonnymuir. A few were wounded and about 40 captured. Andrew Hardie and John Baird were hanged and beheaded at Stirling. A third leader, James Wilson, was executed in Glasgow. The rebels left Bonnybridge by the 'pend' (or vaulted passageway) built under the Forth and Clyde Canal (completed in 1790). The present day road leaves the centre of the town going south and the pend is just beside Mill Garage. Going on south, under two railway lines and straight up the hill on Beam Road towards Drum Farm, the site of the 'battle' is in the field on the left (eastward) before arriving at the public right of way marked 'Drove Loan'.

THE BRAES, facing the Island of Raasay, Isle of Skye, Highland. Here in 1882 occurred the first significant unrest in what came to be known as 'the Highland Land War' or 'the Crofters' War'. The crofters refused to pay rent when Lord MacDonald, the estate owner, removed their grazing rights on the slopes of Ben Lee, above Loch Sligachan. Sheriff's officers sent from Portree with eviction notices were attacked and their summonses burnt. Sheriff William Ivory brought 50 policemen, mostly from Glasgow, ostentatiously on a MacBrayne steamer. They proceeded to the Braes where they were set upon and beaten back, sticks and stones against baton charges. Five men were arrested. In May 1882 the Braes men were tried in Inverness. The charge of 'deforcement' was withdrawn and the men were given fairly lenient fines. But the crofters still refused to remove their livestock from the hill. A messenger at arms, from Portree, with a Court of Session summons arrived at a time when the men were away at sea. The Braes women drove him away. By October Lord MacDonald was prepared to make concessions on rent. A memorial cairn records, in Gaelic and English:

Near this cairn
on the 19th of April 1882,
ended the Battle fought by the
people of Braes
on behalf of the crofters of
Gaeldom

BROADFORD, Isle of Skye, Highland. In 1972 four Dundee University graduates – Brian Wilson, Jim Innes, Dave Scott and Jim Wilkie (with financial support from Don MacIntyre) – set up the *West Highland Free Press*. The paper moved to Breakish in 1974 and in 1987 to Broadford. It was set up as a community newspaper and to revive the traditional radicalism of the area, concentrating immediately on 'anti-land-lordism' and the issue of land ownership. On its masthead are the words, 'An Tir, an Canan, 'sna Daoine', 'The Land, the Language and the People', the motto of the Highland Land League.

CARRADALE, Kintyre, Argyll and Bute. Carradale House. Home of Naomi Mitchison (1897-1999) and Dick Mitchison (1890-1970) from 1937. Dick – later Lord Mitchison of Carradale – was an Old Etonian, a QC, a Labour MP and junior minister in the 1960s. Naomi was a sister of J. B. S. Haldane, the communist scientist, and a niece of Lord Haldane, the Labour Lord Chancellor in 1924. She was a novelist, a feminist and a socialist. She made every effort to break down the traditional relationship between the Big House and the local community and was for 20 years a local councillor. At the birth of her last baby she asked for the Red Flag to be run up on the flagpole. (Sadly the baby did not survive and the flag was taken down again.) She was well to the left of her fellow countryfolk. 'In fact,' she said, 'I doubt if anything short of revolution is going to give the country folk the kick in the pants which they definitely want, or rather need.'

CORRYVRECKAN, Gulf of, Isle of Jura, Argyll and Bute. The most northerly point in Jura looking over to the island of Scarba, the Gulf of Corryvreckan which contains a notorious whirlpool is where George Orwell, his son and their companions nearly came to grief in 1947. They escaped drowning but had to be rescued by local fishermen.

CROIC, Strathcarron, Easter Ross, Highland. Church. In 1845 people were cleared from Glencalvie and took refuge in the graveyard. They scratched on the window panes of the church they were not allowed to enter: 'Glencalvie people the wicked generation . . . Glencalvie people was here . . . Glencalvie is a wilderness blow ship them to the colony.' The names are still visible. The family name of them all was Ross. In March 1854 Strathcarron itself saw the 'Slaughter of Greenyards' when a sheriff and about 35 police attacked a crowd of some three hundred, mostly women. Some were seriously injured and taken to jail in Tain. Some men from Greenyards (Gaelic, Gruinards) were at the time serving in the 93rd Foot, the Sutherland Highlanders. In October that year the 93rd formed the 'Thin Red Line' which repulsed a Russian cavalry charge at the Battle of Balaclava during the Crimean War.

CUMNOCK, East Ayrshire. Lochnorris, on the road to Auchinleck. The home of James Keir Hardie (1856-1915). Father of the Labour Party, Keir Hardie came to Cumnock, to live in a 'room and a kitchen' in 1881 to work on a local newspaper. In 1887 he edited *The Miner*, campaigning for Scottish miners' organisations along with Robert Smillie, the Lanarkshire miners' leader. In 1888 he stood for Mid-Lanark as an Independent Labour candidate and was defeated. He set up a new Scottish Labour Party, with R. B. Cunninghame Graham as President. Adam Birkmyre, a local businessman, who had bought Robert Owen's New Lanark Mills, gave Hardie an interest free loan to allow him to build Lochnorris which became his family home for the rest of his life. His widow, Lillie, lived here until her death in 1924. In that year Emrys Hughes, pacifist and future Labour MP, got a job on *Forward* (in Glasgow), married Nan – the daughter of Lillie and Keir Hardie – and moved here.

CUMNOCK, East Ayrshire. Cemetery. James Keir Hardie is buried here.

CUMNOCK, East Ayrshire. Town Hall. A bust of James Keir Hardie by Benno Schotz stands outside the town hall.

DUMFRIES. St Michael's Churchyard. A mausoleum in the south east corner of the churchyard holds the grave of Robert Burns (1759-96). The mausoleum was paid for in 1815 by public subscription, which included a donation from the Prince Regent, the future George IV. Keir Hardie said, 'I owe more to Burns than to any man living or dead.' Hugh MacDiarmid, in his turn, grumbled,

> Mair nonsense has been uttered in his name
> Than ony's barrin' liberty and Christ.

DUNDEE. D. C. Thomson's. Dundee was built on 'Jam, Jute and Journalism', and has always been a grim place. George Thomson (1921-), later Chancellor of the Duchy of Lancaster in Harold Wilson's second government, with responsibility for negotiations for entry into the Common Market, worked here in the 1940s and was simultaneously editor of *Dandy* and *Beano*. He became disillusioned with the Labour Party, went to Brussels as the first British Commissioner and defected to the Social Democrats.

DUNDEE. J. T. C. Furniture Group, Harrison Road (north of Kingsway), Camperdown. The Labour government attracted new industries to Dundee in the 1960s, most particularly white goods and office equipment. The most prominent was Timex, then a United States-registered multinational owned by a Norwegian, Fred Olsen, which occupied this site. After an economic crisis in 1990 Peter Hall was appointed president of the Scottish concern. Keenly anti-union, he began to sack the workers. The union was prepared to negotiate for rotation of work shifts instead of redundancies, but Hall would not budge. In February 1993 all 343 workers came out on strike and were locked out. Picket lines and mass demonstrations became battle grounds. The Timex dispute became a test case. 'Employers everywhere are waiting to see what the outcome is,' said Willie Lesslie, a union convenor. 'Employers know if the union at Timex can be broken, it might be easier for them to break their own work force.' The workers felt there was not adequate support from their own union – the Amalgamated Engineering and

Electrical Union – and the strike petered out after July 1993. But resentment lingers on in the area as a result of strike-breakers.

EDINBURGH. Assembly Hall, Church of Scotland. Hopes for a Scottish Parliament rose in the 1970s, to be dashed by the Thatcher government of 1979. In May 1997 a Labour government was elected, committed to holding a referendum on devolved government in Scotland. This was held in September 1997 and produced a 75 per cent vote for a Scottish Parliament. The Assembly Hall became the first venue for the new Parliament and on 12 May 1999, Winnie Ewing, the oldest member of the new Parliament, stated: 'The Scottish Parliament, adjourned on the 25th day of March 1707, is hereby reconvened.' On 1 July the Parliament was officially opened (in its temporary location) by the Queen, accompanied by the Duke of Edinburgh and the Prince of Wales (who in Scotland is the Duke of Rothesay). The highlight of the day was Sheena Wellington's singing of Robert Burns's 'A Man's a Man for a' that.' The song, inspired by the French Revolution, is most famous for its resounding finish:

> For a' that, and a' that
> It's comin' yet for a' that
> That Man to Man the world o'er
> Shall brothers be for a' that.

Verses three and four were not sung on that occasion:

> Ye see yon birkie ca'd a 'lord',
> Wha struts, and stares, and a' that,
> Though hundreds worship at his word,
> He's but a coof for a' that,
> For a' that, and a' that
> His ribband, star and a' that,
> The man of independent mind,
> He looks and laughs at a' that.
>
> A prince can mak a belted knight,
> A marquis, duke, and a' that;
> But an honest man's aboon his might,
> Gude faith he mauna fa' that!
> For a' that, and a' that,
> Their dignities, and a' that
> The pith o' Sense, and pride o' Worth,
> Are higher rank than a' that.

The new Scottish First Minister, Donald Dewar, said, 'And in the quiet moments of today we might hear some echoes from the past: the shout of the welder in the great din of the Clyde shipyards, the speak of the Mearns rooted in the land, the discourse of the Enlightenment when Edinburgh and Glasgow were indeed a light held to the intellectual life of Europe, the wild cry of the great pipes and back to the distant noise of battles in the days of Bruce and Wallace . . .'

EDINBURGH. The Scottish Parliament Building, opposite the Palace of Holyrood House. On a site previously occupied by the Scottish and Newcastle Brewery, the cost of the building rose from £40 million to £431 million in five years. It was officially opened in October 2004 – four years after the conceiver of the Parliament building, Donald Dewar, and the architect, Catalan Enric Miralles, both died. The Queen's speech lacked the history of Dewar's speech at the first session of Parliament, but appealed to New Labour ideals of 'accessibility, accountability, equality of opportunity, partnership . . .'

EDINBURGH. Old Calton Burial Ground. Not far from the grave of the philosopher and historian David Hume (1711-76), is an obelisk built to commemorate the five Political Martyrs of the 1793 and 1794 Sedition Trials, the most famous being Thomas Muir of Huntershill. After being sent down from Glasgow University, he studied law at Edinburgh University and became an avid supporter of the French Revolution. He was active in organising electoral reform societies. After a meeting of the Convention of the Scottish Friends of the People in December 1792, he was arrested and tried by Lord Braxfield, the notorious 'hanging judge'. Muir was accused of making seditious speeches and of circulating Thomas Paine's *Rights of Man*, as well as being involved with the United Irishmen movement. He defended himself eloquently. 'I have devoted myself to the cause of the people. It is a good cause, it shall ultimately prevail, it shall ultimately triumph.' But he was up against Braxfield. When another of the martyrs, Joseph Gerrald, said that Christianity was an innovation and that all great men had been reformers, 'even our Saviour himself', Braxfield, in open court, growled, 'Muckle he made o' that. He was hanget.' Muir was sentenced to fourteen years transportation to Botany Bay. In 1796 George Washington sent a ship to rescue him and take him to the United States. After an adventurous voyage Muir was captured by Spanish authorities in Mexico and sent to Spain. He was released and made his way to France, where the Directoire named him as a member of the Directory of the Scottish Republic which would be established after the projected French invasion. Muir died in France in 1799. The other martyrs commemorated are Thomas Fyshe Palmer, William Skirving, Maurice Margarot and Joseph Gerrald.

EDINBURGH. Governor's House. Now used by the Scottish Office, this is all that remains of the Old Calton Gaol. The foundations of the gaol can be seen running east along the bottom of St Andrew's House, built in 1936-39 to accommodate the Scottish Office. The Glendale Martyrs spent two months here in 1883, John Maclean a month in 1916. He was joined by James Maxton, Willie Gallacher, James MacDougall, John Muir and Arthur Woodburn. Emanuel Shinwell spent five months in the building after the demonstration in George Square Glasgow in 1919. During the First World War conditions were grim. For the first 30 days prisoners were on bare boards, without mattresses. They were issued with a Bible and a hymnbook. Breakfast was six ounces of oatmeal and half a pint of buttermilk; dinner, two pints of broth and twelve ounces of dry bread; supper, eight ounces of oatmeal and three quarters of a pint of buttermilk. Prisoners only met during the single exercise hour. In 1916 Arthur Woodburn had agitated, as a member of the No Conscription Fellowship, against the evils of war. He was gaoled in Wormwood Scrubs and the Tower of London before Calton. He later became Secretary of State for Scotland from 1947 to 1950, running the building that stood where his former prison had been.

EDINBURGH. 219 High Street. Two plaques commemorate Dr Elsie Maud Inglis (1864-1917), pioneering doctor and suffragette. In 1889 she set up a nursing home which moved here in 1904. It was called 'The Hospice' but was a maternity hospital, staffed by women only, and was specifically for the poor. She helped to found the Scottish Women's Suffrage Federation. In 1914 she proposed the creation of women's medical units to go to the front. The British authorities showed little interest, but the French government took up her plans with enthusiasm. She set up hospitals in France and organised women's units to go to Serbia, Romania, Malta, Corsica and Russia. She went to Serbia herself in 1915, and was captured and interned by the Austrians. She went on to Russia, fell ill, returned to Britain, died in Newcastle upon Tyne and is buried in Dean Cemetery, Edinburgh.

EDINBURGH. Ramsay Gardens, off Castlehill. In 1890 Patrick Geddes (1854-1932) bought the property which was to be part of his master plan for an 'organic' restoration of Edinburgh's Old Town. His energetic schemes had a huge impact on the regeneration of the Old Town. Geddes was a biologist and sociologist, and had a strong interest in theories of education and knowledge, the arts and history. He encouraged tenement dwellers to plant small gardens, tend window boxes and plant trees and formed the Edinburgh Social Union which became responsible for properties in the area housing 450 families. His most famous follower, Lewis Mumford, called him, 'the professor of things in general'.

EDINBURGH. 6 James Court (East Entry). In 1886 Patrick Geddes moved here and it became the base for his Old Town schemes. James Mavor, who later became Professor of Political Economy and a Russian specialist at the University of Toronto, describes in his autobiography a meeting in Geddes' flat in 1886. Among the guests were Prince Pyotr Kropotkin and Thomas Kirkup. Kropotkin was in Edinburgh staying with his friend, John Stuart Blackie, former Professor of Greek at Edinburgh University, a nationalist and leading figure in the 'Celtic Revival'. Kirkup is best known for his *History of Socialism* (1892), which Mao Zedong said was one of the three works that most influenced his formative thinking, along with *The Communist Manifesto* and *Class Struggle* by Karl Kautsky. Mavor and Kropotkin remained friends after that meeting. In 1899, when Mavor was in Canada, he and Kropotkin were both involved in the negotiations that allowed the Doukhobors to leave Tsarist Russia, where they were being persecuted, for resettlement in Saskatchewan.

EDINBURGH. George IV Bridge. Under the bridge, on the south side of the gloomy sunken street, is a memorial plaque to James Connolly, born in 1868 in the Irish community in Cowgate. He was shot by a British Army firing squad at Kilmainham Gaol, Dublin, in the aftermath of the Easter Rising. He was tied to a chair, unable to stand because of the wounds sustained in the fighting at the Post Office. The plaque reads:

> To the memory of James Connolly
> Born 5 June 1868 at 107 Cowgate
> Renowned International Trade Union
> and working class leader
> Founder of the Irish Socialist Republican Party
> Member of the Provisional Government
> of the Irish Republic
> Executed 12 May 1916 at Kilmainham Jail Dublin

EDINBURGH. East Princes Street Gardens. On the embankment below the National Gallery of Scotland is a large rough block of stone erected by the Friends of the International Brigade Association 'to honour the Memory of those who went from the Lothians and Fife to serve in the War in Spain, 1936-1939.' The accompanying verse is touchingly simple. Thirty men from Edinburgh and Fife joined the International Brigades, and thirteen died. Johnny Rutherford from Newhaven was eighteen years old. He was captured at Jarama and shot by firing squad. George Bridges of the British section of the International Socialist Labour Party was also killed at Jarama. Survivors included Councillor Donald Renton, captured near Madrid, sentenced to death, but saved by a prisoner exchange. Councillor Thomas Murray, his brother George and their sister Annie (a nurse) were at the Ebro Front when the

International Brigades were disbanded.

EDINBURGH. Milne's Bar, Hanover Street. Known as the Poet's Pub, where Hugh MacDiarmid held forth, 'alternating', as Alan Bold says, 'between affability and intensity', often in the company of Norman MacCaig (1910-96) and Sidney Goodsir Smith (1915-75). 'All three poets,' wrote Alan Bold, 'were incessant smokers as well as heavy drinkers so their presence was surrounded by a tobacco cloud of unknowing.'

EDINBURGH, Sandy Bell's Bar, Forrest Road. From 1951 to 1955 the Edinburgh People's Festivals were organised by the Labour movement as an alternative programme to the 'highbrow' emphasis of the official Edinburgh International Festival. They concentrated on folk music and ceilidhs. A key figure was Hamish Henderson from the School of Scottish Studies at Edinburgh University who was a regular at Sandy Bell's. A key component of the revival was tapping into the traditions of the Scottish Travellers ('Gypsies', as they are called in England). Jeannie Robertson from Aberdeen, Betsy Whyte and the 'Stewarts of Blair' (Blairgowrie) became well-known names on the folk scene. Norman Buchan, then a Glasgow teacher, was at the first ceilidh in 1951 representing the Cultural Committee of the Communist Party. He went on to found the Glasgow Folk Club (and became the Labour MP for West Renfrewshire in 1964). Also on the Glasgow side was Morris Blythman (who published poems and songs under the alias Thurso Berwick), a teacher at Allan Glen's School. The folk scene was particularly inventive in supporting the Campaign for Nuclear Disarmament and the protest movements of the 1960s. Hamish Henderson, Norman Buchan and Morris Blythman are names that a generation of musicians, singers and songwriters gladly acknowledge as their inspiration: Archie Fisher, Matt McGinn, Hamish Imlach, Robin Hall and Jimmy MacGregor, Aly Bain on the fiddle, Dick Gaughan from Leith, and many more. The folk revival in Scotland blossomed into a joyous and vigorous part of Scottish life which still flourishes.

EDINBURGH. 1 Buccleuch Place. *The Red Paper on Scotland*, edited by Gordon Brown, was published from here by Edinburgh University Student Publications. Among the contributors were Robin Cook, Jim Sillars, Tom Nairn and John McGrath of 7:84 Theatre Company.

EDINBURGH. George Square Theatre. John McGrath wrote and produced with 7:84 *The Cheviot, the Stag and the Black, Black Oil* for the 1973 conference on 'What kind of Scotland?' organised by Scottish International. McGrath founded 7:84 in 1971, taking the name from a statistic in *The Economist* that said that 7 per cent of the population of the United Kingdom owned 84 per cent of the wealth.

EDINBURGH. Saughton Jail, Gorgie Road. In 1992 Tommy Sheridan, founder of the Scottish Socialist Party, was imprisoned here for refusing to pay the Poll Tax. While in prison he stood as councillor for the Easterhouse ward in Glasgow and won.

EIGG, Inner Hebrides, Highland. In 1997, following the example of crofters at Assynt – see Lochinver – the islanders succeeded in buying out their absentee landlord for £1.5 million.

GARTMORE, Stirlingshire. Stone memorial to R. B. Cunninghame Graham (1852-1936), traveller, writer, socialist. Gartmore was one of three properties inherited by Cunninghame Graham – the others being Ardoch (between Dumbarton and Cardross) and Finlaystone (opposite on the south bank of the Clyde). Cunninghame Graham was sometimes called 'Don Roberto' on account of his exploits in Argentina. He was also called 'the uncrowned King of Scotland'. This was not a title of excessive admiration, but referred to a historical claim by the Graham family of rightful descent from King Robert II, challenging the legitimacy of the Stewart/Stuart line. In 1883, having returned from Argentina, he became involved in socialist politics, having met George Bernard Shaw and William Morris, and became Liberal MP for North West Lanarkshire in 1886 on a programme calling for: the abolition of the House of Lords; universal suffrage; the nationalisation of land and mines; free school meals; the disestablishment of the Church of England; Scottish and Irish Home Rule; an eight-hour working day; graduated income tax; prison reform; and an end to capital and corporal punishment. He became friends with Keir Hardie and helped to get him into Parliament. Along with John Burns, Don Roberto was jailed after the 'Bloody Sunday' demonstration in Trafalgar Square London. He also found himself suspended on a number of occasions from the House of Commons because of unparliamentary behaviour. Keir Hardie invited him to become first president of the Scottish Labour Party in 1888, but he failed to win Glasgow Camlachie for the party in 1892. After a long spell out of politics, he became the first President of the National Party of Scotland (later the Scottish National Party) in 1928. Gartmore House is now a Christian conference centre and retreat. The memorial is on the side of the playing field just as one enters the village from the north on the road from Aberfoyle. It reads:

ROBERT BONTINE CUNNING-
HAME GRAHAM 1852-1936
FAMOUS AUTHOR
TRAVELLER AND HORSEMAN
PATRIOTIC SCOT
AND CITIZEN OF THE WORLD
AS BETOKENED
BY THE STONES ABOVE
DIED IN ARGENTINA
INTERRED IN INCHMAHOME
HE WAS A MASTER OF LIFE
A KING AMONG MEN

GLASGOW. Clydebank Shipyards. John Brown's shipyard was the most famous in the most important shipbuilding area in the world. In 1968 the Labour government set up a consortium of five firms – John Brown's, Fairfield's and Stephen's in Govan, and Connell's and Yarrow's in Scotstoun. This became Upper Clyde Shipbuilders (UCS), with a government 48.4 per cent holding. The labour force was thirteen thousand and there were ample orders on their books. In 1970 the newly elected Conservative government under Edward Heath declared a policy of returning industries to private ownership and getting rid of 'lame duck' firms. Yarrow's was to be privatised and UCS was to receive no further public money. In June 1971 UCS asked the government for £6 million. The government refused. On 14 June a mass meeting took place in Clydebank Town Hall. The next day a train – paid for by Clydebank Town Council – brought hundreds of workers to London to lobby the Prime Minister. The government remained intransigent. The Minister responsible, John Davies, announced on 29 July that UCS was to go into liquidation. The local response was immediate. A work-in began that day at John Brown's. The shop stewards' campaign was led by Jimmy Reid and Jimmy Airlie, both communists. They launched an appeal for money. Support flowed in from all over the world. Jimmy Reid was presented with a huge box of red roses. 'It's from Lennon.' 'Lenin's dead,' shouted a voice from the back. It was from John Lennon and Yoko Ono. Davies visited Glasgow in August. Scottish businessmen told him that they stood to lose millions if liquidation went ahead. The Chief Constable warned he needed five thousand extra police to keep control if the yards closed. There were mass demos in George Square. The work-in continued. Meanwhile the Confederation of Shipbuilding and Engineering Union sought another buyer – Marathon Manufacturing of Houston Texas. By February 1972 Davies was conceding. The government would give £35 million to support the yards. The lame duck policy had been defeated by the work-in and the strength of support given to it. Marathon took over John Brown's. Clydebank was secured. A reformed UCS secured the Scotstoun yards. And Govan Shipbuilders came into being. 'We were victorious,' said Jimmy Reid, 'and we saved thousands of jobs, guaranteeing years and years of employment in the yards and spin-offs in other industries. It was a victory not just for the workers but for the whole Scottish community.' But the industry did fail and today it is non-existent. The Clydeside yards could not build supertankers and there was a failure to invest adequately. 'We were trying to compete with Fred Flintstone tools,' was Jimmy Reid's verdict.

GLASGOW. Custom House, Glasgow Bridge. Spanish Civil

War monument. A black, rusting, graffiti-defiled girder has on top a sandstone statue of a woman with both arms raised in what looks like a nun's habit. It says:

'Better to die on your feet than
live for ever on your knees.'
Dolores Ibaruri (La Pasionaria)
THE CITY OF GLASGOW
AND THE BRITISH
LABOUR MOVEMENT
pay tribute to the courage of
those men and women
who went to Spain
to fight Fascism
1936-1939
2,100 VOLUNTEERS
WENT FROM BRITAIN;
534 WERE KILLED,
65 OF WHOM CAME FROM
GLASGOW

GLASGOW. Shawbridge Street, Pollockshaws. Birthplace of John Maclean (1879-1923). The street is now a canyon among high-rise flats. Maclean started evening classes in 1908 and taught Marxism to large audiences. The classes continued to 1915 when he was dismissed by the local school board for having breached the Defence of the Realm Act. In the square at Shawbridge Arcade, just beyond Bengal Street, a memorial reads:

In memory of John Maclean
Famous pioneer of working class
education,
He forged the Scottish link in the
Golden Chain of World Socialism.

GLASGOW. New Eastwood Cemetery. John Maclean is buried here. The cemetery is to the south of Thornliebank Station. To find the grave, turn right on the tarmacked path entering the gate. When it swings left, count seven grass paths on the left. John Maclean's grave is just down the seventh, under a tall cypress tree. His grave is marked 'John Maclean MA'.

GLASGOW. Queen's Park, Pollockshaws Road. On 6 May 1962 the leader of the Labour Party, Hugh Gaitskell, came to address the Glasgow Labour movement. When he began to speak in support of the United States bases in Holy Loch, there were roars of disapproval. Gaitskell lost control. 'You're nothing. You're just peanuts,' he shouted, and carried on in the vein of 'secret members of the Communist Party . . . tools of Russia . . . Go back to Moscow and demonstrate under Russian tanks.' Matt McGinn wrote a song called 'Boomerang' – to the tune of 'Bless 'em all' – about the protest:

> Boomerang, boomerang,
> Just send them back whaur they belang,
> Alang wi' auld Adenauer, Kennedy's pal,
> Signor Fanfani and Charlie de Gaulle.
> For we dinnae like gifts that go bang.
> Just try one and see if I'm wrang.
> The banners are wavin', wha's next for the shavin',
> So open your boom, boomerang.
>
> Ye aa ken how Gaitskell got shelled at Queen's Park,
> An roasted an salted as well.
> He cried the folks peanuts, but aabody kens
> The only nut there was hissel.
> For he thocht that Polaris could stey in the Loch
> An Scotland wad bow tae the Yanks,
> An back Adenauer and the haill Nato shower
> Wi sodgers, bazookas, an tanks.

GLASGOW. Sighthill Cemetery, Springburn. The Martyrs' Memorial is found about halfway up the hill from the main entrance on the Springburn Road. This commemorates John Baird and Andrew Hardie, two of the leaders of the rising of 1820 at the Battle of Bonnymuir, by Bonnybridge.

GLASGOW. Huntershill House, Crowhill Road. Now used by Dunbartonshire Council, this was the home of the father of Scottish democracy, Thomas Muir of Huntershill (1765-98), who is commemorated by a monument at Old Calton Burial Ground, Edinburgh.

GLASGOW. George Square. The location of major Leftie demonstrations. On 12 December 1915 a large demonstration protested against the introduction of conscription. The demo was not permitted and all the speakers were booked by the police on the grounds that they were causing an obstruction. Charges were later dropped as the meeting passed off peacefully. Among those booked were James Maxton, Emanuel Shinwell, John Maclean and Willie Gallacher. Just over three years later, on 31 January 1919, George Square witnessed 'Bloody Friday', the Battle of George Square. The Ways and

Means Committee which had grown out of the Clyde Workers' Committee had called for a strike to begin on 27 January to press for a 40-hour week. In spite of the demo organisers' recommendation that trams should be off the streets, they were still functioning. A striker pulled down a tram rope, a soldier hit him and fighting started. The police charged and the demonstrators retaliated with fists, iron railings and broken bottles, forcing the police to retreat. David Kirkwood was knocked to the ground by a police baton and was arrested with Willie Gallacher. The 'best fight' of the riot was said to have been in Cathedral Street (at the back of Queen Street station). Fighting continued in and around the city centre streets for many hours afterwards. The Townhead area and Glasgow Green, where many demonstrators had regrouped after the initial police charge, were the scenes of running battles between police and demonstrators. The Secretary of State for Scotland solemnly told the Cabinet that a Bolshevist rising was underway; more troops were sent from England and the city became, in practical respects, under military control. On 10 February the strike was called off and employers settled for 47 hours at the same wages. 'We regarded the 40-hour strike not as a revolution but as a beginning,' said Harry McShane. 'Other things would follow: it was the first rank-and-file agitation to be led by socialists after the war. The working-class movement was bigger at the end of the war than before, and the socialists themselves had hardened.'

GLASGOW. St Enoch Shopping Centre. This is on the site of the old St Enoch Station. On 20 November 1922, following the General Election, the new MPs from Glasgow and the West of Scotland, the 'Red Clydesiders', left in triumph on the night mail train for Westminster. Ten of Glasgow's fifteen seats had gone to Labour. 'What a troop we were!' wrote one of them, David Kirkwood. 'John Wheatley, cool and calculating and fearless; James Maxton, whose wooing speaking and utter selflessness made people regard him as a saint and martyr; wee Jimmie Stewart, so small, so sober, and yet so determined; Neil Maclean, full of fire without fury; Thomas Johnston, with a head as full of facts as an egg's full o' meat; George Hardie, engineer and chemist and brother of Keir Hardie; George Buchanan, patternmaker, who knew the human side of poverty better than any of us: James Welsh, miner and poet from Coatbridge; John W. Muir, an heroic and gallant gentleman; and old Bob Smillie, returned for an English constituency though he was born in Ireland and reared in Scotland.' Some estimates of the crowd say fifty thousand, others a hundred thousand. They sang 'The Red Flag', 'Jerusalem' and Psalm 124 and the moment has been described by Gordon Brown 'as the Scottish Labour Movement's finest hour'.

GLASGOW. Saltmarket. Here, between the High Court and Nelson's Monument in Glasgow Green, six tanks were stationed in February 1919 after the Battle of George Square. The corner of Clyde Street and Saltmarket is the spot, outside the public offices and gaol that stood there, where James Wilson was executed in 1820 after the battle of Bonnymuir. (See Bonnybridge)

GLASGOW. Forge Shopping Centre. This centre, built in 1987, is on the site of the Parkhead Forge, the huge engineering works belonging to Sir William Beardmore. David Kirkwood (1872-1935) was the principal shop steward here during the First World War. Because of the industrial unrest caused by disputes during the war, Kirkwood and other members of the Clyde Workers' Committee were arrested in March 1916 under the Defence of the Realm Act and 'deported' to Edinburgh. He was arrested again after the Battle of George Square in January 1919 but escaped a jail sentence. Elected to the House of Commons in 1922 for Dumbarton Burghs, Kirkwood always had a cordial relationship with Beardmore and ended up as Lord Kirkwood. 'He began to talk a lot of cheap nonsense,' recalled Harry McShane, 'and in one speech actually said that the backbone of the Scottish workers was their love of simple porridge.' After that he was known all over as 'Porridge Davie'.

GLASGOW. St James's Primary School, 88 Green Street, Calton. The Calton was one of the areas of Glasgow most famous for poverty, crime and the indomitable spirit of its people. Calton was mostly knocked down in the 1960s. Much of the earlier street plan has now disappeared in the neat, new crescents and avenues of pleasant little houses. At 88 Green Street stands an elegant, three storey red sandstone with SCHOOL BOARD OF GLASGOW etched in stone on the top, GIRLS above the south door, BOYS above the north. The school was opened in 1895 among the grim tenements and 'backlands', the 'room and kitchens' and 'single-ends', that made up the Calton. A plaque on the north wall reads:

James Maxton MA
1885-1946
Member of Parliament
for Bridgeton
He taught in this school 1909-1912
'A rarer spirit never did steer humanity'

Maxton was involved in strikes in 1916 and was jailed for a year in Edinburgh. He entered Parliament in 1922. One of his biographers is Gordon Brown, whose verdict is that 'Maxton, like many Labour leaders, has suffered the condescension of posterity. He has been belittled and dismissed as "a beloved rebel", picturesque but peripheral . . . But at the height of his powers, in the 1920s, he threatened to change the whole course of politics by offering British socialism a third way between Labour gradualism and Communism.'

GLASGOW. Glasgow Green. The Green has been the site of innumerable demos and protests. The People's Palace and Winter Gardens were built on the north east side off London Road. In 2005 the People's Palace is undergoing reorganisation. It is expected that it will be showing something of the following categories of exhibition: language, drink, dancing, crime and execution, a 'war' section, strikes, poverty, homelessness, marriage, living together, single-end life, football, boxing, industry, and to cap it all, Billy Connolly's banana boots and Billy's portrait by John Byrne. A highlight of the exhibitions is Ken Currie's eight panels produced in 1987 to commemorate the bicentenary of the Glasgow Weavers' Strike. The 1787 strike, when the population of Glasgow was sixty thousand, was caused by a cut in wages following a price collapse in 1786 arising from large scale importation of muslin from India by the East India Company. On 30 June 1787 weavers held a mass meeting on Glasgow Green and resolved to strike. The strike lasted until September and was met with violence. Shooting demonstrators was, for the first time, seen as acceptable. The strike is now regarded as marking the beginning of an effective Labour movement in Scotland, where the weavers emerged as an organised association capable of fighting for their livelihoods. English troops were brought in to restore order. Many weavers were arrested and imprisoned. The most severe sentence was given to one of the principal organisers, James Granger. He was tried in Edinburgh and found guilty of 'forming illegal combinations – the first case of its kind. He was sentenced to be whipped through the streets of Edinburgh by the public executioner and then banished from Scotland for seven years. He returned to Scotland after his banishment and took part in a later strike, in 1811-12.

GLASGOW. Calton Burial Ground. Against the southern wall near the entry at Kerr Place is the Weavers' Lair – two large stones and a plaque commemorating those who were killed during the weavers' strike of 1787. John Page, Alexander Miller and James Ainsley who were killed on 3 September 1787 are buried here, as is James Granger. The stones are in disrepair. A new memorial stone has been placed on the north side of the wall that runs through the middle of the cemetery, with the words:

> They, though dead, still liveth.
> Emulate them.
> We'll never swerve. We'll steadfast be.
> We'll have our rights. We will be free.
>
> They are unworthy of freedom
> Who expect it from hands other than their own.

GLENBUCK, East Ayrshire. Shankly Monument. Bill Shankly (1913-81), miner and football legend, was born here. He represented a time when football was the honest sport of and for the working class; before hooliganism, the tantrums of overpaid stars, corporate corruption and bloated commercialisation. This tiny village had a population of nearly a thousand. Shankly was one of five brothers and five sisters. All five brothers became professional footballers. (The village is said to have produced 49 professional footballers over as many years.) Shankly quotes are famous, and the most famous of all is: 'Some people think football is a matter of life and death. I'm very disappointed with that attitude. I can assure you it is much, much more important than that.' The dedication on the monument is prolix, but the centrepiece says, apostrophe and all:

BILL SHANKLY
THE LEGEND
THE GENIUS
THE MAN
FROM ANFIELD WITH LOVE.
THANKS SHANK'S

GLENDALE, Isle of Skye, Highland. In 1883 crofters began a rent strike because of a lack of grazing land. Five men were arrested, tried in Edinburgh and jailed for two months. On their return, the 'Glendale Martyrs' returned to jubilant celebrations. While they were in prison a Royal Commission was set up – the Napier Commission – to look into the conditions of crofters and cottars in the Highlands and Islands of Scotland. One of the Martyrs, John MacPherson, used to go around the townships addressing crofter meetings, with readings from the Old Testament, Isaiah, 5:8: 'Woe unto them that join house to house, that lay field to field, till there be no place, that they may be placed alone in the midst of the earth.'

GOLSPIE, Sutherland, Highland. Ben Bhraggie Monument. This commemorates the first Duke of Sutherland (1758-1833) who was a vigorous clearer of the County of Sutherland. In John Prebble's words, 'He was coal and wool joined by a stately hyphen and ennobled by five coronets . . . He was the Most Noble George Granville Leveson-Gower, second Marquess of Stafford . . . and the first Duke of Sutherland. His red sandstone effigy, in a red sandstone toga, rears thirty feet from a pedestal seventy-six feet high at the top of Ben Bhraggie . . . Its back is to the glens he emptied, it faces the sea to which his policies committed five thousand people as emigrants or herring-fishers.'

HOLYTOWN, North Ayrshire. Legbranock. The village where Keir Hardie was born has disappeared. The modern bungalow with its thriving cypresses and 'Keir Hardie Cottage' etched in stone on the wall has nothing to do with the founding father of the Labour Party. North Lanarkshire Council has bravely stuck two roadsigns indicating where they think the village might have stood with 'Birthplace of James Keir Hardie, 1856-1915, founder of the Independent Labour Party' underneath. Woodhall Row, where Hardie was born, was part of a double row of miners' cottages running along the edge of what is now the Newhouse Industrial Estate. The three remaining rundown cottages opposite the end of Legbranock Road are called Johnstonhall and are outside the original village.

INVERGORDON, Easter Ross, Highland. Harbour. The natural harbour was used during the North Sea oil boom for oil-rig construction and maintenance services. Before that it was an anchorage for the Royal Navy. In September 1931 the British Atlantic Fleet, as it was then called, arrived there for exercises and for two days a number of ships were in open mutiny. This was in response to pay cuts imposed by Ramsay MacDonald's National government on the navy from 10 to 25 per cent depending on rank. Ten ships had arrived off Invergordon on 11 September. The men had access to newspapers and on the 12th a group of sailors met on shore (on a football pitch) and voted to organise a strike. They left for their ships singing 'The Red Flag'. On the 13th a noisy meeting in the shore canteen was cut short by shore patrols. On the 15th the crews of four ships refused to carry out orders to sail. When officers tried to issue orders (and threats) on the loudspeakers, they were jeered and ignored. The Admiral in charge, Wilfrid Tomkinson, reported to London and recommended concessions.

The Cabinet immediately accepted a compromise. The decision was communicated to the fleet, the exercises were cancelled and all ships left Invergordon that night in perfect order. About two hundred sailors were expelled from the Atlantic Fleet and another two hundred from other units of the Navy. All were accused of subversive activity. The *Daily Worker* had supported the mutineers and their offices were raided and two associates arrested under the Incitement to Mutiny Act of 1797.

INVERIE, Knoydart, West Inverness-shire, Highland. In 1853 Knoydart was the scene of one of the last great clearances. News of the events here inspired the resistance in Strathcarron (see Croic). The widow of Aeneas MacDonell of Glengarry, the sixteenth Chief, wanted the tenants out so that the estate could be sold to a sheep farmer. Although not as notorious as the clearances carried out on the estates of the Duchess of Sutherland in the north, the Knoydart clearance, very well documented, stands out as having been done with particular cruelty. Over three hundred were sent to Canada on a single ship. Another hundred or so were forcibly evicted and had their homes demolished. Many tried to live in shelters but were driven out of these too. In the 1930s, the estate was bought by Lord Brocket, a pro-Nazi, vice president of the Anglo-German Fellowship and a guest of Hitler's at a number of celebrations. Ribbentrop was a visitor to Knoydart. In 1948 'Seven Men of Knoydart', led by the local priest, Father Colin Macpherson, staged the last 'land raid' in Scotland, each man staking out 65 acres. Brocket successfully obtained an interim interdict from the Court of Session against them. Their appeal to Arthur Woodburn, Secretary of State for Scotland in the Attlee government, failed. But Lord Brocket gave up and sold out. Hamish Henderson wrote 'The Ballad of the Men of Knoydart', of which an extract goes:

> 'You bloody Reds!' Lord Brocket yelled,
> Wot's this you're doin' 'ere?
> It doesn't pay, as you'll find today,
> To insult an English Peer.

You're only Scottish halfwits,
But I'll make you understand.
You Highland swine, these hills are mine.
This is all Lord Brocket's land.'

Up spoke the men of Knoydart:
'Och, away and shut yer trap,
For threats from a Saxon brewer's boy,
We just won't give a rap.
O we are all ex-servicemen,
We fought against the Hun.
We can tell our enemies by now;
And Brocket, you are one.'

INVERUGLAS, Loch Lomond, Argyll and Bute. Loch Sloy Dam. Completed in 1945, this was the first built by the North of Scotland Hydro-Electric Board ('the Hydro'), set up by Thomas Johnston (1881-1965), then Secretary of State for Scotland in Winston Churchill's Second World War Coalition government. Johnston, after 1945, became Chairman of the Hydro, until 1959. Born in Kirkintilloch, he had founded the ILP newspaper, *Forward*, in 1906. His writings included *Our Scots Noble Families* (1909) and *The History of the Working Classes in Scotland* (1920). His imaginative initiatives as Secretary of State included setting up a midgie research programme in 1944 to try to find a deterrent to that Highland scourge. His vision of the Hydro was inspired by F. D. Roosevelt's Tennessee Valley Authority. His plan was that the sale of electricity to the south would be used for 'the economic development and social improvement of the North of Scotland'. This was the 1943 Act's 'Social Clause' which was the most radical feature of this, Britain's first nationalised industry. The Hydro was privatised under Margaret Thatcher (at the insistence of her Secretary of State, Malcolm Rifkind). Johnston refused a title, but accepted the Companionship of Honour (CH) in 1953.

IONA, Argyll and Bute. The Iona Community was founded by socialist, pacifist, baronet and life peer George Macleod. In the kirkyard is buried John Smith (1938-94), leader of the Labour Party 1992-94. As his biographer, Andy McSmith has written, 'The paradox about John Smith . . . is that throughout his career he was regarded as being on the party's right wing, but posthumously he became an almost iconic favourite of the left.'

KILMUIR, Isle of Skye, Highland. In November 1884 three hundred marines landed at Uig and marched to the village of Kilmuir to enforce the payment of rents. There was no resistance but the rent strikes continued.

KINGSMUIR, Forfar. Kingsmuir Resource Centre. A plaque on the building commemorates A. S. Neill (1883-1973), educationalist. Neill's father was dominie of the school that once occupied the site of the centre. Neill was a pupil teacher here at the age of fifteen. He went on to be a headteacher at Gretna Green and formed ideas of education without discipline. Then in 1923 he set up a school in Lyme Regis in a house called Summerhill. In 1927 the school was transferred to Leiston, Suffolk. His principle was that children should be allowed to grow emotionally, and to make their own decisions, removing fear and adult coercion. It could not be further from the bleak dour ways of Scottish education as practised at Kingsmuir School in 1900.

KYLEAKIN, Isle of Skye, Highland. Skye Bridge. One of the most important campaigns run by the *Highland Free Press* has been against the tolls on the Skye Bridge, linking Skye to the mainland, across the narrow sound where the ferries used to run. It was Scotland's first Private Finance Initiative, built by Miller Construction. The tolls (£5.70 one way in summer) were the most expensive of any tollbridge in Britain and the profits went directly to the Bank of America who financed the project. After the Bridge was opened in 1995 there was a vigorous no-payment campaign. The organisation of resistance was SKAT (Skye and Kyle Against Tolls). Thousands of charges were issued for refusal to pay, and hundreds have been prosecuted and given criminal records. The Holyrood Parliament had the tolls removed in December 2004 'just in time for Christmas'.

LANGHOLM, Dumfries and Galloway. Cemetery. Christopher Murray Grieve, better known as the communist, nationalist and poet Hugh MacDiarmid (1892-1978), is buried in the cemetery here, a mile south of the town. He was born and brought up in this town, where his father was a postman and his mother looked after the library. On the stone are the words:

> I'll hae nae haufway hoose, but aye be whaur
> Extremes meet – it's the only way I ken
> To dodge the cursed conceit o' bein' richt
> That damns the vast majority o' men.

LANGHOLM, Dumfries and Galloway. MacDiarmid Memorial. This is signposted, on a hill to the east of the town and was created by Jake Harvey in the shape of an open book.

LOCHGELLY, Fife. Chinese Take Away, High Street. Lochgelly is the birthplace of Jennie Lee (1904-88), an MP in 1929, the youngest woman ever elected. She married Aneurin Bevan in 1934 and was Minister for the Arts in Harold Wilson's 1964 government and a founder of the Open University. Lochgelly was in the West Fife constituency that returned William Gallacher as a Communist MP from 1935 to 1950. It is now in the constituency of Gordon Brown. But the town has a grimmer memory in being famous for the Lochgelly tawse. Whereas the cane was the weapon of choice for teachers in England, in Scotland it was the tawse – a leather strap with either two or three tails. Miscreant pupils were thrashed on an extended hand in front of the class. Saddlers provided these instruments as a sideline from their main business, and the most famous was John Dick and Sons of Lochgelly which occupied this site. In the 1970s the business moved to Cowdenbeath prior to the abolition of corporal punishment in Scotland in 1981. Under the pretext of 'collectors' items' there is still an 'adult market' for the Lochgelly tawse.

LOCHINVER, Assynt, Highland. In 1989 the main landowner in the area, Edmund H. Vestey, sold 21,000 acres of this coastal area with thirteen settlements, named it 'North Lochinver Estate' and sold it for over a million pounds to a Swedish land speculator. None of the residents who lived there and worked the land were consulted. In 1992 the Swedish company went into liquidation. The main creditor was a Swedish bank. The selling agents previously employed by the Vestey family were again employed. They broke up the estate into seven lots which were once more put out for sale. Again local residents were ignored. The crofters organised a public meeting, and a proposal was put forward to raise money so that local residents could bid for the lots themselves. A committee was formed, and feasibility study and business plan produced. £300,000 was raised from donations. District and regional councils gave grants and the liquidators finally agreed a deal in December 1992 – six months after the first public meeting. This encouraged other crofters to buy out absentee landlords.

LOSSIEMOUTH, Moray. 1 Gregory Place. Birthplace of James Ramsay MacDonald (1866-1937), first Labour Prime Minister. Born illegitimate, it is not clear whether this or his politics led to the blocking of his application for membership of the local golf club. A local teacher before he went to London, he became secretary of the Labour Representation Committee on its foundation in 1900. He was a charismatic orator and an organiser. He travelled extensively and opposed Britain's involvement in the First World War. He was his own Foreign Secretary in the first Labour government of 1924. He was Labour Prime Minister again from 1929 to 1931, when a financial crisis led him to form a coalition with the other parties. This was seen by most of the Labour Party as a betrayal. In the General Election of 1935 he fought Seaham Harbour but was defeated by Emanuel Shinwell who had earlier been an enthusiastic supporter. He died at sea.

LOSSIEMOUTH, Moray. 17 Moray Street, 'The Hillocks'. The house bought by Ramsay MacDonald.

LOSSIEMOUTH, Moray. Lossiemouth Fisheries Community Museum. This contains a mock-up of Ramsay MacDonald's study in 'The Hillocks'.

NEWCRAIGHALL, City of Edinburgh. Bill Douglas (1937-91) produced three films evoking his childhood here: *My Childhood* (1971), *My Ain Folk* (1973) and *My Way Home*

(1978). The picture of poverty and suffering in this small mining village has moments of humanity and humour. The films are gripping viewing. Bill Douglas's collection of films and other artefacts is held by the Bill Douglas Centre for the History of Cinema and Popular Culture at the University of Exeter.

NEW LANARK, South Lanarkshire. UNESCO World Heritage Village. Robert Owen (1771-1858), partner in a Manchester spinning company, bought the mill here from his father-in-law, David Dale, and moved here in 1800. Dale was an enlightened employer who had tried to improve the conditions of his workers with educational schemes and other community measures, but it was Owen's work that attracted worldwide attention. In the eyes of Marx and Engels, he was the quintessential utopian, and his language of 'harmony', 'co-operation', 'community' and 'union' looked towards an 'organic' society based on authority and obedience. It was very much a paternalistic and hierarchical social order that he envisioned. But given the context of the 'dark satanic mills', what he did has proved an enduring source of inspiration. His fundamental view was that reform depended on education. At New Lanark school classes included music and dancing, and new methods of teaching included pictures, maps and diagrams. He insisted that a child's education should be enjoyable.

NEWTONGRANGE, Midlothian. Scottish Mining Museum. Appropriately near Newbattle Abbey where Cistercian monks started the first coal mine in Scotland in the thirteenth century, this first class museum preserves the best example of a Victorian mine. The museum is on the site of the Lady Victoria Colliery, opened in the 1890s and named after the wife of the Marquess of Lothian. When the mine closed in 1981 most of the men went to nearby Bilston Glen Colliery, south of Loanhead, the scene of some of the most bitter confrontations during the miners' strike of 1984-85. 'I've heard people call it "the great miners' strike in 1984". Well there was fuck all great about it. Thatcher sacked us, the polis beat us up, and the TUC and Neil Kinnock shat on us. It was a year of misery for the miners and their families, and we had a few mair besides trying to get back on oor feet. Some never made it yet.' So said a retired miner from one of the Fife pits.

PLOCKTON, Wester Ross, Highland. School. Sorley MacLean (1911-96) was the schoolmaster here. Born on the Island of Raasay, MacLean was the outstanding Gaelic poet of the twentieth century. He wanted to fight for the Republicans in the Spanish Civil War. In his poem, 'The Cuillin', the magnificent mountain range of the Isle of Skye, he sees the wonderful landscape as a reflection of the heroic spirit of mankind in its struggle to overcome adversity:

> Beyond poverty, consumption, / fever, agony;
> Beyond hardship, wrong, / tyranny, distress;
> Beyond misery, despair, hatred, / treachery;
> Beyond guilt and defilement – / watchfully,
> Heroically is seen the Cuillin
> Rising on the other side of / sorrow.

PORT OF MENTEITH, Stirlingshire. Inchmahome Priory. On the island in the Lake of Menteith lies the body of R. B. Cunninghame Graham (1852-1936), traveller, socialist and writer. He died in Argentina and his body was brought here for burial alongside his wife, Gabrielle de la Balmondiere.

QUARTER, South Lanarkshire. Old Quarry. A former colliery here saw the young James Keir Hardie hone his political skills. He regularly addressed meetings, urging the miners to organise. The Hamilton branch of the Lanarkshire Miners' Union was formed in 1878 and Hardie, aged 21, became secretary. The following year he and two of his brothers, all working at No. 4 Pit in Quarter, were summarily dismissed. Hardie was blacklisted and could get no further work in the mines.

ROUSAY, Orkney. In 1883 the island was owned by General Sir Frederick Burroughs. When interviewed by the Napier Commission investigating the complaints of crofters, he said in his testimony, 'Is the property mine, or is it not mine? If it is mine, surely I can do what I consider best for it? If these people are not contented and happy, they can go away.'

ST ANDREWS, Fife. Cathedral. St Andrews is not a very Leftie place. (Margaret Thatcher's Poll Tax was conceived here.) But in the burial ground by the ruined cathedral is the grave of Adam Ferguson (1723-1816), who gave the world the term, 'civil society'.

SANDAY, Orkney. Over the Water. Stuart Christie, anarchist came to live here in the 1970s, after having been imprisoned in Spain and – having renounced violence – been acquitted as a suspect in the Angry Brigade trial of 1971-72. The house was named by an owner with Jacobite dreams. This became the base for the Cienfuegos Press, Refract Publications and a local radical newspaper, *The Free-Winged Eagle*. The Presbyterian minister on a neighbouring island denounced the paper as the organ of Satan. Alleged satanic practices included: stopping a seal cull, resisting uranium mining, and halting an SAS exercise on the island. The Chief Constable of Inverness opposed Christie having a shotgun licence on the grounds that with it he could arm a local radical militia.

SHOTTS, Lanarkshire. Birthplace of Mick McGahey (1925-99), leader of the Scottish Miners during the 1984-85 miners' strike. His gravelly voice and uncompromising accent became familiar. His father, James, was a founding member of the Communist Party and was imprisoned for a year for activities during the General Strike of 1926.

SPYNIE, Moray. Graveyard. The ashes of the first Labour Prime Minister, Ramsay MacDonald, were interred here, in the family lair of Isabella Allan Ramsay, his mother's mother. His mother, Anne, and the ashes of his wife and two of his children are also buried here. There is no access from the ruins of Spynie Palace. Visitors have to negotiate a housing estate to the north east of Elgin.

STORNOWAY, Isle of Lewis, Western Isles. Aignish. In January 1888 crofters took over land here but found themselves facing the military. Land raids continued until the 1920s. In

1919 ex-servicemen, returning from the Great War, invaded some farms owned by Lord Leverhulme – Tong, Gress and Coll, first of all, and then thirteen others. This led to Leverhulme closing down his enterprises in Lewis. In 1883 members of the Napier Commission, set up to inquire into the position of crofters, were shipwrecked off Stornoway.

SYMBISTER, Whalsay, Shetland. Sodom. Residence, in great poverty, from 1933 to 1942 of Hugh MacDiarmid, his wife Valda and son Michael. It was here that he wrote some of his best poems, and managed, in 1939, to get expelled from the Communist Party – and from the Scottish Nationalist Party. MacDiarmid, always controversial and contrary (in 1956 he rejoined the Communist Party), he could be outrageously petulant. While living in Shetland, he ridiculed its local culture. Shetlanders were 'a boorish people with no more intellectual interests or spiritual perceptions than their own grice'.

TARBERT, Argyll and Bute. Tarbert Cemetery. In 1845, one year before the potato blight, cholera reached Argyll. People in Tarbert noticed that no one had been seen from the tiny village of Allt Beithe to the south. Two men set out first to Baldarroch where they found everyone dead. They then went on to Allt Beithe, high on the hillside. Everyone was dead or about to die, except for a baby, Archibald Leitch, aged two. He was taken back to Tarbert and brought up by relatives. He grew to be a boat-builder and lived to the age of 87. His daughter, Annie, married a man called Smith. Their grandson was John Smith, leader of the Labour Party 1992-94. The gravestone reads:

Erected
to the memory of
John Leitch
later farmer, Altbea
who died Decr 4th 1845
aged 54 years
and of his spouse
Catherine Carmichael
who died Decr 16th 1845
aged 43 years
by
their sons and daughters.

TURRIFF, Aberdeenshire. The Turra Coo Monument, Lendrum Farm. Just over three miles south of Turriff, a road goes to the east to Lendrum Farm, where a monument was unveiled in 1971 to the memory of Robert Paterson, farmer of Lendrum, and to the 'Turra Coo' incident of 1913. Lloyd George's National Insurance Acts of 1911 and 1913 required contributions from employer, including an amount for each employee. Paterson, a prosperous local farmer, refused to pay his workers' contributions. He was tried and convicted. He paid the fine but refused to pay the extra 'arrears'. A sheriff's officer came and poinded (confiscated) a white cow that was taken to Turriff for public auction. Local farmers encouraged workers to attend and a crowd of two thousand were in the square. The cow was brought with slogans painted on it ('frae Lendrum tae Leeks', a derogatory reference to Lloyd George's Welsh origins). In the following revelry the cow bolted and made its way back to Lendrum, and the auctioneer was chased into a stable and had to be rescued by police. A few days later the cow was taken to Aberdeen to be sold. Paterson was tried for breach of the peace and obstruction, and, after a six day trial and moments of frivolity, the verdict was 'not proven'. He returned by train to Turriff and was met at the station by cheering crowds and a pipe band. The cow was bought by a group of local farmers and returned to Paterson, with new slogans painted on her – 'Breath Bad – Gummy Leeks' – and a crowd between three thousand and four thousand gathered. The 'Turra Coo' incident is interpreted in a folksie way, where the local community resists interfering officialdom. Paterson is held to have resisted for the best of motives: the new scheme, it was argued, would make things worse for farm labourers since health was so much better in the countryside and unemployment was not the problem it was in the towns. There are other interpretations.

Index

Ablett, Noah 186, 221
Abraham, William 185, 203
Acland, Richard 34, 164
Addison, Christopher 123, 132
Applegarth, Robert 100, 274
Arch, Joseph 124, 148, 152
Ashbee, C. R. 25
Asquith, H. H. 101, 303
Astor, David 43
Attlee, Clement 3, 8, 32, 40, 64, 69, 70, 79, 84, 85, 86, 87, 88, 95, 99, 100, 101, 105, 107, 110, 117, 122, 123, 126, 132, 149, 154, 165, 188, 276, 347
Attlee, George 54

Baird, John 326, 340
Baldwin, Oliver 64, 72, 151, 153
Ball, John 2, 68, 69, 139, 140
Balls, Ed 162
Bamford, Samuel 5, 226, 246
Barnes, George 15
Bax, Ernest Belfort 148, 149, 150, 159
Bell, John Hyslop 285, 286
Bell, Richard 149, 156
Benn, Hilary 126
Benn, Tony 35, 40, 115, 125, 126, 138, 155, 164
Bentham, Jeremy 90
Besant, Annie 87, 88, 92, 107
Bevan, Aneurin 3, 41, 60, 115, 122, 165, 186, 193, 200, 219, 220, 274, 350
Beveridge, William 40, 97, 99, 107
Bevin, Ernest 16, 32, 60, 79, 105, 115, 165
Biggs, John 147, 159
Birkbeck, George 96, 116
Blair, Tony 41, 71, 84, 101, 109, 111, 112, 126, 129, 154, 161, 162, 281, 284, 287, 292, 296, 303
Blatchford, Robert 13, 15, 134, 230, 247
Blunkett, David 264, 278
Bodichon, Barbara Leigh Smith 59, 66
Bondfield, Margaret 35, 54
Boothroyd, Betty 264, 271
Boughton, Rutland 27, 36
Bourne, Hugh 147, 154, 155, 157
Bower, Fred 240
Bradshaw, John 98
Brandreth, Jeremiah 146, 156, 163
Brine, James 43
Brittain, Vera 98, 150, 160, 161, 163
Broadhurst, Henry 38, 82
Brockway, Fenner 96, 98, 123, 164
Brown, Gordon 102, 111, 162, 319, 321, 335, 342, 343, 350
Buckley, Reginald 36
Bull, George 258, 260, 268
Burns, John 81, 89, 95, 103, 104, 336
Burns, Robert 323, 328, 330
Burt, Thomas 287, 293, 294, 302
Bussey, Peter 253, 260
Butler, Josephine 240-1, 286, 300, 301
Buxton, Noel 124, 129, 130, 140
Byers, Stephen 281
Byron, Lord George 2, 145, 158

Cade, Jack 5, 48, 52, 60, 61, 72, 75
Callaghan, James 41, 84, 101, 102, 126, 131, 150, 155, 161, 166
Campbell, Alastair 154
Carlile, Richard 29
Carpenter, Edward 60, 65, 149, 160
Castle, Barbara 41, 45, 88, 115, 122, 155, 245, 264
Chadwick, Edwin 258, 259, 274
Charles, Thomas 178, 197, 199
Christian, Fletcher 290
Christie, Stuart 354
Churchill, Winston 16, 29, 32, 105, 117, 219, 348
Clark, William 6
Clarkson, Thomas 33
Clifford, John 147, 153, 165
Clowes, William 147, 154, 155, 157
Coates, Ken 150, 162
Cobbett, William 2, 4, 5, 11, 34, 47, 48–54, 56, 58, 59, 61, 62, 64, 65, 70, 73, 115, 259
Cole, G. D. H. 4, 37, 40, 71, 88, 103, 129, 135, 164
Cole, Margaret 5, 103, 107, 123, 129
Connolly, James 333, 334
Cook, Arthur 186, 187, 221
Cook, Henry 69
Cook, Robin 335
Cooper, Thomas 5, 123, 130, 147, 159
Courtenay, Sir William see Tom, John
Cousins, Frank 148, 151, 154, 155
Cradoc, Walter 186, 201, 206
Cripps, Stafford 74, 75, 102, 104, 122
Cromwell, Oliver 20, 34, 40, 98, 104, 120, 123, 175, 206, 223
Crooks, Will 105, 106, 108
Crosland, Anthony 123, 131
Crossman, Richard 40, 79

Dalton, Hugh 4, 99, 102, 113, 123, 129, 158
Dalyell, Tam 4, 64, 129
Davies, John 337, 338
Davies, Ron 71, 194
Davison, Emily Wilding 83, 286, 301, 302
Davitt, Michael 239
Deakin, Arthur 148, 165
Dewar, Donald 330, 331
Dickens, Charles 55, 74
Disraeli, Benjamin 17, 83, 237, 284
Douglas, Bill 351-2
Driberg, Tom 62, 67, 125, 127
Durbin, Evan 30, 40

Edmonds, John 62
Edwards, George 124, 140
Edwards, Ifan ab Owen 206, 207
Edwards, Owen Morgan 185, 207, 217
Ellis, Thomas Edward 184, 198
Engels, Friedrich 9, 13, 92, 95, 112, 238, 243, 352
Ennals, David 165
Evans, Gwynfor 190, 192
Ewing, Winnie 330

Fels, Joseph 90, 133, 134
Ferguson, Adam 313, 354
Foot, Isaac 41
Foot, Michael 41, 54, 71, 88, 89, 115, 116, 167, 200, 220
Forman, John 283, 284, 297
Forster, E. M. 129, 160
Frost, John 33, 181, 212, 213

Gaitskell, Hugh 30, 37, 40, 74, 88, 102, 114, 102, 114, 148, 165, 264, 274, 276, 277, 278, 339
Gallacher, Willie 319, 320, 332, 340, 350
Gandhi, Mahatma 79, 97, 108, 291
Geddes, Patrick 333
Gerrald, Joseph 331
Gibbon, Lewis Grassie see Mitchell,

James Leslie
Gladstone, William 12, 38, 82, 83, 184, 218, 221, 229, 294
Glasier, Katherine Bruce 7
Glyn Dwr, Owain 172, 204, 210, 218
Godwin, William 31, 121
Gollancz, Victor 40, 111, 150, 164
Gooch, Edwin 124, 141
Goodman, Geoffrey 42
Gordon Walker, Patrick 62
Graham, Catherine Macaulay 58
Graham, R. B. Cunninghame 336, 353
Granger, James 344
Grayson, Victor 263, 271
Greenbury, Clement 26
Grieve, Christopher Murray see MacDiarmid, Hugh
Griffiths, James 186

Haldane, Roger 101, 324-5
Hammond, Barbara 5, 114
Hammond, J. L. 5, 114
Hamnet, James 43
Hannington, Wal 99, 299
Hardie, Andrew 326, 340
Hardie, James Keir 14, 15, 32, 81, 94, 96, 103, 109, 124, 135, 136, 149, 156, 163, 186, 200, 211, 239, 263, 272, 277, 318, 320, 336, 341, 345, 346, 353
Harris, Howell 177, 206, 214, 2218, 219, 220, 221
Hattersley, Roy 264, 278-9
Hazlitt, William 2, 49, 72, 89, 95, 144, 167
Healey, Denis 40, 102, 264, 275, 278
Heffer, Eric 122, 178
Henderson, Arthur 14, 15, 81, 115, 285, 295
Henderson, Fred 136
Henderson, Hamish 322, 335, 347
Henson, Gravener 161
Heron, Patrick 26
Hetherington, Henry 181, 214
Hill, Christopher 6
Hobsbawn, Eric 6, 89, 96, 123, 129
Hodgkin, Dorothy Crowfoot 33
Holland, Stuart 62
Holst, Gustav 27, 125, 139
Holyoake, George 53, 59, 60, 95
Hoon, Geoff 162
Horner, Arthur 187, 201, 221
Hosfall, William 253, 256, 274
Howell, Dennis 150, 157
Hudelstone, Trevor 277
Hughes, Emrys 328
Hughes, Victoria 33
Hulton, William 251
Hume, David 313, 331
Hunt, Henry 11, 15, 23, 44, 47, 70, 92, 227, 228, 245, 248
Hurd, Douglas 35
Hutcheson, Francis 313
Hyndman, H. M. 13, 15, 88, 95, 96, 114, 129, 137, 238, 239

Inglis, Elsie Maud 332
Ireton, Henry 98, 104

James, James 196, 216
Jay, Douglas 40, 74
Jay, Margaret 41
Jeger, Lena (née May) 45
Jenkins, Roy 40, 84, 102, 109, 110, 197
Jewson, Dorothy 36
Johnston, Thomas 320, 321, 341, 348
Jones, Elwyn 197
Jones, Ernest 237
Jones, Griffith 177, 205, 206, 214
Jones, Jack 41, 116, 244
Jones, Jenkin 177, 210
Jones, Mari 197
Jones, Michael David 198, 208
Jones, Samuel 177
Jones, William 181, 212, 213

Jowett, Fred 263, 268

Kaufman, Gerald 41
Kenney, Annie 245, 246, 247
Kett, Robert 5, 120, 135, 137, 141
Kingsley, Charles 37
Kinnock, Neil 31, 197, 216, 333
Kirkwood, David 317, 318, 320, 340, 341, 342
Knight, Laura 26
Kroptokin, Pyotr 25, 97, 270, 331

Lansbury, Angela 108
Lansbury, George 7, 37, 38, 60, 81, 83, 86, 88, 95, 99, 102, 107, 108, 125, 127, 128, 129, 131, 133, 134, 295
Lansbury, Minnie (née Glassman) 108
Laski, Harold 38, 40, 88, 135
Lawrence, D. H. 160, 209
Lee, Jennie 3, 122, 220, 350
Lee, Peter 285, 304
Lenin, Vladimir 9, 43, 87, 89, 90, 91, 92, 93, 94, 97, 113, 300, 321, 338
Lever, William 231, 248, 249
Lewis, Richard see Penderyn, Dic
Lewis, Saunders 189, 190, 191, 198, 210, 214, 215, 217
Lilburne, John 34
Lindsay, A. D. 37, 150
Linelli, Alfred 81, 108
Lister, John 263, 272
Lister, Samuel Cunliffe 262, 269
Lloyd George, David 14, 15, 123, 132, 172, 188, 189, 200, 208, 209, 215, 317, 336
Lloyd George, Megan 110, 192, 202, 203
Llwyd, Morgan 223
Lochhead, Liz 307
Loveless, George 43
Loveless, James 43
Lovett, William 5, 22, 39
MacDiarmid, Hugh 324, 328, 334, 349, 350, 355
Macdonald, Alexander 283, 284, 294, 297
MacDonald, Ishbel 84-5, 101
MacDonald, James Ramsay 6, 8, 14, 15, 35, 54, 67, 71, 84, 88, 94, 96, 99, 101, 102, 105, 114, 124, 126, 132, 149, 153, 156, 233, 268, 275, 276, 295, 299, 303, 304, 325, 346, 351, 354
Macmillan, Harold 10, 138, 201
Maguire, Tom 263, 275
Mandela, Nelson 81
Mandelson, Peter 87, 282
Mann, Tom 88, 103, 148, 156, 186, 237, 241, 269, 295
Manning, Leah (née Perrett) 31, 131
Mansbridge, Albert 28, 36, 37
Mansbridge, Frances 28, 36, 37
Martindale, Louisa 35
Marx, Eleanor 88, 92, 116, 237
Marx, Karl 9, 13, 23, 25, 60, 87, 88, 89, 90, 92, 93, 95, 96, 97, 100, 103, 112, 115, 116, 159, 230, 243, 244, 352
Maxton, James 221, 310, 332, 340, 341, 343
Mayhew, Henry 12
Maynard, Joan 37, 44
McGahey, Mick 354
McGinn, Matt 335, 339
McGrath, John 335
Mclean, John 318, 319, 321, 322, 332, 339, 340
McShane, Harry 318, 320, 322, 341, 342
Mellor, George 253, 274, 279
Michael, Alun 158
Milburn, Alan 281
Milburn, Jackie 287
Miles, John 176
Mitchell, Hannah Maria 236
Mitchell, James Leslie 323

Mitchison, Naomi 325, 327
Mitford, Jessica 29
Morgan, Edward 180
Morgan, Kenneth 218
Morgan, William 174, 183, 215, 217
Morgannwg, Iolo 182, 183, 216
Morris, William 2, 19, 24, 27, 36, 37, 39, 81, 87, 88, 92, 95, 98, 108, 110, 111, 116, 124, 135, 159, 272, 336
Morrison, Herbert 87, 105, 282
Morton, A. L. 125, 130, 134
Mowlam, Mo 156
Muir, Thomas 331, 340
Mundella, Anthony 147, 162
Murray, Len 148, 166, 167, 211

Neale, Edward Vansittart 30
Neill, A. S. 125, 134, 312, 323, 348
Nesbit, Edith 164
Nicholson, Ben 26
Nicholson, Norman 289
Noonan, Robert see Tressell, Robert

O'Connor, Feargus 12, 86, 116, 117, 146, 161, 253, 260, 279
Oastler, Richard 253, 258, 259, 268, 273, 276, 278
Orwell, George 2, 4, 43, 47, 57, 58, 62, 64, 74, 79, 111, 114, 125, 137, 140, 160, 164, 324, 327
Owen, David 84, 109, 278
Owen, Hugh 198, 200
Owen, Robert 47, 53, 71, 73, 181, 198, 203, 213, 214, 243, 249, 328, 352

Paine, Thomas 29, 34, 47, 49, 50, 51, 56, 57, 67, 68, 70, 73, 89, 98, 124, 139, 140, 178, 331
Pankhurst, Christabel 100, 245, 246, 247
Pankhurst, Emmeline 81, 100, 217, 244-5, 247, 277
Pankhurst, Sylvia 88, 104, 108, 117, 127, 245
Paterson, Robert 356
Patterson, William 283, 284, 297
Penderyn, Dic 196, 201, 211
Penny, John 173, 174, 175, 183, 205
Pethick-Lawrence, Emmeline 27, 32, 68
Philipps, Wogan 27, 36
Picton-Turbervil, Edith 156
Pollitt, Henry 99, 239
Ponsonby, Arthur 7
Potter, Beatrice see Webb, Beatrice
Potter, Dennis 30
Potter, George 148, 158
Powell, Vavasor 186, 201
Prescott, John 41, 216, 217
Price, Richard 178, 206
Price, William 183, 204, 207, 213
Priestley, J. B. 2, 34, 264, 269, 270, 273
Pugh, Arthur 148, 164

Rainborrow, Colonel 21
Reid, Jimmy 337-8
Reid, Thomas 313
Richard, Henry 184, 211, 221
Robertson, William 313, 314
Robinson, Kenneth 163
Rodgers, Bill 40, 84, 109
Romilly, Esmond 29
Rossetti, Dante Gabriel 24
Rowland, Daniel 206, 221
Rude, George 6
Ruskin, John 2, 25, 40, 97, 211, 288, 290, 291, 294, 295, 296
Russell, Bertrand 81, 98, 162, 215-6, 222

Sassie, Victor 115
Saville, John 6
Scargill, Arthur 266, 268, 279
Seacole, Mary 79, 116
Shankly, Bill 344-5
Shaw, George Bernard 13, 97, 122,

127, 159, 209, 336
Shelley, Percy Bysshe 2, 4, 31, 38, 49, 56, 60, 66, 67, 74, 97, 113, 123
Shinwell, Emanuel 7, 69, 115, 186, 319, 332, 340, 351
Shore, Peter 123, 129
Short, Clare 154, 158
Skinner, Dennis 41, 149, 155
Smiles, Samuel 12
Smillie, Robert 7, 328, 341
Smith, Adam 243, 313, 314
Smith, Chris 87, 158
Smith, Claude Stuart 133
Smith, Herbert 265, 275
Smith, Herbert 265, 275
Smith, John 3, 105, 324, 348, 355
Snowden, Philip 6, 15, 102, 264, 266, 274, 275, 277
Solly, Henry 44
Soper, Donald 100, 220
Soskice, Frank 40, 114
Spooner, William 299
Standfield, John 43
Standfield, Thomas 43
Stephens, J. R. 250
Stonehouse, John 97
Strachey, John 40, 64, 70

Tawney, R. H. 37, 40, 97, 99, 107, 132, 150, 164
Taylor, A. J. P. 40, 86, 114
Thatcher, Margaret 17, 33, 81, 125, 129, 148, 257, 307, 317, 319, 329, 348, 353, 354
Thistlewood, Arthur 93, 95, 115
Thomas, George 192, 197
Thomas, J. H. 149, 156
Thomas, Margaret Haig 208-9
Thomas, Morgan 216
Thomas, Theodore Parker 210
Thomas, William 210
Thompson, E. P. 6, 21, 37, 145, 146, 254, 267
Thorne, Will 88, 103, 109
Tillett, Ben 32, 88, 103, 127, 237, 262, 269, 270, 295
Tolstoy, Leo 26, 128, 291
Tom, John 52, 63
Towle, James 145, 146, 153
Tressell, Robert 50, 66, 72, 242
Trevelyan, Charles 7, 129, 303
Trotter, James 287, 293, 294
Tyler, Wat 5, 48, 52, 54, 61, 68, 95, 105, 120, 268

Valentine, Lewis 189, 200, 215
Vincent, Henry 12, 29, 207, 212, 213

Walshe, Christina 36
Wardle, George 15
Warwick, Countess of 103, 125, 130, 134-5, 139, 140, 166
Webb, Beatrice (née Potter) 3, 5, 13, 28, 31, 42, 47, 71, 99, 101, 103, 114, 135
Webb, Philip 25
Webb, Sidney 3, 5, 13, 14, 42, 47, 71, 99, 101, 103, 114, 135
Wedgewood, Josiah 149, 152, 153, 165
Wells, H. G. 2, 3, 13, 41, 47, 48, 54, 69, 72, 75, 77, 83, 100, 117, 125, 135, 164
Wesley, John 120, 178
West, Rebecca 60, 209
Westwood, Joseph 165
Wheatley, John 318, 320, 321, 341
Wilkes, John 89, 96
Wilkinson, Ellen 264, 299
Wilks, Mark 136-7
Willey, Thomas 24, 30
Williams, D. J. 189, 204, 215, 217
Williams, Edward see Morgannwg, Iolo
Williams, Hugh 181, 203
Williams, Marcia 150, 161
Williams, Shirley 41, 84, 98, 102, 109, 150, 161

Williams, Tom 149, 154
Williams, Waldo 170, 190, 212, 215
Williams, Zephaniah 181, 199, 212, 213
Wilson, Harold 40, 41, 42, 62, 74, 84, 85, 88, 101, 102, 115, 123, 126, 150, 155, 157, 161, 163, 166, 216, 254, 264, 273, 274, 277, 303, 329, 350
Wilson, John 283, 297
Wilson, Mary 42
Winstanly, Gerard 20
Wollstonecraft, Mary 31, 58, 89, 104, 109, 113
Woodburn, Arthur 95, 320, 332, 347
Wordsworth, William 289, 290, 298, 299
Wrobel, John 115

Wroth, William 175, 208
Zedong, Mao 333